Restorative justice from a children's rights perspective

Restorative justice from a children's rights perspective

Annemieke Wolthuis and Tim Chapman (Eds.)

eleven

Published, sold and distributed by Eleven
P.O. Box 85576
2508 CG The Hague
The Netherlands
Tel.: +31 70 33 070 33
Fax: +31 70 33 070 30
e-mail: sales@elevenpub.nl
www.elevenpub.com

Sold and distributed in USA and Canada
Independent Publishers Group
814 N. Franklin Street
Chicago, IL 60610
USA
Order Placement: (800) 888-4741
Fax: (312) 337-5985
orders@ipgbook.com
www.ipgbook.com

Eleven is an imprint of Boom uitgevers Den Haag.

ISBN 978-94-6236-227-7
ISBN 978-90-8974-993-2 (E-book)

About the series

Restorative justice offers a unique approach to crime and victimisation and a change of course from the traditional preoccupation with retribution and transgression of rules in the criminal justice system. It focuses on acknowledging and amending the hurt and injustice experienced by victims, support for offenders to promote desistance from wrongdoing, and the concerns of the society for safety and efficient conflict resolution. Essentially, restorative practices involve a facilitated, voluntary and respectful dialogue between the parties affected by crime. Many different practices have been developed that meet restorative justice requirements, including, but not limited to, victim-offender mediation, restorative conferencing, peace-making circles, and peer mediation. These practices are being utilised in response to property and violent crime, adult and youth offending, school bullying and workplace conflicts, cultural conflicts and mass victimisation. This book series aspires to highlight the many accomplishments achieved through the use of restorative justice practices in response to crime and social conflict.

It is a collection of ground-breaking theoretical essays on the principles, uses and versatility of restorative justice as well as state-of-the-art empirical research into the implementation of restorative justice practices, experiences in these programmes and evaluation of their impact on victim recovery, reoffending and community capacity building. Contributors include established scholars and promising new scholars.

The series in practice: While the primary aim of the series is to publish different types of academic books, thereby giving the floor to researchers, both emerging and well-established ones, we also wish to use it to support and give a platform to painters we admire and who have accepted that we use their unique work for our covers. Each is mentioned within the four different branches our books fit under as described below:

Branch 1: MONOGRAPHS and EDITED COLLECTIONS
These are original academic works based on particular empirical or theoretical research into restorative practices, and edited collections around a specific topic in the field of restorative justice.

The covers for this branch are paintings by Sasa Saastamoinen. Further work by this painter can be found at https://www.sasasaastamoinen.com.

Branch 2: ANTHOLOGY
This branch aims to publish 'anthologies' of work by invited authors, who choose a number of their own publications that have shaped the discourse and debates on restorative justice. They will, within the anthology, be able to reflect on their impact on the field, on the controversies and debates that they have contributed to and how they have responded and evolved. They will also reflect on the future of restorative justice.

The covers for this branch are original portraits by Abigail McGourlay. Further work by this painter can be found at https://www.instagram.com/mcgourlayart/.

Branch 3: TRANSLATIONS
This branch will publish translations of seminal books in the field of restorative justice having originally been published in other languages than English.

The covers for this branch are paintings by Kittie Jones. Further work by this painter can be found at http://www.kittiejones.com/.

Branch 4: THE INTERNATIONAL ENCYCLOPAEDIA OF RESTORATIVE JUSTICE by general editors Ivo Aertsen and Jennifer Llewellyn and a large group of regional editors

The International Encyclopaedia of Restorative Justice will present, for the first time, an encompassing picture of restorative justice worldwide. The origins, development, legislation and practical implementation of restorative justice will be described and critically analysed for a broad range of countries in Africa, Asia, Europe, Latin America, Anglo-America and Oceania, while a variety of challenges and issues related to the developments in the respective regions will be discussed comparatively. The *International Encyclopaedia* explores the complexity of information and analysis into six volumes that will both broaden and deepen our understanding of this innovative field of justice practices.

The covers for this branch are original paintings by Michelle Campbell. Further work by this painter can be found at https://www.chellecampbell.co.uk.

Please see the last page of this book for a list of published volumes in this series.

Acknowledgments

Annemieke Wolthuis

It was in 1997 when my boss Stan Meuwese, who was the director of Defence for Children International in Amsterdam back then, returned from a child justice conference in Fort Lauderdale, USA, and informed us that there was a new movement called 'restorative justice' and that we should look into it. I was young and enthusiastic and immediately started to study up. I dove into the subject, got hooked and never let go. I soon found out that the family group conferences in New Zealand played a central role in juvenile justice over there, and that children's hearings in Scotland, and mediation and restorative group consultations in Belgium were also emerging. We soon came into contact with Lode Walgrave and colleagues from the KU Leuven and we attended conferences they organized on restorative justice for youth offenders. Meanwhile, in the Netherlands, a number of people were working on restorative justice pilot projects, including John Blad, who taught criminal law at Erasmus University Rotterdam, and Rob van Pagée and Jan van Lieshout, who were busy rolling out 'Real Justice conferences' (family group conference model) of people with a conflict and their network, which later became 'Eigen Kracht', inspired by American and New Zealand examples. The subject has continued to fascinate me, both in research and in practice. I wrote contributions about this in a Dutch/Flemish journal on restorative justice and Defence for Children International publications and looked at pilots with mediation and conferencing. At some point, I envisaged more academic ambitions. In 2006, I discussed an idea for a PhD study on restorative justice with Jaap Doek, Emeritus Professor at the Free University of Amsterdam (VU), and with John Blad, one of our most celebrated national restorative justice experts. In 2007, I joined the Open University on a research position, which allowed me to do the PhD study I had envisioned a year earlier. In 2012, I delivered my thesis on restorative justice and children's rights. I enjoyed those early years of pioneering.

The Netherlands was not a frontrunner on restorative justice, but I think we have improved. Much has happened since the early 2000s, with the input of organizations like Restorative Justice Nederland where I now work, and many other academics and practitioners in the field. I became a mediator myself to gain insight into what happens on the other side of the table. And I only recently started working as a substitute youth judge in the Court of Rotterdam, where I can also see if mediation is an option in the criminal youth cases we are handling. Today, in 2021, restorative justice has gained a more established position in law, policy and practice, not only in the Netherlands, but throughout the world. The focus of this book is how restorative justice has developed for children and young people, which I am proud to present to you.

Restorative justice, a child's right, was the title of my doctoral dissertation (in Dutch), which I defended in 2012. It was published as a book with Boom publishers. The focus was partly on how to integrate restorative justice into the Dutch child justice system. However, it also contained an analysis of international standards, theory and practice worldwide. Since the defense, I have been thinking that I would like to write a book in English on the same topic, but only 2 years ago I finally took further steps in this direction. I decided to make it a joint initiative. Tim Chapman, my dear colleague on the board of the European Forum for Restorative Justice, and our current chair, who is an expert in many aspects of restorative justice, including children's rights, agreed to be my co-author and co-editor. Colleagues at Eleven International Publishing, also publishing *The International Journal on Restorative Justice*, were immediately interested. And that is when we started approaching the authors. They all reacted in such an enthusiastic way! I feel honored to have been able to work with such a wonderful team. They are all experts who advance restorative thinking, theory and practice, especially for the benefit of children and young people around the globe. Having said that, readers should approach these contributions with a critical mind and ask themselves: will they inspire good restorative justice practices and do they reflect what children would want?

Tim Chapman

I think that I first met Annemieke on a long coach journey through the Basque Country to the beautiful town of Oñati where we were going to participate in a symposium. We spoke not only of the relevance of children's rights to restorative justice, but also of the tensions between those who campaign for children's rights and those who practice restorative justice. We agreed that we should write something about it one day. Many years later this book has finally arrived.

As a practitioner in youth justice in Northern Ireland, I had always championed the rights of the child. But once the new law introducing restorative justice into the core of the Northern Irish youth justice system was implemented in 2002, I experienced significant resistance to it from people whom I had previously seen as allies. They found it difficult to conceive of children and young people as victimizing others, including other children. They viewed rights as a protection against being victims of state oppression for young people in conflict with the law. They imagined the restorative process of meeting with those who have harmed as re-traumatizing already vulnerable children.

Much has changed since then. The restorative justice approach is considered a success and is no longer a strange and slightly threatening innovation. There has been a rapid expansion of restorative approaches throughout the world as reported in the chapters of this book. The professional discourse recognizes that children and young people are often victims of crime who require the same protection and support to participate as children in conflict with the law.

Joint message

We would like to thank Tinneke Van Camp and Estelle Zinsstag, Co-Editors in Chief of the book series *Studies in Restorative Justice*, published by Eleven and Selma Soetenhorst, Publisher, who all worked with us in a very productive and cordial way. All comments or suggestions shared have been taken into consideration. We would like to thank all the authors, who were patient with us and shared their expertise in a professional and friendly way. And Lode Walgrave, who inspired us all with his views on child justice and the need for a restorative switch since the eighties. Finally, we would also like to thank our families for their support and understanding during the process of putting this together. We are proud the book is out.

Beyond rhetoric on children's rights and restorative justice

A critical foreword

Lode Walgrave

For several reasons, a volume like 'Restorative justice from a children's rights perspective', edited by Annemieke Wolthuis and Tim Chapman, is more than welcome. The initiative has yielded a thought-provoking collection of chapters written by excellent scholars. It is informative and inspirational for all who are involved in doing justice after the occurrence of an offense committed by, or victimizing a child or a young person. As all good texts do, this book will also provoke comments and thoughts. Here are mine.

1 The meaning of rights

A Belgian newspaper of 11 December 2019 (De Morgen, 2019: 7) reported that a boy of 9 (!) dropped out of his bachelor studies at the Technical University of Eindhoven, because he found the trajectory proposed by the university to be too slow. According to the father of this 'wonder child', the boy wanted to finish his trajectory a few months earlier, which was, according to his father, 'his right'. I wonder which system, law, rule, declaration or convention assigns, directly or indirectly, the right to a boy to dictate his university curriculum himself. The claim of the father illustrates the inflation of the notion of 'rights'.

Sometimes indeed, rights are claimed as part of a demanding rhetoric, while they are not recognized as such by others. Trade Unions claim the right to post strikers' pickets. Independence movements claim the right of autonomy for their region. By calling their interests or wishes 'rights', they suggest that it is inherent to their position, that the legitimacy of their claim is not up for discussion.

A right suggests a legitimate due, a just claim that cannot be disputed. The Universal Declaration of Human Rights states that all human persons possess entitlements by the simple fact that they are humans. The *Convention on the Rights of the Child (CRC)* proclaims by authority that all children have special rights which are inseparably linked to the status of being a child. It is as if humans and children have rights by nature.

But they do not. Rights are granted by the relevant community, based on acknowledged claims or on moral grounds. Rights are transformations of needs, interests and/or wishes, recognized as being legitimate. The consequence is twofold:

recognized rights create more freedom and entitlements for the rightsholders, and obligations to respect them for the others.

Some interest groups do not have the power or the authority to claim rights for themselves. The powerful then may assign rights to the weaker, out of a concern for protection. They want to avoid abuse of those who are weaker. In an ethical move, the assigners of the rights then freely submit their own interests, liberties and wishes to the needs and interests of the weaker population.

2 Children's rights as protective rights

Rights for children are typically protective rights. Children are too dependent to voice claims, but the adults in the international community have decided to assign them rights. The most fundamental text is the *Convention on the Rights of the Child (CRC),* which was adopted unanimously in 1989 by the United Nations General Council.

The CRC reflects a shift in the vision on children and young people during the 20th century. In 1947, an authoritative Belgian lawyer obtained general approval with his statement that the child 'has one right only, the right to be educated, and one duty only, the duty to be docile in the hands of his educator' (Dabin, 1947: 11). Much has changed since then. From being considered as 'not yet fully-fledged human beings', as dependent and vulnerable objects of law, children have turned into autonomous and responsible subjects of law, competent and bearing all human rights.

Contrary to the Universal Declaration of Human Rights, the CRC is not just a moral declaration, but a convention, including a juridically enforceable status. All citizens can claim certain dispositions before their national courts and a few of these dispositions even have priority over national law. At least this is the case in theory, which is very often not respected in the jurisdictional practices of many countries. International control over the implementation is executed by the *Committee on the Rights of the Child.*

3 Restorative justice in youth justice

Restorative justice practices have been piloted, tried out and implemented mostly in responding to youthful offending (see for example Foussard et al. Chapter 6, and Dünkel & Păroşanu Chapter 7 in this volume). The more flexible procedures in youth justice systems leave more space for alternatives, including victim-focused programs. Moreover, the public at large is more prepared to accept experiments in dealing with youths. It is believed, indeed, that experimenting with youthful offenders is less risky than with adults, and that young people are more responsive to rehabilitative initiatives. However, as several chapters in this volume indicate, the practices in the field do not always reflect the legal possibilities. Restorative justice is a relatively new approach that continues to provoke hesitation and skepticism among (especially judicial) practitioners.

The option for more restorative justice in responding to youth crime is a good thing. In a nutshell, the main positive and negative reasons for this are the following:

First of all, it is pure logic. For many scholars, including myself, social harmfulness of behavior is the crucial reason to criminalize it. Offenses are forbidden because they cause prejudices to victims and because they hurt dominion, the set of assured rights and freedoms in society (Braithwaite & Pettit, 1990). Consequently, it is logical to focus on trying to repair these harms if an offense occurs. What may have seemed to be a naïve position appears to be increasingly feasible through growing experience all over the world.

Second, it is ethically right to involve victims in the settlements of their victimization. It is *their* case. As Christie (1977) argued, the criminal justice system has stolen the conflict from its owners and restorative justice returns the ownership to where it belongs. To be clear, that does not invalidate the role of the criminal justice system. I shall come back to this.

Third, it is socially more constructive to give priority to inclusion and respectful dialogue over exclusion and authoritative infliction of pain. But this priority cannot always be achieved. That is why restorative justice is a priority, not a monopoly.

In addition, many publications have elaborated on the dysfunctional effects of the punitive premise. Intentional infliction of pain is unethical. It leads the focus away from the essence, being the harm the offense has caused. It is ineffective to assure public safety, to deter potential offenders and to rehabilitate offenders. It is increasingly at odds with procedural and other institutional tangles (Walgrave, 2008). It is time to reflect on a possible alternative, and restorative justice offers a pathway toward more constructive responses.

But also, the purely rehabilitative responses to youthful offending are not without problems. Basically, the welfare-oriented youth justice systems are subjected to four criticisms: (1) the effectiveness of the treatment-oriented interventions in youth justice is generally poor, (2) the focus on the needs of the offender, rather than on the characteristics of the offense, removes the grounds for legal safeguards, (3) priority for 'the best interest of the child' lacks credibility in the response to serious youth crime, (4) the rehabilitative orientation for young offenders neglects the legitimate needs and interests of victims.

It is, of course, humane and ethical to pursue the social rehabilitation of young people who have committed an offense or who are drifting into a lifestyle in which offending is part of life. The question is, however, if this pursuit must be the priority in responding to crime. My position is that it is not. Responding to (youth) crime must first of all focus on repairing the harm resulting from the crime. But we may assume that rehabilitation of (young) offenders is probably a secondary effect. The face-to-face confrontation about the harm and suffering caused, the respect and support by significant others experienced during the encounter, the chance offered to make amends and to be re-accepted as a law-abiding citizen, the satisfaction felt when the reparative gestures have been carried out successfully and are valorized by significant others, are all elements that may facilitate the offender's awareness and his or her motivation to conform and/or to accept rehabilitative support. Restorative encounters may function as ideal steps toward rehabilitative initiatives carried out by specialized agencies (Pleysier, Vanfraechem & Walgrave, 2017; Walgrave, Ward & Zinsstag, 2019). This assumption is confirmed by extensive empirical research (Bonta, Jesseman, Rugge & Cormier, 2006; Sherman, Strang, Mayo-Wilson, Woods & Ariel, 2015; Walgrave, 2011). Several theoretical models are available to explain such outcomes (reintegrative shaming, procedural justice, social bonds, interaction rituals, the Good Lives Model). Moreover, other initiatives aiming explicitly at the offender's social (re)integration can run parallel with or after the restorative justice intervention.

4 Restorative justice is not a children's right

While implementing restorative justice in response to youthful offending is a good thing, it is not a right in the strict sense of the word. The only legal rights of restorative justice are those provided for in legal systems. Most youth justice systems offer the possibility to refer youth crime to restorative processing, but they do not oblige it. Being referred to restorative processes is a favor according to most legislators, rather than a mainstream response. Only a few youth justice systems explicitly prioritize restorative responses (Dünkel, Grzywa, Pruin & Selih, 2011). What is more, for children as victims, nothing is stipulated. Just like adults, child victims are dependent on the goodwill of the judicial gatekeepers and/or the offender.

Several chapters in this volume (Wolthuis Chapter 1, Winter Chapter 3, Gal, Chapter 4, Bolivar et al. Chapter 11, Moore Chapter 5, Czarnecka-Dzialuk Chapter 13) suggest that restorative justice for youth is congruent with the CRC, or that restorative justice is 'child-friendly' (Filippi Chapter 12, Berger & Wolthuis, Chapter 14). The 'watchdog' of the CRC, the Committee on the Rights of the Child, even promotes the option for restorative responses (Wolthuis Chapter 1 and Winter Chapter 3 in this volume). The CRC and the Committee do not, however, issue an enforceable right. It is a claim, a kind of pressure by an authoritative international body. It may strengthen the arguments of restorative justice advocates, it may impress some legislators, but it may also leave other legislators indifferent.

And practice may still not fully comply with legislation (Cartuyvels & Bailleau, 2010; Dünkel et al., 2011; McAra, 2017; see also Foussard et al. Chapter 6, Dünkel & Păroşanu Chapter 7, Sloth Nielsen Chapter 8 and Berger & Wolthuis Chapter 14 in this volume).

Accompanying measures, such as providing persuasive information, organizing appropriate training and establishing capable agencies, are needed to make sure that the option for restorative justice is appropriately implemented in practice (Păroşanu & Lynch Chapter 10, Czarnecka-Dzialuk Chapter 13, Chochua Chapter 9 in this volume). Morrison et al. describe an experiment in British Columbia in that sense (Chapter 15 in this volume) and Gellin discusses preventive aspects of restorative education in Finland (Chapter 16 in this volume).

The claim for more restorative justice is based on the belief that a restorative starting point is more ethical than a punitive one and more balanced than the rehabilitative premise, and that restorative processes offer better constructive opportunities for both victims and offenders and for community life as well. As just mentioned, ample empirical data are available to support this belief. While it is more than worthwhile to advocate the transformation of youth justice into a predominantly restorative justice system (Wolthuis, 2012), it is actually not a right; it is currently not an obligation for the legislator and for the judiciary to give priority to restorative responses to youthful offending.

In any case, the introduction of restorative models in youth justice must be accompanied by measures to protect child victims in their encounters with the offender and to guard the rights of youthful offenders (as mentioned also in this volume, among others in Chapman Chapter 2 and Gal Chapter 4).

5 Weak legal safeguards in rehabilitation-oriented youth justice

More than criminal justice systems do for adult offenders, current youth justice systems include rehabilitative concerns in their response to youth crime. The sanction imposed on a youthful offender is oriented more toward his or her needs and interests, and less motivated by the characteristics of the offense.

Aligning sentencing with the needs of the offender rather than with the characteristics of the offense inevitably erases enforceable limits on judicial intervention. The judgment is passed in view of achieving rehabilitative aims in the future and is less based on available checkable characteristics of the offense committed.

The *United Nations Standard Minimum Rules for the Administration of Juvenile Justice* (1985) do not resolve this ambivalence. These rules, also known as the Beijing Rules, stipulate, for example, that the judicial response 'shall always be in proportion to the circumstances of both the offenders and the offence' (Beijing Rules, Art. 5.1.). Proportionality is applied not only to the offense, but also to the peculiar individual needs of the child. But it is difficult to assess this kind of proportionality. To which standard does proportionality refer if the offense committed is benign but reveals huge underlying psychological and social problems? And it is unclear how to 'allow appropriate scope of discretion at all stages of the proceedings' (Bejing, Art. 6.10) and to assure at the same time 'the principles of fair and just trial' (Bejing, Art. 14.10).

The CRC states that all judicial interventions must be taken 'in the best interest of the child' (CRC, Art. 40.1) but what does equality mean if two youngsters who committed a harmful act together appear to have very different needs and interests?

The 'prospectiveness' in the response to youth crime (Feld, 1993) and its extension with preventionist ambitions risk making youth justice 'insatiable'. The need for treatment and prevention are infinitely large. Traditional legal safeguards, on the contrary, are based on retrospection, looking backwards to the offense, as a yardstick for measuring the permissible degree of restriction of freedom. The future-oriented rehabilitative ambitions of most youth justice interventions are hard to combine with the retrospective basis of legal safeguards. Current youth justice tries to combine what cannot be combined satisfactorily.

The question is whether a restorative justice approach offers a better pathway for this issue.

6 RESTORATIVE JUSTICE AND THE LEGAL CONTEXT

The relation between restorative justice and the legal context is a matter of discussion. Originally, Anglo-Saxon scholars, living under a common law regime, saw restorative justice as a way to escape the overly formal institutional responses. They saw restorative justice as 'a form of insurgency because it competes with the state' (Sullivan & Tift, 2006: 5) and they strongly believed in the community as the niche in which conflicts would be resolved. Others, however, especially on the European continent with civil law regimes, almost immediately tried to embed restorative practices within a legal and judicial frame (Walgrave, 2002). This opposition is currently much less sharp. As restorative justice practices are gaining credibility, many legislations position them in pre-sentential or post-sentential judicial procedures.

It is apparent in several chapters in this volume that most restorative initiatives are located in the margins of the criminal/youth justice system, as a kind of diversion. Consequently, restorative schemes risk being co-opted as ornaments of a system that remains primarily punitive, or as alternatives to treatment models for youngsters.

Diversionary schemes, in fact, circumvent the fundamental problems raised by the restorative justice approach. How to combine informal confidential encounters with a high emotional dimension, with the requirements of formality, publicity and rationality that are characteristic in judicial procedures? How to assure legal safeguards, such as presumption of innocence, right of defense, due process, proportionality, equality and others, in a restorative approach that rests upon voluntary face-to-face dialogue between the direct stakeholders? Where is the public dimension of the offense if the encounter brings only the concrete victim in dialogue with his or her offender? How to represent the interests of the community if the state is marginalized?

That is why I have since long advanced what is now called a 'maximalist' vision on restorative justice (Walgrave, 2008). One might also call it a 'straightforward' or a 'consequential' vision on restorative justice. The social, ethical and instrumental reasons to opt for the restorative premise do not disappear in case of serious crime or if the restorative dialogue does not yield satisfying outcomes. And the fundamental problems with the punitive premise do subsist. A consequential vision on restorative justice is not limited to offering pathways of diversion from the penal justice procedures. It aims at changing the punitive criminal justice system itself into a restorative criminal justice system that gives priority to the possibilities of achieving reparation and restoration.

In a restorative criminal justice system, the judicial institution has three functions: (1) to assure that offenses are not left without consequences for the victim, for the offender and for public order and peace, (2) to safeguard legal rights for all stakeholders, by controlling checks and balances and by offering the possibilities for all stakeholders to submit their case to judicial judgment if they cannot agree with the outcomes of the encounter, and (3) to exert pressure to motivate offenders to participate in encounters and to possibly use coercion if restorative processes cannot or do not yield satisfying results. But even in such cases the judicial sanctions must try to repair as much as possible the harm and suffering caused by the crime.

Compared to traditional criminal justice, restorative justice is inspired by a clearly distinct philosophy; it conceptualizes the essentials of crime differently, aims at different goals, involves other key actors, uses other tools and operates in a different social and juridical context. Restorative justice, therefore, is based on a different paradigm. It is hard then to keep exactly the same ground rules for a clearly different game. Instead of trying to submit restorative justice to traditional criminal justice principles, the legal criteria need to be revised and reformulated in order to preserve the socially constructive potentials of restorative justice. But two ground principles will remain: (1) the protection of all citizens against abuses of power by fellow citizens and by the societal institutions, and (2) the equal treatment of all citizens by the legal institutions.

7 Restorative justice may help to improve legal rights in youth justice

Basically, consequential restorative justice has better potential to respect legal safeguards than does rehabilitative justice. Its focus on the harm and suffering caused is retrospective. Harm caused by the offense is a more controllable yardstick for the intervention than the offender's needs in the future.

Restorative justice, in fact, can be considered as a form of inverted retribution. Traditional punitive retribution has three components: the expression of blame on the unlawful behavior, the indication of the responsibility of the offender and the attempt to restore the moral balance through a proportionate response. We find these three components also in restorative justice, but in a more constructive sense.

Restorative justice clearly articulates the limits of social tolerance. It intervenes because a crime has been committed, and the crime is disapproved. But while punitive retribution focuses on the transgression of the criminal law as the reason to condemn the offender, restorative censuring focuses on the harm caused to another person and to social life. Restorative censuring refers explicitly to the obligation to respect the quality of social life.

As in punitive retributivism, restorative justice raises the responsibility of the offender. But punitive responsibility is passive. The offender is confronted by the criminal justice system with his or her responsibility and she or he must submit to the punitive consequences imposed on him/her by that system. Passive responsibility is retrospective. It is imposed because of an act committed in the past. Restorative justice, on the contrary, relies on a concept of active responsibility. The offender is invited (under pressure) to take active responsibility, by participating actively in the deliberations and to make active gestures that contribute to the reparation of this harm. Active responsibility is raised because of the act committed in the past, but also oriented toward an action or a situation in the future. Active responsibility, therefore, is both retrospective and prospective.

Also, the balance principle is essential in restorative justice, maybe even in a more genuine form than in punitive retributivism. Punitive retributivism tries to restore the balance by paying back to the offender the same amount of suffering and harm she or he has caused. It is assumed that things are then evened out. The amount of suffering in the world is doubled, but equally spread (Wright, 1992). In restorative justice, the offender must himself or herself pay back by repairing as much as possible the harm and suffering caused. Again, the balance is now restored, not by doubling the total amount of suffering, but by taking suffering away.

All in all, restoration and retribution appear to have much in common. They 'may be seen as two sides of a coin, rather than a pair of opposites' (Baehler, 2007: 290; see also Walgrave, 2004; Zehr, 2002). Facing the common concerns of both punitive and restorative justice to rebalance the consequences of a wrong clearly indicates that restorative justice also contains a sanctioning dimension, including a kind of retrospectivity and the idea of a balance between the illegal act and the response to it. It is the ground on which a system of restorative law enforcement can be constructed, leaving ample space for deliberation among the stakeholders if possible, but also providing a judicial response that serves reparation if needed.

8 Rights for restorative justice as an objective

While restorative justice can currently not be advanced as a children's right in the strict sense of the word, the sections here above provide good arguments to claim them. Ethical, social and instrumental reasons exist to argue for restorative justice to become the mainstream response to offending, a right for children and adults, victims as well as offenders. If done well, systematic application of restorative practices offers the most beneficial pathway toward repairing a victim's losses and suffering, for the rehabilitation of an offender and for preserving public peace in social life. Restorative justice must be considered and implemented consequentially in a fully-fledged system that assigns the right to all stakeholders to try out the potentials of a restorative response to the offending, and that obliges all agents of the system to facilitate such a response. In a restorative criminal justice system and in a restorative youth justice system, the potentials of responding restoratively to offending are always considered a priority. But it may appear not to be possible, for reasons of security or because of the mental state of (one of the) stakeholders. Only then, may other measures of security or of treatment be necessary.

The chapters in this book provide an excellent collection of illustrations and arguments in support of the claim to construct restorative justice as a fully-fledged right for all youthful stakeholders in the aftermath of an offense, including victims, offenders and members of the communities of care. Annemieke Wolthuis and Tim Chapman did a wonderful job in conceiving and editing this volume.

References

Baehler, K. (2007). Justifying restorative justice. In G. Maxwell & J. Liu (eds.), *Restorative justice and practices in New Zealand: towards a restorative society* (pp. 289-299). Wellington: Institute of Policy Studies, Victoria University.

Bonta, J., Jesseman, R., Rugge, T. & Cormier, R. (2006). Restorative justice and recidivism. Promises made, promises kept? In D. Sullivan & L. Tift (eds.), *Handbook of restorative justice* (pp. 108-120). London: Routledge.

Braithwaite, J. & Pettit, Ph. (1990). *Not just desert. A republican theory of criminal justice.* Oxford: Oxford University Press.

Cartuyvels, Y. & Bailleau, F. (2010). Youth criminal justice in Europe. At the intersection of protective thinking, a neo-liberal turn, and neo-conservative ideology. In F. Bailleau & Y. Cartuyvels (eds.), *The criminalisation of youth. Juvenile justice in Europe, Turkey and Canada* (pp. 263-284). Brussel: VUBPress.

Christie, N. (1977). Conflicts as property. *British Journal of Criminology*, 17(1), 1-15. doi: 10.1093/oxfordjournals.bjc.a046783.

Dabin, J. (1947). *Le contrôle de la puissance paternelle en droit Belge*. Bruxelles: Larcier.

Spoormakers, S. 'Hoogbegaafde Laurent (9) stopt studies aan Nederlandse unief', *De Morgen*, 10 December 2019. Retrieved from https://www.demorgen.be/nieuws/hoogbegaafde-laurent-9-stopt-studies-aan-nederlandse-unief-ze-beschuldigen-hem-van-plagiaat~b746bf4b/ (last accessed 13 October2021).

Dünkel, F., Grzywa, J., Pruin, I. & Selih, A. (2011). Juvenile justice in Europe – legal aspects, policy trends and perspectives in the light of human rights standards. In F. Dünkel, J. Grzywa, P. Horsfield & I. Pruin (eds.), *Juvenile justice systems in Europe. Current situations and reform developments* (Vol. 1, 2nd ed., pp. 1839-1898). Mönchengladbach: Forum Verlag Godesberg.

Feld, B. (1993). Criminalizing the American juvenile court. In M. Tonry (ed.), *Crime and justice: a review of research* (Vol. 17). Chicago: Chicago University Press.

McAra, L. (2017). Can criminologists change the world? Critical reflections on the politics, performance and effects of criminal justice. *British Journal of Criminology*, 57(4), 767-788.

Pleysier, S., Vanfraechem, I. & Walgrave, L. (2017). Restorative justice and adolescent health. In A.L. Cherry et al. (eds.), *International handbook on adolescent health and development* (pp. 115-142). Cham: Springer.

Sherman, L., Strang, H., Mayo-Wilson, E., Woods, D. & Ariel, B. (2015). Are restorative justice conferences effective in reducing repeat offending? Findings from a Campbell systematic review. *Journal of Quantitative Criminology*, 31, 1-24. doi: 10.1007/s10940-014-9222-9.

Sullivan, D. & Tift, L. (2006). Introduction: the healing dimension of restorative justice: a one-world body. In D. Sullivan & L. Tift (eds.), *Handbook of restorative justice* (pp. 1-16). Oxon: Routledge.

Walgrave, L. (2002). Restorative justice and the law: socio-ethical and juridical foundations for a systemic approach. In L. Walgrave (ed.), *Restorative justice and the law* (pp. 191-218). Cullompton: Willan Publishing.

Walgrave, L. (2004). Restoration in youth justice. In M. Tonry & A. Doob (eds.), *Youth crime and youth justice. Comparative and cross-national perspectives* (Vol. 31, pp. 543-597). Chicago: University of Chicago Press, Crime and Justice.

Walgrave, L. (2008). *Restorative justice, self-interest and responsible citizenship.* Cullompton: Willan Publishing.

Walgrave, L. (2011). Investigating the potentials of restorative justice practice. *Washington University Journal of Law & Policy*, 36, 91-139.

Walgrave, L., Ward, T. & Zinsstag, E. (2019). When restorative justice meets the good lives model: contributing to a criminology of trust. *European Journal of Criminology*, 1, 1-17. doi: 10.1177/1477370819854174.

Wolthuis, A. (2012). *Herstelrecht, een kinderrecht, Voorstellen voor integratie van herstel in het hart van het jeugdstrafrecht* (diss.). Boom Lemma uitgevers, Den Haag.

Wright, M. (1992). Victim-offender mediation as a step towards a restorative system of justice. In H. Messmer & H.U. Otto (eds.), *Restorative justice on trial. Pitfalls and potentials of victim-offender mediation* (pp. 525-539). Dordrecht and Boston: Kluwer Academic Publishers.

Zehr, H. (2002). *The little book of restorative justice*. Intercourse: Good Books.

Table of Contents

Introduction

Annemieke Wolthuis and Tim Chapman

> Safety and security don't just happen, they are the result of collective consensus and public investment. We owe our children, the most vulnerable citizens in our society, a life free of violence and fear. – Nelson Mandela

1 The structure

This book is divided into three parts. Part I covers international standards and reflections on restorative justice for children. The five chapters deal with restorative justice and children's rights, the importance of value-led and evidence-based standards, the relevant international standards and work of the Committee on the Rights of the Child, the needs and rights of child victims and child perpetrators and rights-based restorative justice.

Part II is about the global and regional developments and trends in restorative justice for children. In Europe, there is a variety of types of legislation for restorative justice and there are different restorative processes for children and young people including mediation and restorative conferences. This book also reviews practices in Africa, Asia, Latin America and the Pacific. Differences can be found, but common features are that many systems recognize the potential for restorative justice for young people, and yet the actual involvement of young people as either victims or perpetrators is disappointingly low. In other words, there is much to be done to realize the potential.

Part III addresses national practices and challenges for restorative justice approaches with children. Experiences, promising practices and challenges are shared from Georgia, Chile, France, New Zealand, Poland, Canada, Finland and the Netherlands. While the main focus is on the use of restorative justice within child justice, there are also two chapters that go beyond this or can be seen as more preventive work, and that is the use of mediation in education, as Maija Gellin describes in Finland, as well as the work that Brenda Morrison and colleagues are doing in Canada within their youth project, Shaking the Movers.

2 Terminology

Even though many prefer the terms 'the harmed person' and 'the person responsible', we will use the better known terms 'victims' and 'offenders' or 'perpetrators' as is also commonly used by other authors. For us, these terms relate to the child's relationship to a specific offense and are not used to label or describe the identity of any individual. Sometimes it is specified if we are dealing with suspects or accused persons/children. The term 'children', as per the definition of the UN Convention on the Rights of the Child, includes everyone under the age of 18. Young people are those aged between 12 and 24. They may also be referred to as adolescents or young adults.

For a long time, it was common to use the term 'juvenile justice', but the word 'juvenile' has a negative connotation in some contexts. The Committee on the Rights of the Child and other UN bodies started using the term 'child justice' recently. We have also tried to use that in this book, as well as the terms 'youngsters' and 'young people'. The word juvenile is still used when we refer to international instruments still using that term.

Restorative justice is an umbrella concept, but the main features are that the harm is central and that victim, offender and the community should be involved in trying to find a solution for a conflict. The definition used by the European Forum for Restorative Justice is for both of us a workable one: Restorative justice is an approach of addressing harm or the risk of harm through engaging all those affected in coming to a common understanding and agreement on how the harm or wrongdoing can be repaired and justice achieved. There may be some differences in terms used by the different authors, since each term operates in its own local context.

3 An introduction of each chapter

In the first chapter Annemieke Wolthuis, researcher, teacher and mediator in the Netherlands, explores what restorative justice is in relation to children's rights and child justice. Can it be defined as a right against the position Lode Walgrave has taken in his foreword, where he argues that not everything can be seen within a rights discourse? And can children's rights protect children from the risks of restorative practices described by Tim Chapman in Chapter 2?

Both authors conclude positively though, in favor of a rights approach. Walgrave ends with these promising words: 'to construct restorative justice as a fully-fledged right for all youthful stakeholders in the aftermath of an offense, victims, offenders and members of the communities of care'. Chapman concludes that children's rights are compatible with restorative justice, although not automatic. There needs to be an awareness of how the values and strategic priorities of systems can influence practitioners to abuse or neglect children's rights. Tensions between children's rights and the values of restorative justice can, in his eyes, be resolved through distinguishing rights designed to protect children and those that promote their active participation in society.

Wolthuis agrees with these reflections. She starts by pointing out that reactions to criminal behavior by young people include more and more restorative measures worldwide. What does this trend entail and what are the core values of restorative justice for young suspects or accused persons and young victims? What practices and rules are in place and what can be used with them?

Wolthuis explores and explains the needs and possibilities of the use of restorative justice for young suspects and young people who have been harmed. She first goes back to the basics: What is restorative justice, where does it come from and what is special about it in relation to children and young people? Developments in restorative work among youth are explained, as well as relevant international children's rights and standards on child justice and restorative justice. She then moves on to the following aspects: What do experts say about how states should deal with criminal behavior of youngsters and the rights of young people in conflict with the law? How can or should it be integrated in child justice systems around the globe?

The UN Committee on the Rights of the Child considers that restorative measures are a priority above retributive reactions and that reintegration and learning from mistakes are especially important, for example, as also explained in more details by Renate Winter in Chapter 3. Wolthuis argues that restorative justice can be seen as a children's right and that all children should have access to restorative justice measures. At the same time, the implementation should also be rights-proof and protect against risks. Special emphasis is given to how restorative interventions can best be integrated in child justice systems.

And an ideal situation of what such a child restorative justice system should look like in law and in practice is envisaged. Wolthuis concludes that restorative justice should be accessible for all children and adolescents at all stages, from prevention until after detention.

Tim Chapman, visiting professor at the University of Strathclyde and at the University of Sassari, continues in his Chapter 2, entitled 'Restorative practices can steal the rights of children too: the importance of value-led and evidence-based standards', by exploring research that also has reported on what can go wrong when involving children in restorative justice, and what is needed to use it in an effective and useful way. To what extent does the practice of restorative justice enable children to exercise their rights? Informed by a rights-based approach, how can the practice of restorative justice be improved? To answer these questions, Chapman reviews research evidence into violations of key children's rights in restorative practices. He offers an analysis of how these abuses occur and then suggests how children's rights can become an integral part of restorative practice through value-led and evidence-based standards of practice. He also reiterates that restorative processes aim to restore both personal dignity and just relations.

He describes that best practices in restorative justice are based upon the inclusion and active participation of victims and perpetrators of harm, and their supporters, in a process of mutual understanding and agreement on what action to take to address the harm and its consequences. These practices conform to children's rights such as protection from discrimination, having their views heard and being treated according to their best interests. However, there is increasing evidence that restorative practices do not always respect these rights. He analyzes the structural and philosophical conditions that enable this to happen. Research results in different countries show also how it can fail if the right preparations or circumstances are not met, but these can be addressed. Chapman concludes with the proposal that if restorative processes are to be truly rights-based, the quality of practice should be assured by standards based upon robust values and research, and upon the quality of the professionals involved.

We were honored that Renate Winter, an international champion of children's rights, agreed to explain (in Chapter 3) the work of The UN Committee on the Rights of the Child and Restorative Justice. In her own personal style, she demonstrates how the Committee, the treaty body that has the mandate to watch over the implementation of the rights of children according to the Convention in all member states of the UN that have ratified the CRC, is engaged with the theme of child justice and restorative justice, and how it can address children's well-being.

She is critical of states which have not complied with the Convention. She does so because she believes that the Convention and other international instruments are tools for change.

Winter explains the influence of the main principles of the Convention on the child justice system and the importance of restorative justice for upholding these principles. To find alternatives for children in conflict or in contact with the law, she explains that Article 37, dealing with the protection of children deprived of their liberty has to be read in conjunction with Article 39, dealing with child victims (they might become witnesses as well and have then also to be protected), and Article 40, dealing with offending children. The more recent General Comment 24 on child justice mentions restorative justice more in detail. Restorative justice can, in the words of Winter, also be seen as a real alternative to the imprisonment of young people, that is still in far too many countries a fact even for minor incidents. Consequently, the Committee does its utmost to convince member states of the advantages of restorative youth justice, diversion, alternatives, mediation and community service in the best interest of children and society.

In Chapter 4, Israeli child expert and head of the criminology department of the University of Haifa, Tali Gal, writes about Child victims and child perpetrators in restorative justice: a Needs-Rights Model. She emphasizes the relevance of the EU Victims Directive of 2012, which creates an obligation for all EU members to ensure that restorative justice programs are accessible for any interested victim. In particular, the Directive stipulates that restorative justice must be tailored according to the unique needs of vulnerable populations, particularly children.

These are exciting times for restorative justice proponents. But they are also challenging. How should restorative justice programs operate in cases involving child victims? How can they avoid secondary victimization and achieve therapeutic goals for them? Additionally, any restorative justice program must also meet the needs and rights of young offenders.

Gal's chapter presents the Needs-Rights Model for child victims and considers its application to young offenders or children as offenders. The model integrates legal and psychosocial terminology in order to map the various interests of victimized children, and, once broadened, those of victimizing children as well. To shift from theory to practice, the chapter reconsiders the eight heuristics for working with victimized children and discusses their implementation when working with young offenders. She clearly states that the needs-rights of young offenders and young victims are closely related. Gal points at an urgent need to regulate the implementation of child-inclusive restorative justice programs. Restorative justice programs addressing childhood victimization are more likely to emerge within the juvenile justice context, where the focus is on the rehabilitation and reintegration of young perpetrators. A universal model that can be applied to victims as well as to perpetrators provides a useful framework for regulation in these contexts, as it does not require a full-blown diversion from existing restorative justice programs with young offenders. Gal concludes by giving three areas where this needs-rights model is significant, and a research agenda for the coming period.

Chapter 5 is entitled 'Rights-based restorative justice: questioning and decolonizing our ways of knowing, doing and being in Canada and beyond', and is written by Shannon Moore, associate professor in the Department of Child and Youth Studies and Director of the Centre for Women's and Gender Studies at Brock University in Canada. She focuses upon rights-based restorative justice for youth and offers a critical analysis of both the limits and the potential of integrating two United Nations frameworks: the United Nations Convention on the Rights of the Child and the United Nations Basic Principles on the Use of Restorative Justice Programmes in Criminal Matters. A model of rights-based restorative justice has been developed by her to articulate a framework to link the theoretically, ontologically and methodologically congruent principles of child rights and restorative justice. Child rights and restorative justice practices similarly encourage the voices of victims, offenders and young people to be heard through non-discriminatory, safe and authentic participation. Restorative justice and children's rights are premised on similar principles of human worth and dignity. One may reasonably assume that their interconnection in practice may facilitate more ethical and democratic responses to young people in conflict with the law.

Notwithstanding these arguments, this chapter interrogates the limits of both child rights and restorative justice at the threshold of translating international and national policy narratives into meaningful and direct practice with young people. Without such critical questioning, child rights and restorative justice processes risk, for instance, becoming a destructive tool to reify dominant power relations such as settler colonialism in countries such as Canada. Currently in Canada, there is an overrepresentation of indigenous and black young people and adults in contact with provincial and federal security and custody systems. This fact has been directly linked to the assimilation and cultural genocide of indigenous peoples through colonization processes and the residue of Enlightenment ideas that propelled the international slave trade for 500 years. In response, Moore presents an argument for decolonizing restorative justice and for a child rights policy and praxis to understand how complex systems are structurally formed, how power is exercised and how language shapes policy and practice interpretations. It also offers guidance on how to use restorative justice in such complex contexts.

Chapter 6 is entitled 'Restorative justice for children around the globe: international perspectives and trends'. It is written by Cedric Foussard, child justice expert at Terre des Hommes, in cooperation with other experts in the world. The first focus is on how restorative justice presents a shift in paradigm in North and Central America and also on how restorative justice is a return to roots in the Middle East and North Africa region, and Southeast Asia. During the autumn of 2019, the results of the Global Study on Children Deprived of Liberty were presented at the United Nations General Assembly. Following a two-year investigation, it was found that the initial number of children deprived of liberty around the globe exceeded one million. This concurs with an estimation made by UNICEF ten years ago. It is now internationally recognized that children who come into conflict with the law are more likely to have experienced violence or adversity than their non-offending peers. Exacerbating the deleterious effects of this childhood trauma, children's contact with the criminal justice system poses undue risks of physical, sexual and psychological violence.

Meanwhile, in the past decade, impelled by international and regional standards, guidelines and recommendations, justice systems for children have been reformed and improved to divert children away from the formal justice system and to implement alternatives to the deprivation of liberty. It is in this context that in different continents, simultaneously, a growing interest in restorative justice has been noted. Restorative justice practices for children are now more widespread than ever and are applied to cases of children who become involved with the justice system, both for minor and serious offenses.

This chapter gives an overview of the trends in restorative justice for children on an international and regional level, including recent changes in Central America, where the concept of restorative justice is being integrated in national legislation, and in North America, where civil society is playing an important role in promoting the use of restorative justice. In Southeast Asia, and the Middle East and North Africa (MENA) regions, restorative justice for children is evolving as part of the recovery of indigenous and customary justice practices, both in a secular and non-secular context.

Chapter 7, entitled 'Restorative justice in European youth justice systems: contextual, legal, practice-related and analytical aspects' is written by emeritus professor Frieder Dünkel of the University of Greifswald in northeast Germany and Andrea Păroşanu, currently Research Fellow with the Diana Unwin Chair in Restorative Justice, Victoria University of Wellington. Both have been involved in European comparative research on child justice and restorative justice for many years.

Elements of restorative justice have been incorporated into youth criminal law in most Western and recently also in Eastern European countries. Victim-offender mediation has become an important alternative to more repressive sanctions, and not only in youth justice systems. Recently, different forms of conferencing have been implemented in some jurisdictions (Belgium, Northern Ireland, etc.). As Western European countries review their experiences of restorative justice over longer periods, it will be possible to present some data on 'good, promising, questionable or bad practices'. The practice in Europe seems to be rather diverse. Specific attention is given to restorative justice in Belgium, Finland, Northern Ireland, France and Germany. At the same time, the numbers of referrals in most countries remain modest. The experience in Eastern Europe remains only 'symbolic' in most cases, but some interesting developments deserve to be mentioned.

This chapter summarizes the results of two projects conducted and coordinated at the Department of Criminology at the University of Greifswald. The first (EU-funded) project covered 36 countries and jurisdictions in order to draw a restorative justice-landscape concerning historical and legal backgrounds as well as the practice of implementation and use of restorative justice-elements in penal matters (see Dünkel, Grzywa-Holten & Horsfield, 2015). The second project covered 30 jurisdictions representing the 28 EU member states. It was focused on developments in youth justice (see Dünkel, Horsfield & Păroşanu, 2015). The results are encouraging on the one side, as restorative justice more and more becomes an integral part of youth (and adult) criminal justice systems. On the other hand, numbers remain low and legal professionals are still reluctant and concerned about the new approach.

The driving forces for reform, such as abolitionist thinking, the emphasis on victims' rights, the shift toward more rehabilitative youth justice measures, or just the pragmatic orientation to international human rights standards in the process of integrating into the

EU have shaped the need for youth justice reforms. Such reform has seen expansions in the powers of decision-makers throughout the criminal justice system to divert cases from prosecution, conviction and/or sentencing into alternative procedures and measures that bear superior reintegrative and rehabilitative potential than purely retributive intervention. Overall, the picture that remains is that the availability of restorative justice decreases the deeper one delves into the criminal procedure, with a few exceptions to this rule that provide access to victim-offender mediation or conferencing, regardless of the stage of criminal proceedings and regardless of offense and offender characteristics.

Evaluation results are also summarized, which indicate that restorative justice measures have a great potential to satisfy victims, improve offenders in terms of desistance and social reintegration and reduce reoffending.

In Chapter 8, Julia Sloth Nielsen, professor at the Faculty of law, University of the Western Cape, and professor of children's rights and the developing world at Leiden University, addresses restorative child justice in South Africa, Namibia and Zimbabwe. This chapter gives the current state of play of restorative justice for children in conflict with the law in the three neighboring southern African countries of South Africa, Namibia and Zimbabwe. It describes the way in which restorative justice entered the public arena in the three countries and provides background information on law reform processes which seek to further restorative justice principles and practices in the child justice domain. Finally, an assessment of the current situation as regards the penetration of restorative justice in child justice in the sub-region is made. Sloth Nielsen shows that restorative justice has gained a toehold in the southern African sub-region in child justice legislation and, to an extent, in practice.

However, sustaining promising initiatives seems to present challenges, as the South African experience, in particular, shows. Support in practice has wavered, as illustrated by the diminishing use of restorative justice practices, even though they appear in, and are adequately regulated by, legislation. In contrast, commitment to restorative justice in neighboring Namibia and Zimbabwe continues unabated, as evidenced in recent draft child justice law proposals which continue to be received positively by stakeholders from all quarters at workshops (non-governmental organizations, police authorities, prosecutors and so forth). Reasons for this must necessarily be speculative, but it could be that the ties that restorative justice has to indigenous values is still felt more strongly in these countries, by comparison to South Africa. It could simply be that South African functionaries prefer the 'easier' diversion options which the Child Justice Act provides, as less time-consuming and labor-intensive.

Sloth Nielsen concludes by expressing worries about the effects of the COVID pandemic in the region. With the digital deficit in Africa, the replacement of 'in-person' mediated meetings with online versions is simply not a prospect in the foreseeable future. This then poses considerable challenges for 'in-person' meetings. At the same time, COVID has exposed huge flaws and gaps in child protection systems across the continent, rendering children far more vulnerable to violations of their physical and psychological integrity as they remain concealed at home, out of school, and as frontline responders are unable to detect or get access to children in need. This also affects children in conflict with the law.

The remaining chapters are about the development of restorative justice with children in eight countries. Reading them, one becomes aware of different stages of development and how each stage presents new challenges. Some countries, such as Chile, France, the Netherlands and Georgia are in the process of implementing new legislation. Other countries have well-established provisions for restorative justice. These include Finland, Poland, Canada and New Zealand.

Maia Chochua, a lawyer who has supported the development and implementation of the Juvenile Justice Code of Georgia, writes about introducing restorative practices in the child justice system of Georgia. Maia Chochua traces the history of reform in her country from a retributive to a restorative system and acknowledges the support of international bodies, such as the European Union and UNICEF, and of international experts. The new Juvenile Justice Code is based upon the CRC and international models such as the UNODC Model Law on Juvenile Justice and the Model Law on Justice in Matters involving Child Victims and Witnesses of Crime.

Readers will be informed and encouraged by Chochua's detailed account of the change process and its tangible outcomes. It is also made clear through the description of the procedures how the CRC supported the transformation and how children's rights are threaded throughout the Code's provisions. In just 10 years, the life chances of Georgian children and young people involved in offenses as both perpetrators and victims have been significantly improved.

The next chapter, Restorative justice and children's rights in Aotearoa New Zealand: Convergence and divergence, is written by Andrea Păroşanu, research fellow at Victoria University of Wellington, and Nessa Lynch, associate professor, Victoria University of Wellington. They report on the family group conference approach in New Zealand (Aotearoa), focusing on the points of convergence and divergence between restorative justice and children's rights. They provide a useful profile of children and young people in conflict with the law in their country, demonstrating their needs and vulnerability to being victims of abuse.

New Zealand's youth justice system emphasizes well-being and recognizes the rights and interests of victims, with the aim of preventing offending. It also respects whānau, hapū, iwi or a family group, in accordance with tikanga Māori [custom]. The system prioritizes diversion from prosecution. The primary restorative process used is the family group conference, though, as the authors explain, its restorative nature is limited by its lack of voluntariness and low participation by victims. They also provide evidence that the right to participate in a process that relies so much upon communication can disadvantage children with language difficulties and learning disabilities. This can be addressed through specialist support.

Daniela Bolivar, assistant professor at the School of Social Work at the Catholic University of Chile, Alejandra Mera, a Chilean lawyer and professor of criminal justice in Diego Portales University, and Iván Navarro Papic, who works in the Ministry of Justice and Human Rights of Chile and lectures at Alberto Hurtado University, outline their ideas in the chapter 'The potential of restorative justice to fulfil the children's right to be heard: the experience in Chile'. They describe the implementation of restorative justice with children and young people in Chile, stressing the critical importance of the right of the child to be heard. The chapter was written in the context of the law on the Chilean juvenile justice system that is being reformed to introduce restorative justice and to emphasize social reintegration.

An evaluation of one of the pilot mediation programs found substantial evidence that children and young people were enabled to participate actively in the justice process by sharing their narratives. This experience also contributed to the young people's emotional development. Significant factors in the young person's experience included skillful mediation and not being judged by the mediator, having their needs addressed, the child's developmental stage being taken into account. The authors also value restorative justice as a contribution to a democratic society.

Jessica Fillipi is a researcher in criminology with the Ministry of Justice in France, and is associated with the Centre of Research in Criminology at the University of Law and Criminology in Brussels. In her chapter, When child-friendly justice meets restorative justice in a welfare model: the case of France, she examines critically a law introduced in 2014, which put in place provision for restorative justice at all stages of the criminal justice process. The author is particularly interested in how the French 'welfare model' of youth justice limits the potential of restorative justice.

Fillipi argues that the 'child-friendly' model of justice is more compatible with children's rights and restorative justice. However, the procedures for restorative justice with children and young people in France are framed within a welfare model through which professionals take responsibility to protect the well-being of children, thus severely limiting their participation and power to make their own choices.

Beata Czarnecka-Dzialuk, assistant professor at the Department of Criminology of the Institute of Law Studies in the Polish Academy of Sciences, describes the development of restorative justice in Poland and the importance of children's rights in supporting these developments in her chapter titled Restorative justice for young people in Poland: the law, current practices and prospects for improvement. However, like Fillipi, she demonstrates how various institutional obstacles have limited the use of mediation with children and young people. These include the way that the law is framed, the conservatism of judges, the lack of availability of mediation service and low public awareness.

Czarnecka-Dzialuk concludes with a useful list of recommendations to improve the situation including the importance of standards of practice.

Maartje Berger is legal advisor for Children's Rights and Child Protection at Defence for Children and Annemieke Wolthuis is an independent consultant, researcher, trainer and mediator in the field of human rights, children's rights and restorative justice. This chapter, Child justice in the Netherlands: a boost for restorative and child-friendly interventions?, offers the reader an overview of developments in the Netherlands regarding mediation in criminal cases involving youth with respect to children's rights.

The authors present current statistics, practices and research. They address current challenges and describe how new ideas are making the Dutch child justice system more restorative and child-friendly. Berger and Wolthuis usefully link the rights of children to be heard and to enter into meaningful participation in the restorative process. They conclude with a list of recommendations which may have relevance to many countries beyond the Netherlands.

Arrangements for restorative justice in Canada are among the most developed in the world. Consequently, we were very pleased that Brenda Morrison, the Director of the Centre for Restorative Justice and an associate professor in the School of Criminology, Simon Fraser University, Canada, Virginia Caputo, an anthropologist, Angie Mapara-Osachoff, the Senior Regional Program Manager for Equitas, and Daniella Bendo, an Assistant Professor in Childhood and Youth Studies at King's University College at Western University in Canada, chose to describe an innovative project based upon restorative principles that enables children to know their rights through experiential exercises in their contribution, 'Rights, restoration and justice for children: *Shaking the Movers* in Canada'.

The *Shaking the Movers* model is based upon the premise that children are full rights holders. It represents a restorative encounter between young people's lived experience and authority. The overlap between children's rights and restorative justice is demonstrated by the degree of active participation, by processes of accountability and by system change. The authors invite readers to expand their understanding of the potential of the practices of restorative justice. The chapter is also a strong tribute to the vision, commitment and persistence of one woman, the Hon. Landon Pearson, a true champion of children's rights.

Maija Gellin, director of the program for restorative approach and mediation in education (*VERSO-program*) in Finland, has contributed the last chapter, titled Strengthening rights and participation of children: a Finnish perspective on a restorative approach to education. She also invites us to imagine rights-based restorative practices beyond the youth justice system. Similar to the previous chapter, the author demonstrates that schools can be sites in which children can learn and practice their rights though engaging in restorative practices.

Finland has an international reputation for high standards of education. But as Gellin states, conflicts, bullying and misbehavior are part of daily life in Finnish schools, as they are throughout the world. Unlike most countries, mediation and conflict resolution is part of the Finish core curriculum for schools. There has been a restorative approach in Finnish schools since 2001 and the Verso program has been collecting statistics to evaluate its effectiveness.

4 In conclusion

This book has brought together 23 people from many different countries in the field of restorative justice for young people in a children's rights perspective to share a rich and diverse range of research, theory, legal contexts and experiences. Readers should bear in mind that most of the contributors are not writing in their own language.

The rights and needs of children have been clearly connected with the practices of restorative justice. Risks of abuse of rights in restorative practices have been identified. But the chapters have demonstrated the potential of the use of high-quality restorative justice in the whole spectrum from prevention to the detention of young people who come in conflict with the law or are harmed by such an act. Both the Canadian and Finnish experiences inform us that it is not enough to have children's rights in place within the youth justice system. For rights to be embedded in society, children must have the opportunity to become aware of their rights and to develop their confidence to assert their rights when they need to.

This gives us reason to be positive about what has been achieved in the field of restorative justice and child justice since the nineties. At the same time, there is a need to continue to research, lobby and build active support, and continuously improve practices to make these children's rights into reality. We call upon all of you to make this a joint initiative and to make sure child justice is not the unwanted child of government policy in many states any longer. It is for our children and our future.

Part I

International standards and reflections on restorative justice for children

Chapter 1
Restorative justice, a child's right

*Annemieke Wolthuis**

1 Introduction

Consider this scenario that I experienced as a mediator in a criminal case (names and some details are changed):

> *On a Saturday afternoon, Marco (16) and his girlfriend went to the theatre to watch a movie. Some boys behind them started throwing popcorn and candy at them. When Marco said something about it, they got into an argument. When they left the cinema, a few of the boys were waiting for them. All of a sudden, Marco found himself surrounded by several of them. Davy (15) kicked him. Marco got terribly mad and took out a knife he had in his jacket. He stabbed Davy who started bleeding heavily.*
> *The police were called by some bystanders and an ambulance rushed Davy to the hospital. Marco spent that night in police custody and, after the court trial, was sentenced to a few months in youth detention. During his detention, he was invited to consider participating in victim-offender mediation. Davy, who had sustained a serious shoulder injury, had recovered in the meantime and also received the request to take part in a guided encounter with Marco. With the support of their parents, they both accepted the invitation. A restorative journey started.*

This example gives an introduction on how a restorative encounter can take place within a child justice system. But there are many more examples. In this chapter, I will first address some basic questions: What is restorative justice in relation to children's rights and youth justice? Can governments be obliged to ensure that restorative interventions are in place for children in conflict with the law? Can young people (victims and offenders) themselves or their parents claim it as their right to be allowed to take part in a restorative encounter?

In order to explore this more in depth, we have to look at what international and European legal instruments say about the role of restorative justice when it comes to

* I would like to thank Jaap Doek, Ivo Aertsen and Lode Walgrave for their useful comments and suggestions.

child justice and reactions to delinquent behavior and harm. What do these rights entail? We also need to consider what rights and needs victims have, and, in the context of this book, child victims specifically. In what follows, I will first give a short introduction to restorative justice, its main principles, background and forms and on the specific aspects of restorative justice related to children and adolescents. Relevant international and European conventions and guidelines will then be explained, followed by an analysis of the guiding aspects. Of course, the main starting point when referring to children's rights is the UN Convention on the Rights of the Child (CRC). I will mention the most important rights in relation to child justice within the CRC, but for a more in-depth clarification and the importance of those articles and comments I refer to Chapter 3 by Renate Winter, judge and member of the UN Committee on the Rights of the Child. There are many other regional and international standards relevant for youth justice and restorative justice that will be addressed, although some will be explored in more depth in other chapters of this volume. In the final part of this chapter, I will explore how restorative justice could be positioned in relation to criminal justice and youth justice and what needs to be done to implement it to a maximum extent. An ideal situation is envisaged.

2 RESTORATIVE (YOUTH) JUSTICE

2.1 *Definitions and concepts*

To put restorative justice, and more specifically restorative youth justice, into context, I will give a short overview of what it entails. Restorative justice is an umbrella concept with many definitions. Its ancient origins go back to times where people tried to solve conflicts within their own community. Later, criticism of the criminal justice system and the emancipation of victims and children created new or renewed attention for restorative (youth) justice, especially since the 1970s. A central notion of restorative justice is its focus on the restoration of the damage and/or harm done through dialogue between victim and offender and eventually those within their networks. In a traditional criminal justice process the main focus is on the offense and the offender.

The following definition by Vanfraechem (2007), which was adapted from a definition provided by Walgrave (Walgrave, 2000, 2004) to reflect a more practical angle and which I find useful and adequate, is:

> Restorative justice is an option for doing justice that is primarily focused on repairing the harm that has been caused by the crime. It is best accomplished through cooperative processes that include all stakeholders. (Vanfraechem, 2007: 18, 35)

On its homepage, the European Forum for Restorative Justice states in 2020 that

> Restorative justice is an approach of addressing harm or the risk of harm through engaging all those affected in coming to a common understanding and agreement on how the harm or wrongdoing can be repaired and justice achieved (see: https://www.euforumrj.org/en).

Again, it shows that the focus is on harm and how that harm can be restored. It is also a humane approach, and, in the words of Nils Christie (1977), about giving the conflict back to the parties who own it.

A commonly used tool to visualize the parties involved is the restorative justice triangle. In this triangle, the harm is placed at the center and the three parties that can play a role, or can be influenced by what happened, are: the person who is harmed (often referred to as the victim), the person who caused the harm (often referred to as the offender) and the society or community. It is about relinking what has gone wrong. Criminal offenses are often committed when there is little bonding of young persons with their environment, and sometimes when there is too much bonding, so there is a broken link that needs to be restored. Restoration with society and/or those directly involved in the criminal offense is needed (Deklerck, 2007). This is relevant for both the harm doer and the harmed person.

Figure 1.1. Restorative triangle (Restorative Justice Nederland).

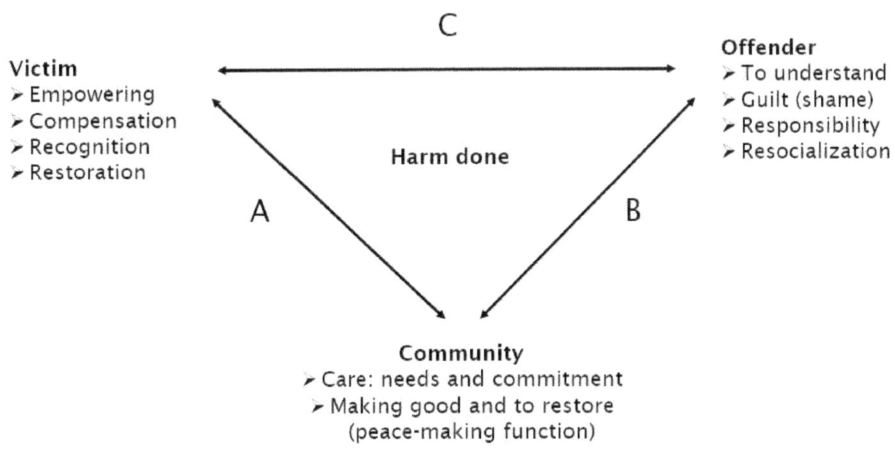

This triangle shows the possible needs of victims, who often want to be listened to, be empowered and be able to share their experiences and anger. Sometimes, they want restoration and compensation. The offender can be in need of a better understanding of what happened, and what the effects of his or her behavior were. Sometimes shame and guilt play a role. Being made a part of a restorative encounter or process means that they are enabled to take responsibility, and in a later stage – if detention is involved – to reintegrate into society. Concerning the impact of criminal offenses on the community, it is also important to point at the threat such events create for the general feelings of safety and security. This results in the need for public action.

The role of the community may vary in different (criminal justice) systems and per case, but it is a fact that in most cases there are more people affected than only the victim and offender. The affected community consists, for example, of bystanders. Think, for instance, of the people outside the movie theater where the violent incident between Davy and Marco took place. Staff at the theater and bystanders may also have been shocked or affected by what they saw or felt. In other cases, the entire community, municipality or society can be affected (Braithwaite, 2002). In addition, there is also the supportive community (of care) around a child, consisting of parents, other family members, friends, a teacher or a youth worker.

2.2 Roots

The origins and background of relatively new initiatives for child justice have different roots (Weitekamp, 1999). More recent factors that have contributed to the development of restorative justice since the 80s include the following: a growing criticism of the existing child justice systems which were malfunctioning, not rights-based enough and where the rehabilitative or educational approach showed its limitations, and the emancipation of victims who have received more rights and a more serious role in criminal cases since the eighties. Also, the development of children and young people in society as being subjects of rights and having their voices heard – especially since the adoption of the UN Convention on the Rights of the Child in 1989 – has played a role (Wolthuis, 2012).

In most literature on restorative justice, reference is also made to ancient roots, going back to how aboriginals and indigenous peoples dealt with conflicts or misbehavior within their communities. In those societies, the elderly played often a role in getting people to talk, share and heal (Johnstone & Van Ness, 2007; Morris & Maxwell, 2001; Weitekamp, 1999). In New Zealand, the youth justice system is oriented toward first trying a family group conference when a young person enters the child justice system and it is based on a Maori tradition, mainly because they had many Maori youngsters in the criminal justice system (Morris & Maxwell, 2001). The experiences there have inspired other systems too.

What is known as the first modern restorative justice project with young people is the Kitchener project in Canada that was set up in 1971, as also described by Shannon Moore in Chapter 5. Restorative justice started in many countries with experiments and pilots with children. This is partly because judicial actors and public opinion are more open toward alternatives when children and young people are involved. They are the ones who should, and can still, learn from their mistakes. Also, for politicians this was an easier target (Wolthuis, 2012).

2.3 *In a circle*

The most common forms of restorative justice – at least in a European context – are victim-offender mediation (VOM) and (family group) conferencing. VOM is a meeting where the victim and the offender meet in a well-prepared and coordinated session by one or two trained mediators, often around a round table. Sometimes support persons like parents, partners or other family members may join (Bradshaw, Roseborough & Umbreit, 2006). In a conference, from the first moment people from the network of both parties are involved. The emphasis is on family or broader network involvement and a conference is often described as more outcome-oriented than a VOM. The participants all sit in a circle. Sometimes, representatives of the community or public institutions like a police officer are also involved. Often two facilitators lead the conference.

How many people can attend and whether or not a script is used may vary according to the model in use (Zinsstag & Vanfraechem, 2012b). A third form is restorative circles, which can include much larger groups, after problems or conflicts in a community, for example in cases of discrimination or hate crime in order to make peace. Also, in issues in schools or neighborhoods where more pupils or students are involved or affected, youth circles can be used (Fellegi & Szego, 2013; Pranis, 2005).

Today in almost all countries in the world, restorative justice practices are used, especially for young people in conflict with the law (Aertsen, 2021; Wolthuis, 2012). The forms differ and also who initiates or refers cases differs as can be found in the other chapters of this book. There is no need to call an intervention restorative only when a real encounter is taking place between parties involved in a conflict. Sometimes people are not ready to meet, but happy if the facilitator brings messages back and forward, a so-called shuttle mediation. Interventions can vary from fully, mostly and partly restorative, depending on the active involvement of three major stakeholders in the aftermath of a crime: victims, offenders and communities (McCold & Wachtel, 2003).

2.4 *Does it work?*

Results of the evaluations and meta-studies of restorative justice interventions, including possible effects, show that restorative youth justice works. Research into different forms of restorative justice (mainly victim-offender mediations (VOM) and conferencing) reveals high satisfaction rates for both victims and offenders. Most evaluations indicate a decrease of recidivism, especially in more severe cases, and in no cases have higher numbers of recidivism been found. Restorative processes generally engage victims and perpetrators more effectively than the traditional justice system. Offenders appreciate the opportunity to meet the victim, to actively participate and to express remorse. They have been found to have a more positive attitude toward police and law through participating in restorative justice. Restorative justice often helps to strengthen relationships with their friends or relatives, encouraging desistance. Victims' needs and interests are taken into account. However, as it is a voluntary process, there is also a large group not interested. About 50 percent of the victims approached agree to participate. Once they become involved in a restorative justice process, they experience less fear and feelings of revenge, and satisfaction rates are high. Feelings of safety also seem to increase. Both parties associate restorative justice with fair treatment. Entering into a safe and truthful dialogue with others enhances each participant's understanding of what has happened from each person's point of view and leads to a sense of responsibility to repair or restore the consequences of the harm. Furthermore, the use of restorative justice can save costs by preventing youngsters from entering the court system, and by diminishing incarceration rates (Bergseth & Bouffard, 2007; Bradshaw et al., 2006; Claessen et al., 2015; Shapland et al., 2008; Shapland, Robinson & Sorsby 2011; Sherman & Strang, 2007).

2.5 *Current*

As Moore also states in her chapter, Abrahamson's (2001) assertion that youth justice is 'the unwanted child of state responsibilities' is in most states still valid. There are many governments that too easily put children and young people who get in conflict with the law in closed correctional youth institutions instead of helping them to meet their needs. Instead of assisting them to learn, we put them away. Think of the famous James Bulger case in the UK where two teenagers kidnapped a toddler from a shopping mall,went to a railway where they tortured him and left him for death. An awful act, of course, but the harsh reaction by the British media and criminal justice system was also questioned a lot and challenged before the European Court on Human Rights. The boys were sentenced to imprisonment as if they were adults. The system made them worse and not socially better integrated boys. The European Court of Human Rights ruled that the UK had violated Article 6 ECHR (*T and V v. United Kingdom*, ECHR, 16 December 1999). The question is what the impact of restorative justice could be for society and for the boys, or kids in similar situations.

At the same time, there is a tendency in some countries and there are efforts on the part of the United Nations, the European Commission, the Council of Europe and other regional bodies to make the system more humane and child-friendly, including the use of restorative justice practices. The question is what place the restorative justice interventions have in the system and how many cases are referred. Unfortunately, the figures indicate that restorative justice interventions are still marginal compared to other legal sanctions (Dünkel, Grzywa-Holten & Horsfield, 2015; Dünkel, Horsfield & Păroşanu, 2015; Lee & Dandurand, 2020; Marder, 2020; Put, Vanfraechem & Walgrave, 2012; Shapland, Burn, Crawford & Gray, 2020).

2.6 Child offenders and child victims

In relation to restorative child justice, more attention in research has been given so far to child suspects or offenders than to child victims. Roles can vary since child offenders may also be victims or deal with similar experiences as victims. Furthermore, as both parties have similar needs in many ways, understanding the experience of child offenders can offer some insights into the situation of child victims. It is important to combine the needs and rights of young people in this as described by Gal in Chapter 4 and in her previous work (Gal, 2011).

Restorative justice is being implemented in child justice and consequently also in cases involving child victims. It is important to note that restorative justice is also being implemented in the regular criminal justice system for adult offenders who have victimized a child victim. In such cases the set of principles and values for restorative youth justice should be fully applied. While many countries have recognized the importance of this type of conflict resolution in cases involving children, a more comprehensive understanding of the pitfalls, challenges to access and good practices for child victims is lacking. Recently, more research has been initiated on child victims, for example by the i-RESTORE project, coordinated by Terre des hommes and funded by the EC, emphasizing this need for more attention and training for professionals that are initiated in the next stage of the project.[1] Promoting the use of restorative justice for child victims will result in benefits for them, but only if conducted by following the appropriate methods and safeguards , to ensure that no further harm is caused to the victim. This is especially important, because children may be placed in vulnerable situations, for example when they do not receive adequate preparation, support and follow-up. Furthermore, power imbalances are more likely to arise when dealing with child victims and adult offenders (Wolthuis, Laxminarayan & Biffi, 2020).

---

1 https://tdh-europe.org/our-work/i-restore-protecting-child-victims-through-restorative-justice/7143, last consulted on 14 January 2021.

3 International human rights standards

3.1 UN Convention on the Rights of the Child

What do human, and more specifically children's, rights say about how to deal with young people who make a mistake that can result in a harmful event or an offense? And how to deal with young victims? What is child-friendly justice? What is a rights-based restorative justice? On the side of the offender, it is the pedagogical aspect what makes restorative justice for children special. Restorative justice programs can offer effective alternatives to formal and stigmatizing sanctions/punishments. This is mainly because of the learning aspects involved, the use of diversion and the provision of alternatives for the imprisonment of youngsters. The development of children's rights has contributed to this end (Wolthuis, 2012).

The UN Convention on the Rights of the Child (CRC) offers rights and protection with the intention that every child should be able to grow up and become a well-balanced adult. A child, according to the CRC is a 'subject of rights', and states have an obligation to make sure that these rights of the child are respected, protected and fulfilled while taking into account the evolving capacities of the child. Youngsters who come into contact with the police and justice authorities need special attention. Just like any other child, they need guidance and training while growing up.

Three pillars already identified by Cantwell in 1995 are: *provision, protection and participation*. Children have the right to protection, to provisions and to take part in society (Cantwell, 1995). The forms of restorative justice used in criminal procedures clearly contain, in addition to the restorative function for the victim, a pedagogical character for the accused. The CRC was adopted in 1989 and does not use the wording 'restorative justice', but largely reflects restorative thinking given the fact that in Article 40, para. 1 CRC all states parties to the CRC recognize the desirability of promoting the child's reintegration and the child's assuming a constructive role in society. The term 'restorative justice' became much more known and accepted in the 1990s. All international and European instruments dealing with youth crime or related aspects that were launched after 1996 use the term restorative justice and see it as a preferred intervention (Lynch, 2010; Wolthuis, 2012). The CRC is the common thread throughout the various contributions in this book and so will be addressed repeatedly. The various chapters need to be accessible on their own, so discussion of the CRC might be repetitive. For an overview of the relevant articles of the CRC and the work of the UN Committee on the Rights of the Child, see Chapter 3 by Renate Winter.

The following section will provide an overview of other relevant child rights regulations in relation to child justice focused both on child victims as well as child offenders. It is important to have a 'child justice' system that addresses the situation of victims and offenders equally. A really 'inclusive' child justice system is a system with a balanced approach to all stakeholders. The content of relevant human rights standards for child justice, including victims and offenders and restorative justice, are explained and relevant provisions for child restorative justice are cited. Explanatory comments from the Committee on the Rights of the Child give further explanations, as well as new implementation tools such as the Handbook on Restorative Justice Programmes of 2020.

3.2 *Other UN instruments*

In addition to the CRC (1989), the following child justice guidelines were issued by the UN in the same period that provided a more in-depth understanding of the CRC: the Riyadh Guidelines (1990) that deal with the social policy to protect young people and to prevent them from committing criminal offenses; the Beijing Rules (1985) that call upon progressive youth justice systems to be installed and the Havana Rules (1990) that guarantee the fundamental rights and include measures that should be initiated for the social reintegration of children deprived of their liberty (Wolthuis, 2012).

There are other UN recommendations that were adopted later and make reference to restorative justice, for example, the UN Guidelines on Justice in Matters involving Child Victims and Witnesses of Crime that was issued in 2005. These guidelines recognize the particular vulnerability of children who are victims and/or witnesses of a crime and are exposed to a significant risk of secondary victimization as a result of their participation in the criminal proceedings. The guidelines encourage specifically the use of 'informal and community practices, such as restorative justice' (Art. 36).

The United Nations Principles and Guidelines on Access to Legal Aid in Criminal Justice Systems (2013) in its definition of 'legal aid', includes restorative justice processes as a type of service that should be provided at no cost to those offenders, victims and witnesses without sufficient means or when the interests of justice so require (para. 8).

Also, in 2013, the Office of the Special Representative of the Secretary-General on Violence Against Children published a report[2] supporting restorative justice. The report provided several recommendations, arguing that it is time to move from a punitive model to a more restorative model, particularly for children (UN, 2013).

The United Nations Model Strategies and Practical Measures on the Elimination of Violence against Children in the Field of Crime Prevention and Criminal Justice (2014) recommend the provision of legal aid and legal information to children participating in alternative dispute resolution mechanisms and restorative justice processes (para. 6 (l)). Recognizing the merits of restorative justice programs, particularly as alternatives to

2 To access the report, click here: https://violenceagainstchildren.un.org/news/promoting-restorative-justice-children. Last accessed on 14 January 2021.

criminal proceedings, the strategies recommend also the use of diversion programs and the implementation of restorative justice programs for children as alternative measures to judicial proceedings (para. 31). Because of the serious nature of violence against children and the severity of the physical and psychological harm caused to child victims, the strategies urge caution and Member States are encouraged to ensure that through such mechanisms:

> violence against children is appropriately denounced and deterred, that perpetrators of violence against children are held accountable for their actions and that redress, support and compensation for child victims is provided. (para. 25)

The new UNODC Handbook on Restorative Justice Programmes (2020) that updated the 2006 version is a practical guide related to the UN Basic Principles on the Use of Restorative Justice Programmes in Criminal Matters (2002). The Handbook makes references to child victims and offenders in many chapters, but in Chapter 6 on more serious crimes it states:

> Restorative justice may also be an appropriate response in cases where children are victims of violence. Restorative justice can offer an environment where child victims, with the support of family, friends or a support person/ advocate, can participate in a process that meets their varying needs, be accommodated in terms of their coping capacity and level of development and avoid further trauma for children through exposure to difficult and unfriendly adversarial justice processes that may otherwise occur. The success of such an approach, from a child's rights and needs perspective, depends on the extent to which the child is participating voluntarily, is adequately prepared and is supported along the way.

These last preconditions are relevant in all cases concerning children in restorative justice interventions. When addressing violence against children, it is important to recognize that children who are victims of violence are in a unique position of powerlessness compared with adult victims of crime. Power imbalance between the child victim and the offender may result in pressure to participate or forgive the offender and it also affects the bargaining power of the participants in the process. It is concluded that in cases involving children, the best interests of the child and in particular the safety of the child victim must always be a precondition and central goal of the restorative process. Child victims must be thoroughly clinically assessed prior to any participation in restorative justice (Wolthuis et al., 2020).

In other chapters in this book other, regional guidelines such as the European guidelines on child-friendly justice, binding EU Directives and the Council of Europe Recommendation CM/Rec (2018)8 concerning restorative justice in criminal matters offer scope and content in relation to encourage states to develop and use restorative justice with respect to their criminal justice systems, for example Dünkel & Păroşanu (Chapter 7). The relevant laws and regulations for countries in Africa are addressed by Slot Nielsen (Chapter 8) in this issue. For other regions, see Foussard (Chapter 6).

4 Key principles and laws & regulations

4.1 The underlying principles of a children's rights-based approach

The international instruments discussed above contain key principles for a 'rights-based' child justice system. For child offenders, they can be summarized as:
- Children to have the opportunity to learn from their mistakes; thus pedagogy as a leading concept;
- The rights of the child to be the determining consideration;
- The best interests of the child as a primary focus;
- Diversion (alternatives for entering the criminal procedure) where possible;
- Special attention for the development of personal responsibility;
- Reintegration of the child back into society as the main goal of the reaction given;
- Victims to be involved in the procedure;
- Use of restorative justice where possible;
- Detention to be used only as a measure of last resort;

In my PhD dissertation, I identified that these principles could be formed with the first letters in Dutch: the words PROBEER HET, meaning TRY it OUT. I called it a TRY OUT model in order for the Dutch context to give restorative justice for children and young people a real boost and to take it seriously (Wolthuis, 2012). The mentioned instruments give diversion and the use of restorative justice a prominent place in response to criminal cases. Restorative justice becomes a priority when dealing with youth delinquency. In my opinion, we can speak about a restorative duty and a children's right. It is about the duty of governments to make the use of restorative methods in penal cases possible, including the task of monitoring its realization. Young people themselves, even if they make mistakes, have the right to be treated in a child-friendly and educational way, with restorative justice as one of the clear options spelled out in many international human rights instruments.

For child victims, the following principles are relevant:
- Attention for their needs;

- Proper protection from violence and other harmful acts;
- Right to recover from harm done to them;
- Assistance for this recovery and reintegration;
- An environment which fosters the health, self-respect and the dignity of the child;
- Prevention from re-victimization;
- Attention for power imbalances;
- Individual needs assessment to identify specific protection;
- Legal safeguards and a rights-based approach;
- The importance of good and regular training in all these aspects for professionals working with child victims (and or child suspects);
- The right to legal and social assistance for a victim involved in either a criminal law or a civil law procedure;
- The right to privacy.

Also, these needs and rights need to be taken into account by states and institutions when dealing with children in conflict with the law (Wolthuis et al., 2020).

At the same time, there are risks in using restorative justice interventions with young people, such as power differences and secondary victimization. Chapman in the next chapter addresses the risks and pitfalls that need to be addressed in order to make the use of restorative interventions a safe and sound choice.

4.2 National laws and regulations

International law provides a frame, but much is still left for further arrangements at the national level. Laws and regulations can promote restorative justice in a country, but whether and how these regulations can be used depends on local context and its social ecology; how does the implementation of legal rules run in a country and, more specifically, how do formal rights function in practice? Critical victimology (and criminology) has criticized the rights approach to victims for being selective, discriminatory, polarizing, etc. How this is all settled also influences how children's rights function in practice.

Procedural safeguards, guidance and control are important points to take into account when drafting bylaws. Specific laws regulating restorative justice stimulate continuity and a central policy, which often involves financial support and security of the progress and evaluations of the interventions. How restorative justice is placed at the heart of the juvenile justice system in Northern Ireland is a very successful example (Zinsstag & Chapman, 2012a). At the same time, too many regulations concerning details do not correspond to the characteristics of restorative justice itself, which is essentially about giving people the opportunity to take ownership of their personal responsibility and finding just solutions for the harm done (Wolthuis, 2012).

Much inspiration can be learned from abroad. However, Zehr and Mc Rae have written when they were explaining the New Zealand model that no model should be simply copied and plugged into another context. It is better to adapt the principles of restorative justice as necessary to each setting (MacRae & Zehr, 2004). It is important to observe and obtain insight about the good aspects and the problems faced elsewhere, and accordingly adapt and apply this information to our own cultural and legal context.

5 Restorative justice and criminal (youth) justice

5.1 *What position*

The question of how to position restorative youth justice in relation to criminal (youth) justice has been addressed since the beginning of the movement. Restorative justice has a different objective from the traditional criminal law approach. The objective of restorative justice is to repair or restore the damage caused by a crime. To restore means to focus on the future and finding solutions. It puts an emphasis on the harm that has been caused and relationships that may have been damaged as a result. This implies a different perspective than that of the traditional criminal law system in which retribution, deterrence and preventing reoffending dominate. Restorative justice can be described as 'a horizontal-oriented discourse' as the offender and the victim participate in working toward a solution by taking part in the decision-making throughout the joint communication process. Interaction between the victim and the offender and restoration/reparation are the leading factors in the settlement (Johnstone & Van Ness, 2007; Zehr, 1990).

How can restorative justice, with its own specific objectives, function in relation to child justice? Opinions on how to position restorative justice – within or outside the criminal justice system – and how to design the ideal system partially overlap. However, there are some who call for a complete replacement of criminal justice by restorative justice. Walgrave has named this 'the restorative paradigm'. He argues that restoration in youth justice should be a first choice based on meta-evaluations and especially in more serious cases (Walgrave, 2009). He has built on that 'maximalistic vision' and now calls it a 'consequential vision of restorative justice' – in short, recovery where possible and only in extreme cases in which offenders are a danger to themselves or to society proceed to sanctioning in the form of imprisonment. Furthermore, in his vision, the recovery goal is central and not the process (Walgrave, 2009, 2020).

Those who disagree, feel that restorative justice should be positioned outside of the criminal justice system, or next to it. This line of thinking can be described as the 'minimalistic' view (McCold & Wachtel, 2003). Von Hirsch and Ashworth express worries about the fairness of a restorative approach, because no limitations can be made on the kind of sanctions that are agreed or imposed (Ashworth, 2005; Von Hirsch, Roberts, Bottoms, Roach & Schiff, 2003). Weijers is also critical and promotes in his 'revisionistic' vision that a restorative encounter should stay outside ('in the shadow of') the criminal law. It can get a legal position in the frame of a suspended sentence. The encounter itself can focus on what is happening between the parties, where guilt, empathy and the relationship of trust are important moral criteria for success (Weijers, 2005).

However, the most common approach is that of a compromise that leaves room for both retribution and restorative justice, and searches for ways to integrate restorative justice into the existing youth justice system; the 'dualistic model' (Cornwell, 2010; Dignan, 2002; Duff, 2002; Van Ness, 2002). In practice, these integration models meet in the middle, where they come together with the slogan 'restore if possible, punish if necessary'. Nevertheless, the integrative approaches do vary in regard to the extent to which retribution and recovery must be awarded a place in the reaction to an offense. Other main points that are often mentioned are: a central role for communication, attention for the victim and avoiding detention as much as possible. I agree with Aertsen that 'integrating' restorative justice into the existing youth justice system does not necessarily imply that the underlying rationale of the existing system is adopted, or that two rationales would exist besides each other within the system. The integration of restorative justice into the system has maybe also the potential to challenge the underlying rationale or principles and to reorient or to reform them fundamentally. The question should not be how two rationales within the system can coexist, but how they relate to each other, and how to evolve dynamically in an ongoing interaction. In that way maybe the system can develop fundamentally into another direction from within (Aertsen, 2021).

However, just a few authors write explicitly about youth. In my opinion, for the positioning of restorative justice in relation to child justice, a link should be sought with the pedagogical aspects of youth justice and its focus on prevention and reintegration. Furthermore, a relational approach is in order because of the central focus on human interaction (Van Garsse, 2007). I opted for a pragmatic dualistic choice to integrate restorative justice into current criminal youth law ('not separately, but together') and to work toward an increasingly restorative justice model. In such a model, restorative justice options should be given priority on the basis of children's rights. This means only switching to other sanctions if a restorative justice intervention is not seen as suitable, not identified in the best interests of the child (Wolthuis, 2020). Attention to the principle of subsidiarity is important, as also is alertness to a pull effect of getting more cases into criminal justice system as needed. If a case can be settled with a warning or reprimand, that is preferred. With Walgrave, I am not against restorative justice interventions that are (partly) coerced and/or compulsory, as is also used in current punishments and measures (Blad, 2020; Walgrave, 2020). I want to work step by step toward a restorative youth sanction law, with an active perspective for change and a long-term vision (Claessen et al., 2018). John Blad puts it nicely in the last interview after his retirement I held with him in 2019:

> There seems to be too little awareness that a different legal system can be made. A good example of this is New Zealand, where criminal youth law has been adapted and tailored to restorative justice. But then you also have to keep going and create volume in a quantitative sense. As in New Zealand, you could handle all youth affairs through the Family Group Conferences system. Another option: just as the conditional dismissal is a commonly used 'sub-procedure' in criminal justice, so can mediation be in criminal cases. Judicial policy can then maximize its use for reasons of public interest. Especially when it comes to criminal youth law. (Kool & Wolthuis, 2019)

So indeed, we should not be afraid of changing the system and be creative in using current legal possibilities.

My goal is to continue until restoration is at the heart of juvenile criminal law, with restorative justice as a first option to be tried. In my PhD dissertation I gave the Dutch ten years to get this in place (Wolthuis, 2012). So, there's still one more year to go.

5.2 *Rights-based*

Working toward a restorative youth justice system, in which restorative justice fulfils this central role, requires a change of law whereby participation, reintegration and interventions benefit both the victim and the accused. It is important to design and incorporate the restorative justice interventions in a good and transparent manner, in order to prevent abuses and legal inequality (see also the next chapter by Chapman). Human rights dictate the boundaries. Human rights instruments have made it clear that the protection of the best interest of the child implies that the traditional aims of criminal justice, repression and retribution are subordinate to the aims of rehabilitation and reintegration, central to the restorative justice view, as clearly stated by the Committee on the Rights of the Child in its General Comment No 10 on children's rights in juvenile justice (2007).[3]

Child rights and restorative justice practices similarly encourage the voices of victims, offenders and young people to be heard in socially just sorts of ways through non-

3 UN Doc. CRC/C/GC/10, 25 April 2007, para. 10.

discriminatory, safe, authentic and complete participation as is well worked out by Moore and Mitchell in 2009 and further explained by Moore in Chapter 5 of this volume.

On the other hand, it is also necessary to review restorative justice in the light of children's rights (Moore & Mitchell, 2011). Restorative justice is not always the appropriate means and the way it is executed also has risks. For example, one must always be aware of risks of abuse, power, discrimination or excess punishment. Children should first of all be seen as subjects of rights, as rights-holders. Article 39 and 40 of the general principles laid down in the Convention provide a strict framework and a guideline on how to apply 'rights-based' child restorative justice. Other rules and guidelines, as well as legal practice, serve to support this framework (Moore & Mitchell, 2011; Wolthuis, 2012). It concerns the balancing of interests and is one of tailor-made solutions. Legal guarantees play a role, but they should be balanced with the unique flexibility of restorative justice. Principles of proportionality, equality and the presumption of innocence are relevant, although they are not always evident in the existing criminal justice systems. Furthermore, when reviewing human rights, it is not always clear which rule has priority. In these cases, a solid balancing of interests is decisive. Even the restorative guarantees – neutrality, confidentiality and voluntariness have not always been evident in restorative justice proceedings. This is partly due to the criminal law context, but also because of the complexity of the principles (Lauwaert, 2009). A concrete balance of interests in each case, based on children's rights, proves necessary, as well as further research into the principles and their consideration (Wolthuis, 2012).

Chapman et al. (2015a) summarized in the European model for restorative justice with children and young people three crucial aspects: protecting rights, restoring respect and strengthening relationships. Justice is based upon rights that protect, in line with the CRC. This also means that the safety of children and young people engaged in restorative processes must be at the core of any model. It is important to recognize that children are often the victims of crimes committed by other children (Chapman et al., 2015a).

In fact, that is what a good, functioning restorative justice model should look like, also taking into account the needs-rights model of Tali Gal (see Chapter 4). The practice should also be child-friendly, child-centered and child-participatory. Child-friendly procedures need to be in place and the child should be at the center of the decision-making which must be based on what the child wants. Making the justice system more child-friendly means

> that child victims must not experience restorative justice as negative and, should be given the opportunity and be supported to participate actively in the restorative process. They too should be heard with respect and sensitivity and protected from further harm. (Chapman et al., 2015a)

The Lundy model of participation is intended to focus decision-makers on the distinct and interrelated elements of the provision. Its four elements in this order should be taken seriously: space, voice, audience and influence (Lundy, 2007).

6 Conclusions and ways forward

6.1 *Restoration at the heart of child justice systems*

On the basis of my PhD research, I made suggestions on how to implement restorative justice in general and more specific in relation to the Dutch juvenile justice legal system. The current Dutch developments are described in Chapter 14 by Maartje Berger and me, where we also included some ideas for improvement. Much of it can be used for many countries. The ideas can be worked out in six stages, from prevention to detention. The tasks of the involved professionals and organizations should be described, as well as the conditions and criteria involved for the implementation of restorative justice for juveniles. Here I make the suggestion of more general use for all systems.

Restorative justice should be in a very strong position in all countries according to international standards. Those human rights standards promote the use of restorative justice in cases of offending by children and young people and with that, restorative justice can be seen as a children's right. I concluded in 2012 on the basis of my PhD research that restorative justice is a government obligation and a children's right in the sense of an obligation to investigate whether a restorative process is possible in each specific case involving young person(s) (Wolthuis, 2012, 2020). This applies to the young suspect, but the young victim also deserves those rights (Gal, 2011).

By slightly altering our way of thinking, it is possible to change the content of the child justice systems, whereby the best interests of the child, its education and its rehabilitation prevail and where the use of restorative justice is a primary consideration.

I propose that child justice laws should be created whereby the use of restorative justice needs to be a first option for the police, the public prosecutor and/or the judge. Finally, the use of restorative justice can form a premise before other penal sanctions are considered and also an intervention for reintegration after trial. The focus in such a youth system must be on prevention. However, if youngsters make mistakes, the police need to be able to use restorative justice as a conditional discharge. And in existing alternatives, where young people carry out community service tasks, these tasks should where possible be linked more closely to their actual criminal behavior. It can also entail initiatives for making apologies. Within the criminal procedure, I see most possibilities at the level of the public prosecutor. In the advisory stage, the Council for Youth Protection and the probation office need to check if a restorative justice option is suitable and can offer a solution in the current case. If this does not work – for whatever reason, (i.e. if a victim is not willing to participate) – then the judge should still have the option to refer the youngster to mediation or a conferencing program.

The introduction of restorative justice in youth justice programs needs to take place in the framework of the children's rights principles that are also important for the implementation of the youth justice system. In my PhD research and explained in this chapter, I put this framework under the motto TRY IT (Wolthuis, 2012). Now we need to go further and replace it by REALIZE IT.

My idea is to regulate restorative justice through all of the phases of youth criminal behavior, from prevention to detention and even beyond. This is in line with Braithwaite's notion of responsive regulation (Braithwaite, 2016) which is a meta-strategy for arranging problem-solving strategies in a hierarchy of coerciveness and then implementing a presumptive preference for trying the less coercive, less interventionist, and cheaper solutions first, moving up the hierarchy of strategies until one of them succeeds in fixing the problem.

To achieve access to restorative justice for all children and young people, the youth sanction system must give restorative justice a prominent place, as has been done in Northern Ireland and New Zealand. Belgian juvenile law also offers an emancipated system with priority for restoration and mediation or conferencing at level of the public prosecutor and via the youth judge (Aertsen, 2021; Wolthuis, 2020).

6.2 *How it should be*

In an ideal situation, children are well aware of restorative ways of working since they learn how to deal with conflicts through peer mediation in school. Prevention and participation projects with and for youngsters are available in all cities. All police staff are trained in restorative justice methods. They should know how to mediate informally, and they can refer more serious cases to mediation or conferencing. If a case is not dealt with in a diversionary way, as soon as the public prosecutor has a file in front of him/her, he/she delegates the investigation and the referral to an independent mediation service. The facilitators need to have a certificate to be able to give a legal proof of quality guarantee, as well as in-depth knowledge on how to work in a child-friendly way. Monitoring is important, as well as paying attention to the proportionality of the outcomes. A coherent and inclusive vision on the qualities of mediation and is needed. The specialized youth judge should review whether restorative methods have not yet been used and if there is still this possibility. When a young person is in the almost unlikely situation that he must be placed in a closed detention center, because this should be really used as a measure of last resort, he should be placed in a small-scaled house where reintegration and restoration are core methods. If this is all well in place, the youngster gets out with a package that prepares him well for a new and better life. And if he makes another mistake, this is well taken care of in a restorative way.

Also, the subsidiarity principle should be given due weight. The starting point is that the least invasive means for the suspect is used, that is sufficient to achieve the intended goal.

To create such a place in the current youth justice systems that exist, changes are needed. Many systems have included children's rights and often changes are feasible but rather limited. In other places, more needs to be done, but assistance can be provided by UN bodies and/or organizations like the European Forum for Restorative Justice. It will take policy decisions by governments and judicial authorities, who can be bureaucratic and not so open to change. What we have seen is that in countries where judges and prosecutors became convinced that a restorative approach was the way forward and started lobbying within the system, that changes got more easily accepted. At the same time, a good (set of) law(s) also helps to make the system aware that certain things should happen. Creating working groups with various stakeholders in the justice chain as well as child rights experts also helps. For the people on the work-floor, it is important to keep trying new initiatives and monitor those. Ideally, changes come both from the bottom as well as from the top. Raising awareness needs to happen along three lines: the general public, the professionals and the parties in a conflict.

The words I concluded my PhD dissertation with are still valid: Child justice and restorative justice; combine, integrate and implement. And as my promoter and previous chair of the Committee on the Rights of the Child Jaap Doek told me again recently when I interviewed him for an online world conference on restorative justice: 'the law in books is not the same as the law in action.' So even if the laws are in place, we need to work hard to inform and train people to get that knowledge to implement these laws and regulations. We must also not forget to involve children themselves. Their stories are the most powerful. Think again of Marco and Davy. They got together when they were invited by the court mediators, were able to listen and to share and were said to be able to better continue with their lives afterwards. First, they were asked what they wanted. See children and listen to them; put them and restorative justice at the heart of the system.

REFERENCES

Abrahamson, B. (2001). *The unwanted child.* Geneva: Defence for Children International.

Aertsen, I. (2021). Evoluties in het Vlaams herstelrechtelijke beleid sinds 2000. *Tijdschrift voor Herstelrecht,* 21(1), 36-50.

Ashworth, A. (2005). Verantwoordelijkheden, rechten en herstelrecht. In I. Weijers (red.), *Het herstelgesprek bij jeugdige delinquenten, Sleutelteksten uit het internationale debat* (pp. 171-187). Amsterdam: SWP.

Bergseth, K. & Bouffard, J. (2007). The long-term impact of restorative justice programming for juvenile offenders. *Journal of Criminal Justice*, 35, 433-451. doi: 10.1016/j.jcrimjus.2007.05.006.

Blad, J. (2020). Twintig jaar Tijdschrift voor Herstelrecht. *Tijdschrift voor Herstelrecht*, 20(4), 3-7.

Bradshaw, W., Roseborough, D. & Umbreit, M.S. (2006). The effect of victim offender mediation on juvenile offender recidivism: a meta analysis. *Conflict Resolution Quarterly*, 24(1), 87-98. doi: 10.1002/crq.159.

Braithwaite, J. (2002). *Restorative justice and responsive regulation*. New York: Oxford University Press.

Braithwaite, J. (2016). *Restorative justice and responsive regulation: the question of evidence*. RegNet Working Paper No. 51, School of Regulation and Global Governance (RegNet) (update of an earlier 2014 version of this paper. Also available at SSRN).

Cantwell, N. (1995). *United Nations convention on the rights of the child, international standards concerning the rights of the child*. Geneva: Defence for Children International 1995.

Chapman, T., Gellin, M., Aertsen, I. & Anderson, M. (2015a). *Protecting rights, restoring respect and strengthening relationships: European model for restorative justice with children and young people*. European Council for Juvenile Justice, Brussels: International Juvenile Justice Observatory.

Chapman, T., Gellin, M. & Anderson, M. (2015b). *Toolkit for professionals: implementing a European model for restorative justice with children and young people*. European Council for Juvenile Justice, Brussels: International Juvenile Justice Observatory.

Christie, N. (1977). Conflicts as property. *British Journal of Criminology*, 17, 1-15. doi: 10.1093/oxfordjournals.bjc.a046783.

Claessen, J., Blad, J., Slump, G. J., van Hoek, A., Wolthuis, A. & de Roos, T. (2018). *Legislative Proposal to Introduce Provisions Governing Restorative Justice Services into the Dutch Code of Criminal Procedre and Explanatory Memorandum*. Oisterwijk: Wolf Legal Publishers.

Claessen, J., Zeles, G., Zebel, S. & Nelen, H. (2015). Bemiddeling in strafzaken in Maastricht II, Onderzoek naar de samenhang tussen bemiddeling en recidive. *NJB*, 29, 2015-2025.

Cornwell, D.J. (2010). Reparatieve en herstelgerichte strafrechtspleging: een goed argument voor tweesporigheid in strafrechtelijk beleid? *Tijdschrift voor Herstelrecht*, (1) 7-20. Vertaald uit: Cornwell, D.J. (2009). Reparative and restorative criminal justice: a respectable case for 'bifurcation' in contemporary penal policy? In

D.J. Cornwell (ed.), *The penal crisis and the Clapham omnibus: questions and answers in restorative justice*. Sherfield on Lodden: Waterside Press.

Deklerck, J. (2007). Re-link-ing de-linq-uency: why the mediation process works. In R. Mackay, M. Bošnjak, J. Deklerck, C. Pelikan, B. van Stokkom & M. Wright (eds.), *Images of restorative justice theory* (pp. 186-204). Frankfurt am Main: Verlag für Polizeiwissenschaft.

Dignan, J. (2002). Restorative justice and the law: the case for an integrated systemic approach. In L. Walgrave (ed.), *Restorative justice and the law* (pp. 168-190). Devon: Willan Publishing.

Duff, A. (2002). Restorative Punishment and Punitive Restoration. In L. Walgrave (ed.), *Restorative Justice and the Law* (pp. 82-100, 2002), Devon: Willan Publishing.

Dünkel, F., Grzywa-Holten, J. & Horsfield, P. (2015). (eds.) *Restorative justice and mediation in penal matters – a stocktaking of legal issues, implementation strategies and outcomes in 36 European countries*. Mönchengladbach: Forum Verlag Godesberg.

Dünkel, F., Horsfield, P. & Păroşanu, A. (2015). *European research on restorative juvenile justice. Volume 1: research and selection of the most effective juvenile restorative justice practices in Europe: Snapshots from 28 EU member states*. Brussels: International Juvenile Justice Observatory.

Fellegi, B. & Szego, D. (2013). *Handbook for facilitating peacemaking circles*. In the framework of the project entitled 'Peacemaking Circles in Europe,' No. JUST/2010/JPEN/AG/1609 financed by the Criminal Justice Programme 2010, European Commission, DG Justice, Freedom and Security.

Gal, T. (2011). *Child victims and restorative justice: a needs-rights model*. Oxford: Oxford University Press.

Johnstone, G. & Van Ness, D. (2007). *Handbook of restorative justice*. Devon: Willan Publishing.

Kool, R. & Wolthuis, A. (2019). Vormingswerker, rechtstheoreticus en herstelrechtelijk pionier – interview met John Blad. *Tijdschrift voor Herstelrecht*, 19(4), 50-63. doi: 10.5553/TvH/1568654X2019019004006.

Lauwaert, K. (2009). *Herstelrecht en procedurele waarborgen* (PhD dissertation). Apeldoorn, Maklu.

Lee, J.A. & Dandurand, Y. (2020). Twenty years of growing support for restorative justice: presenting the second edition of the UN Handbook. *International Journal on Restorative Justice*, 3(3), 419-430. doi: 10.5553/IJRJ.000052.

Lundy, L. (2007). 'Voice' is not enough: conceptualising Article 12 of the United Nations Convention on the Rights of the Child. *British Educational Research Journal (BERA)*, 33(6), 927-942.

Lynch, N. (2010). Restorative justice through a children's rights lens. *The International Journal of Children's Rights*, 18(2), 161-183. doi: 10.1163/157181810X12592206285646.

MacRae, A. & Zehr, H. (2004). *The little book of family group conferences: New Zealand style, a hopeful approach when youth cause harm.* Intercourse: Good Books.

Marder, I.D. (2020). The new international restorative justice framework: reviewing three years of progress and efforts to promote access to services. *The International Journal on Restorative Justice*, 3(3), 95-418. doi: 10.5553/IJRJ.000048.

McCold, P. & Wachtel, T. (2003). In pursuit of paradigm: a theory of restorative justice, Paper presented at the XIII World Congress of Criminology, 10-15 August 2003, Rio de Janeiro, Brazil, International Institute for Restorative Practices, 12 August 2003.

Moore, S. & Mitchell, R. (2011). Theorising rights-based restorative justice: the Canadian context. *The International Journal of Children's Rights*, 19(1), 81-105. doi: 10.1163/157181810X508483.

Morris, A. & Maxwell, G. (ed.). (2001). *Restorative justice for juveniles. Conferencing, mediation and circles.* Oxford: Hart Publishing.

Pranis, K. (2005). *The little book of circle processes: a new/old approach to peacemaking.* Intercourse: Good Books.

Put, J., Vanfraechem, I. & Walgrave, L. (2012). Restorative dimensions in Belgian youth justice. *Youth Justice*, 12(2), 83-100. doi: 10.1177/1473225412447159.

Shapland, J., Atkinson, A., Atkinson, H., Dignan, J., Edwards, L., Hibbert, J., Howes, M., Johnstone, J., Robinson, G. & Sorsby, A. (2008). *Does restorative justice affect reconviction? The fourth report from the evaluation of three schemes.* Sheffield: Centre for Criminological Research, University of Sheffield.

Shapland, J., Burn, D., Crawford, A. & Gray, E. (2020). From victimisation to restorative justice: developing the offer of restorative justice. *International Journal on Restorative Justice*, 3(2), 194-214. doi: 10.5553/IJRJ.000034.

Shapland, J., Robinson, G. & Sorsby, A. (2011). *Restorative justice in practice – evaluating what works for victims and offenders.* Routledge: London.

Sherman, L.W. & Strang, H. (2007). *Restorative justice: the evidence.* London: The Smith Institute.

Van Garsse, L. (2007). Herstel in de schaduw van het jeugdstrafrecht? Reflecties op een revisionistische benadering. Respons op Weijers. In E. Claes, J. Declerck, A. Marchal & J. Put (eds.), *Herstel en jeugd: nu in het (r)echt* (pp. 127-141). Brugge: die keure.

Van Ness, D. (2002). Creating restorative systems. In L. Walgrave (ed.), *Restorative justice and the law* (pp. 136, 137). Devon: Willan Publishing.

Vanfraechem, I. (2007). *Herstelgericht groepsoverleg: een constructief antwoord voor ernstige jeugddelinquentie* (diss. Leuven). die keure, Brugge.

Von Hirsch, A., Roberts, J., Bottoms, A.E., Roach K. & Schiff, M. (2003). *Restorative justice and criminal justice, competing or reconcilable paradigms.* Oxford and Portland: Hart Publishing.

Walgrave, L. (2000). *Met het oog op herstel. Bakens voor een constructiefjeugdsanctierecht.* Leuven: Universitaire Pers Leuven.

Walgrave, L. (2004). Restoration in youth justice. In M. Tonry & A. Doob (eds.), *Youth crime and youth justice. Comparative and cross-national perspectives* (Vol. 31, pp. 543-597). Chicago: University of Chicago Press, Crime and Justice.

Walgrave, L. (2009). 'Een maximalistische visie op herstelrecht'. *Tijdschrift voor Herstelrecht*, 9(3), 19-38.

Walgrave, L. (2020). Waarheen stuurt het Tijdschrift het herstelrecht? *Tijdschrift voor Herstelrecht*, 20(4), 8-10. doi: 10.5553/TvH/1568654X2020020004002.

Weitekamp, E. (1999). History of restorative justice. In G. Bazemore & L. Walgrave (eds.), *Restorative justice for juveniles. Repairing the harm by youth crime* (pp. 75-102). Monsey: Criminal Justice Press.

Weijers, I. (2005). Herstel in het Nederlands jeugdstrafrecht. *Tijdschrift voor Herstelrecht*, 4, 39-50.

Wolthuis, A. (2012). *Herstelrecht, een kinderrecht. Voorstellen voor een integratie van herstel in het hart van het jeugdstrafrecht* (PhD Dissertation). Boom juridische uitgevers, Den Haag.

Wolthuis, A. (2020). Is herstelrecht voor jeugdigen volwassen geworden? *Tijdschrift voor Herstelrecht*, 20(4), 81-90. doi: 10.5553/TvH/1568654X2020020004011.

Wolthuis, A., Laxminarayan, M. & Biffi, E. (2020). *i-RESTORE project: research review, supporting child victims through restorative justice with a focus on Albania, Greece and Romania*. Budapest: Terre des hommes.

Zehr, H. (1990). *Changing lenses: a new focus for crime and justice.* Scottdale: Herald Press.

Zinsstag, E. & Chapman, T. (2012a). Restorative youth conferencing in Northern Ireland. In: Zinsstag, E. & Vanfraechem, I. (eds.). *Conferencing and restorative justice, international practices and perspectives.* Oxford: Oxford University Press.

Zinsstag, E. & Vanfraechem, I. (eds.). (2012b). *Conferencing and restorative justice, international practices and perspectives.* Oxford: Oxford University Press.

Chapter 2
Restorative practices can steal the rights of children too

The importance of value-led and evidence-based standards

Tim Chapman

1 Introduction

Approaches to children in conflict with the law have tended be a blend of rehabilitation, risk management and detention. While very different in purpose and method, each share the dominance of professional expertise, services and authority and a blind spot for the victims of crime. Each model can be criticized from a human rights point of view: the detention model for excessive punitiveness and neglect of the best interests of the child; rehabilitation for professional pathologizing of children and intervening intrusively in their lives and the managerialist safeguarding system for stigmatizing and institutionalizing children.

In many jurisdictions, restorative justice is made available to young people in conflict with the law as an alternative to these models. Many chapters of this book (specifically, Chapter 1) argue that restorative justice and children's rights are very compatible. Children's rights and restorative justice share a common concern over the arbitrary or abusive use of power to dominate, intimidate, silence and render invisible children. It is the contention of this chapter that restorative justice does not always protect children from such abuses. Informed by a rights-based approach, how can the practice of restorative justice be improved? To answer this, I will review research evidence into violations of key children's rights in restorative practices. I will offer an analysis of how these abuses occur and then suggest how children's rights can become an integral part of restorative practice through value-led and evidence-based standards of practice.

2 How restorative justice practices can steal the rights of children

Let us consider evidence from research on the children's rights most relevant to restorative justice. Article 2 of the UN Convention on the Rights of the Child (CRC) is designed to protect children from discrimination whatever their ethnicity, sex, religion, language, abilities or any other status, whatever they think or say, whatever their family background. In relation to the large volume of literature on theory and research in the field of restorative justice, relatively little attention has been paid to race, ethnicity, gender (Miles, 2013; Österman & Masson, 2018), sexual orientation or disability. Some research has found that restorative justice has not been effective in countering the economic and social disadvantages of indigenous young people in the New Zealand and Australian youth justice systems (Hayes & Daly, 2003; Jackson & Henderson, 2006; Little, Stewart & Ryan, 2018; Maxwell & Morris, 2001). Family Group Conferences, based upon indigenous concepts and practices in New Zealand, were actually found to be less effective in meeting the needs of young Māori people (Moyle & Tauri, 2016). Cunneen (2002) concluded in relation to the politics of decolonization that changes brought about by restorative justice have at best been superficial and at worst have reinforced existing power relationships. Given the lack of empirical research in this area, it is likely that restorative practices broadly reflect the patterns of discriminatory and oppressive practices throughout the criminal justice system in many countries.

Article 3 of the CRC places primary consideration on the best interests of the child. This principle has led to policies that young people who offend should be treated as children first and offenders second (Haines & Drakeford, 1998; Welsh Assembly Government and Youth Justice Board, 2004). Young people's participation in restorative justice has been criticized (Haines, 2000; Hayes & Hayes, 2008; Lynch, 2010; Maruna et al., 2007; Newbury, 2011) on the grounds that their immaturity and stage of cognitive development disadvantages them in a process which demands verbal ability, empathy and concentration.

For some (Haines, 2000; Wood, 2020), the best interests of the child are incompatible with the restorative value of responsibility and the process of making oneself accountable to the person whom one has harmed. Children in conflict with the law tend to have had higher rates of adverse childhood experiences than those who do not offend (Abram et al., 2004; Dierkhising et al., 2013). Wood (2020) refers to research which has found that not only does restorative justice not address the symptoms of serious trauma, but it may aggravate them through the stress of disapproval and shame (Bazemore, 1998). Wood (2020) maintains that a traumatized young person reacts to triggers and, thus, is not a rational and accountable actor. The experience of participating in a restorative process may be perceived as a punishment and reinforce the young person's hypersensitivity to threat.

Much of this research has been conducted from the point of view of the interests of the young person who has perpetrated harm rather than the young person who suffered harm. It has been reported that young victims can be significantly less satisfied with restorative conferences than adult victims (Gal, 2011; Gal & Moyal, 2011). This may be due to adults protecting children whom they perceive as vulnerable rather than as persons with a voice. There has tended to be a poor level of victim participation in family group conferences (Levine, 2000).

Can the principle of the best interests of the child conflict with Article 12, which refers to respect for the views of the child? Who defines what is in the best interests of a specific child? This means that not only should there be opportunities for children to express their views on matters that have an impact on them, but that their views must be heard and taken seriously.

The right to be heard is crucial in relation to restorative justice, as Christie (1977: 9) states:

> The offender gets a possibility to change his position from being a listener to a discussion – often a highly unintelligible one – of how much pain he ought to receive, into a participant in a discussion of how he could make it good again.

However, the reality of a restorative dialogue involving children often does not reach this lofty ideal.

Barnes (2015) observed young people in Northern Ireland feeling vulnerable and ill-equipped to express their views in a 'room full of adults' (Haines, 2000). Consequently, they can be intimidated, orchestrated or coerced into doing what is expected of them. On observing restorative conferences, it often seemed to Barnes that the process was scripted to lead to an apology and to agreeing to a predictable reparation plan.

Applying the knowledge and methodology of the discipline of linguistics to the process of the restorative conference, Martin, Zappavigna and Dwyer (2007: 230) found that 'the flat ideational focus of the young person's Record of Events means that convenors and liaison officers take responsibility for interpreting what happened.' Their interpretation includes the attitudes and emotional reactions of young people and value judgments on their actions and consequences. They may also try to direct the young person to a proper restorative utterance (such as empathy or responsibility) using tactical questions and statements: 'how would you feel if it happened to you' or 'so you know you did the wrong thing'. The practitioner controls the communication: 'The convenor initiates virtually all exchanges and introduces virtually all explicit evaluation, to which the young person responds compliantly a word or a phrase at a time.' (2007: 235)

According to Rosenblatt (2015), during youth offender panel discussions, the community panel members do most of the talking and the Youth Offending Team worker dominates the decision-making through a report that recommends what the young person must do. Hoyle, Young and Hill (2002) observed police officers pursuing their own preferred outcomes on many occasions rather than enabling the participants' wishes to emerge from their dialogue. Often victims were not asked what they wanted to happen. Hoyle et al. (2002) interviewed 'non-participating victims', many of whom had not been well informed about the restorative process or prepared for participation. They felt that they were not in a position to make an informed decision to participate and that the police were not eager that they should attend. Rosenblatt (2015) found that, in the case of referral orders, community panel members received no training in how to engage victims. Consequently, they attempted to represent victims' experiences based upon their own. These attempts at victim empathy rarely convinced the young perpetrators.

To address young people's lack of power and confidence when participating in restorative processes, they will normally be accompanied by parents or carers who offer them support (Bradt, Vettenburg & Roose, 2007). Research (Bradt, 2005) found that mediators decide who a young person should bring to support them in a mediation. This may include deciding which friends are appropriate and whether divorced parents should be invited. Bradt (2005) and Vanfraechem (2003) found that mediators were less likely to encourage the attendance of supporters for victims than for the perpetrators of harm. While carers are invited to prevent the young person being dominated, they may themselves dominate the process of dialogue by talking excessively on behalf of their children (Claes, 1998; Roche, 2003). This may be due to over-protectiveness toward either the victim or the perpetrator. It may also be caused by their own feelings of shame (Prichard, 2002) or anger over the harmful incident.

It is clear from Article 40 CRC, which relates to youth justice, that the Convention did not envisage the rapid development of restorative justice throughout the world since it was ratified in 1989. Nevertheless, the quality of justice depends upon children in conflict with the law being treated with dignity and respect and enabled to reintegrate into society. Doubts have been expressed about adults exerting undue influence over the child's admission of responsibility for the harm and over the child's agreement to participate in the process. Skelton and Frank (2004: 205) stated

> Because most current restorative justice processes require the offender to acknowledge responsibility before referral to a restorative justice program, the rights to be presumed innocent until proven guilty and to remain silent are no longer applicable. Some argue that the offender is voluntarily relinquishing these rights in order to benefit from the restorative justice option, but the extent to which these decisions are made voluntarily is in doubt.

The reintegration of young people is considered to be at the core of the restorative process. Family members and supporters and members of the community are a resource for generating reintegrative shame (Braithwaite, 1989) through which the perpetrator of harm feels shame for what he or she has done and is enabled to reintegrate within society through making amends. However, there are risks. Maxwell and Morris (2004) observed that when shaming becomes a strategy, it risks stigmatization and the reinforcement of criminality. It may stimulate the need to deny or minimize (Sykes & Matza, 1957) responsibility for harm. Hayes (2006) concluded that this can result in apologies that are perceived as insincere by victims. Similar findings were reported by others (Choi & Severson, 2009; Daly, 2002; Newbury, 2011).

This may be due to what Wood (2020) refers to as the problem of getting to accountability, considered to be an essential element of restorative justice (Braithwaite, 2006; O'Mahony & Doak, 2017). Young people in restorative conferences have been observed to struggle expressing themselves and to give a full account of the harm that they have caused (Beckett, Campbell, O'Mahony, Jackson & Doak, 2005; Bolitho, 2012; Hayes, 2006). As a consequence, their meaning may be misinterpreted, and their sincerity may be distrusted. Partly this may be due to language and communication problems which tend to be more prevalent among disadvantaged young people who offend (Bryan, 2004; Sanger, Moore-Brown, Magnuson & Svoboda, 2001) and partly because the dialogue process, based on respectful conversation, empathy and taking responsibility, tends to privilege middle-class styles of communication (Willis, 2020).

Reparation, addressing in a practical way the damage, loss or violations caused to the victim or the affected community by the harmful act, is a key outcome for restorative justice (Rosenblatt, 2015; Walgrave, 2008; Zehr, 1990). Bazemore (2000: 48) is very clear on this:

> unless repairing harm is at the core of the definition of restorative justice, … stakeholders and staff will often slip into the traditional and comfortable mode of simply trying to help or hurt the offender.

Hoyle et al. (2002) found in the study of the Thames Valley Police restorative justice initiative that material reparation was rarely agreed on and that most reparation took the form of an apology irrespective of the victims' wishes. As a result, victims were often unmoved by written apologies. Many had been led to expect financial compensation. Where this was agreed on, there were cases in which the commitment to compensate was not kept. Rosenblatt (2015) found that referral orders, a restorative provision for young people in conflict with the law in England and Wales, consisted of a program of activities designed for rehabilitation rather than for reparation. Even when reparation was part of an agreed plan, the young person was referred to a pre-existing reparation project rather than one designed to meet the victim's or community's needs arising from the harm. In some cases, it was decided that the referral order could be discharged even though the young person had not completed the agreed reparation. Rosenblatt (2015) discerned a tendency to use a so-called reparation activity, such as writing a letter of apology, as a rehabilitative method. As a consequence, the value of reparation to victims and communities is diluted.

It is hardly surprising that many schemes report a very low level of direct victim participation in restorative processes. Newburn et al. (2002) found 13 percent victim attendance, Crawford and Burden (2005) found an average of 9 percent and Rosenblatt

(2015) observed only one out of 39 panel meetings in which a victim participated. Hoyle et al. (2002) calculated that victims participated in 14 percent of the processes in the Thames Valley Police restorative program. This led to practitioners constructing surrogate victims or imaginatively describing the impact of the offense without any direct evidence. Such tactics can take the process away from its restorative and reintegrative principles toward shaming and stigmatizing the young person.

Research suggests that in Northern Ireland (Barnes, 2015) the Public Prosecution Service has the controlling role over the conference plan, regardless of stakeholder satisfaction. Facilitators were heard to say: 'I need enough in this plan to get it through the Public Prosecution Service' or 'at the end of the day, the Public Prosecution Service have to decide if they want to agree with the plan'.

The concept of *stealing* children's rights originates in Christie's influential article, *Conflicts as Property* (1977), in which he argues that the state and its professionals steal the conflict from the victim, the offender and communities by excluding them from participation and decision-making in the process of justice.

Since this article was published, thinking and practice in the restorative justice field has developed and caused Christie's concepts, conflict and property, to become problematic. The focus of restorative justice is now on harm rather than on conflict. Most victims feel wronged by the injustice of the crime and do not see themselves as morally equivalent to the perpetrator. To frame a conflict as a property, something that can be owned and be at risk of being stolen, is to adopt the language of the market and the law, rather than the way people speak of wrongs.

The experience of victimization that a restorative process should be examining is often experienced as a significant disruption to one's preferred life narrative (Crossley, 2000), which can violate and shatter important values and assumptions (Janoff-Bulman, 1992). This interruption in the continuity and stability of life can undermine one's sense of control over events and cause disconnections in one's social relations. Restorative processes aim to restore both personal dignity and just relations.

However, restorative justice processes may reconstruct or distort the victim's story to make it fit a simpler or thinner restorative narrative. As Pemberton, Pauline, Aarten and Mulder (2019: 414) observe: 'They prioritize values of restorative justice theory over victimological experience by introducing a preferred plotline for victims to follow.' Professionals, even when they are engaged in restorative justice, find it difficult to recognize and correct the biases that originate in their position of relative power and privilege. As the cultural and social theorist, bell hooks (hooks, 1990: 152) wrote:

> No need to hear your voice when I can talk about you better than you can speak about yourself. No need to hear your voice. Only tell me about your pain. I want to know your story. And then I will tell it back to you in a new way. Tell it back to you in such a way that it has become mine, my own. Re-

> writing you, I write myself anew. I am still author, authority. I am still the colonizer, the speaking subject and you are now at the center of my talk.

This form of colonization by restorative practitioners can be very subtle. Emotional distress may be skillfully soothed or neutralized by expressions of empathy. Where the participants' stories begin and end may be determined by the questions that practitioners ask to structure the process, thus, avoiding the context in which the harm took place. Concepts such as closure through healing avoid facing the reality of an injustice, a 'wrong' that should be righted. Whoever has power over the narrative is able not only to control the process and its outcomes but also to conceal their power and control. The process is presented as reasonable, respectful and righteous. Even when participants do not experience it as such, they may find it difficult to explain their 'resistance'. While the practices described in this section are not typical of all restorative practice, how do such abuses emerge from a process of justice which places such value on enabling participants to tell their story in their own way?

3 What causes these abuses?

Restorative justice is still a minor and, in its modern form, a relatively new field of practice. To survive and grow it must seek and gain the support of much larger, more powerful and established systems such as the criminal justice system, social services and education. Even in those countries where laws and regulations on the use of restorative justice have been implemented, low levels of referrals may be caused by gatekeepers such as judges, prosecutors or police officers who are not sufficiently aware of the value of restorative justice or are distrustful of the restorative philosophy (Campbell et al., 2006; Clairmont & Kim, 2013; Shapland, Robinson & Sorsby, 2011).

Inevitably, efforts to promote restorative justice and to gain the authority and resources to practice it lead to a degree of institutionalization of restorative practices along with compromises over values, aims and processes (Aertsen, Daems & Robert, 2006; Archibald & Llewellyn, 2006; Hudson, 2007; Maglione, 2018). Furthermore, the bureaucratic, organizational and efficiency needs of the institution may predominate over the needs of people who choose to participate in restorative processes (Umbreit, 1995).

Professional culture, whether it is derived from a policing, teaching or social work perspective, can dilute and even distort the values and principles of restorative justice. The criminal justice system has a vocabulary based upon a set of assumptions which are rarely examined or challenged but have a substantial influence on how professionals think and practice. Concepts such as offender, risk and the prevention of offending as the primary measure of effectiveness are taken for granted and applied to restorative justice. Pavlich (2005) argues that this way of thinking determines what types of crimes (generally low-risk) may be appropriate for restorative justice, what types of offenders and victims should be permitted to participate in restorative processes and what types of outcomes are acceptable. Each of these decisions is an exercise of power which dilutes the rights of people to have a voice about issues that affect them. The price for the acceptance and growth of restorative justice is often paid in relation to the quality of practice and outcomes and the exclusion of victims. For example, a report by the New Zealand Children's Commissioner (2017) on family group conferences in New Zealand concluded that they were under-resourced and of inconsistent quality in relation to the participation of young people. This was because they were generally driven by the department, not the family.

Restorative justice does not fit comfortably within the prevailing managerialist and market orientation of modern public services. When studying the facilitation of youth conferences in Northern Ireland, Barnes (2015) observed a 'MacDonaldization' tendency (see also Umbreit, 1999), based upon managing through predictability, calculability, efficiency and control (Ritzer, 2008). These principles appeared to dominate many, though not all, of the conferences, producing a thin, prescribed and less human version of the ideal (Umbreit & Armour, 2011).

The dilution of restorative values and principles by organizational priorities and professional culture resonates with Habermas's theory (1981, 1987) of the colonization of the 'lifeworld' by economic and political systems. Restorative justice engages the lived experience of people (Kremmel & Pelikan, 2017) who have been affected by harmful actions, and its process is communicative rather than strategic. Yet, the power of criminal justice professionals to make strategic decisions will often override the active participation and the voices of the parties in a restorative process.

There may also be philosophical tensions between restorative values and children's rights. Ward and Langlands (2008) argue that the core values which human rights are designed to protect (Gewirth, 1996; Griffin, 2008) are incompatible with the flexibility and informality of restorative justice. This may result in the offender being coerced to participate in the interests of the victim and having their own needs and experience of victimization being neglected. Furthermore, the collective nature of the restorative process may introduce cultural relativism into the decision-making process and the influence of punitive attitudes and prejudices such as racism. Although there is little evidence presented to support these assertions and although the rights and needs of victims are not considered relevant to their argument, the authors have identified a real tension between rights based upon respect for the dignity of human beings and the restorative process which is designed to activate participants' responsibilities for each other.

One source of this tension is the focus of restorative justice on a specific injustice or harmful act and the specific emotions, needs and values that arise from this act. Consequently, the restorative process will be driven by the subjectivity of lived experience rather than universal rights, laws and procedures. In this sense, restorative justice is more individualist and idiosyncratic (Schiff, 2007; Shapland et al., 2006) than a rights-based practice. During a restorative process, the participants do not argue for their entitlements but enter into a respectful dialogue out of which mutual understanding and agreement emerge. The restorative justice process is inevitably a subjective process. Yet it is the experience of encounter and dialogue between people who may have negative feelings toward each other that usually generates mutual understanding and collaborative decision-making. The logical and often binary thinking of professionals working in systems, especially in individualistic cultures, struggles to engage with, as Nancy (2000) puts it, the simultaneous singular/plural nature of the restorative process. By this he means that *being* is always *being with*. To be a perpetrator or a victim of a crime is to be connected through a common narrative which places them in relation to each other, whether they wish to be or not.

Three key insights from the theory of restorative justice reflect this relational philosophy. One is that a crime is not simply a breach of the criminal law, but an unjust act of harm against a person. Another insight, the 'ripple effect' of harm beyond the perpetrator and victim, requires restorative justice to be less individualistic and to engage with the ecosystems which both sustain harmful behaviors and offer resources which can prevent further harm and support the victims' recovery and the reintegration of the perpetrator. Thirdly, harm incurs obligations to restore what has been lost, damaged or violated (Zehr, 2002).

According to Esposito (2010), community is defined by our obligations to each other. Laws and rights enforced by the state are designed to offer immunity from abuse and oppression. The danger is that this immunity may lead people to believe that they are released from fulfilling obligations to others. He argues that a regime of rights leads to a strong state and a weak civil society, the antithesis of the restorative ideal of people taking responsibility for restoring obligations when they are breached (see also Harvey, 2011). A society focused upon immunizing itself from threats leads to rights-bearing individuals pursuing self-interest and organizing themselves according to identity. The modern legal concept of the private person as the bearer of rights replaces the impersonal subject of *communitas*, an inclusive sense of solidarity based upon social obligations. Rights protected by the law may have the effect of reversing the 'affirmative bond of common obligations into the purely negative right of each individual to exclude all others from using what is proper to him or her' (Esposito, 2011: 30).

Rights can become proprietary, privately owned (Gaus, 2010) and used strategically according to how much power and resources one can mobilize. We speak of *having* rights. The restorative process is about *being in relations*. The assertion and protection of rights through strategic, and often political, action within systems represents a contradiction with the restorative process of communicative action within the world in which we live. Such a dialogical process can transform a conflict or narratives of harm from being held as private property into something relating to the common good.

To an extent the wide-ranging and often contradictory quality of restorative justice theory reflects its vulnerability and uncertainty as a communicative practice located in powerful strategic systems. This makes it an easy target for criticism. To become confident and effective, restorative practices must resolve inconsistencies with children's rights. This means addressing the two problems identified in this chapter. One relates to its external environment – the tendency of more powerful host systems to impose their priorities and values on the practice of restorative justice. The other problem concerns its internal conflict between its aim of restoring individual dignity and its process of activating solidarity and obligation toward others.

4 The importance of values and standards

Shklar (1964, 1990) argues that *doing* justice and *undoing* injustice are qualitatively different.[1] Doing justice is based upon a complex system of laws and procedures based upon rights and universal principles which require the understanding and practices of highly trained professionals. The aim of such a system is *to bring the perpetrator of a crime to justice.* To this end it strives for rationality, fairness and impartiality. However, this form of doing justice cannot address the full range of harms and contextualized individual suffering that arise from an injustice. Most victims are absent for most of the process. Most offenders are represented by professionals speaking on their behalf. Neither party is offered the opportunity to participate and to express their emotions, needs and what they want to happen.

Restorative justice is distinct from other equally valid approaches toward children who have harmed others and who have been harmed by others. A needs-based approach may ask: *what has happened and what is the matter with you and what do you need?* A risk-focused approach may ask: *what has happened and what are the risks of it happening again and how can we manage these risks?* Both of these approaches require experts who can use their knowledge to think and act strategically to achieve planned outcomes. Restorative justice is value-led and focuses on the following questions: *what has happened* and *what is it that matters to each of you that needs to be restored?* Restorative justice focuses primarily on the specific act of harm that has brought the parties together and the subjective experience, understanding and wishes of each person affected by the harm. In that sense the process is designed *to undo an injustice.*

1 For an excellent explanation of these distinctions see Pemberton, 2015. Retrieved 5 January 2017 from https://pure.uvt.nl/portal/files/9026843/150760_oratie_Pemberton_def.pdf.

The value of respect for human dignity leads to the premises that the participants are experts on their lived experience and that they are capable of participating in a process designed to address a harmful incident that has had an impact on the quality of their lives. The value of solidarity leads to the conclusion that no matter how estranged or hostile the participants are, they need to collaborate to repair the harm and to move on in their lives. In restorative justice, the potential conflict between these values is resolved through a process of justice that is based upon the value of truth and the practice of facilitated dialogue.

Agreed standards of practice can protect and sustain such values. Standards within the various agencies of the criminal justice system are designed to define the quality of service that the public can expect from its professional services. They are often framed so as to determine the activities of professionals and can be rigidly prescriptive and bureaucratic. At an early stage of the development of the modern restorative justice movement, Minow (1998: 2) argued that

> alternatives such as mediation, restorative justice conferences, and truth and reconciliation commissions depart from precedent and professional scripts to invite humane encounters, deepened interpersonal ties, and the involvement of people's hearts and commitments.

Unfortunately, many restorative practitioners have adopted scripts to ensure that the stories of perpetrators and victims conform to a restorative discourse. Barnes' (2015) research into Northern Irish youth conferencing practice found that the restorative process is often a highly scripted and predictable process. This seems to indicate the prescience of Beckett et al.'s warning in 2005, that conferencing in Northern Ireland was in danger of becoming 'standardised' and 'prescribed' (Beckett et al., 2005: 149). Pelikan concludes (2000: 150-151) that

> the danger I perceive lurking in the tightly woven web of regulations is that the very special nature of the mediation procedure and its potential for furthering self-activity and democratic participation is set aside, smothered, by a diversionary measure that consists in the establishment of some secondary and second-rate criminal procedure.

It seems clear that, to use Piaget's (1985) words, restorative justice has often been assimilated within systems rather than being accommodated within them. Assimilation refers to how new information or knowledge is made to fit within existing discourses such as the aim of reducing offending. Accommodation requires existing cognitive and cultural discourses to make space for a new approach to operate effectively.

Accommodating restorative justice implies boundaries which protect the values of the restorative process.

Gearty (2006) distinguishes between rights which protect people from oppression and those which support human flourishing. This is an important distinction as rights can create boundaries within which restorative processes can be accommodated. They resonate with Braithwaite's (2002) constraining standards which provide participants protection from domination by others. Yet these boundaries cannot be so closed that they inhibit interaction between restorative justice and the institutions which host it.

Two children's rights can act as filters through which children can enter the restorative space. *The principle of the best interests of the child* should ensure that children are fully informed about the restorative process in ways that they understand, so that they can make a free and informed choice whether to participate. It follows that the process must be designed and facilitated so that it is safe, avoids degrading or humiliating treatment and addresses the needs of the child arising from the harmful incident. A restorative process cannot work unless the child accepts responsibility for committing the harmful act. It is critical that children who deny responsibility are not advised or persuaded to participate in a restorative process because it would be in their best interests. The principles of voluntary consent to participation and confidentiality are also important protections of the best interests of the child.

The protection from discrimination is a right that reparative justice must pay much more attention to. It means that the restorative process should not only be inclusive, flexible and adaptable to diversity including gender, sexual orientation, race, ethnicity, religion, language, class, disability and domestic circumstances, but also should be designed to counter systemic discrimination. Restorative justice should not absent itself from harms caused by imbalances of power. It should actively seek ways of rebalancing power and restoring just relations. More specifically, victims should be invited to participate to address their needs and not to contribute to the rehabilitation of the perpetrator.

Other standards are required to activate the restorative process through the participants' engagement in dialogue. Such standards are guided by Article 12 (respect for the views of the child), and Articles 39 and 40 which emphasize the dignity of the child and recovery from harm and reintegration. These rights promote the flourishing of the child, rather than protection, by animating a process of justice based upon accountability, truth and dialogue.

Braithwaite (2002) asserted that quality assurance is more important than training. Standards of practice must be in place to balance the protection of the integrity and effectiveness of restorative justice with the need for support from the system. Following Shklar's distinctions above and to avoid domination by the system, standards should be framed from the participants' perspective – what they can expect from a restorative process and what the system has a responsibility to assure. This shifts the power to the people whom restorative justice is designed to serve. The standards (in italics below) are designed to achieve this balance while conforming to children's rights.

> ***Restoration***: The focus of the restorative process is to understand the harm and to agree on action to restore whatever has been lost, damaged or violated.

Making a distinction between the young person and the harm, the problem, which restorative justice addresses, is not the young person but a specific act of harm and its consequences. It follows, then, that young people are seen as children whose rights and agency are respected (cf. Haines & Drakeford, 1998) and not as offenders or, for that matter, as victims. The restorative process does not define children by their relationship to the harmful act. Indeed, they and their supporters are the active participants in a process to repair and restore what has been damaged by the harm.

> ***Inclusion***: Restorative processes are inclusive and are available and accessible to all who wish to participate.

The discretion of professional gatekeepers, such as judges, prosecutors, police officers and social workers to determine who is suitable as a participant in a restorative process raises the problem of professional privilege and the power arising from the system's strategic priorities. The professional role is to facilitate the restorative process, not to take control of it. As Christie (1977: 12) argued:

> Let us try to get them to perceive themselves as resource-persons, answering when asked, not domineering, not in the centre. They might help to stage conflicts, not take them over.

The venue should be accessible, taking into consideration disability, travel and other commitments in the child's life. The process should be inclusive of diverse cultures and ways of communicating and address any concerns that participants may have over their safety.

> ***Participation***: People who choose to participate in a restorative process will be offered appropriate support and preparation.

Much of the criticism of restorative justice in relation to children and young people relates to their ability to participate in a process in which they are expected to articulate what has happened and how it has affected them, usually among a group of adults. This is a valid criticism if one views the child as lacking the ability to learn and the restorative process as fixed rather than flexible. Sen (1999) maintains that it is not enough to offer equitable access to justice. People require capabilities to participate actively in society. Alexander (2008) argues, on the basis of the Republican principle of non-domination (see also Braithwaite, 2002), that such capabilities should not depend upon the goodwill of others but should be guaranteed by rights and the individual's own power to choose.

While restorative justice processes offer children the opportunity to have their voice heard, practitioners must go further to ensure that the process is adapted to that individual's circumstances and that she or he is well prepared and supported to do themselves justice. To this end children must understand the process and how they might benefit from participation. This requires skilled preparation and child-friendly language. In relation to support, parents and carers are assumed to be the appropriate persons to accompany the child. This may not be perceived as such by all young people. While parents may have a right to attend, the young person should also have a choice and may also choose a friend, a youth worker or a favorite grandparent or aunt. Furthermore, if the process identifies capabilities and resources that are missing in a child's life, there should be a commitment to address these as an outcome of the process.

Some young people may have adapted to traumatic experiences through abandoning hope of respect, kindness or justice from the adult world. If this is not recognized and accommodated, they will find the process very difficult and unsatisfactory. On the other hand, a deeply respectful, sensitive and fair process could be a small contribution toward improving adaptive functioning and restoring normal development. As Pranis (2000) observed, the power of individuals over their lives and their environment is enhanced by the number of people who truly and respectfully listen to their story. Mika, Achilles, Halbert, Amstutz and Zehr (2004) engaged in a process of listening to victims who had experience of restorative justice. They found that victims' voices and needs had, in general, been marginalized in restorative processes. Their proposals included to tailor approaches to the diversity of victims and to establish standards of practice which maximize victim participation and outcomes.

Comprehensive preparation enables participants to hold practitioners accountable for the quality of the restorative process. Hoyle et al. speculated that (2002: 29)

> if all our participants had been given a good grasp of restorative justice principles through preparation they would, we think, have been far more critical of the level of procedural fairness they experienced within the session itself.

It is important that both child victims and perpetrators have a sense of control over their participation and not experience the restorative process as reported by Hoyle et al. (2002: 13): 'In the interim study our main conclusion was that only two out of the 23 cases merited the label of restorative justice' according to the criteria laid down by the

Thames Valley Police model. Facilitators dominated the process, apologies seemed to be coerced and there was evidence of shaming.

Zernova (2007) found that victims who participated in family group conferences often perceived that the facilitators were more sympathetic toward the person who had harmed them, that perpetrators had more support available to them and that the process focused predominantly on rehabilitation rather than victims' needs. The restorative process should enable victims not only to state the needs that arise from their suffering but to see that their needs are addressed as far as it is possible. Bolivar's study (2019) found that victims value participation in a just process in which their narrative of harm is taken seriously, and their emotions are heard and validated with respect. It is important to recognize that each victim experiences harm in a very specific way and requires an individually tailored approach.

Perpetrators should be facilitated to give an account of their actions in their own way, to listen to the victim's account of their suffering, to answer the victim's questions and to take active responsibility to repair the harm. The quality of the facilitation of processes matters (Maxwell & Morris 2004). Young people were less likely to commit more harmful actions after they had had an experience that was 'fair, forgiving, allowing them to make up for what they had done and not stigmatising or excluding them' (Maxwell & Morris 2004: 214). A skillfully facilitated process motivates young people to accept support. If the process is followed by support for the offender, the risk of further harm is much lower (Maxwell & Morris, 2004).

A restorative process is akin to an enquiry into injustice undertaken by those most affected by the injustice. This is consistent with Article 39 of the CRC, relating to recovery from harm and the aim of reintegrating children who have experienced neglect, abuse, exploitation, torture or who are victims of violent conflict. This right is not only clearly relevant to child victims, but also to many perpetrators whose harmful behavior is associated with a history of trauma. A rights-based restorative process should address both how the victim's suffering can be alleviated and how past injustices suffered by the perpetrator can be restored.

> ***Commitment to act***: Agreements on how to repair harm emerge from the process of dialogue and understanding between the participants.

This can create anxiety among professionals who believe that their expertise should define what is in the best interests of the child more effectively than the lived experience of those closest to the harm, its causes and its consequences. The restorative justice process generally does examine responsibility for harm more rigorously than the court process. It does not, however, force a young person to take responsibility. The process invites individuals to define how much responsibility they are willing to take for the harm as described by the people affected by it. It should also offer the young person responsible for the harm, and their carers, the opportunity to state what resources and support they need to have a better life. Rights protect children's safety and well-being only insofar as potential abusers understand and fulfil their obligations in relation to them. Restorative processes are designed to activate and reinvigorate these obligations.

While Daly (2000: 35) states that 'restorative justice practices assume mentally competent and hence morally culpable actors, who are expected to take responsibility for their actions', good restorative practice with young people should be designed to enable them to develop the capacity to understand the moral context of their actions and to take a level of personal responsibility appropriate to their cognitive development and mental health.

Once the restorative process has produced an agreed action plan, victims have complained that they are not kept informed of progress toward completing the plan (Shapland et al., 2006; Zernova, 2007). It is important for the credibility of restorative justice that those who have participated in a process believe that the agreement is being implemented.

Perpetrators may need practical and emotional support to fulfil their commitments to repair the harm that they have caused and to take steps to avoid further harmful actions. When actions are not being taken as agreed, there should be an accountability process designed to understand and solve the problem. Once the agreement has been completed, the perpetrator's efforts and integrity should be recognized and communicated to the victims and other significant people.

5 Conclusions

This chapter has argued that children's rights are compatible with restorative justice. This compatibility is not automatic. It needs to be based upon an awareness of how the values and strategic priorities of systems can influence practitioners to abuse or neglect children's rights. To resist this tendency, restorative justice must be accommodated within systems rather than assimilated by them. The tensions between children's rights and the values of restorative justice can be resolved through distinguishing rights designed to protect children and those that promote their active participation in society. In the final analysis, the responsibility to deliver high-quality restorative justice that is congruent with children's rights lies with practitioners who should be competent and accountable for their standards of practice. If these conditions can be put in place and sustained, we can state more confidently that children's rights should include the right of access to high-quality restorative justice.

References

Abram, K.M., Teplin, L.A., Charles, D.R., Longworth, S.L., McClelland, G.M. & Dulcan, M.K. (2004). Posttraumatic stress disorder and trauma in youth in juvenile detention. *Archives of General Psychiatry*, 61(4), 403-410. doi: 10.1001/archpsyc.61.4.403.

Aertsen, I., Daems, T. & Robert, L. (2006). *Institutionalizing restorative justice.* Cullompton: *Willan Publishing.*

Alexander, J.M. (2008). Capabilities and social justice. Farnham: Ashgate Publishing.

Archibald, B.P. & Llewellyn, J.J. (2006). The challenges of institutionalizing comprehensive restorative justice: theory and practice in Nova Scotia. *Dalhousie Law Journal*, 29(2), 297-343.

Barnes, O.M. (2015). *Restorative justice in the criminal justice system: the MacDonaldisation of diversionary youth conferencing* (unpublished PhD thesis). Faculty of Social Sciences, Ulster University, UK.

Bazemore, G. (1998). Restorative justice and earned redemption: communities, victims, and offender reintegration. *American Behavioral Scientist*, 41(6), 768-813. doi: 10.1177/0002764298041006003.

Bazemore, G. (2000). Rock and roll, restorative justice, and the continuum of the real world: a response to "purism" in operationalizing restorative justice. *Contemporary Justice Review*, 3(4), 459-477.

Beckett, H., Campbell, C., O'Mahony, D., Jackson, J. & Doak, J. (2005). *Interim evaluation of the Northern Ireland youth conferencing scheme.* Belfast: Northern Ireland Office.

Bolitho, J. (2012). Restorative justice: the ideals and realities of conferencing for young people. *Critical Criminology*, 20(1), 61-78. doi: 10.1007/s10612-011-9150-z.

Bolivar, D. (2019). *Restoring harm: a psychosocial approach to victims and restorative justice.* London: Routledge.

Bradt, L. (2005). *De Betekenis van Relevante Derden Binnen Herstelbemiddeling en Herstelgericht Groepsoverleg.* Onuitgegeven Licentiaatverhandeling, Gent, Belgium: Universiteit Gent.

Bradt, L., Vettenburg, N. & Roose, R. (2007). Relevant others in restorative practices for minors: for what purposes? *The Australian and New Zealand Journal of Criminology*, 40(3), 291-312. doi: 10.1375/acri.40.3.291.

Braithwaite, J. (1989). *Crime, shame and reintegration.* Cambridge: Cambridge University Press.

Braithwaite, J. (2002). Setting standards for restorative justice. *British Journal of Criminology*, 42, 563-577. doi: 10.1093/bjc/42.3.563

Braithwaite, J. (2006). Accountability and responsibility through restorative justice. In M. Dowdle (ed.), *Public accountability: designs, dilemmas and experiences* (pp. 33-51). Cambridge: Cambridge University Press.

Bryan, K. (2004). Preliminary study of the prevalence of speech and language difficulties in young offenders. *International Journal of Language and Communication Disorders*, 39(3), 391-400. doi: 10.1080/13682820410001666376.

Campbell, C., Devlin, R., O'Mahony, D., Doak, J., Jackson, J., Corrigan T. & McEvoy K. (2006). *Evaluation of the Northern Ireland youth conference service.* Northern Ireland: Northern Ireland Office.

Choi, J.J. & Severson, M. (2009). 'What! what kind of apology is this?': the nature of apology in victim offender mediation. *Children and Youth Services Review*, 31(7), 813-820. doi: 10.1016/j.childyouth.2009.03.003.

Christie, N. (1977). Conflicts as property. *British Journal of Criminology*, 17(1), 1-15. doi: 10.1093/oxfordjournals.bjc.a046783.

Claes, M. (1998). The juvenile mediation project in Leuven (Belgium). In L. Walgrave (ed.), *Restorative justice for juveniles. Potentialities, risks and problems* (pp. 367-385). Leuven: University Press.

Clairmont, D. & Kim, E. (2013). Getting past the gatekeepers: The reception of restorative justice in the Nova Scotian criminal justice system. *Dalhousie Law Journal*, 36(2), 359-391.

Crawford, A. & Burden, T. (2005). *Integrating victims in restorative youth justice.* Bristol: The Policy Press.

Crossley, M.L. (2000). Narrative psychology, trauma and the study of self/identity. *Theory and Psychology*, 10(4), 527-546. doi: 10.1177/0959354300104005.

Cunneen, C. (2002). Restorative justice and the politics of decolonization. In E.G.M. Weitekamp & H. Kerner (eds.), *Restorative justice: theoretical foundations* (pp. 32-43). Devon: Willan Publishing.

Daly, K. (2000). Revisiting the relationship between retributive and restorative justice. In H. Strang & J. Braithwaite (eds.), *Restorative justice: philosophy to practice* (pp. 33-54). Aldershot: Ashgate Publishing.

Daly, K. (2002). Restorative justice: the real story. *Punishment & Society*, 4(1), 55-79. doi: 10.1177/14624740222228464.

Dierkhising, C.B., Ko, S.J., Woods-Jaeger, B., Briggs, E.C., Lee, R. & Pynoos, R.S. (2013). Trauma histories among justice-involved youth: findings from the National Child Traumatic Stress Network. *European Journal of Psychotraumatology*, 4(1). Retrieved from www.tandfonline.com/doi/pdf/10.3402/ejpt.v4i0.20274.

Esposito, R. (2010). *Communitas: the origin and destiny of community.* Stanford: Stanford University Press.

Esposito, R. (2011). *Immunitas: the protection and negation of life.* Cambridge: Polity Press.

Gal, T. (2011). *Child victims and restorative justice: a needs-rights model.* Oxford: Oxford University Press.

Gal, T. & Moyal, S. (2011). Juvenile victims in restorative justice: findings from the reintegrative shaming experiments. *British Journal of Criminology*, 51(6), 1014-1034. doi: 10.1093/bjc/azr052.

Gaus, G. (2010). The idea and ideal of capitalism. In , G. Brenkert & T. Beauchamp (eds.), *The Oxford Handbook of Business Ethics* (pp. 73-99). Oxford: Oxford University Press.

Gearty, C. (2006). *Can human rights survive?* Cambridge: Cambridge University Press.

Gewirth, A. (1996). *The community of rights.* Chicago: The University of Chicago Press.

Griffin, J. (2008). *On human rights.* Oxford: Oxford University Press.

Habermas, J. (1981). *The theory of communicative action: lifeworld and system: a critique of functionalist reason.* Boston: Beacon Press.

Habermas, J. (1987). *The theory of communicative action, Vol. 2: lifeworld and system: a critique of functionalist reason.* Boston: Beacon Press.

Haines, K. (2000). Referral orders and youth offender panels: restorative approaches and the new youth justice. In B. Goldson (ed.), *The new youth justice.* Lyme Regis: Russell House Publishing.

Haines, K. & Drakeford, M. (1998). *Young people and youth justice.* Basingstoke: Macmillan.

Harvey, C. (2011). Reconstructing and restoring human rights. In T. Gavrielides (ed.), *Rights and restoration within youth justice.* Whitby: de Sitter Publications.

Hayes, H. (2006). Apologies and accounts in youth justice conferencing: reinterpreting research outcomes. *Contemporary Justice Review*, 9(4), 369-385. doi: 10.1080/10282580601014292.

Hayes, H. & Daly, K. (2003). Youth justice conferencing and reoffending. *Justice Quarterly*, 20(4), 725-764. doi: 10.1080/07418820300095681.

Hayes, S. & Hayes, H. (2008). Developing ethical identities in young offenders through restorative justice practice in Australia. *Queensland University of Technology Law & Justice Journal*, 8(2), 380-391. doi: 10.5204/qutlr.v8i2.49.

hooks, b. (1990). *Yearning: race, gender, and cultural politics* (pp. 145-153). Boston: South End.

Hoyle, C., Young, R. & Hill, R. (2002). *Proceed with caution: an evaluation of the Thames Vally police initiative in restorative cautioning.* York: Joseph Rowntree Foundation.

Hudson, B. (2007). The institutionalisation of restorative justice: justice and the ethics of discourse. *Acta Juridica*, 1, 56-72.

Jackson, M.A. & Henderson, A.D. (2006). Restorative justice or restorative health: which model best fits the needs of marginalized girls in Canadian society? *Criminal Justice Policy Review*, 17(2), 234-251. doi: 10.1177/0887403405281185.

Janoff-Bulman, R. (1992). *Shattered assumptions: towards a new psychology of Trauma.* New York: Free Press.

Kremmel, K. & Pelikan, C. (2017). Lifeworld, law and justice. In I. Aertsen & B. Pali (eds.), *Critical restorative justice*. Oxford: Hart Publishing.

Levine, M. (2000). The family group conference in the New Zealand children, young persons, and their families act of 1989 (CYP&F): review and evaluation. *Behavioral Sciences & the Law*, 18(4), 517-556. doi: 10.1002/1099-0798(2000)18:4<517::AID-BSL402>3.0.CO;2-E.

Little, S., Stewart, A. & Ryan, N. (2018). Restorative justice conferencing: not a panacea for the overrepresentation of Australia's indigenous youth in the criminal justice system. *International Journal of Offender Therapy and Comparative Criminology*, 1-24. doi: 10.1177/0306624X18764524

Lynch, N. (2010) Restorative justice through a children's rights lens. *International Journal of Children's Rights*, 18, 161-183. doi: 10.1163/157181810X 12592206285646.

Maglione, G. (2018). Pushing the theoretical boundaries of restorative justice: non-sovereign justice in radical political and social theories. In T. Gavrielides (ed.), *Routledge international handbook of restorative justice*. London: Routledge.

Martin, J.R., Zappavigna, M. & Dwyer, P. (2007). Youth justice conferencing in New South Wales Australia. *Linguistics and Human Sciences*, 3(2), 221-253.

Maruna, S. (2006). Who owns resettlement? Towards restorative re-integration *British Journal of Community Justice*, 4, 23-34.

Maruna, S., Wright, S. Brown, J. van Marle, F., Devlin, R. & Liddle, M. (2007). *Youth conferencing as shame management: results of a long-term follow-up study*. Brentford: ARCS.

Maxwell, G. & Morris, A. (2001). Family group conferences and reoffending. In A. Morris & G. Maxwell (eds.), *Restorative justice for juveniles: conferencing, mediation and circles* (pp. 243-263). Oxford: Hart Publishing.

Maxwell, G. & Morris, A. (2004). What is the place of shame in restorative justice? In H. Zehr & B. Toews (eds.), *Critical issues in restorative justice* (pp. 133-142). Boulder: Criminal Justice Press.

Mika, H., Achilles, M., Halbert, E., Amstutz, L.S. & Zehr, H. (2004). Listening to victims – a critique of restorative justice policy and practice in the United States. *Federal Probation*, 68(1), 32-38.

Miles, R. (2013). *Restorative justice: female offenders in restorative justice conferences*. London: The Griffins Society.

Minow, M. (1998). *Between vengeance and forgiveness: facing history after genocide and mass violence*. Boston: Beacon Press.

Moyle, P. & Tauri, J.M. (2016). Māori, family group conferencing and the mystifications of restorative justice. *Victims & Offenders*, 11(1), 87-106. doi: 10.1080/15564886. 2015.1135496.

Nancy, J.-L. (2000). *Being singular plural*. Stanford: Stanford University Press.

New Zealand Children's Commissioner. (2017). Fulfilling the vision: improving family group conference preparation and participation. Retrieved from www.occ.org.nz/publications/reports/state-of-care-2017-family-group-conferences/.

Newburn, T., Crawford, A., Earle, R., Goldie, S., Hale, C., Hallam, A., Masters, G., Netten, A., Saunders, R., Sharpe, K. & Uglow, S. (2002). *The introduction of referral orders into the youth justice system: final report.* Home Office Research Study 242. London: Home Office.

Newbury, A. (2011). 'I would have been able to hear what they think': tensions in achieving restorative outcomes in the English youth justice system. *Youth Justice*, 11 (3), 250-265. doi: 10.1177/1473225411420531.

O'Mahony, D. & Doak, J. (2017). *Reimaging restorative justice: agency and accountability in the criminal process.* London: Bloomsbury.

Österman, L. & Masson, I. (2018). Restorative justice with female offenders: the neglected role of gender in restorative conferencing. *Feminist Criminology*, 13(1), 3-27. doi: 10.1177/1557085117738326.

Pavlich, G. (2005). *Governing paradoxes of restorative justice.* London: Glasshouse Press.

Pelikan, C. (2000). *Victim-offender-mediation in domestic violence cases: a research report.* United Nations Crime Congress Ancillary Meeting, Vienna, Austria. Retrieved from http://restorativejustice.org/10fulltext/pelikan-christa.-victim-offende r-mediation-in-domestic-violence-cases-a-research-report.html.

Pemberton, A. (2015). *Victimology with a hammer: the challenge of victimology Inaugural lecture.* Tilburg: Prismaprint. Retrieved 16 September 2020 from https://pure.uvt.nl/portal/files/9026843/150760_oratie_Pemberton_def.pdf (last accessed 10 November 2020).

Pemberton, A., Pauline, G.M., Aarten, P.G.M. & Mulder, E. (2019). Stories as property: *narrative ownership* as a key concept in victims' experiences with criminal justice. *Criminology and Criminal Justice*, 19(4), 404-420. doi: 10.1177/1748895818778320.

Piaget, J. (1985). *The equilibrium of cognitive structures: the central problem of intellectual development.* Chicago: University of Chicago Press.

Pranis, K. (2000 Spring). Empathy development in youth through restorative practices. *Public Service Psychology*, 25(2). doi: 10.1037/e553302012-003.

Prichard, J. (2002). Parent-child dynamics in community conferences: some questions for reintegrative shaming, practice and restorative justice. *The Australian and New Zealand Journal of Criminology*, 35(3), 330-346. doi: 10.1375/acri.35.3.330.

Ritzer, G. (2008). *The MacDonaldisation of society.* Los Angeles: Pine Forge Press.

Roche, D. (2003). *Accountability in restorative justice.* Oxford: Oxford University Press.

Rosenblatt, F.F. (2015). *The role of community in restorative justice.* Abingdon: Routledge.

Sanger, D., Moore-Brown, B., Magnuson, B. & Svoboda, N. (2001). Prevalence of language problems among adolescent delinquents. *Communication Disorders Quarterly*, 23, 17-26. doi: 10.1177/152574010102300104.

Schiff, M. (2007). Satisfying the needs and interests of stakeholders. In G. Johnstone & D.W. Van Ness (eds.), *Handbook of restorative justice* (pp. 228-264). Devon: Willan Publishing.

Sen, A. (1999). Development as freedom. Oxford: Oxford University Press.

Shapland, J., Atkinson, A., Atkinson, H., Colledge, E., Dignan, J., Howes, M., Johnstone, J., Robinson, G. & Sorsby, A. (2006). Situating restorative justice within criminal justice. Theoretical Criminology, 10(4), 505-532. doi: 10.1177/1362480606068876.

Shapland, J., Gwen Robinson, G. & Angela Sorsby, A. (2011). *Restorative justice in practice – evaluating what works for victims and offenders*. Routledge: London.

Shklar, J. (1964). *Legalism: law, morals and political trials*. Cambridge: Harvard University Press.

Shklar, J. (1990). *The faces of injustice*. New Haven: Yale University Press.

Skelton, A. & Frank, C. (2004). How does restorative justice address human rights and due process issues? In H. Zehr & B. Toews (eds.), *Critical issues in restorative justice* (pp. 203-213). Cullompton: Willan Publishing.

Stenning, P. (2010). Whose conflict is it anyway? A critique of restorative justice. In J. Blad, M. Hildebrandt, K. Rozemond, M. Schuilenburg & P. Van Calster (eds.), *Governing security under the rule of law* (pp. 125-138). The Hague: Eleven International Publishing.

Strang, H. (2002). *Repair or revenge: victims and restorative justice*. Oxford: Oxford University Press.

Stubbs, J. (2009). Restorative justice, gendered violence, and indigenous women. In J. Ptacek (ed.), *Restorative justice and violence against women* (pp. 103-122). New York: Oxford University Press.

Sykes, G.M. & Matza, D. (1957). Techniques of neutralization: a theory of delinquency. *American Sociological Review*, 22(6), 664-670. doi: 10.2307/2089195.

Umbreit, M. (1995). *Mediation of criminal conflict: an assessment of programs in four Canadian provinces*. St. Paul: Center for Restorative Justice and Mediation.

Umbreit, M. (1999). Avoiding the marginalization and "McDonaldization" of victim offender mediation: a case study in moving toward the mainstream. In G. Bazemore & L. Walgrave (eds.), *Restorative juvenile justice: repairing the harm of youth crime*. Monsey: Criminal Justice Press.

Umbreit, M. & Armour, M.P. (2011). *Restorative justice dialogue: an essential guide for research and practice*. New York: Springer Publishing.

Vanfraechem, I. (2003). *Herstelgericht groepsoverleg in Vlaanderen. Verslag van een wetenschappelijkbegeleid pilootproject: Onuitgegeven onderzoeksrapport*. Leuven, Belgium: K.U. Leuven.

Walgrave, L. (2008). *Restorative justice, self-interest and responsible citizenship.* Cullompton: Willan Publishing.

Ward, T. & Langlands, R.L. (2008). Restorative justice and the human rights of offenders: convergences and divergences. *Aggression and Violent Behavior*, 13, 355-372. doi: 10.1016/j.avb.2008.06.001.

Welsh Assembly Government and Youth Justice Board. (2004). *All Wales youth offending strategy.* Cardiff: Welsh Assembly Government.

Willis, R. (2020). 'Let's talk about it': why social class matters to restorative justice. *Criminology & Criminal Justice*, 20(2), 187-206. doi: 10.1177/1748895818804307.

Wood, W.R. (2020). The indecent demands of accountability: trauma, marginalisation and moral agency in youth restorative conferencing. *The International Journal of Restorative Justice*, 3(2), 168-193. doi: 10.5553/IJRJ.000038.

Zehr, H. (1990). *Changing lenses: a new focus for crime and justice.* Scottdale: Herald Press.

Zehr, H. (2002). *Little book of restorative justice.* Intercourse: Good Books.

Zernova, M. (2007). *Restorative justice: ideals and realities.* Aldershot: Ashgate Publishing.

Chapter 3
The UN Committee on the Rights of the Child

How we work and what child victims and offenders need

Renate Winter

1 Presentation of the Committee of the Rights of the Child

For several years now, I have worked as a member of the Committee on the Rights of the Child. In this contribution, I will describe the work we do, the issues we come across and how I experience this work, including the child justice systems and the need for a more restorative approach.

The Committee on the Rights of the Child has been established for the purpose of examining the progress made by States parties to the Convention on the Rights of the Child (CRC) in the realization of their obligations under the CRC – an activity also known as 'monitoring'.

The Committee consists of eighteen members elected by the States parties for a period of 4 years. States parties (currently 196) can nominate a candidate for the election and that person has to be a national of the State party nominating her or him. After 4 years, a member of the Committee can be renominated (by her or his state of nationality) for another election (Art. 43 CRC).

We, the members of the Committee, are from different continents, from different nations, speak different languages, have different professions – albeit always connected to working with children – come from different backgrounds and are currently in a 50-50 ratio of males and females.[1]

Members of the Committee serve in their personal capacity and not as representatives of the State that has nominated her or him. They are independent from everyone and every institution and have to be impartial in every decision they make and shall be seen by a reasonable observer to be so.[2]

The Committee meets three times a year for a period of 4 weeks. During the first 3 weeks, the Committee meets in public with delegations of about five to seven States parties for a discussion of the reports they submitted to the Committee while taking

1 See www.ohchr.org/EN/HRBodies/CRC/Pages/Membership.aspx, (last consulted on 24 July 2020).
2 See also The Addis Ababa Guidelines, 2012.

into account reports from non-governmental organizations (NGOs), UN agencies and others.[3] The fourth week is devoted to the preparation of the next session – it is a meeting behind closed doors with NGOs and UN agencies, such as UNICEF.

The UN General Assembly adopted in May 2000 two optional protocols to the CRC: one on the involvement of children in armed conflict (OPAC, ratified by 170 States)[4] and the other one on the sale of children, child prostitution and child pornography (OPSC, ratified by 177 States).[5] The CRC Committee is also in charge of monitoring the implementation of these two optional protocols.

In 2011, the UN General Assembly adopted a third optional protocol to the CRC on a communications procedure (OPCP).[6] This protocol makes it possible for children to submit complaints about the violation of their right(s). However, this possibility exists only for children living in countries which have ratified this third optional protocol (currently 46). Since 2014 the CRC Committee has dealt with such complaints, and so far have considered more than 40 cases. A majority of these cases were considered inadmissible because the conditions for admissibility are rather strict. Many complaints were submitted by or on behalf of refugee and/or asylum-seeking children.

A country becomes a State party to the CRC after it has deposited with the UN Secretary General the instrument of ratification or accession. The CRC entered into force on 2 September 1990, that is the 30th day after the 20th instrument of ratification or accession was deposited (Art. 49 para. 1 CRC). All countries can at the time of their ratification or accession make reservations on the applicability of one or more articles of the CRC. A reservation incompatible with the object and purpose of the CRC shall not be permitted (Art. 51 CRC). In the beginning, many States parties made a lot of reservations, some because they did not quite understand, some out of mistrust, some because they wanted first to arrange their own legislation and then have their reservations removed, some because the reservation was, according to them, in line with their constitution or religion. A reservation means that a State party is not bound by a specific article of the CRC (e.g. on Art. 21 dealing with adoption, or something more general like stating that 'the Convention shall be interpreted in the light of the principles of the Islamic Laws and values'). In 1996, out of the 175 States parties, 47 had made a reservation, some very broad and others more specific.[7] It is the well-established policy of the CRC Committee to recommend to States parties to withdraw reservations they have made, with some

3 These meetings are known as the (official) sessions of the Committee.
4 OPAC (2002).
5 OPSC (2002).
6 OPCP (2011): Optional Protocol to the Convention on the Rights of the Child on a communications procedure. Adopted and opened for signature, ratification and accession by General Assembly resolution A/RES/66/138 of 19 December 2011 entered into force on 14 April 2014.
7 Schabas (1996).

success. By 2014, 6 States with a rather broad reservation and 23 with a specific reservation had withdrawn these reservations.[8]

The CRC is almost universally ratified. Out of the 197 States, 196 ratified the CRC.[9] This makes the Committee confident with regard to its work. However, the Committee feels unable to do its work in a satisfactory manner due to a lack of manpower, time and funding.

The Committee is assisted by a Secretariat that provides information on the situation in a given State and aids in drafting documents, decisions, answers to questions, etc.

2 Presentation of the work of the CRC

States parties have to report regularly to the CRC Committee on the implementation of the CRC and the Optional Protocols 1 (OPAC) and 2 (OPSC). The first report has to be submitted within 2 years of the CRC or the optional protocol entering into force in that country. Thereafter, reports on the implementation of the CRC have to be submitted every 5 years (Art. 44 para. 1 CRC). Second and further periodic reports on the implementation of the optional protocols have to be part of the periodic reports on the implementation of the CRC (Art. 8 para. 2 OPAC and Art. 12 para. 2 OPSC).[10] The Committee has issued reporting guidelines to provide the States parties with information about the structure of the report and the issues that have to be addressed in the report. Reporting is not on the implementation of every article separately but on a group of articles covering a certain theme, for example, family environment and alternative care, violence against children and child protection measures.[11] Most States parties do submit their reports on time. But if a State party does not report on time, the Committee will remind it that its report is overdue. This reminder will be repeated if necessary. If all that has no effect, the Committee can, as a measure of last resort, inform the State party that its progress in implementing the CRC will be examined at a specified date without a report. This measure was used at the beginning of this century for States parties with a delay of many years in the submission of its first report and it proved to be effective. The State party in question submitted its report well before the date that was set for the examination of the State's progress.

8 Arts (2014).

9 The USA is the only State that did not ratify the CRC. But it did ratify OPAC and OPSC.

10 This rule applies to all State which are a party to the CRC. There is only one State, the USA, that is not a State party to the CRC but the USA did ratify the OPSC and the OPAC. It means that the USA has to submit periodic reports on the implementation of the OPSC and OPAC every 5 years (Art. 12, para 2 OPSC and Art.8, para 2 OPAC. Under Art. 44, para 1 (b), of the Convention on the Rights of the Child, UN Doc. CRC/C/58/Rev.3, 3 March 2015.

11 The first guidelines were issued in 1991 and revised a couple of times. The most recent is treaty-specific guidelines regarding the form and content of periodic reports to be submitted by States parties.

If we receive a State party report on the implementation of the CRC or of OPAC or OPSC, we will inform national and international NGOs, UN specialized agencies like UNICEF and the OHCR and national human rights institutions and (children's) ombudspersons (also known as stakeholders in the field of children's rights) about it with an invitation to submit complementary or alternative reports.[12] In their reports, the stakeholders inform the Committee about the situation of children as they perceive it. In most cases there are a lot of differences between the view of a State party and the view of the stakeholders. Some States parties like to look good and may avoid mentioning certain problems, some tell the Committee that they know what needs to be done to improve the situation but cannot do so because of a lack of human and/or financial resources, while others state that according to their constitution or religion they cannot comply with what the CRC articles ask for. These State parties have most likely made a rather general reservation (see above on reservation). Stakeholders inform the Committee not only about the problems in the country concerned but also about what should be and has not been done. Sometimes they have political reasons to complain, sometimes they have personal interests and sometimes they just want to inform the Committee about a very important point that is missing in the official report.

With the assistance of the Secretariat, which also prepares 'country information' reports, compiles the statistics available, etc., we now have to consider all the reports and make some kind of 'blueprint' to identify the differences among countries and the possible reasons for these differences.

When we have defined them, a task force will deal with a specific State, to which several members of the Committee are allocated, and establish a list of questions to be sent to the Member State with the request to provide answers. This task force usually has at least one member who speaks the language of the Member State, if it is one of the six UN languages, one member who knows the region and one male and one female member, all from countries different from the one under investigation. The Committee member from the country under discussion is excluded from the whole procedure, meaning that he or she has no voice and no vote.

Furthermore, we invite the stakeholders who provided us with information through their reports to meet with the Committee in Geneva to have a discussion about their reports and the most recent developments in the country. It is a meeting behind closed doors to allow a frank discussion without representatives of the State party concerned present. In the meantime, the Secretariat schedules a meeting with a delegation of the State party concerned in Geneva to answer our questions and to provide further explanations about ongoing problems, measures taken, legal changes, etc. In case a

12 See, for example, www.ohchr.org/_layouts/15/WopiFrame.aspx?sourcedoc=/Documents/HRBodies/CRPD/Future/GroupNGOs_Ukraine_CRPDFuture.doc&action=default&DefaultItemOpen=1 (last consulted on 24 July 2020).

State is very far away and its delegation finds it difficult to travel to Geneva, we can have this meeting via videoconferencing. Such virtual meetings are challenging, as technical problems arise rather often due to the multitude of participants, especially if the delegation speaks a language that is not one of the official UN languages and additional interpreters must be provided.[13]

When everything is set up, first the task force, and then other members of the Committee, try to involve the delegation in a fruitful open discussion about their report and the overall situation of the children in their country. Sometimes we get answers, sometimes we do not, but together with the reports there is a good basis for drafting our concluding observations,[14] our reactions to what we have been informed of'. The COBs, as we call them, reflect, in a specific order, all the issues concerning children in a given State, following the articles of the Convention. It starts with reflections on general measures of implementation, such as reservations, declarations, legislation, policy and strategy, coordination, resources, data collection, independent monitoring, dissemination of the Convention and training and cooperation with civil society and the business sector. For instance:

- Can reservations and declarations be withdrawn? Is there perhaps a time frame to be negotiated for when this can happen?
- Has legislation that is adverse to children or excluding them been changed? Are there plans to do so? Are there obstacles? Which ones? Why?
- Is there a policy and a strategy to implement all rights of children, as no right can stand alone by itself without connection to the other ones?
- Is there coordination among the different ministries and State institutions concerning actions for children?
- Are there enough budgetary resources for implementing a given strategy and action plan?
- Is there systematic data collection about every action concerning children and its outcome/consequence? There is really no country where data collection is done in a way that the data can be compared correctly.
- Is there an institution like an independent ombudsperson (with the emphasis on 'independent'!) or another independent institution to monitor State actions?
- Has anything been done to make the Convention known to all children, parents, teachers, judges, police, etc. Very often, in discussions with children, for example, we find that they have never heard of a convention that protects their rights, and neither have parents or teachers.

---

13 There are six official languages of the UN. These are Arabic, Chinese, English, French, Russian and Spanish. The correct interpretation and translation of these six languages, in both spoken and written form, is very important to the work of the organization, because this enables clear and concise communication on issues of global importance.

14 See https://tbinternet.ohchr.org/_layouts/15/treatybodyexternal/TBSearch.aspx?Lang=en&TreatyID=5&DocTypeID=5, last consulted on 24 July 2020.

- Is there some training for persons dealing with children? Are there specialists to deal with them correctly as required by the Convention?
- What about the business sector? Can a company violate children's rights in the name of profit (even for the whole population, but mostly for the stakeholders)? Under which conditions, for instance, can an oil company extract oil from a piece of land where children live?

As evidenced here, a lot of questions are addressed, and such exploration continues when we have to consider, for instance, the definition of who is a child in a specific country. Is the right to enjoy all rights mentioned in the Convention granted to all persons between 0 and 18 years of age? Or are there exceptions? Can a girl be married at the age of 10? Can someone who committed a crime as a child be hanged for it when he or she turn 18? Can a child lose his or her rights during a pandemic? What do we mean by the general principles of the Convention? What is the meaning of Articles 2, 3, 6 and 12? (These four articles are discussed in depth in the next section of this chapter.)

What about civil rights? Do children have the same civil rights as adults? Are they humans in the making or are they an equal part of the civil society? Do they 'legally' exist at all? Do they have a nationality, a name, can they talk freely, decide about their religion, associate freely, access information, protect their privacy and image? How do media behave vis-à-vis children – do they respect children's privacy?

Then, regarding violence against children, which is a terrible issue on the rise in every country: Is torture against children allowed? Is corporal punishment permitted? What about abuse, neglect, sexual exploitation? Are there harmful practices such as female genital mutilation? What is done against all of these by the State? Are there plans for recovery and reintegration of children? If so, what are the real aims of these plans? Are there helplines and are they reachable for children?

We look into family environment and alternative care as well, check how families are protected and what happens to children deprived of a family in foster care/institutional care, read adoption laws, address illicit transfer of children and non-return caused by family members or any other people/institutions and discuss the difficulties faced by children of incarcerated parents.

The life of children with disabilities is another concern of our Committee, as is basic health and welfare. Health services, adolescent health issues, mental health of children, drug and substance abuse, HIV/Aids, the impact of climate change on children's health, social security and standard of living have to be evaluated, if enough information is provided.

The next issue to deal with is education and cultural activities. To whom is education available and until when – from early childhood through to university? Possibilities for vocational training and time for leisure, play and artistic activities have to be evaluated. There are many, many children who can never rest and play, be it because their parents want them to become excellent in order to have a better life in their future, or because they have to work hard to assist their families.

The last chapter in the COB, Chapter 10, deals with various highly problematic issues, such as asylum seeking, refugees, migrant children, children belonging to a minority, children in street situations, exploited children through child labor, sexual exploitation and abuse, sale, trafficking and abduction, and, finally, child justice for young offenders, victims and witnesses.

We have other work to do as well, such as drafting General Comments[15] – an interpretation of specific provisions of the Convention, preparing statements when exceptional (mostly terrible) situations arise in a given country, such as due to the consequences of war, environmental disasters or personal tragedies like imminent death penalty and working for transparency and collaboration, such as for the 'days of general discussion', where we share information about our achievements and failures to civil society and States parties.

The Committee found that different Member States interpreted the CRC articles differently. Sometimes they interpreted them in the interest of the given State, sometimes in the interest of pressure groups and sometimes they did not understand the meaning of some definitions or articles. Thus, the Committee, as many other treaty committees, started to issue comments on specific articles, explaining the meaning, the aim, the methodology and the measures to be taken to grant the fulfilment of the respective obligations as well as the indicators allowing a Member State to find out where it stands with regard to the implementation for a given right for its children. At the moment we have 24 General Comments, dealing with different provisions of the Convention, e.g. one concerning the right to health, another one concerning the right to education, another one concerning the right of girls (drafted together with CEDAW, the treaty body for women's rights)[16] and so on. Whatever we do, we always have to ground our work in the main principles on which the Convention is based and which are guiding us.

3 The main principles on which the CRC's work is based

All rights in the Convention are linked and must be considered as a whole. The four articles that the Committee considers as the General Principles of the CRC and can be

15 See https://tbinternet.ohchr.org/_layouts/15/treatybodyexternal/TBSearch.aspx?Lang=en&TreatyID=5&DocTypeID=11, (last consulted on 24 July 2020).

16 CEDAW (1979). It entered into force as an international treaty on 3 September 1981 after the twentieth country had ratified it. By the tenth anniversary of the Convention in 1989, almost one hundred nations had agreed to be bound by its provisions.

seen as overarching rights that are needed for the fulfilment of all other rights,[17] are Article 2, on non-discrimination, Article 3, para. 1 on the best interests of the child as a primary consideration in all actions concerning children, Article 6 on the inherent right to life and the right to survival and development and Article 12 on the right to express views and be listened to. What do these main principles tell us and what do they mean?

> ***Article 2***
> 1. States Parties shall respect and ensure the rights set forth in the present Convention to each child within their jurisdiction without discrimination of any kind, irrespective of the child's or his or her parent's or legal guardian's race, color, sex, language, religion, political or other opinion, national, ethnic or social origin, property, disability, birth or other status.
> 2. States Parties shall take all appropriate measures to ensure that the child is protected against all forms of discrimination or punishment on the basis of the status, activities, expressed opinions or beliefs of the child's parents, legal guardians or family members.

This article protects the rights of all children in any situation that the Convention mentions, as it addresses 'all forms of discrimination', the obvious ones and hidden ones alike.

A child has the right to have a birth certificate notwithstanding if his/her parents have a nationality or not. A child has the right to go to school, notwithstanding if she or he is a girl or a boy. A child has the right to live in a clean environment, notwithstanding if he or she comes from a minority background or from a majority. A child has the right to live like any other child in the community, notwithstanding that his or her parents are in prison.

That seems to be obvious so far. But what about the hidden discrimination? Let's illustrate with a case in a youth court: Two boys are accused of having stolen several items. They both declare that they have stolen a few of those items, but not all of them. One of the boys, coming from a well-to-do family, tells the judge that he has stolen out of boredom and really does not need all the stuff the victim claims was stolen. The judge can accept this explanation. The other boy, from a Roma family, says that he has stolen a few items but not all of them and took the stolen items to his mother. The judge considers the family of the boy and his upbringing and has difficulties believing this boy. Maybe he will believe him in the end, maybe not. The most interesting part of the judge's thinking, though, is the fact that he has doubts because of the family and the upbringing of the boy. This can be a form of 'hidden' discrimination, which is something that every one of

17 See, for example, www.unicef.org/armenia/en/stories/four-principles-convention-rights-child (last consulted in March 2021).

us has internalized, be it because of education, environment, culture or religion. It is a dangerous issue, and many children are victims of such beliefs. As soon as we know about the danger, we can avoid falling into the trap, but it takes a lot of self-assessment to always stay away from this form of discrimination.

> ***Article 3***
> 1. In all actions concerning children, whether undertaken by public or private social welfare institutions, courts of law, administrative authorities or legislative bodies, the best interests of the child shall be a primary consideration.

Article 3, para. 1 is the most well-known provision of the Convention, but also the most difficult to interpret. Many politicians, people working with children, NGOs and judicial personnel use this article to declare that they act only for children.

Is it really true that their primary consideration is the best interests of the child? Or is it maybe only an excuse to cover other interests? Who decides, using which criteria, at what time, to declare that a decision taken is in the best interests of a child? What legislative or administrative decision can be taken to ensure that the primary consideration was the best interests of the child? Who can tell what is in the best interests of a child? Competent authorities? The parents? The institutions dealing with the child? Witnesses? Victims? What about the idea of consulting the child? Is it in the best interests of a child to stay together with his or her migrant parents in administrative detention? Or is it in the best interests of the administrative authorities to keep the whole family together for easier deportation? Is it in the best interests of the child to be taken from h parents to stay with a foster family outside of detention? Or is it in the best interests of social services to be able to control that family? What if the child were asked and said that he and she would prefer to stay with the family in the same community environment?

A judge has to decide in a family dispute about child custody and the person with whom the child shall live. Parents fight, their lawyers fight, the grandparents as witnesses fight. Finally, the judge declares that he will put the child in an institution for his or her security until the dispute is settled. Is this decision in the best interests of the child? Or in the best interests of the judge to finalize a case? Or in the best interest of the parents to learn about their behavior that traumatizes the child?

What about a decision of a ministry of education that a pregnant girl has no right to continue her education? Is it in the best interests of the girl to concentrate on her future motherhood instead of school? Is it in the best interests of the other girls at the school, not to be 'contaminated by a bad girl'? Or is it in the best interests of the school to keep a good reputation? Or of the politicians to show that they uphold the prescriptions of their religious leaders? Or is it just plain discrimination? Difficult to decide, is it not? What about asking the girl what she thinks is best for her?

A closed institution for children has to decide whether a child can be released prematurely or be denied release. Is this decision in the best interests of the child, as his or her rehabilitation is not yet completed? Or is it in the best interests of the institution that gets paid by the State per capita, according to the number of inmates? What about consulting the child on his or her future?

These were a lot of questions. Maybe there is somewhere a definition of the best interests of a child to be found as guidance? But how would it be possible to find such a definition as every child is different, has different needs at different times in different environments and different situations? The Committee has provided a General Comment (GC 14) on the best interests of a child in the form of a checklist to assist decision-makers, reminding them of where to look and what to consider when taking a decision. More does not seem to be possible, neither legally nor in practice.

> ***Article 6***
> 1. States Parties recognize that every child has the inherent right to life.
> 2. States Parties shall ensure to the maximum extent possible the survival and development of the child.

There are fortunately not many States that deny a child the right to life. There is just one State where the decision of allowing a child to be born can lie in the hands of the authorities. There are seven other Member States where the death penalty for children still exists. Some of them execute children below the age of 18; some take 16 years to decide about the death penalty, some wait until the child becomes an adult. In all of these countries the argument is that persons after puberty are not children anymore. There is no consideration about when puberty starts or has ended, nor if the development of that given child allows the conclusion that this particular child fully understood not only what is right or wrong, but also the consequences of his or her behavior. In some countries the argument comes from the religious side, in others from the political one, depicting a child as a terrorist who has to be treated like an adult due to special legislation about terrorism.

In a lot of States, the second part of this article is not always taken into consideration. What about the survival of minority children in ghettos? Is the maximum extent of survival granted for children in war situations? As child soldiers? As workers in hazardous environments in copper mines, or in ammunition factories? Do all these children have any kind of possibility for development, not to speak about a maximum extent possible? When will a child in a street situation be able to learn mathematics? When can a child collecting cacao beans at least 12 hours a day develop his or her reading ability? Do all children in prison have good teachers? Do all those in medical confinement have the assistance of trained social workers to be better equipped for a self-sustained life? Are all parents (not only those in difficult situations) willing to give their children the possibility to develop the skills they are born with, or will they be allowed to develop only those in the best interests of their parents? Do Articles 2 and 3 of the Convention have to be considered when discussing problems of a Member State with Article 6? When Articles 2 and 3 are discussed, Article 6 should be evaluated as well, as the different rights are mutually dependent.

> ***Article 12***
> 1. States Parties shall assure to the child who is capable of forming his or her own views the right to express those views freely in all matters affecting the child, the views of the child being given due weight in accordance with the age and maturity of the child.
> 2. For this purpose, the child shall in particular be provided the opportunity to be heard in any judicial and administrative proceedings affecting the child, either directly, or through a representative or an appropriate body, in a manner consistent with the procedural rules of national law.

It seems to be rather clear that if one has to decide what is in the best interests of a child, what is his or her protection against discrimination, to which extent his/her development is granted, to ask the very person who is the subject of this decision about their best interests.

In the majority of countries worldwide this is not the case, be it because of tutelary legal systems, be it because tradition dictates that a child can be seen but not heard, be it because children beyond a certain age do not have the legal right to be heard, be it because people believe that they know better anyway and that they have the right 'not to follow the orders of a child'. The last part of para. 1 is quite often misinterpreted or not considered at all in such cases, as 'giving due weight' means to consider and evaluate, but not to follow blindly a wish or a whim.

Very often one also hears that there is no need to address a child, as para. 2 provides the possibility to hear representatives of the child instead. What about a case where the parents ask the judge to allow them to sell the property of their child to profit from a given situation? Will the judge then ask these parents about the opinion of the child? Will the judge ask the youth protection agency, the social workers of which have never seen that child, but have sent a report? General Comment No. 12 of our Committee defines very clearly that representatives of a child can be heard instead of the child only if this child is not available at all, e.g. because he or she is in hospital and the matter is urgent.

It is really very difficult to convince people dealing with children, including judges, parents, lawyers, police and community members, to get the opinion of the child for whom they have to make a decision.

4 The influence of these principles on the child justice system

So, if we think about discrimination according to Article 2 of the Convention, will discussion with the child according to Article 12 have to be considered as well? Is discrimination ever in the best interests of a child according to Article 3 and grants ever full development according to Article 6?

Discrimination has to be looked at, for example, when deciding about access granted to health, education, leisure time, a safe environment and the justice system. One has to see if prevention of violence, child labor, child marriage or corporal punishment has taken place, and if the right to have an identity and protection of privacy has been provided, when it comes to examining discrimination.

The same methodology applies when the use of Article 3 has to be evaluated, which is on the best interests of a child; decisions of governments, the justice system and the administrative authorities on all issues just mentioned, have to be considered in order to establish if Article 3 has been recognized. Thus, especially Article 6, concerning life and development, has to be included in this evaluation. One has to check furthermore if Article 12, the right to have the child's voice heard and his or her opinion taken into consideration, has been taken into account as well.

None of the four general principles stand alone, as none of the rights of the child can be granted without granting the others, if the implementation of the rights of the child should be considered as achieved.

When we try now to deal with the justice system and all the examples mentioned above, it will be seen that the guarantees of Articles 2, 3, 6 and 12 are not easy to uphold at all.

How to grant equality before the law in a country where minorities are discriminated against? How to grant access to the court system when child victims do not have access to a lawyer? How to grant the best interests of a child victim vis-à-vis an offender, child or not? How to make sure that a child is not held longer than allowed in police custody or in pre-trial detention, or does not get an disproportionately high prison sentence, because the law allows for it and the prosecutor argues that it is in the best interests of all children to see harsh punishment happening to deter others? How to protect a child witness from second victimization due to a confrontation with an aggressive offender at court? How to give the Roma boy (and the bored rich boy as well) in Section 3 the possibility to understand what they have done to the victim?

5 The importance of restorative justice for upholding these principles

To find answers to all these questions I have just raised, and to find alternatives for children in conflict or in contact with the law, we have to look into our most important document, the Convention. Maybe there is something to be found there.

There are, indeed, three articles that are very helpful in this regard. Article 37 mentions the protection of children deprived of their liberty and has to be read in conjunction with Article 40. Article 39 deals with child victims (who might become witnesses as well and then also have to be protected) and Article 40 deals with offending children.

> ***Article 37***
> States Parties shall ensure that:
> (a) No child shall be subjected to torture or other cruel, inhuman or degrading treatment or punishment. Neither capital punishment nor life imprisonment without possibility of release shall be imposed for offenses committed by persons below 18 years of age;
> (b) No child shall be deprived of his or her liberty unlawfully or arbitrarily. The arrest, detention or imprisonment of a child shall be in conformity with the law and shall be used only as a measure of last resort and for the shortest appropriate period of time;
> (c) Every child deprived of liberty shall be treated with humanity and respect for the inherent dignity of the human person, and in a manner which takes into account the needs of persons of his or her age. In particular, every child deprived of liberty shall be separated from adults unless it is considered in the child's best interest not to do so and shall have the right to maintain contact with his or her family through correspondence and visits, save in exceptional circumstances;
> (d) Every child deprived of his or her liberty shall have the right to prompt access to legal and other appropriate assistance, as well as the right to challenge the legality of the deprivation of his or her liberty before a court or other competent, independent and impartial authority, and to a prompt decision on any such action.

Article 37 deals with the most difficult and cumbersome part of the legal reactions to children in conflict with the law or otherwise (arbitrarily) deprived of liberty. These children are the most vulnerable in the whole justice system and need maximum protection. Unfortunately, there are still Member States to the Convention that are not inclined to provide such assistance, as seven Member States still apply the death penalty for children (sometimes waiting until the children are adults to execute them, in order to be able to claim that they do not kill children), despite the fact that Article 37a explicitly states that anyone having committed a crime under the age of 18 cannot be subjected to the death penalty. Some States are converting the death penalty into life imprisonment without parole, which is not permitted by the Convention either. The main reason for punishing children is to (re)educate them and (re)insert them into society. A lifelong imprisonment without parole contradicts this endeavor. Furthermore Article 37 establishes the most important legal guaranties for imprisonment (Art. 37 b and d) and explicitly mentions that children deprived of liberty are not children deprived of basic rights (Art. 37 c). It seems clear in any case that alternatives to deprivation of liberty, as offered by the restorative justice system for children, have solutions that would make these difficulties obsolete in many cases.

> ***Article 39*** of the CRC states:
> States Parties shall take all appropriate measures to promote physical and psychological recovery and social reintegration of a child victim of: any form of neglect, exploitation or abuse; torture or any other form of cruel, inhuman or degrading treatment or punishment; or armed conflicts. Such recovery and reintegration shall take place in an environment which fosters the health, self-respect and dignity of the child.

The usual measures provided by the legal system, like restitution of damages and payment for treatment and recovery, are first and foremost not easy to get, as mostly additional civil procedures are necessary, and second, they do come rather late due to often lengthy procedural prescriptions and the overburdening of the civil justice system. Regaining self-respect and dignity are usually not in the list of measures. It will thus be difficult to uphold the four basic principles without viable alternatives.

> ***Article 40*** of the CRC states:
> 1. States Parties recognize the right of every child alleged as, accused of, or recognized as having infringed the penal law to be treated in a manner consistent with the promotion of the child's sense of dignity and worth, which reinforces the child's respect for the human rights and fundamental freedoms of others and which takes into account the child's age and the desirability of promoting the child's reintegration and the child's assuming a constructive role in society.
> 2. To this end, and having regard to the relevant provisions of international instruments, States Parties shall, in particular, ensure that:
> (a) No child shall be alleged as, be accused of, or recognized as having infringed the penal law by reason of acts or omissions that were not prohibited by national or international law at the time they were committed;

> (b) Every child alleged as or accused of having infringed the penal law has at least the following guarantees:
> (i) To be presumed innocent until proven guilty according to law;
> (ii) To be informed promptly and directly of the charges against him or her, and, if appropriate, through his or her parents or legal guardians, and to have legal or other appropriate assistance in the preparation and presentation of his or her defense;
> (iii) To have the matter determined without delay by a competent, independent and impartial authority or judicial body in a fair hearing according to law, in the presence of legal or other appropriate assistance and, unless it is considered not to be in the best interest of the child, in particular, taking into account his or her age or situation, his or her parents or legal guardians;
> (iv) Not to be compelled to give testimony or to confess guilt; to examine or have examined adverse witnesses and to obtain the participation and examination of witnesses on his or her behalf under conditions of equality;
> (v) If considered to have infringed the penal law, to have this decision and any measures imposed in consequence thereof reviewed by a higher competent, independent and impartial authority or judicial body according to law;
> (vi) To have the free assistance of an interpreter if the child cannot understand or speak the language used;
> (vii) To have his or her privacy fully respected at all stages of the proceedings.
> 3. States Parties shall seek to promote the establishment of laws, procedures, authorities and institutions specifically applicable to children alleged as, accused of, or recognized as having infringed the penal law, and, in particular:
> (a) The establishment of a minimum age below which children shall be presumed not to have the capacity to infringe the penal law;
> (b) Whenever appropriate and desirable, measures for dealing with such children without resorting to judicial proceedings, providing that human rights and legal safeguards are fully respected.
> 4. A variety of dispositions, such as care, guidance and supervision orders; counselling; probation; foster care; education and vocational training programs and other alternatives to institutional care shall be available to ensure that children are dealt with in a manner appropriate to their well-being and proportionate both to their circumstances and the offense.

The first paragraph of this article already mentions the key problems that an average justice system, especially if not specialized for children, will encounter. It mentions the most important reasons underpinning the existence of a youth justice system: dignity and reintegration.

When we look into the whole list of rights in the additional paragraphs, when we consider all rights an offending child should be provided with, it is easy to see that once again, as soon as discrimination is an issue, as long as the best interests of a child are not respected, when opportunities for development are not foreseen in a justice setting and when the right to be heard is not granted, these principles will not apply.

The solution upheld by the Committee for all these problems is mentioned in para. 4 of Article 40 when alternatives are addressed. It is restorative justice as an alternative that we recommend to each and every Member State.

There is another document that helps to find solutions for many of the problems mentioned and that is General Comment No. 24,[18] which I will address here. For an overview of other relevant UN instruments related to child victims and/or child offenders, see the first chapter by Wolthuis.

GC 24 deals with children's rights in the justice system. It mentions all the dispositions that an appropriate child justice system should have, from prevention of youth criminality to investigation, accusation, trial and measures to be taken on the rights of the children when deprived of liberty.

> Point 74 of this states:
> A wide range of experience with the use and implementation of non-custodial measures, including restorative justice measures, exists. States Parties should benefit from this experience and develop and implement such measures by adjusting them to their own culture and tradition. Measures amounting to forced labor or to torture or inhuman and degrading treatment are to be explicitly prohibited and penalized.

This is exactly what we recommend to every Member State that we have to evaluate. A lot of problems arise when religious, political or traditional reasons are mentioned that would 'force' the Member State to harshly punish a child, often a very young one, 'in the best interest of the child' for educational purposes or in the interest of protecting the society against 'criminal/ bad/ depraved/ abnormal/ unruly/ dangerous' children.

18 See document CRC/C/GC/24 (2019).

Restorative youth justice[19] functions in continental law as well as in case law, in customary law (where quite a few ideas are taken over already or have developed simultaneously) as in Sharia law.

Restorative justice principles have no problem whatsoever with Article 12 of the CRC, as listening to (child) offenders as well as (child) victims and witnesses and having a dialogue between them is a condition *sine qua*.

There is also no problem with Article 2 CRC, as every child, offender, witness or victim coming from whatever entity, religion, gender, etc. (see the whole list in Art. 2) is invited to that dialogue and its consequences, namely to find agreed, practicable solutions for both parties and the community they live in.

Article 3 CRC will be respected easily as well in restorative youth justice, as it is certainly in the best interest of a child to have the problem underlying the offense settled, once and for all. Only this way can lasting peace between parties, their families and their communities be established. Dignity can come back to both victim and offender. Restoration can take place in a form acceptable for all participants in this procedure; self-esteem will be boosted after having reached and implemented a consensus.

Life and development according to Article 6 CRC will be granted as well. The use of the death penalty or lifelong prison without parole is not a tool recommended by restorative justice for children. Furthermore, dialogue between victim and offender and offers for reparation by the child ensure by itself the development and understanding of a young person. Measures agreed on, such as training, treatment, assisting others or helping out in communities, will strengthen self-esteem and dignity in a positive way, showing and leading the way to a non-criminal future.

Article 12 is crucial for restorative youth justice. Without hearing what a child victim, witness or offender, has to say, there is no restorative justice. It is exactly the dialogue – the fact that a child is listened to and taken seriously when taking over responsibility – that grants the healing factor of this procedure.

Peter was a very aggressive boy of sixteen, having had to appear at court for the third time because of violence at school, this time for breaking chairs and benches. His family had a history of violence as well and his father tried to shame and belittle the boy whenever possible. Peter offered to the court after participation in a restorative program, to do

19 "The roots of what has come to be called restorative justice run deep into our history and into the strengths of diverse cultures from around the world. As articulated by Howard Zehr (1990), Daniel Van Ness and Karen Heetderks Strong (1997), Kay Pranis (1998), and others, restorative justice requires that we look at crime as causing harm and injury to the relationships that bind our families, neighborhoods, and communities together. Van Ness and Heetderks Strong specifically suggested that *if crime causes injury, justice ought to be about repairing that harm.* Numerous children grow up in the constant dread of being laughed at. Ridicule of children is well-nigh criminal. It retains its effect on the soul of the child, and is transferred into the habits and actions of his adulthood" (Moeser, 1999).

something positive and agreed to visit elderly people in a care home who never had anyone visit them on four Saturdays and Sundays. When Peter arrived, he was greeted by an old man: 'Sir, thank you very much for having come to us and spending your time with us, Sir'.

When telling his story to the prosecutor later on, Peter almost cried. 'Can you imagine,' he said, 'He said "Sir" to me, he accepted me, he was even grateful of such one like me.' Peter felt valued for the first time in his life, understood that violence is weakness and that taking responsibility means to be strong. He took his own proper responsibility very seriously. He visited the old man regularly for two years, until the old man died.

If sentenced to prison (after three times of breaking the law) what would Peter have learned? His dignity would certainly not be respected; he would have to obey without discussion and would have no responsibility himself at all. He would have developed for sure, but in the direction of the law of the jungle, to say the least.

Worldwide, thousands and thousands of Peters have to languish in prisons, very often for a long time and more often than not for not very serious offenses.

It is for them that the Committee does its utmost, over and over again, to convince Member States, all Member States, of the advantages of restorative youth justice, diversion, alternatives, mediation and community service being in the best interests of children and society.

References

Addis Ababa Guidelines. (2012). Guidelines on the independence and impartiality of members of human rights treaty bodies, Annex to the UN General Assembly Resolution A/67/222.

Arts, K. (2014). Twenty-five years of the convention on the rights of the child: achievements and challenges. *Netherlands International Law Review*, 61(3), 267-303. doi: 10.1017/S0165070X14001272.

CEDAW. (1979). Convention on the Elimination of All Forms of Discrimination against Women (CEDAW), adopted in 1979 by the UN General Assembly.

CRC/C/GC/24. (2019). General comment No. 24 (2019) on children's rights in the child justice system.

Moeser, J.P. (1999). Reclaiming juvenile justice for the 21st century. *Reclaiming Youth and Children*, 8(3), 163-164.

OPAC. (2002). Optional Protocol to the Convention on the Rights of the Child on the involvement of children in armed conflict adopted and opened for signature, ratification and accession by General Assembly resolution A/RES/54/263 of 25 May 2000 entry into force 12 February 2002.

OPSC. (2002). Optional Protocol to the Convention on the Rights of the Child on the sale of children, child prostitution and child pornography, adopted and opened for signature, ratification and accession by General Assembly resolution A/RES/54/263 of 25 May 2000, entered into force on 18 January 2002.

(OPCP) Optional Protocol to the Convention on the Rights of the Child on a communications procedure. Adopted and opened for signature, ratification and accession by General Assembly resolution A/RES/66/138 of 19 December 2011 entered into force on 14 April 2014.

Schabas, W. (1996). Reservations to the convention on the rights of the child. *Human Rights Quarterly*, 18(2), 472-491. doi: 10.1353/hrq.1996.0023.

Chapter 4
Child victims and child perpetrators in restorative justice

A Needs-Rights Model

Tali Gal

1 Introduction

Moran's father died when she was ten years old. Her mother's boyfriend began sexually abusing her when she was thirteen. Her mother knew of the abuse but did nothing to stop it. At age fifteen, when she could not take the abuse any longer, Moran confronted them, but her mother took her boyfriend's side. Moran moved to a boarding school, and a friend assisted her in filing a police complaint. I met Moran in 1998. She was seventeen years old at the time, and I was a young children's rights lawyer working in a non-governmental organization. A judge had just sentenced her abuser to six months of community work as an alternative to incarceration. It turned out that since her report to the police was incomplete and developed over time (as is common in such cases), the indictment included only minor sexual offenses, to which the offender pleaded guilty. Moran was neither notified of the plea negotiations, nor was she invited to the sentencing hearing. Needless to say, nobody sought her opinion about the plea agreement. When she came to me, all she wanted was that somehow an appeals court should alter the six-month community work sentence to an equivalent term of incarceration. A letter she had written to the judge with this appeal was disregarded since it was 'delivered to court against procedural rules'. All she wanted was for her voice to be heard, even at that late stage, even just for a minor revision of the decision.

Ten years later, in the summer of 2018, I was contacted by the social worker who had been Moran's supporter in the years that followed the trial. I remembered Moran immediately despite the time that had passed since then. She told me that Moran had suffered from severe physical injury following a failed suicide attempt a few years back. In a wheelchair, suffering from chronic pain and with no prospects for relief despite strong medication, she approached Dignitas, a Swiss non-profit member society which support assisted dying, in 2017. After a lengthy process, Moran orchestrated her own death, with her two closest friends around her. I was surprised to hear that while preparing for her death, Moran wanted to find me; that the fact that I persuaded the prosecution to appeal for a revised sentence was one of the happiest moments in her dark adolescent years. During those years I was working with Moran, she was yearning for her mother's acknowledgment, validation and support. She wanted the police and the trial judge to recognize her story. None of those things happened, but at least she found a lawyer – myself – who acted on her behalf, and an appellate court that accepted her request to revise the sentence. Another victory was a torts claim she had filed against her mother and abuser, which led to a large sum of damages paid to her – not the acknowledgment she had hoped for, but at least a court statement validating her story.

In her short life, as well as in her self-orchestrated death, Moran represents the desperate needs many young victims share: having their voice heard, their story validated, regaining some level of control over their lives (or death, as in this tragic story) and having supportive adults around them. Moran stood out in the unique combination of great strength and extreme vulnerability she demonstrated at the same time. But many young victims are both strong and vulnerable; they wish for their opinions to be respected and need their families to stand by them. Moran, as well as many other child victims who I escorted through the criminal process as a lawyer, inspired me to study the field of restorative justice and the involvement of child victims in it. In 2011, after eight years of doing research,[1] I published *Child Victims and Restorative Justice: A Needs-Rights Model* (Gal, 2011), offering a theoretical framework for the development of child-inclusive restorative justice for child victims. As an advocate and a researcher, I naturally hoped that the book would make a difference. Perhaps it did, but very little. While restorative justice programs addressing juvenile offenders have proliferated globally in the past twenty years, the involvement of victimized children in restorative justice has remained largely undeveloped and under-researched.

In the absence of restorative justice programs specifically targeting victimized children, very few studies examined how children and youth experience their involvement. Gal and Moyal (2011) performed a secondary analysis of the findings from the Reintegrative Shaming Experiments (RISE) conducted in Canberra, Australia, by Heather Strang and Lawrence Sherman (Strang, 2002). Comparing the experiences of young victims with those of adult victims regarding their involvement in restorative justice conferences following violent and property crimes, we found that unlike adult victims who experienced the process as fair, young victims were less satisfied with restorative justice conferences. A complementary qualitative analysis identified adult domination and program insensitivity to youth's special needs as recurring themes. The conclusion of the study was that in order to fulfil the potential of restorative justice to achieve just outcomes for victimized children and youth, restorative justice processes must be specifically tailored to their needs, vulnerabilities and capabilities.

---

1 Much of the research was conducted during my PhD studies at the Australian National University, under the inspirational supervision of Prof. John Braithwaite, with Drs. Heather Strang and John Seymour as advisors. It was completed while I was a post-doctorate fellow at the Hebrew University in Jerusalem.

An Australian report for the Royal Commission into Institutional Responses to Child Sexual Abuse (Bolitho & Freeman, 2016) found only a small number of restorative justice programs addressing sexual violence, and none of them targeted specifically victimized children. Based on the limited existing experience, the authors proposed five recommendations for achieving positive outcomes for victims: specialism – including training and skills; screening – careful selection of appropriate cases and suitable participants; expertise – involving experts in sexual offenses and family violence; flexibility – responding to victims' needs; timing – adjusting the timing to victims' readiness; and services – targeted programs for offender rehabilitation.

A recent EU-funded collaboration between the University of Leuven, the European Forum for Restorative Justice and the International Juvenile Justice Observatory led to the publication of a practical guide for implementing restorative justice with victimized children (Pali & Randazzo, 2018). The guide was based on a learning process from three European states implementing restorative justice regularly: Belgium, Northern Ireland and Finland. Despite their systematic search, the authors found very little and mostly anecdotal information about the involvement of victimized children in restorative justice processes. They concluded that the focus of attention of the programs and their evaluation studies was typically the perpetrator rather than the victim, particularly if the perpetrator was a minor; information about victims' involvement only seldom refers to young victims separately from the general victim population. Despite the limited empirical findings, the authors extracted, based on anecdotal experiences and interviews with professionals, ten recommendations for the involvement of victimized children in restorative justice: 1. Develop accessible, safe and high-quality restorative justice programs for child victims; 2. Provide restorative justice facilitators training on children's rights, needs and effective forms of communication with children; 3. Ensure full and clear information and free consent; 4. Give priority to the best interests of the child; 5. Ensure children's safety; 6. Provide multiple ways of participation for victimized children; 7. Use child-friendly techniques; 8. Ensure that process outcomes are proportional to the deeds; 9. Collect information and research about the involvement of child victims in restorative justice; 10. Involve community members.

To further contribute to the discourse about restorative justice involving children and youth, this chapter attempts to expand the Needs-Rights Model (NRM) beyond child victims as originally envisioned, to child perpetrators as well.[2] It begins by presenting the NRM as a comprehensive theoretical framework for understanding the experiences of victimized children and youth, and promoting their interests. It then considers how the

---

2 This chapter offers a universal framework and does not focus on child victims or child perpetrators in a specific locality. However, considering that the introduction referred to an Israeli case, it may be relevant to provide details about the Israeli law concerning juvenile offending: the minimum age of criminal responsibility in Israel is 12. The Youth (Care and Supervision) Law, 14 LSI 44 (5720-1960), applies to children aged 12-18 at the time of the offense.

NRM can be applied, with some modifications, to address the needs-based rights of children and youth who commit a criminal offense. Next, the chapter offers practical starting points, or heuristics, for conducting restorative justice with children and youth as victims and victimizers, based on the NRM. The chapter ends with suggesting directions for future research.

2 The Needs-Rights Model (NRM) for victimized children and youth

The NRM (Gal, 2011) is a double-layered structure, with a first layer of child victims' rights and a second layer of child victims' needs integrated together and creating an interdisciplinary framework for developing and evaluating justice-related programs addressing childhood victimization.

The motivation to develop such an interdisciplinary model was based on my impression that legal practitioners and scholars use completely different terminology than that used by mental-health professionals and scholars, even when they address the same issues regarding victimized children and youth. On the one hand, human rights lawyers are preoccupied with advocating for the legal rights of their clients, and children's rights advocates are no different. A 'strictly rights' discourse can be criticized for being too abstract, for increasing dispute and tension, and for failing to offer solutions between competing rights. At the same time, a purely needs-based discourse, with the terminology often used by psychologists and social workers is also problematic, tending to paternalism and lacking the power of a rights-based discourse. An integrated language of needs-rights is stronger; based on empirical findings about human nature, human needs and human behavior, we can better understand the specific meanings of certain rights with regard to certain children, and at the same time benefit from the unique status that international human rights and children's rights hold.

The 1990 United Nations Convention on the Rights of the Child (CRC) offers an authoritative and compelling Bill of Rights for children, as the other chapters in this book demonstrate (Wolthuis, 2021; Winter, 2021), and was thus used as the first and normative layer in the NRM (Gal, 2011: 192).

Six provisions from the Convention were selected as key elements in the model: the Conventions' four 'guiding principles' and two specific rights targeting victimized children. The guiding principles are the following: (a) the equality principle (CRC Art. 2); (b) the best interests of the child principle (CRC Art. 3); (c) the life, survival and development principle (CRC Art. 6); and (d) the principle of participation (CRC Art. 12). The specific victimization-related provisions are these: (e) the right to protection against any form of abuse and maltreatment at the hands of caretakers (CRC Art. 19), and (f) the right to rehabilitation of those who have been victimized (CRC Art. 39).

Of course, this is not an exhaustive list of child victims' rights. Other specific rights are included elsewhere in the Convention, as well as in other UN, European or regional treaties. But most of the other rights can be understood as derived from these six provisions.

The second layer of the model includes existing empirical knowledge regarding the various needs of child victims. The extended body of psychosocial research relating to children facing stress, trauma, victimization and legal processes was organized in four clusters: (I) findings regarding elements that promote children's well-being (the corresponding term to the legal phrase 'best interests'); (II) findings regarding the importance of active involvement and a sense of control, a concept closely related to the legal term of participation; (III) findings regarding children's perceptions of procedural justice – the importance of having their voice heard, being able to understand the process, and having a respectful, neutral decision-maker; and (IV) knowledge drawn from developmental victimology (Finkelhor, 2008) – the different ways children and youth of various ages are vulnerable to crime and cope with it.

The combined model, integrating the six normative elements (a-f) and the four groups of empirical knowledge (I-IV), was then organized, for the sake of simplicity, to four needs-rights clusters. Each cluster was informative as to the ways restorative justice programs can best meet the needs-rights of victimized children:

The child well-being cluster. The child's unique developmental needs and interests should shape the restorative justice process, the format of participation of the child in it, and its outcomes. For example, the child's specific interests and wishes should shape, to the extent possible, the invitee list for the process and how the process is to be carried out. Possible outcomes, such as restitution, an apology or other reparative measures, should be similarly determined largely by the child victim's needs and wishes. Welfare considerations of victimized children should shape program design at the systemic level.

The control/partnership cluster. Children should be listened to throughout the process, and their participation in it must be tailored according to their individual needs, wishes and capabilities. Although full participation in the process may sometimes be impossible or undesirable, for most children, some level of participation, while challenging, may actually have therapeutic benefits. Accordingly, participation-enhancing techniques as well as child representation should be implemented to encourage children's involvement.

The procedural justice cluster. Restorative justice processes must be equally available and accessible for all child victims, with special measures available to secure the safe and positive involvement of children with special needs. Information regarding the restorative justice process must be clear and age-appropriate, children's voices should be heard throughout, and facilitators must act professionally and without bias.

The protection/development cluster. Restorative justice processes involving victimized children must be specifically designed for certain age groups and types of crime. Safety must be a precondition and a goal. Post-process monitoring is crucial to ensure the fulfilment of the reparation agreement.

3 EXPANDING THE NRM TO CHILD PERPETRATORS

Children's rights do not apply to child victims only. No matter what type of crime a youth perpetrated, he or she is still benefiting from the international and national human rights governance, granting special protections as well as self-determination rights to all children and youth. Similarly, child perpetrators of crime hold unique needs, vulnerabilities and interests. Empirical knowledge about such needs, vulnerabilities and interests may inform us as to how to implement their internationally acknowledged rights. Accordingly, a Needs-Rights Model may be just as applicable to child perpetrators.

A first stage of constructing a child-perpetrator NRM involves identifying the international human rights that may be used as the normative layer of the model. Here, too, the CRC provides the most suitable template, and the four guiding principles are the central normative elements relevant for child perpetrators. Two additional provisions specifically apply to child perpetrators: Article 37 (the right against torture and inhumane treatment or punishment), and Article 40 (the right to due process and a preference for alternative measures to criminal proceedings).

Once the set of these six provisions has been identified, the next step is to identify existing psychosocial knowledge about young offenders. A full review of the research about young offenders across ages, gender, culture and special needs is beyond the scope of this chapter, but using the same clusters that were used in the context of victimized children to explain what young offenders might need is helpful in highlighting some examples.

Starting with studies exploring **what promotes the well-being** of young perpetrators of crime, a well-established fact is that children and youth who commit crime are at risk of being labelled as criminals. Therefore, as the systematic review by Petrosino, Turpin-Petrosino, Hollis-Peel and Lavenberg (2013) found, oftentimes 'doing nothing' is better than 'doing something', and formal processing often has a criminogenic effect on juveniles. Restorative justice models, in contrast, construct a strong framework in which *reintegrative shaming* (Braithwaite, 1999) can be communicated: the involvement of family members and other meaningful people in the child perpetrator's life facilitate a combined message of strong denunciation of the action and strong support for the person. The separation between the action and the actor enables child perpetrators to take responsibility, recognize the wrongfulness of their deeds, and make amends. This, in turn, opens the door for them to return to a normative lifestyle and be reaccepted by their communities. It is also known, based on the studies of Ahmed, Harris, Braithwaite and Braithwaite (2001) in the context of school bullying, that the opportunity to *manage shame* – to acknowledge it and find constructive ways to discharge it – may make it easier for young victimizers to desist from their offensive behavior.

Moving to psychosocial knowledge about child and youth **participation and sense of control**, the most basic premise is that young perpetrators have the same developmental need to take an active part in decision-making processes affecting them, as do young victims (Buss, 2011). The question remains *how* child participation should take place when the child is the perpetrator of an offense. One of the strongest lessons drawn from studies involving interviews with children on participation is that children strive to have *ongoing relationships* with those who hold legal power over them, and this applies to a range of contexts such as special education, child protection, juvenile court and public policy. Sharon Bessell (2015), for example, indicated that out-of-home children felt frustrated with the high turnover of caseworkers; meaningful participation occurred only with known, trusted adults with whom they had ongoing conversations in non-formal settings. Accordingly, a child advocate representing a young offender should be someone the child knows and trusts. Child-friendly *temporal elements* – when the participation takes place, for how long, and how often – are also crucial for children to be able to meaningfully participate in decision-making processes affecting their lives (Tisdall, 2015).

Moving next to the **procedural justice** cluster, according to Tom Tyler's theory (1990), people who experience the process against them as fair are more likely to accept its outcomes, and consequently are less likely to reoffend. A study by Penner, Viljoen, Douglas and Roesch (2014) with Canadian youths on probation, found that children aged 12-17 who perceived their overall experience of the criminal justice system as fair, were less likely to reoffend in the short term than those who experienced it as unfair. Many children and youth, when asked about their understanding of a just process, mention the importance of voice, understanding the process, being treated respectfully, and having a neutral decision-maker (Murphy, 2015). Having parents around is also important for children, for protecting their rights and for emotional support (Lawrence, 2003). In addition, the above-mentioned RISE experiments demonstrated the importance of being culturally sensitive when conducting restorative justice with young people belonging to minority groups (Sherman & Strang, 2007). Restorative justice programs that are not culturally sensitive can lead to frustration, a sense of injustice, and possibly an increased risk of reoffending.

Finally, the **protection cluster** includes knowledge about the need to be particularly careful when working with young offenders with special needs. The term inclusiveness refers to an understanding that children and youth differ in their capabilities, and that each process must be accessible and inclusive to all (Gal, 2015: 455). The integration of the non-discrimination principle with relevant empirical knowledge regarding certain disabilities or populations leads to a duty to adjust processes so that any child perpetrator can meaningfully participate in them. The study by Hennessey Hayes and Pamela Snow (2013) provides a strong reminder that, considering the large rate of oral language impairments among young offenders (up to 50 percent), expecting them to effectively communicate remorse and empathy during restorative justice conferences might be unrealistic in many cases. Tailor-made processes preceded by thorough preparations that include expectation management are more likely to be successful.

4 Young victims and young offenders: empirical and normative overlaps

A large body of research shows that young victims and young offenders share similar characteristics, and that there is a significant overlap between the two population groups (Jennings, Higgins, Tewksbury, Gover & Piquero, 2010; Mulford et al., 2017; Posick & Zimmerman, 2015; Regoeczi, 2000). The overarching humanistic approach championed by the CRC implies that classifying children and youth as either 'victims' or 'perpetrators' would not only be empirically inaccurate but also normatively wrong, because the event that marked them as such should not define who they are. Indeed, the above analysis demonstrates the similarity between the needs-rights of those who are considered, for the sake of the current analysis, as child victims and of those who are considered child perpetrators. Both population groups are protected by the Convention and its guiding principles. Victimized children are also protected by the right against abuse by caretakers and the right to rehabilitation following victimization. Offending children are also protected against cruel and unusual punishment and have a right to due process which favors the use of alternative measures to the use of criminal proceedings. Not surprisingly, these specific provisions share similar goals: to prevent harm and promote rehabilitation and reintegration among children and youth.

There are also significant overlaps in the psychosocial literature relating to the needs and wishes of victimized and offending youths. The support of family members is important for both groups, whether to ensure a reintegrative shaming experience (Braithwaite, 1989) or to provide a platform for acknowledgment and validation (Herman, 2005). Participation in decision-making is considered by children and youths in various circumstances as desirable, including those who broke the law (Roesch-March, 2014) and those who are considered in-need of protection (Van Bijleveld, Dedding & Bunders-Aelen, 2013). Children and youth assign importance to the *ways* in which they are involved in decision-making, highlighting the importance of continuous relationships (Bessell, 2011), adequate timing (Tisdall, 2015), and age-appropriate information (Piamenta, 2019). Procedural justice is considered important for victimized as well as offending youth. For example, juvenile offenders wanted to have their voices heard in juvenile courts in order to validate their experiences and to affirm their membership in the community (Pennington & Farrell, 2019). Child victims of sexual assault were influenced, in their contact with justice professionals, by family and community perceptions of the fairness of the legal system (Hlavka, 2014). Cultural sensitivity and competency are important when working with juvenile offenders (Strang, 2002) as well as with victimized children and youth (Pennell & Anderson, 2005). Similarly, research relating to children with special needs refers to the need for processes of all kinds to be child-inclusive (Badham, 2004).

Accordingly, the NRM can be applied, with only minor revisions, as a framework for applying restorative justice with children and youth in conflict with the law. The same four needs-rights clusters appear: needs-rights relating to their best interests in restorative justice; those relating to their participation in restorative justice processes; needs-rights relating to the practice of restorative justice in a procedurally fair manner; and finally, those relating to the protection of children and youth of all population groups and developmental stages in restorative justice settings.

Instead of repeating the content of each of these needs-rights clusters, the following section translates the NRM to practical heuristics for working with children and youth in restorative justice settings. These heuristics were developed in the context of child victims (Gal, 2011: 183-188), and are broadened here to include child perpetrators as well.

5 From theory to practice: eight heuristics for applying restorative justice with young victims and young offenders

The following paragraphs present the eight heuristics and discuss how they apply to young offenders as well. For greater clarity, I add actual examples from restorative justice processes conducted with youth, which I either observed or heard about through interviews and conversations with facilitators.

The eight heuristics are:

1. Holism
2. Tailor-made process
3. Children as partners
4. Participation as a continuum
5. Liberating children's voices
6. Let go
7. Restorative process as a goal
8. Empowering advocacy

1. *Holism*: If holism in the case of child victims means treating them as whole human beings with strengths and interests other than the victimization they endured (Minow, 1993), holism with offenders means seeing them as human beings who

conducted a wrongful act, not as criminals. In restorative justice terminology, a holistic approach is manifested through separating the wrong from the wrongdoer. Participants at restorative justice processes condemn the actions of the perpetrator, but at the same time express support and belief in him or her as a human being. An experienced facilitator once told me: 'We learn to be non-judgmental', meaning that they approach the perpetrator without bias, notwithstanding what they are accused of.

2. A *tailor-made process:* Every victim is different, and so is every offender, and restorative justice processes must be tailored to meet their specific capabilities, wishes and interests. Similar to victims, young perpetrators should be able to determine who they would like to invite as supporters. Specifically, the preparation phase is crucial, among other things, for evaluating the ability of the perpetrator to talk about their actions and express their feelings about them. Following Hayes and Snow's (2013) discussion about oral language impairments, facilitators preparing young victims and perpetrators should use validated tools for evaluating oral language competence of all young participants. Young victims and perpetrators alike should be supported in planning what they want to say and should be assisted in developing realistic expectations of what would be expressed by the other side. A young victim of a cyber-sexual assault felt too ashamed to attend the restorative conference that followed the offense, but wanted to hear the perpetrator's apology. She was called in from the next room where she was waiting just as the perpetrator was ready to apologize. As he talked, she did not look at him, and once he finished, she got up and left the room.
3. *Children as partners:* It is well established that the criminal justice system regularly excludes victims from decision-making (Englebrecht, 2011). Child victims are particularly side-lined and silenced (Powell, Hlavka & Mulla, 2017), either out of concern for their well-being or due to disbelief about their ability to contribute a valid viewpoint that is different from those already expressed by others. The concept of children as partners (Gal, 2011: 185-186) suggests that when reaching decisions regarding young victims, adults depend on them for providing the most expert knowledge about their needs, interests and wishes. Young offenders are also appreciative when they are supported to choose their desired level of participation, instead of being silenced (Peterson-Badali, Care & Broeking, 2007). In restorative justice, it is much easier to treat both victims and offenders as partners to a joint, consensual decision. In fact, when both the victim and the perpetrator are young (as is frequently the case, particularly in violent offenses), they are often the most suitable people to craft a reparation plan, provided that their shared dialogue is monitored and supported by others. Treating young people as partners means respecting their own viewpoints, interests and capabilities throughout the restorative process.

4. *Participation as a continuum:* Partnerships differ from each other and they depend on the ability and motivation of the stakeholders; they can also change over time, as participants gain confidence and trust in themselves and in others. Victims might not want to be present throughout the whole encounter, but as long as they are offered a range of options, the term 'partnership' applies. With young offenders, significant differences in capacities exist and not everyone can lead the discussion, write on the whiteboard and present a detailed account of their feelings. The level and form of participation should suit the particular child at each stage of the process.
5. *Liberating children's voices*: Children of different ages and developmental stages express themselves differently and this is true for both victims and offenders. Adults carry the role of being 'translators', rather than authors, of what young participants say. This is a challenging role, because oftentimes youths' expressions are short and vague. An experienced facilitator told me that many young offenders are concerned that they will not be able to effectively convey their remorse during the restorative encounter, worrying that their limited verbal abilities will simply not suffice. Despite these common concerns, facilitators should avoid talking on behalf of young perpetrators during the encounter, but instead, encourage and support them until they find the right words. Oftentimes this means being quiet for a while or giving space for non-verbal gestures, which are crucial. Parents too tend to speak on behalf of their children, and they are often more articulate and 'easier to work with'. But when parents take their children's place, many of the benefits of restorative justice are missed. Adults need to let the youths express themselves in any possible way, as long as their message is authentic and non-dominating.
6. *Let go:* Legal professionals and social workers typically want to protect young victims from further harm – thus often deciding to exclude them from the decision-making process. The *let go* principle means that a *difficult* experience is not necessarily a *harmful* one. Restorative justice conferences are often intense, difficult and challenging, but at the same time meaningful, transformative and positive. This is true for young people who committed the offense as well. Many perpetrators are terrified of meeting 'their' victims and the victims' parents. It is important not to force them to agree to attend but to provide them with all the information about the process and its potential benefits and risks. Facilitators should remember at all times that whether to attend or not to attend a restorative justice conference is a decision completely at the hands of the young participants. *Letting go* also means allowing young participants to 'take risks' during the restorative encounter, while remaining at an arm's length. At one of the family group conferences held in Israel following the dissemination of an indecent photo of a teenaged girl, the victim and the perpetrator left the room and jointly constructed a list of invitees for a group talk where the victimizer agreed to take responsibility and apologize for her deed. Such a constructive solution would have not been possible if the adults were overprotective.

7. *Restorative process as a goal:* No matter what the outcomes are, the process itself, when conducted well – being non-dominating, egalitarian and safe – is often a life-changing experience and can become a model for children and their parents in reaching decisions and communicating emotions and expectations. I was told by numerous facilitators that a single encounter cannot always repair everything; but it is almost always the case that the young people feel a significant positive change following the process.
8. Finally, *Empowering advocacy:* One of the challenges faced by advocates representing youth is to provide zealous representation on the one hand – to seek the best result for their client – while keeping the youth at the forefront. To maintain this fine line, those representing children should avoid professional jargon, provide detailed and clear information to their clients, and maintain non-dominating dialogue with them throughout the process. Even if the legal results are impressive, if that victory was achieved with the young victim or offender sidelined, it is not a success from the perspective of the child's needs-rights, and the young client is likely to be frustrated and unsatisfied (Peterson-Badali et al., 2007).

6 Conclusion: a universal NRM for children and youth in restorative justice

The scant literature on restorative justice in the context of child victims demonstrates that there is an urgent need to regulate the implementation of child-inclusive restorative justice programs. Realistically speaking, restorative justice programs addressing childhood victimization are more likely to emerge within the juvenile justice context, where the focus is on the rehabilitation and reintegration of the young perpetrators. A universal model that can be applied to victims as well as to perpetrators provides a useful framework for regulation in these contexts, as it does not require a full-blown diversion from existing restorative justice programs with young offenders. The significance of the NRM, as applied to both child victims and child perpetrators, is three-fold:

First, the NRM helps build discursive bridges between lawyers and social workers, and between legal scholars engaged with norms and social-scientists engaged with empirical findings. Once integrated within joint clusters of needs-rights, 'participation' is linked with 'control', 'best interests' with 'well-being', and 'respect' with 'procedural justice'. As a result, our knowledge about what works is broadened, as well as our understanding of what needs to be improved.

Second, the NRM creates a discursive bridge between youth victimization and youth offending, based on normative and empirical arguments. Very often, those who are involved in supporting victimized children promote a 'tough on crime' approach toward their victimizers, while those working in the juvenile justice field focus on the rehabilitation of young offenders. But more often than not, both the victim and the perpetrator are minors. The NRM, which is naturally compatible with the basic notions of restorative justice, offers an integrated framework for addressing the needs-rights of child victims as well as those of child offenders.

Third, from a practical perspective, the heuristics ensuing from the NRM provide helpful guidance for conducting restorative justice with children and youth. Specific programs targeting certain offenses or certain populations must develop their own working principles, but the eight heuristics are solid starting points that are grounded within an international normative framework as well as existing empirical research.

The NRM offers a research agenda that integrates different fields of scholarship and calls for further research in the various directions set by the needs-rights clusters. Questions arising from the model and requiring further research include the level of adherence to the needs-based rights of victimized and victimizing children in restorative justice processes, the manifestation of certain needs-based rights of child victims and child offenders in restorative justice processes, the identification of other needs-based rights not included in the model that are important for either victimized or victimizing youth, and promising practices fulfilling specific needs-based rights of children and youth in restorative justice processes.

References

Ahmed, E., Harris, N., Braithwaite, J. & Braithwaite, V. (2001). *Shame management through reintegration*. Cambridge: Cambridge University Press.

Badham, B. (2004). Participation – for a change: disabled young people lead the way. *Children & Society*, 18, 143-154. doi: 10.1002/chi.821.

Bessell, S. (2011). Participation in decision-making in out-of-home care in Australia: what do young people say?. *Children and Youth Services Review*, 33(4), 496-501. doi: 10.1016/j.childyouth.2010.05.006.

Bessell, S. (2015). Inclusive and respectful relationships as the basis for child inclusive policies and practice: the experience of children in out-of-home care in Australia. In T. Gal & B. Duramy (eds.), *International perspectives and empirical findings on child participation* (pp. 183-206). New York: Oxford University Press.

Bolitho, J. & Freeman, K. (2016). The use and effectiveness of restorative justice in criminal justice systems following child sexual abuse or comparable harms. *Royal Commission into Institutional Responses to Child Sexual Abuse, Sydney*.

Braithwaite, J. (1989). *Crime, shame and reintegration*. Cambridge: Cambridge University Press.

Braithwaite, J. (1999). Restorative justice: assessing optimistic and pessimistic accounts. *Crime and Justice, 25*, 1-127.

Buss, E. (2011). Failing juvenile courts and what lawyers and judges can do about it. *Northwestern Journal of Law and Social Policy*, 6(2), 318-333.

Englebrecht, C.M. (2011). The struggle for 'ownership of conflict': an exploration of victim participation and voice in the criminal justice system. *Criminal Justice Review*, 36(2), 129-151. doi: 10.1177/0734016811399419.

Finkelhor, D. (2008). *Childhood victimization: violence, crime, and abuse in the lives of young people*. Oxford: Oxford University Press.

Gal, T. (2011). *Child victims and restorative justice: a needs-rights model.* New York: Oxford University Press.

Gal, T. (2015). From social exclusion to child-inclusive policies: toward an ecological model of child participation. In T. Gal & B. Duramy (eds.), *International perspectives and empirical findings on child participation* (pp. 451-463). New York: Oxford University Press.

Hayes, H. & Snow, P. (2013). Oral language competence and restorative justice processes: refining preparation and the measurement of conference outcomes. *Trends and Issues in Crime and Criminal Justice*, 463, 1-7.

Herman, J.L. (2005). Justice from the victim' perspective. *Violence Against Women*, 11(5), 571-602. doi: 10.1177/1077801205274450.

Hlavka, H.R. (2014). Legal subjectivity among youth victims of sexual abuse. *Law & Social Inquiry*, 39(1), 31-61. doi: 10.1111/lsi.12032.

Jennings, W.G., Higgins, G.E., Tewksbury, R., Gover, A.R. & Piquero, A.R. (2010). A longitudinal assessment of the victim-offender overlap. *Journal of Interpersonal Violence*, 25(12), 2147-2174. doi: 10.1177/0886260509354888.

Lawrence, J.A. (2003). *Safeguarding fairness for children in interactions with adults in authority: computer-based investigations of the judgments of secondary school students, technical report.* Report to Criminology Research Council. School of Behavioural Science, The University of Melbourne. Retrieved from www.aic.gov.au/sites/default/files/2020-05/200001-35.pdf (last accessed 1 August 2021).

Minow, M. (1993). Surviving victim talk. *UCLA Law Review*, 40(6), 1411-1446.

Mulford, C.F., Blachman-Demner, D.R., Pitzer, L., Schubert, C.A., Piquero, A.R. & Mulvey, E.P. (2017). Victim offender overlap: dual trajectory examination of victimization and offending among young felony offenders over seven years. *Victims & Offenders*, 13(1), 1-27. doi: 10.1080/15564886.2016.1196283.

Murphy, K. (2015). Does procedural justice matter to youth? Comparing adults' and youths' willingness to collaborate with police. *Policing and Society*, 25(1), 53-76. doi: 10.1080/10439463.2013.802786.

Pali, B. & Randazzo, S. (2018). *Practical Guide: Implementing Restorative Justice with Child Victims*, 1-120. Retrieved from https://www.oijj.org/sites/default/files/archivospaginas/implementing_practical_guide_eng.pdf (last accessed 1 August 2021).

Pennell, J. & Anderson, G. (2005). *Widening the circle: the practice and evaluation of family group conferencing with children, youths, and their families.* Washington: NASW Press.

Penner, E.K., Viljoen, J.L., Douglas, K.S. & Roesch, R. (2014). Procedural justice versus risk factors for offending: predicting recidivism in youth. *Law and Human Behavior*, 38(3), 225-237. doi: 10.1037/lhb0000055.

Pennington, L. & Farrell, A. (2019). Role of voice in the legal process. *Criminology*, *57*(2), 343-368. Doi: 10.1111/1745-9125.12205.

Peterson-Badali, M., Care, S. & Broeking, J. (2007). Young people's perceptions and experiences of the lawyer-client relationship. *Canadian Journal of Criminology and Criminal Justice*, 49(3), 375-401. doi: 10.3138/cjccj.49.3.375.

Petrosino, A., Turpin-Petrosino, C., Hollis-Peel, M.E. & Lavenberg, J.G. (2013). Scared straight and other juvenile awareness programs for preventing juvenile delinquency: a systematic review. *Campbell Systematic Reviews*, 9, 1-55. doi: 10.4073/csr.2013.5.

Piamenta, J. (2019). *The perspectives of young victims of sexual assault regarding the criminal process* (PhD Dissertation). University of Haifa, Israel.

Posick, C. & Zimmerman, G.M. (2015). Person-in-context: insights on contextual variation in the victim–offender overlap across schools. *Journal of Interpersonal Violence*, 30(8), 1432-1455. doi: 10.1177/0886260514540327.

Powell, A.J., Hlavka, H.R. & Mulla, S. (2017). Intersectionality and credibility in child sexual assault trials. *Gender & Society*, 31(4), 457-480. doi: 10.1177/0891243217716116.

Regoeczi, W.C. (2000). Adolescent violent victimization and offending: assessing the extent of the link. *Canadian Journal of Criminology*, 42(4), 493-505.

Roesch-March, A. (2014). 'Out of control': making sense of the behaviour of young people referred to secure accommodation. *British Journal of Social Work*, 44(2), 197-213. doi: 10.1093/bjsw/bcs102.

Sherman, L. & Strang, H. (2007). *Restorative justice: the evidence.* Oxford: Smith Institute.

Strang, H. (2002). *Repair or revenge: victims and restorative justice.* Oxford: Clarendon Press.

Tisdall, E.K.M. (2015). Addressing the challenges of children and young people's participation. In T. Gal & B. Duramy (eds.), *International perspectives and empirical findings on child participation* (pp. 381-404). New York: Oxford University Press.

Tyler, T.R. (1990). *Why people obey the law.* New Haven: Yale University Press.

Van Bijleveld, G.G., Dedding, C.W.M. & Bunders-Aelen, J.F.G. (2013). Children's and young people's participation within child welfare and child protection services: a state of the art review. *Child & Family Social Work*, 20(2), 129-138. doi: 10.1111/cfs.12082.

Chapter 5
Rights-based restorative justice

Questioning and decolonizing our ways of knowing, doing and being in Canada and beyond

Shannon A. Moore

1 Restorative justice – recalling the roots

The nomenclature *restorative justice* signifies a social response to violations of the law. The actual term is just three decades old, yet the philosophy and processes underpinning it may be traced back in millennia to Indigenous ways of knowing (Cunneen, 2007; Moore, 2007, 2020; Ross, 1996; Tauri, 2016). The term restorative justice was first coined by Canadians Mark Yantzi and Dave Worth as an outcome of their work with Community Justice Initiatives. Community Justice Initiatives thrives today as a small local organization in Ontario, Canada. Programs facilitated through Community Justice Initiatives formed the catalyst for the international movement now found in over 100 countries around the globe (Moore, 2007, 2020; Nyp, 2004). Yantzi was one of many Canadians and other delegates (Moore & Mitchell, 2009) that helped shape the development of the United Nations basic principles on the use of restorative justice in criminal justice matters (United Nations Economic and Social Council, 2002). In addition, the growth in the use of restorative justice over the past three decades has been supported by prison abolition movements, faith communities, transformation justice initiatives and alternative dispute resolution movements (Hadley, 2001; Moore, 2004).

The principles of restorative justice may be summarized through five dimensions and are expressed in the United Nations Basic Principles on the Use of Restorative Justice Programmes in Criminal Matters (United Nations Economic and Social Council, 2002). First, the perpetration of crime and the infliction of harm are fundamentally the violation of a human being or human relationships as they rupture the well-being of individuals, communities and societies. Second, the goals of restorative processes involve the repairing of harm done and restoring relationships between individuals and community with an aim of facilitating movement of all participants toward greater equilibrium. Third, all restorative processes must be voluntary and respect the rights of individuals to free choice. This is achieved through sensitive consideration of power relationships, and social and structural inequities within society. Fourth, victims of crime must always be of central concern and given free choice to participate in the process. Fifth, perpetrators of wrongdoing are given the opportunity to accept responsibility for the harm they have caused and a choice to participate in a restorative process. The above five aspects emphasize the importance of human interpersonal and social relationships (Moore, 2004, 2007). Restorative justice is shaped by the needs of the communities impacted by harm while also guided by values of empowerment, accountability, honesty, respect, engagement, volunteerism, restoration, inclusiveness, collaboration and problem solving (Clarysse & Moore, 2017; Moore, 2007).

As an approach to addressing conflict with the law or in community, restorative justice practices value humanity and relationality (Vaandering & Reimer, 2019) as a key axiological standpoint. Restorative justice as epistemology, a framework for how we know the world, is dialogical and participatory as 'it is knowable through our efforts to speak to one another' (Woolford & Nelund, 2019: 69). Ontologically, restorative justice shapes our experiences of being in the world, with the viewpoint that change is possible for ourselves and in the world around us and that communication is the keystone to transformation. Restorative justice is teleologically driven toward greater balance in relationships through liberated communication 'so that humans can collectively re-create society for the betterment of each and everyone of us' (Woolford & Nelund, 2019: 69). Restorative justice focuses on teaching and healing in response to wrongdoing and engages all parties impacted by violations to the law and social relationships.

Ross (1996) petitions us to take this understanding of restorative justice further by keeping 'an eye on the past to understand how things have come to be, an eye on the future to design measures that show the greatest promise of making it healthier for all concerned' (15). This non-linear conception of time, articulated so many years ago, is to unlearn, relearn and learn again the histories and context that shape legal and social systems in our nations. In Canada, that history is indelibly entangled with colonization, which has 'touched everything' (Ross, 1996: 14). In the context of colonial histories, it is essential to understand the difficult truths of our nations as the first step toward decolonizing our relationships as well as legal and social systems. The second step is to appreciate the Indigenous roots of restorative justice. Woolford and Nelund (2019: 20-21) emphasize that such a step reflects a commitment to the transformative politics of restorative justice and a refusal to reproduce structures of domination:

> Racialized, gendered, classed, heteronormative and settler-colonial biases are easily imported into restorative justice processes. Given the general persistence of these patterns of domination, this should be expected. The restorative justice movement cannot simply assume that it is outside of these patterns of domination, they must be addressed directly in restorative justice practice. (20-21)

Given the reality of structural injustice within our institutions, it follows that participants' experiences of restorative justice are a reflection of the power relations in programs and processes shaped by the texts that guide facilitation and mediation. To be restorative, heteropatriarchy must be abandoned, because otherwise processes risk reinforcing gender domination, settler colonialism and heteronormativity (Woolford & Nelund, 2019; see also Arvin, Tuck & Morrill, 2013).

Notwithstanding the articulation of the Indigenous roots of restorative justice, it is important to note that Chartrand and Horn (2016) emphasize the complex and nuanced relationship between contemporary restorative justice and Indigenous legal traditions:

> There are important features that make Indigenous legal traditions quite different from restorative justice processes, including how Indigenous legal traditions often use proactive/preventative strategies mediated through kinship networks (Gray and Lauderdale 2007), how they place a high importance on spirituality (Cameron 2005; Borrows 2010), and the historic use of punitive/retributive sanctions (Milward 2012; Napolean and Friedland 2014). (Chartrand & Horn, 2016: 3)

Given the arguments above, it is clear that restorative justice and Indigenous legal traditions should not be conflated but these instruments can be used to enrich contemporary understanding of how justice may be a tool for healing relationships and build toward reconciliation among settler and Indigenous ways of knowing.

2 Contextualizing colonialism

Canada is a colonial nation, and that fact is entangled with the systematic cultural genocide of Indigenous populations by European colonization that has, in turn, woven the fabric of services (social, justice, health, education) and the interpretation of human rights in this country (Moore, 2017, 2020). Cultural genocide and the manifest devastation of First Nations, Inuit and Métis populations throughout Indigenous communities in Canada are documented within the final report of the Truth and Reconciliation Commission of Canada (2015):

> For over a century, the central goals of Canada's Aboriginal policy were to eliminate Aboriginal governments; ignore Aboriginal rights; terminate the Treaties; and, through a process of assimilation, cause Aboriginal peoples to cease to exist as distinct legal, social, cultural, religious and racial entities in Canada. The establishment and operation of residential schools were a central

> element of this policy, which can best be described as 'cultural genocide' ... cultural genocide is the destruction of those structures and practices that allow the group to continue as a group. States that engage in cultural genocide set out to destroy the political and social institutions of the targeted group. Land is seized, and populations are forcibly transferred and their movement is restricted. Languages are banned. Spiritual leaders are persecuted, spiritual practices are forbidden, and objects of spiritual value are confiscated and destroyed. And, most significantly to the issue at hand, families are disrupted to prevent the transmission of cultural values and identity from one generation to the next. In its dealing with Aboriginal people, Canada did all these things. (1)

Truth precedes reconciliation and is essential in processes with a set intention to decolonize (Absolon, 2019) our relationships, communication, politics and practices.

Prior to colonization, Indigenous communities in Canada were socially and spiritually vibrant (Moore, Tulk & Mitchell, 2005) and date back at least 30 millennia (Bourgeon, Burke & Higham, 2017) before Europeans first arrived on the shores of what is now called Canada. This truth-telling is a call to policymakers and practitioners to make a crucial shift toward appreciating the institutionalization of inequity that has perpetuated the silencing of minority voices, including Indigenous and Black young people in Canada, who are disproportionally represented in our justice systems (De Finney, Dean, Loiselle & Saraceno, 2011; Pon, Gosine & Phillips, 2011). Recent figures from Canada's federal Department of Justice (2017) confirm the state of structural injustice as revealed through Indigenous incarceration rates:

> In 2014/2015, Indigenous youth (aged 12-17) accounted for 37% of provincial/territorial custody admissions. The proportion of Indigenous youth in provincial/territorial custody was about 5 times higher than their representation in the youth population (7%). Indigenous youth were overrepresented in provincial/territorial custody in most jurisdictions, especially British Columbia, Manitoba, and Ontario. (para. 2)

If we deny the terrible truths of colonization strategies, then we will most certainly do harm and continue to perpetuate elevated rates of overrepresentation of non-white individuals in contact with mental health services, social services and justice systems. The suggestion here is that restorative justice would benefit from a reciprocal relationship with decolonizing processes, facilitated through truth-telling regarding hegemonic power relations that shape the development of policy and implementation of practice.

The practice of restorative justice reflects the values of Indigenous or Aboriginal systems of justice in Canada (and elsewhere) and implies both a certain process and outcome. The motive behind restorative justice is practical: it aims at restoring balance back to the lives of victims of wrongdoing as well as peace within the community, while allowing offenders the chance to be accountable for their actions and develop a sense of responsibility for being the perpetrators of harm (Moore, 2007). The focus is on responding to disharmonies in relationships and building up accountability, respect and capacity. The inverse, yet parallel process, is the diminishment of antagonism. Restorative justice is defined by principles that focus on healthy human relationships and on healing the effects of wrongdoing through the promotion of dialogue among individuals within communities. In this way, restorative justice is context-bound and co-constructed within the social worlds of those impacted by crime, harm and conflict (Braithwaite, 2002; Cunneen, 2007; Moore, 2007; Moore et al., 2005; Strang & Braithwaite, 2000).

The challenge of meaningfully bringing forward restorative justice practices in a retributive child justice system is beyond measure. Retributive justice focuses on a single criminal act, is adversarial and punitive, and can increase the isolation and alienation of an offender in relation to his or her community (Moore & Mitchell, 2009, 2012). Historically, Canada's retributive justice system was inherited from Europeans during colonization in the 17th and 18th centuries. A further complicating factor emerges when we acknowledge that Christian missionaries were the conduits of colonization and in a contemporary sense, Canada as a nation is predominantly Christian. Today, volunteerism predominantly drives the organization, promotion and deployment of restorative justice in courts, schools and the community at large, with a patina of Christian ethos. In Canada, and elsewhere, this has been attributed to the long-standing history of prison ministry volunteerism within systems of justice (Stansfield, Mowen & O'Connor, 2018) and flows from the established links within the philosophy of restorative justice to spirituality (Brunk, 2001). In the same instance, an apparent void of critical consciousness of the harms caused by organized religion through the processes of colonization continues to obscure efforts to decolonize our institutions.

3 Child rights and child justice

In countries across the globe, efforts to integrate the United Nations Convention on the Rights of the Child (CRC) (United Nations, 1989) into systems of youth justice remain largely aspirational as interventions in the lives of young people engaged in behaviors in conflict with the law are slow to change, even after three decades of effort (Moore & Mitchell, 2009, 2012). Abramson's (2006) assertion that juvenile justice is the unwanted child of the child rights movement holds true. Notwithstanding this abeyant action

(Moore, 2020, the CRC serves as an umbrella treaty, has influenced the development of a majority of international child justice standards, and offers basic guidance to a more coordinated implementation on the level of practice in youth justice (Denov, 2007). Although the CRC is often described as the most universally ratified human rights instrument, it is arguably the most violated (Moore & Mitchell, 2009; Muncie, 2008). For instance, analysis of Canadian child justice, similar to its American and European counterparts, shows evidence that integrating the CRC into juvenile justice contexts is mired with competing and contradictory aims. Child rights discourses of innocence are incommensurate with the reality of young people's actions that have been found to violate the law.

In countries that have both ratified the CRC and successfully integrated its principles in legislation, policy and practice, it follows that all young people in those contexts would have an equal birthright to experience their human rights as articulated under the CRC. Young offenders' views would be heard through meaningful participation in the justice proceedings that impact them, and robust supports that recognize their increased vulnerability to risk due to age and context would be in place during all stages of contact with the juvenile justice system. For instance, Canada may be credited with integrating principles of the CRC within the *Youth Criminal Justice Act* (YCJA) of 2003 (Denov, 2007; Moore, 2007, in press). The *Youth Criminal Justice Act* was a replacement for the *Young Offenders Act*, which was criticized for its overly punitive approach to young offenders. The YCJA was targeted to provide a 'legislative framework for a fairer and more effective youth justice system' (Department of Justice Canada, 2013:1). In theory, the intent was a more effective and fair system of child justice, yet in practice this has not been fully realized. Denov (2007) reinforces this point from a Canadian perspective as she argues,

> guaranteeing the rights of young offenders enables young people to exercise choices, ask questions, challenge procedures, and have the opportunity to be heard in proceedings: all this may defy assumptions about young people and the criminal justice process. (53-54)

The suggestion here is that Canada likely is not alone in its struggle with complication, contradiction and compromise in the context of bringing forward a human rights perspective to juvenile justice.

Around the globe, the CRC could be the standard-bearer within youth justice programming and holds the potential for influence in any juvenile context precisely because it is legally binding at the international level and regularly evaluated by the United Nations. Human rights-based approaches to engaging with youthful offenders supports democratic practices that are in compliance with international law (Moore & Mitchell, 2009, 2012). Unfortunately, it remains a challenge to move principles of child rights into practice. Child justice as a hierarchical system remains reified by legitimizing power relations (Clarysse & Moore, 2017) lacking appreciation of the innate citizenship coupled with the increased vulnerability to risk of young offenders (Moore & Mitchell, 2012). Child rights discourses are tied to global humanitarian discourses where notions of children being innocent and vulnerable are read 'through colonial and neoliberal categories of age, gender, race and culture' (Sinervo & Cheney, 2019: 1). This manifests similarly in restorative justice processes in Canada with established links among religious ministries and volunteerism to the justice systems that reinforce moral codes imbedded in humanitarianism and charity (Sinervo & Cheney, 2019).

4 RIGHTS-BASED RESTORATIVE JUSTICE

Rights-based restorative justice was developed in response to the need for a framework to link the theoretically, ontologically and methodologically congruent principles of child rights and restorative justice (Moore, 2007; Moore & Mitchell, 2007, 2009, 2011, 2012). Child rights and restorative justice practices similarly encourage the voices of victims, offenders and young people to be heard in socially just sorts of ways through non-discriminatory, safe, authentic and complete participation. The integration of the principles found within these two sets of United Nations instruments is the foundation of rights-based restorative justice, as summarized by Moore (2007) and Moore and Mitchell (2009):

> *Non-discrimination, equality and mutuality:* All young people have the same human rights regardless of social-cultural context or whether they are victims or perpetrators of harm; processes address the balance between equality and mutuality among stakeholders.
>
> *Best interests, well-being and restoration:* For all young participants involved there is a concern for their best interests, their well-being and a restoration of equilibrium for all stakeholders. The aim is to heal harm done in the context of human relationships.
>
> *Survival, development and safety:* For young participants, there is an appropriate consideration for healthy development, especially in the context of vulnerabilities and power relations typical in circumstances of victimization. Participants must feel a sense of safety.

Participation, voice, and volunteerism: All stakeholders must voluntarily engage in all processes and be given opportunity to have their views meaningfully heard.

From the perspective of the UN Convention on the Rights of the Child, restorative justice and children's rights may be understood as theoretically congruent as they are premised from similar principles. Moreover, through their interconnection in practice, more ethical and democratic responses to young people in conflict with the law may be facilitated. Practices based on restorative justice and children's rights also may be seen to correspond with Canada's domestic and international legal commitments, including those of the CRC and the United Nations basic principles of restorative justice (United Nations Economic and Social Council, 2002). Both of these United Nations meta-narratives were adopted by Canada and drafted with significant Canadian input (Moore & Mitchell, 2009).

Rights-based restorative justice (Moore & Mitchell, 2009) as a framework for domestic policy and practice may be understood in the context of recent legislative developments in Canada and a practical focus on fair, proportionate and democratic interventions with young people in conflict with the law. With Canada's ratification of the CRC in 1991, adoption of the United Nations basic principles of restorative justice and with the federal government's enactment of the *Youth Criminal Justice Act* in 2003, Canadian policy is committed to a system of youth justice that integrates the principles of restorative practice and children's human rights (Denov, 2007). The YCJA has emerged as a major legislative development for rights-based initiatives, notwithstanding the substantial obstacles that have to be addressed if restorative practice and children's rights are to be actualized in practice.

Further analyses of relevant UN instruments focused upon juvenile justice reveal complementary thinking to this conceptual underpinning for a rights-based restorative justice paradigm. These include the following: the Riyadh Guidelines (United Nations, 1990); the Beijing Rules (United Nations, 1985); and the Vienna Guidelines (United Nations Economic and Social Council, 1997) (see also Wolthuis and Winter in this volume). These international instruments emphasize non-judicial interventions, and community, family and school-based responses along with prevention strategies. Adapting such approaches could facilitate movement from an overreliance on retributive systems and partisan political responses perennially invoked to solve youth criminal justice issues, in the direction of more holistic, even preventive measures.

5 Toward decolonizing discourses

Our ways of thinking as scholars and practitioners reciprocally and autopoietically impacts our ways of being and acting. Epistemology, ontology and methodology are entwined. Our conceptual frameworks and theories shape our choices for behaviors and our interpretations of social and political worlds. Decolonization is a complex conceptual framework that has a range of definitions and implications for policy and practice. Drawing on Tuck and Yang's (2012) arguments, for the purpose of this chapter, decolonization has a goal of eradicating the impact and processes of colonization – decolonization is not a metaphor. Decolonization is a commitment to respond to structural and procedural injustice and build new ways of thinking, being and doing in a postcolonial context. Indigenous scholars Lyn Trudeau and Amos Key Jr. (2020) expand on this definition of decolonization with an emphasis on the role of education:

> Decolonization, within this particular context, is a call to reexamine hierarchal structures and disseminating knowledge within our institutions and educative spaces. Decolonization is a process that asks each of us, individually and collectively, to explore our perceptions of what Decolonization means and to further invoke a new understanding of our relationships together and what this means moving forward if we all want to actively engage in Reconciliation. The questions that are often asked and explored are: what is/was Colonization and what is/was Conciliation in these conversations. Asking these questions at the very beginning, allows all to unpack and examine historic settler 'privilege', practices and record of colonization, so to restore and reconcile Indigenous Human Rights in Canada. (10)

Arguably, the first best step toward decolonization is education and a process of un-learning, learning and re-learning the impact of our social and political histories on who is defined as a full citizen (Truth and Reconciliation Commission of Canada, 2015).

In Canada, Indigenous peoples are legislated and regulated under the race-based Indian Act of 1876 (Indian Act, 1985) limiting their citizenship in Canada as other than white settler and reinforcing Indigeneity as colonial subjectivity. This furthers social isolation, a central instrument of colonizers (McCallum, 2017). Notwithstanding this fact, efforts to move forward decolonizing discourses in the context of human rights restorative justice have recently become evident through two high-profile processes within Canada. The principles and process of restorative justice form the basis for the truth and reconciliation proceedings, which Canada has recently concluded, in response to the cultural genocide of Indigenous peoples in Canada documented during processes of colonization (Truth and Reconciliation Commission of Canada, 2015). Restorative justice principles also informed Canada's National Inquiry into Missing and Murdered

Indigenous Women and Girls (2017) which is guided by three goals: finding the truth; honoring the truth; and giving life to the truth as a path to healing. This inquiry states an intention to find the truth by:

> Gathering many stories from many people. These truths will weave together to show us what violence really looks like for Indigenous women and girls in Canada. The work of the National Inquiry is not to hear one single truth, but many truths. This will help us understand the far-reaching effects of violence, as well as solutions to end it. (5)

These processes of inquiry have aided Canadians in documenting the ongoing, multi-generational effects of colonization and cultural genocide and uncovering the direct links between acts of structural injustice and the disproportionately high representation of Indigenous peoples (First Nations, Métis, and Inuit) within Canada's child welfare and criminal justice systems as both victims and offenders (Moore & Mitchell, 2009; Senate of Canada Standing Committee on Human Rights, 2007).

Indigenous young peoples are described by researchers, policymakers and advocates as the 'most vulnerable group of children and youth in Canada today, and in the future' (Finlay, Parker-Loewen & Mirwald, 2005: 10). Testifying during the Senate human rights hearings, Finlay et al. (2005) noted that Indigenous peoples in Canada are more

> likely to be born into poverty, suffer health problems, be victims of maltreatment, be placed away from their families and communities in provincial and territorial child welfare systems or be incarcerated in youth correctional facilities. (10)

These factors impacting Indigenous young people in Canada (and Indigenous and Aboriginal young people around the globe) reinforce structural injustices imbedded in political and social systems in postcolonial countries such as Canada. The increased risk for Indigenous young peoples to be involved in the justice system is evidenced by incarceration rates eight times higher than for non-Indigenous youth. It is also evident that young people in contact with the welfare system often 'cross-over' into justice systems (Finlay et al., 2005: 10). These authors further argue that increased states of risk faced by Indigenous young peoples are indicative of 'an element of racism – if the same circumstances existed for non-aboriginal people, I am wondering if we would be as tolerant' (10).

In a Canadian context of engaging restorative justice, it is important to note that the Royal Canada Mounted Police (RCMP) oversees the formal implementation of many restorative justice programs. In the same instance, the RCMP historically had a mandate to control Indigenous communities and is a manifestation of settler colonial policing policy and practice. In a contemporary sense, the RCMP has been critiqued for over-policing Indigenous communities and for racial profiling (Howe & Monaghan, 2018). If restorative justice is simply another tool in response to violations of the law for settler colonial policing, then the ideals of colonization are perpetuated rather than mitigated. To ignore the historical roots of restorative justice in Indigenous communities around the globe, and the diversity of restorative justice as cultural formation, the communitarian values and emphasis on relationships will likely also be negated. This erasure of history and context allows restorative justice to then become a tool of the oppressor rather than an instrument to heal harm (Hunt & Holmes, 2015; Tauri, 2014, 2016).

A rights-based restorative justice framework, however, has the potential to transcend binary notions of right-doing and wrongdoing, to consider community context and our shared histories, and to account for the underlying drivers of racism, distributive and structural injustices that are the greatest causes of harm, suffering and risk for Indigenous young peoples in our society. This process of acknowledging the benefits of a comprehensive approach to restorative justice has recently been evidenced by the Government of British Columbia as they made a commitment to enact a province-wide restorative justice system (Bailey, 2017), which could clear the way for other provinces and territories in Canada to engage in similar legislative action.

In light of Canada's international commitments to the CRC and the United Nations basic principles of restorative justice, the lens provided by rights-based restorative justice could provide an effective standard of practice for rights-based youth justice. Certainly, viewing restorative practice in the context of children and young people's rights reveals several links between these constructs. Similar to human rights, restorative justice is not a new concept; both have roots that may be traced through the millennia, notwithstanding their recent appearance in discourses influencing how we relate and create space for children and young people in mainstream society (Johnstone & Van Ness, 2007; Moore et al., 2005). In Canada, this is demonstrated through community-based initiatives, provincial restorative justice programs, and the YCJA that reflects an openness to seriously engage restorative justice processes (Moore, 2007). Similarly, an interest in rights-based policy and practice has slowly evolved across service sectors in Canada over the past decade. Globally, restorative justice principles are evident in Indigenous and ancient cultures the world over, not only in North America but also in ancient Celtic traditions as well as in practices in various regions of Africa and Asia (Moore, 2007). Through recognition of the complexity of justice within the context of our history, politics and power relations, we will be more likely to realize a rights-based approach that is responsive to the challenges of equality and structural injustice within systems of youth justice. Further, youth justice stakeholders have a responsibility to ensure ethical practice with everyone, perhaps most especially individuals who have been victimized or are vulnerable, including young people, Indigenous peoples, individuals living with disabilities, and 2SLGBTQQIA+ (Two-Spirit, lesbian, gay, bisexual, transgender, queer, questioning, intersex and asexual and other sexual orientations and genders).

6 Conclusion

This chapter argued for decolonizing both restorative justice and child rights discourses in order to transcend the impasse of moving theory to local practice. It would be a mistake to understate the challenge of decolonization. Uncovering and facing difficult truths is often traumatic. Decolonization hurts before it can heal, because it forces all stakeholders to question the benevolence of those who retain the privilege and power to actually make meaningful change and bring forward the voices and views of less privileged speakers. The process of truth-telling demands an un-learning of unconscious biases that shapes our world views and how we ask and answer questions about our social worlds. Similarly, change processes driven by restorative justice principles are often mistakenly dismissed as an easy resolution route in comparison to retributive systems of justice. Restorative justice, like decolonization, propels participants to question what one holds to be true and calls on participants to sit with the hurt directly caused to relationships and community. To achieve lasting change that attains the goal of healing relationships, space must be created to bring forward the vulnerability and humanity of all participants to the forefront of dialogue and conscious thought. This is only likely to be achieved through an attitude of humility.

As an academic writing about rights-based restorative justice for almost two decades, critical awareness of how my efforts have resulted in a rich output in relation to the products of academe is a reality, while I question whether positive change for young people most in need has resulted from my scholarly efforts. Given my position of power and privilege, I find myself compelled to write honestly about the shortcomings of rights-based restorative justice. It seems more necessary than ever to approach this work with humility and to dive deeply into re-learning, un-learning and learning again the meaning of restorative justice and child rights in Canada as a so-called postcolonial state, yet still mired by heteropatriarchy, gender domination and settler colonialism. Decolonizing rights-based restorative justice will be uncomfortable and messy and will demand a long view in relation to investments in time to meaningfully transform our institutions, policy and practices with young people. To be successful, young people must have space to meaningfully participate and, in the same instance, privileged stakeholders must step aside in an act of allyship, so that key stakeholders and young people from equity-seeking communities including black, Indigenous and people of color may directly shape decolonization of restorative justice practices.

References

Abramson, B. (2006). Juvenile justice: the "unwanted child" - why the potential of the convention on the rights of the child is not being realized, and what we can do about it. In E. Jensen & J. Jepsen (eds.), *Juvenile law violators, human rights, and the development of a new juvenile justice system* (pp. 15-38). Oxford: Hart.

Absolon, K. (2019). Decolonizing education and educators decolonizing. *Intersectionalities: A Global Journal of Social Work Analysis, Research Polity and Practice*, 7(1), 9-28. Retrieved August 20, 2021, from https://journals.library.mun.ca/ojs/index.php/IJ/article/view/2073/1709.

Arvin, M., Tuck, E. & Morrill, A. (2013). Decolonizing feminism: challenging connections between settler colonialism and heteropatriarchy. *Feminist Formations*, 25(1), 8-34. doi: 10.1353/ff.2013.0006.

Bailey, I. (30 July 2017). B.C. NDP government seeks restorative justice system. *The Globe and Mail.* Retrieved from www.theglobeandmail.com/news/british-columbia/bc-ndp-seeks-restorative-justice-system-for-some-offences/article35840730/.

Bourgeon, L., Burke, A. & Higham, T. (2017). Earliest human presence in North America dated to the last glacial maximum: new radiocarbon dates from Bluefish Caves, Canada. *PLoS ONE*, 12(1), 1-15. doi: 10.1371/journal.pone.0169486.

Braithwaite, J. (2002). Setting standards for restorative justice. *British Journal of Criminology*, 42(3), 563-577. doi: 10.1093/bjc/42.3.563.

Brunk, C. (2001). The spiritual roots of restorative justice. In M. Hadley (ed.), *Restorative justice and the philosophical theories of criminal punishment* (pp. 31-56). Albany: New York Press.

Chartrand, L. & Horn, K. (2016). *A report on the relationship between restorative justice and indigenous legal traditions in Canada.* Department of Justice Canada, Minister of Justice and Attorney General of Canada, ISBN 978-0-660-27826-1. Retrieved from www.justice.gc.ca/eng/rp-pr/jr/rjilt-jrtja/index.html.

Clarysse, L.B. & Moore, S.A. (2017). Restorative justice, peacebuilding practices, and educational praxis: critical analysis of Canadian and United Kingdom discourses. *Journal of Leadership, Accountability and Ethics*, 14(5), 123-138. doi: 10.33423/jlae.v14i4.1494.

Cunneen, C. (2007). Reviving restorative justice traditions? In G. Johnstone & D. W. Van Ness (eds.), *Handbook of restorative justice* (pp. 113-131). Portland: Willan Publishing.

De Finney, S., Dean, M., Loiselle, E. & Saraceno, J. (2011). All children are equal, but some are more equal than others: minoritization, structural inequities, and social justice praxis in residential care. *International Journal of Child, Youth and Family Studies*, 2(3/4), 361-384. doi: 10.18357/ijcyfs23/420117756.

Denov, M. (2007). Youth justice and children's rights. In R.B. Howe & K. Covell (eds.), *A question of commitment: children's rights in Canada* (pp. 153-178). Waterloo: Wilfrid Laurier University Press.

Department of Justice Canada. (2013). *The youth criminal justice act: summary and background*. Ottawa: Minister of Justice and Attorney General of Canada. Retrieved from www.justice.gc.ca/eng/cj-jp/yj-jj/tools-outils/pdf/back-hist.pdf.

Department of Justice Canada. (January 2017). Indigenous people overrepresented as homicide victims and accused. In *Research on justice issues, just facts* (para. 2). Ottawa: Department of Justice. Retrieved August 20, 2021, from www.justice.gc.ca/eng/rp-pr/jr/jf-pf/2017/jan02.html.

Finlay, J., Parker-Loewen, D. & Mirwald, J. (21 February 2005). *Submission to the senate standing committee on human rights*. Ottawa: Canadian Council of Provincial Child and Youth Advocates.

Hadley, M. (ed.). (2001). *The spiritual roots of restorative justice*. Albany: State University of New York Press.

Howe, M. & Monaghan, J. (2018). Strategic incapacitation of indigenous dissent: crowd theories, risk management, and settler colonial policing. *Canadian Journal of Sociology/Cahierscanadiensde sociologie*, 43(4), 325-348. doi: 10.29173/cjs29397.

Hunt, S. & Holmes, C. (2015). Everyday decolonisation: living a decolonising queer politics. *Journal of Lesbian Studies*, 19(2), 154-172. doi: 10.1080/10894160.2015. 970975.

Indian Act (R.S.C., 1985, c. I-5). Retrieved August 20, 2021, from http://laws-lois.justice. gc.ca/eng/acts/i-5/.

Johnstone, G. & Van Ness, D. (eds.). (2007). *Handbook of restorative justice*. London: Willan.

McCallum, M.J. (2017). Indigenous historical perspectives starvation, experimentation, segregation, and trauma: words for reading Indigenous health history. *Canadian Historic Review*, 98(1), 96-113. doi: 10.3138/chr.98.1.McCallum.

Moore, S.A. (2004). Towards an integrated perspective: restorative justice, cross-cultural counselling and school-based programming. In M.H. France, M.C. Roderiguez & G.G. Hett (eds.), *Diversity, culture and counselling: a Canadian perspective* (pp. 347-355). Calgary: Detselig.

Moore, S.A. (2007). Restorative justice. In R.B. Howe & K. Covell (eds.), *A question of commitment: children's rights in Canada* (pp. 179-208). Waterloo: Wilfrid Laurier University Press.

Moore, S.A. (2017). Restorative justice education, policy and practice: transdisciplinary reflections on mental health implications. In L. Evans (ed.), *Restorative and transitional justice: perspectives, progress and considerations for the future* (pp. 1-24). New York: Nova Science.

Moore, S.A. (2020). Young people, justice, and children's rights in Canada: critical reflections at the edge of abeyant action. In T. Waldock (ed.), *The status of children in Canada: a children's rights analysis* (2nd ed., pp. 87-106). Toronto: Canadian Scholars Press.

Moore, S.A. & Mitchell, R.C. (2007). Rights-based restorative justice: towards critical praxis with young people in conflict with the law. In A. Ang, I. Delens-Ravier, M. Delplace, C. Herman, D. Reynaert, V. Staelens, R. Steel & M. Verheyde (eds.), *The UN children's rights convention: theory meets practice* (pp. 549-563). Proceedings of the International Interdisciplinary Conference on Children's Rights, 18-19 May 2006. Ghent, Belgium: Intersentia. doi: 10.1177/1473225408101430.

Moore, S.A. & Mitchell, R.C. (2009). Rights-based restorative justice: evaluating compliance with international standards. *Youth Justice: An International Journal*, 9(1), 27-43.

Moore, S.A. & Mitchell, R.C. (2011). Theorising rights-based restorative justice: the Canadian context. *The International Journal of Children's Rights*, 19(1), 81-105. doi: 10.1163/157181810X508483.

Moore, S.A. & Mitchell, R.C. (2012). Rights-based restorative justice in Canada: from silence to citizenship. In M. Freeman (ed.), *Oxford law and childhood studies current legal issues* (Vol. 14, pp. 202-218). Oxford: Oxford University Press.

Moore, S.A., Tulk, W. & Mitchell, R.C. (2005). Qallunaat crossing: the southern-northern divide and promising practices for Canada's Inuit young people. *First People's Child and Family Review*, 2(1), 117-129. doi: 10.7202/1069541ar.

Muncie, J. (2008). The "punitive turn" in juvenile justice: cultures of control and rights compliance in Western Europe and the USA. *Youth Justice*, 8(2), 107-121. doi: 10.1177/1473225408091372.

National Inquiry into Missing and Murdered Indigenous Women and Girls. (2017). *Interim report: our women and girls are sacred*. Ottawa: Government of Canada. Retrieved August 20, 2021, from www.mmiwg-ffada.ca/files/ni-mmiwg-interim-report-en.pdf.

Nyp, G. (2004). *Pioneers of peace: the history of community justice initiatives in the Waterloo Region 1974–2004*. Kitchener: Pandora.

Pon, G., Gosine, K. & Phillips, D. (2011). Immediate response: addressing anti-native and anti-black racism in child welfare. *International Journal of Child, Youth and Family Studies*, 2(3/4), 385-409. doi: 10.18357/ijcyfs23/420117763.

Ross, R. (1996). *Returning to the teachings: exploring aboriginal justice*. London: Penguin.

Senate of Canada Standing Committee on Human Rights. (2007). *Children: the silenced citizens. Final report on effective implementation of Canada's international obligations with respect to the rights of children*. Ottawa: Senate of Canada. Retrieved August 20, 2021, from https://sencanada.ca/content/sen/committee/391/huma/rep/rep10apr07-e.htm.

Sinervo A. & Cheney, K. (2019). NGO economies of affect: humanitarianism and childhood in contemporary and historical perspective. In K. Cheney & A. Sinervo (eds.), *Disadvantaged childhoods and humanitarian intervention* (pp. 1-35). Palgrave Studies on Children and Development. London: Palgrave Macmillan.

Stansfield, R., Mowen, T. & O'Connor, T. (2018). Religious and spiritual support, reentry, and risk. *Justice Quarterly*, 35(2), 254-279. doi: 10.1080/07418825.2017.1306629.

Strang, H. & Braithwaite, J. (2000). *Restorative justice: philosophy to practice*. New York: Routledge.

Tauri, J. (2014). An Indigenous commentary on the globalisation of restorative justice. *British Journal of Community Justice*, 12(2), 35-55.

Tauri, J. (2016). Indigenous peoples and the globalization of restorative justice. *Social Justice*, 43(3), 46-67.

Trudeau, L. & Key Jr., A. (2020). *Decolonization committee. Brock University, Canada, President's advisory committee on human rights, equity and decolonization final report 2020*. Brock University, Ontario, Canada.

Truth and Reconciliation Commission of Canada. (2015). *Honouring the truth, reconciling the future*. Summary of the Final Report of the Truth and Reconciliation Commission of Canada. Winnipeg: Author. Retrieved August 20, 2021, from https://publications.gc.ca/collections/collection_2015/trc/IR4-7-2015-eng.pdf.

Tuck, E. & Yang, K.W. (2012). Decolonisation is not a metaphor. *Decolonisation: Indigeneity, Education and Society*, 1(1), 1-40.

United Nations. (1985). *United Nations standard minimum rules for the administration of juvenile justice: the Beijing rules*. New York: United Nations.

United Nations. (1989). *Convention on the rights of the child*. New York: United Nations.

United Nations. (1990). *United Nations guidelines for the prevention of juvenile delinquency: the Riyadh guidelines*. New York: United Nations.

United Nations Economic and Social Council. (1997). *United Nations resolution 1197/30: administration of juvenile justice. The Vienna guidelines*. Geneva: United Nations.

United Nations Economic and Social Council. (2002). *United Nations basic principles on the use of restorative justice programmes in criminal matters*. New York and Geneva: United Nations. Retrieved from www.un.org/en/ecosoc/docs/2002/resolution%202002-12.pdf.

Vaandering, D. & Reimer, K. (2019). Listening deeply to public perceptions of restorative justice: what can researchers and practitioners learn? *The International Journal of Restorative Justice*, 2(2), 186-208. doi: 10.5553/IJRJ/258908912019002002002.

Woolford, A. & Nelund, A. (2019). *The politics of restorative justice: a critical introduction* (2nd ed.). Halifax: Fernwood Publishing.

Part II

Global developments & trends of restorative justice for children

Chapter 6

Restorative justice for children around the globe

International perspectives and trends

Cedric Foussard[*]

1 Introduction

It is internationally recognized that children who come into conflict with the law are more likely to have experienced some form of violence or adversity than their non-offending peers (O'Brien & Foussard, 2020). Children's contact with the formal criminal justice system poses undue risks of physical, sexual and psychological trauma, which exacerbates the deleterious effects of previous childhood trauma.

In addition, longitudinal studies (McAra & McVie, 2010) show that, to some extent, contact with formal justice systems can increase re-offending and deepen a child's subsequent criminal justice involvement. Since the adoption of the UN Convention on the Rights of the Child (CRC), international and regional standards therefore call on states to divert children in conflict with the law away from formal justice systems following the principle of the best interests of the child and ask states to improve participation of children in judicial proceedings.

Indeed, as underlined in the General Comment 24 of the CRC on 'children's rights in the child justice system', the aim of child justice systems should be to protect the best interests of the child, by avoiding retributive measures of formal criminal justice systems and, instead, encouraging the rehabilitation of child offenders, in line with restorative justice objectives. The Council of Europe's Child-Friendly Justice guidelines further stress the fact that child justice systems should be accessible, age-appropriate, efficient, diligent, adapted to and focused on the needs of the child (Council of Europe, 2011). In its conclusion, the Global Study on Children Deprived of Liberty recalls several international children's rights standards, which urge states to divert away 'children as much as possible and providing a variety of options for this', such as 'community programs and restorative justice practices' (Nowak, 2019).

* With Razwana Begum, Diane Geragthy, Marta Gil Gonzalez and Ignacio Valentín Mayoral Narros.

The CRC, in its Article 12, recalls as well, that all children have the right to express their views and to have them taken seriously in all matters affecting them. This right applies as well to children in conflict with the law and to victims, thus requiring that they are consulted in the decision taken in their best interests. Effective child participation in judicial proceedings implies, also, that children can enjoy their right to information to

> comprehend the charges, and possible consequences and penalties, in order to direct the legal representative, to challenge witnesses, to provide an account of events, and to make appropriate decisions about evidence, testimony and the measure(s) to be imposed. (CRC Committee, 2019: para. 46).

In order to preserve the well-being of the child, the Beijing rules (United Nations Standard Minimum Rules for the Administration of Juvenile Justice, 1989) in Article 14 also emphasize the importance of maintaining an atmosphere of understanding to allow the child to participate and to express himself or herself freely.

Yet, in spite of international agreement on the need to ensure that children's rights are protected in their interactions with the criminal justice system, international standards and best practices are not sufficiently being followed. During the autumn of 2019, the results of the Global Study on Children Deprived of Liberty were presented at the United Nations General Assembly. After more than 2 years of investigation, the first results show that the number of children deprived of liberty around the globe far exceeds the million children behind bars that was estimated a decade ago by UNICEF (Nowak, 2019).

Restorative approaches in child justice, that are based on the concept of voluntary and effective participation of children wherever they are offenders or victims, have great potential for diverting children from criminal justice systems. Widely encouraged by international standards (ECOSOC, 2002), they can help to avoid a number of negative consequences for children in conflict with the law, including physical and psychological harms and increased criminality. Furthermore, restorative practices are based on the principle of effective participation of children in conflict with the law, in a non-adverse environment that fosters communication with other stakeholders, including the victim, other affected parties and the wider community, in order to address and repair the harm caused.

The modern concept of restorative justice is based on the idea that the formal criminal justice process is often an inadequate forum for resolving conflicts between victims and offenders and for meeting both their needs and those of the broader community in which their conflict is situated. In this conceptual approach to restorative justice, participation and involvement are essential to focus on the harm, needs and obligations of all parties involved, within a framework that incorporates international human rights, including proportionality and confidentiality.

Restorative justice is a complex and evolving concept, which enables the peaceful resolution of conflicts and contributes to a better cohesion of societies. At a global level, it can be observed that in recent years, restorative justice for children has been applied in different contexts, both judicial and non-judicial. This chapter explores the different ways in which different groups of states have developed their use of restorative justice, the common challenges that they have faced, and the results that they have seen. It will explore North and Central America, where restorative practices are used as a complement for children who have been convicted and sometimes even deprived of liberty, and as a measure to avoid recidivism. In other settings, notably MENA and Southeast Asia, this article will look at how restorative justice approaches are used as a way to create synergies, collaboration or even sometimes merge aspects of different legal systems.[1]

While the flexibility of restorative justice measures is promising in those cases and can contribute to the broader goals in the development of the criminal justice systems in different countries, the question of their effectiveness remains. Ongoing efforts to assess their impact in practice across a range of different objectives, including diversion, education, reintegration, reducing recidivism and victim participation, will therefore be important.

2 Switching of paradigms: from a punitive to a restorative vision of justice in North and Central America for children

2.1 *Toward a wider implementation of restorative justice practices for children in North America*

Over the last fifty years, Canada, Mexico and the United States have, to varying degrees, embraced restorative justice as a more developmentally appropriate and effective alternative to the formal child justice system (Federal-Provincial-Territorial Working Group on Restorative Justice, 2016).[2] While Canada and Mexico have formally incorporated reparative principles and practices into their national laws, restorative justice remains largely at the margins in most U.S. jurisdictions.

Canada is credited with being the home of the modern restorative justice movement in North America (see Amour, 2012 citing a 1,974 case in which two youth paid

1 This article will not look at Europe, since that is done in Chapter 7 by Frieder Dunkel and Andrea Păroşanu and not at South Africa, Namibia and Zimbabwe, which are covered in Chapter 8 by Julia Sloth-Nielsen.

2 Although there is widespread agreement that restorative justice plays an increasingly prominent role in North American youth justice systems, little data exists to support this consensus due to limited capacity, a lack of uniform definitions and multi-level governance structures in Canada, Mexico and the United States. See, for instance,

restitution to their victims as an alternative to formal prosecution). It is also the country that has made the most progress in embedding restorative justice processes in its child justice system in this region. The roots of Canada's embrace of restorative justice are a blend of 'aboriginal' traditions of justice, faith-based ideals of forgiveness and healing, and concerns about the country's increasingly punitive and ineffective responses to youth crime, as well as its failure to adequately address the needs of victims (Canadian Resource Centre for Victims of Crime, 2011; see also Leung, 1999).

Canada's national Youth Criminal Justice Act (S.C. 2002, c.1) incorporates restorative justice at several stages of the child justice system (see, generally, Department of Justice Canada, 2013). A key component of the Act is the favored use of 'extrajudicial measures' outside the justice system to respond to less serious offending (Department of Justice Canada, 2013). The goals of these alternatives are to hold youth accountable for their actions, provide opportunities for early intervention, conserve resources for more serious cases and reduce recidivism. Examples of alternatives to court involvement include police warnings, prosecutorial cautions and referrals to community-based programs. In addition, other sort of alternatives dispositions may be imposed if extrajudicial measures are not sufficient to meet the Act's reparative goals. Sanctions include victim compensation, mandatory participation in services and community volunteering. Unlike in the case of extrajudicial measures, extrajudicial sanctions may be imposed only after a youngster accepts responsibility for his or her actions and agrees to the sanctioning process. Because of the more serious consequences of failure to satisfy sanction requirements, the Act provides for certain procedural protections in extrajudicial sanctioning, including an opportunity to consult with an attorney. In addition to these diversionary and deflection strategies, the Act also provides for the use of restorative justice approaches at various stages of the judicial process, from post-charging to pre-parole revocation. Throughout Canada, individual provinces have also adopted restorative justice programming (see Wong, 2020 discussing Manitoba's use of restorative justice to respond to the overrepresentation of indigenous youth; but see Ellis, 2009 arguing that standardized restorative justice practices do not adequately respond to the needs of First Nations peoples). A focus of many of these programs is to reduce the overrepresentation of indigenous youth in the justice system (Wong, 2020). Chapter 5 and Chapter 15 of this volume also contain information on Canada.

In 2016, Mexico adopted the National Law on the Integral System of Criminal Justice for Adolescents.[3] This comprehensive legislation favors the use of deferred prosecution mechanisms in cases involving children between the ages of twelve and eighteen (Wright & Montoya Gonzales, 2016: 34). Restorative options can be used at each stage of a child justice case, including after sentencing (Wright & Montoya Gonzales, 2016: 35). Mechanisms include victim-offender mediation, restorative boards and restorative

3 Ley Nacional del Sistema Integral de Justicia Penal Para Adolescentes.

circles. Each process requires the accused youth to acknowledge responsibility for his or her actions, although acknowledgement cannot be used as evidence of guilt in a later proceeding. In addition, each alternative measure entails a structured preparatory process, overseen by a facilitator. Agreements may include compensation (except in cases of domestic violence), restorative justice plans or other provisions designed to repair the harm caused by a youth's actions. If the offending youth fails to comply with the terms of an agreement, the case will be reverted to the formal justice system.

In addition to national laws, several Mexican states have incorporated restorative justice approaches in their response to youth crime. The State of Oaxaca, for example, was an early adopter of mediation and other reparative processes for use in child justice matters (see, generally, Caldwell, 2011 discussing Oaxaca's early adoption of restorative justice conferences as an alternative to the adversarial justice system). In Sonora State, conciliation and mediation are options for willing participants, while Nuevo Leon State supports a range of restorative practices designed to repair the harms experienced by victims and communities (see Frías Armenta & Gómez Martínez, 2014: 588).

While restorative justice was taking hold in many parts of the world in the 1970s and 1980s, in the United States the main response to youth crime was to adopt more punitive approaches, including harsher youth court penalties and, for some young people, long periods of incarceration in adult prisons (Feld, 2018). Rather than increasing public safety and meeting the needs of victims, however, these measures proved to be more expensive, more racially discriminatory and less effective than the traditional child justice system responses (Feld, 2018). As the negative effects of the 'get tough on crime' policies became increasingly obvious, a small number of researchers began to advocate for the type of restorative approaches being used in Canada, New Zealand and elsewhere (Beale, 2003). In the 1990s, the federal Office of Juvenile Justice and Delinquency Prevention (OJJDP) funded a national demonstration project to encourage states to adopt a 'balanced and restorative' approach to youth crime, with the goal of holding young offenders accountable, repairing harm to victims and increasing community safety (see OJJDP, n.d.). Civil society organizations such as the American Bar Association also endorsed the use of restorative justice in schools and in the justice system (American Bar Association Resolution 107B).

As a result of these efforts, today the majority of states in the U.S. have incorporated restorative justice principles into their youth codes. In addition, many state and local jurisdictions employ a variety of restorative mechanisms to resolve mostly low-level crimes such as shoplifting, criminal damage to property, theft and drug possession. Depending on the jurisdiction, these processes may include victim-offender mediation, restorative justice courts, community panels, peer juries and peace circles. Restorative justice practices are also increasingly used in schools as a means of disrupting the 'school to prison pipeline' and as an alternative dispute mechanism in prisons and community corrections settings.

In some states, such as Delaware and Colorado, restorative justice practices are embedded in state-level statutes and overseen by state agencies, courts and other system stakeholders (Pavelka, 2016). In other states, restorative justice practices have emerged organically from neighborhoods struggling to find new approaches to interrupt conflict. Some of the more innovative restorative justice organizations include Common Justice in New York, Impact Justice in Oakland and Washington DC, and the Restorative Justice Hubs in Chicago (Adler School Institute on Public Safety and Social Justice, 2011). Some non-profit organizations have been very active in promoting the use of restorative justice for children and young adults. One example is the Juvenile Justice Initiative, an organization based in Chicago, which has created bridges among Illinois officials and European experts by organizing field visits, exchanges of practices and training on restorative justice approaches.[4]

Despite the expanding use of restorative justice, however, the U.S. continues to lag behind other jurisdictions in the systematic implementation and funding of restorative justice alternatives in the child justice system. Instead, over the last two decades, proponents of child justice reform have relied principally on emerging adolescent development research to raise the age of youth court jurisdiction, reduce overreliance on jails and prisons, end the use of the youth death penalty and substantially limit life without parole sentences (Models for Change n.d.).[5] Whether a wholesale paradigm shift to a child justice system grounded in restorative justice principles will take place in the future remains an open question.

2.2 *Toward more child-friendly justice and restorative justice approaches for children in Central America*

The restorative approach is not an unusual element to encounter throughout the legal frameworks on Child Law in the Central American region, especially through the child justice systems. A deeper analysis of this approach in each country is needed to assert adjusted proposals, in order to promote an effective implementation of restorative justice as opposed to a punitive approach, which 'does not bring neither short nor long-term societal solutions, but generally violates the rights of the child in conflict with the law' (Terre des hommes, n.d.).

As established in the Costa Rica Declaration of Restorative Justice in Latin America,[6] the Latin American region has the highest rates of social exclusion, violence and imprisonment (see Carranza, 2017). Furthermore, the World Bank (2011; see also Terre

4 For more information at https://jjustice.org/resources/restorative-justice/.

5 Models for Change is a decade-long effort by the MacArthur Foundation to create a more fair and just juvenile justice system by changing law, policy and practice.

6 Declaración de Costa Rica sobre la Justicia Restaurativa en América Latina (2005).

des hommes, 2014: 10) identifies three main drivers behind crime and violence in Central America specifically: a) drug trafficking, b) youth violence and c) gangs and availability of firearms. In addition, weak criminal justice institutions also affect crime and violence.

In this context, it can be asserted that restorative justice could contribute in both a direct and indirect way to reducing violence and crime rates in Central America.[7] Restorative justice is more than an approach to justice or a way of diversion; it is a philosophy of culture to implement in all areas of life, when possible, according to its main principles. Regarding the criminal justice system,

> alternative dispute-resolution mechanisms can play an important complementary role, although they should not be seen as taking the place of formal criminal procedures. Youth mediation and reconciliation programs, as well as the establishment of peace centers (Centros de Convivencia), justice houses, municipal mediation and reconciliation centers, judicial facilitators and mobile justice of the peace courts are all successful initiatives in Latin America. (World Bank, 2011: 30-31)

The Concluding Observations on the 'administration of juvenile justice', adopted by the UN Committee on the Rights of the Child, can assist in developing an overview of the situation of restorative justice in the region. Regarding Panama, the Committee recommends that the State Party 'promote non-judicial measures in the case of children accused of criminal offences, by expanding the re-education program with measures including diversion, mediation and counselling' (CRC Committee, 2018c: 13). Likewise, the Committee recommends that El Salvador 'take the measures necessary to establish a specialised juvenile criminal justice system in accordance with the law, encompassing non-custodial measures such as diversion, mediation and counselling' (CRC Committee, 2018a: 13). As in Panama and El Salvador, the Committee recommends that Guatemala promote 'mediation, diversion or non-custodial sanctions, including probation, counselling or community service' (CRC Committee, 2018b: 14). The latest Concluding Observations about Belize (adopted in 2005) recommended that the state establish a juvenile justice system itself, so no specific references are made to restorative justice (CRC Committee, 2005: 16). Regarding Costa Rica, Nicaragua and Honduras, there are no specific references, either positive or negative, to restorative justice mechanisms in the latest Concluding Observations for the situation of Children

---

7 According to Zumbado and Herrero (2010) 'the restorative focus on alternative measures helps to diminish violence indices by making youth responsible and allowing the victim of the crime to feel a sense of justice. … I think the restorative justice vision is a moral, ethical and social responsibility'. Parker (2002) asserts: 'the need to lower prison populations, increase transparency in the administration of justice, and ease the overload in the judicial system, is creating impetus for reform. Civil society values of healing and reintegration, as well as the desire to transform Latin American society from a culture of violence to a culture of peace, are moving those reform efforts in a restorative direction'.

Rights (see CRC Committee, 2010, 2011, 2015). According to the Committee, it can be concluded that a special effort has to be carried out in Panamá, El Salvador, Guatemala and Belize in order to promote and apply restorative justice measures in the administration of child justice. Moreover, Central American countries, along with 23 other countries in the region, have recently renewed their commitment to develop integral and comprehensive policies to strengthen a restorative approach within child justice systems.[8]

Regarding the implementation of restorative justice mechanisms through Central America, the Costa Rican experience must be highlighted due to its efforts to reform the justice system since the end of the 1990s (see Parker, 2002; see also Burgos Mata, 2018; Espinach Rueda, 2018; Jimenez Bolaños, 2015; Mena Pacheco, 2008). It was in 1997 when Ley N° 7727 Law of alternative conflict resolution and promotion of social peace (Ley N° 7727, Ley de Resolución Alterna de Conflictos y Promoción de la Paz Social) established the basis for negotiation, conciliation, mediation and arbitration. Prior to that, in 1996, the youth criminal justice law (Ley N° 7576, Ley de Justicia Penal Juvenil) was passed, which promotes the use of conciliation between the victim and the offender. Finally, it was in 2018 when the Restorative Justice Law (Ley N° 9582, Ley de Justicia Restaurativa) was passed introducing the application of restorative justice in general terms through all the phases of criminal proceedings.[9]

Different methods of diversion coexist in the child justice systems in Central America. Among others, the law in Costa Rica, El Salvador, Guatemala, Honduras, Nicaragua and Panama recognizes conciliation as a restorative justice approach. In addition, reparation to the victim is found in laws in Costa Rica, Guatemala, Honduras, Nicaragua and Panamá (Tiffer Sotomayor, 2012).

Some good practices can be highlighted regarding the implementation of restorative justice through Central America: a) Restorative Juvenile Justice Program in Latin America (Terre des hommes)[10], b) Youth Justice Program & Programa Niñez sin Rejas

8 'Declaración Iberoamericana de Justicia Juvenil con enfoque restaurativo' signed by the Iberoamerican Conference of Ministries of Justice – COMJIB, signed in 2016, 'Decálogo Iberoamericano de Justicia Juvenil con enfoque restaurativo', signed in 2018 by Iberoamerican Judicial Conference (Cumbre Judicial Iberoamericana).

9 The purpose of the law is 'definir un marco conceptual y procedimental para instaurar la justicia restaurativa en el ordenamiento jurídico costarricense, como un instrumento que contribuya a resolver los conflictos jurídicos generados por los hechos delictivos, con la participación activa de las partes intervinientes, a fin de restaurar los daños a la víctima, procurar la inserción social de la persona ofensora, con soluciones integrales y promover la paz social' (to define a conceptual and procedural framework to establish restorative justice in the Costa Rican legal system, as a tol that contributes to resolve legal conflicts generated by criminal acts, with the active participation of the parties involved, in order to restore the damage to the victim, look for the social insertion of the victim, with integral solutions and promote social peace).

10 See the website project at www.tdh.ch/en/media-library/documents/thematic-policy-2014-restorative-juvenile-justice.

(BICE) in Guatemala[11] and c) Restorative Youth Justice Program del *Poder Judicial* in Costa Rica.[12] Other valuable experiences on restorative justice in Central America are mentioned by the World Bank (2011: 31), including 'municipal mediation centers and the mobile justice of the peace courts in Honduras, the centers for the administration of justice in Guatemala, and the judicial facilitators in Nicaragua'.

In addition, it is relevant to highlight some good practices referred to by the Commission on Crime Prevention and Criminal Justice regarding the use and application of the United Nations Basic Principles on the Use of Restorative Justice Programs in Criminal Matters (UN CCPCJ, 2017): a) training programs for criminal justice officials concerning the concept of restorative justice and how it may be implemented within criminal justice systems in Nicaragua, Costa Rica and Panama (Prison Fellowship International), b) communities of restoration in El Salvador, Guatemala, Belize and Costa Rica (Prison Fellowship International), c) several activities on restorative justice in Costa Rica (Defence for Children International), d) Victim-Offender Mediation and restorative justice processes for children in the child justice system practices in Guatemala (Organismo Judicial). In Honduras, Terre des hommes foundation is developing new integrated models aimed at strengthening the reintegration policy. The objective of this intervention is to facilitate an integrated system involving different institutions, to create a common restorative vision to be embedded in the child justice system.

Finally, the considerable efforts made by NGOs and universities in Central America in order to promote restorative justice mechanisms for children have to be highlighted, although the implementation at field level is still not widespread.

3 Back to the roots: when recent developments on restorative justice for children are based on customary justice practices

3.1 *Restorative justice in the Middle East and North Africa (MENA) region*

Restorative Justice in the MENA region has strongly emerged in the last decade as an approach to administer justice for children within the States' Rule of Law. The regulatory developments have been enacted within 'youth laws' across the region, while enforcement of these laws is taking shape slowly but progressively. Nonetheless, restorative justice, as currently conceptualized and practiced in the region, is influenced in many of its essential elements by community-based alternative dispute resolution mechanisms, also known as customary justice practices, both secular and faith-based. These justice mechanisms

11 See the website project at https://bice.org/es/justicia-juvenil-en-guatemala/.

12 See the website project at https://justiciarestaurativa.poder-judicial.go.cr/.

reflect the roots, the history and the different wars, conflicts and social processes the different countries in the region have experienced. They are nurtured by traditions and social norms and are grounded in the need to safeguard the social cohesion of their communities. Since community-based justice processes have often developed in the absence of, or separately from, child justice legal frameworks, in some cases there is a need to adapt and codify them. From the origins of community peace as a primary objective, restorative justice practices in the MENA region have evolved to extend their goals to the protection of child welfare and child rights. It is now framed within the child justice systems, although the recognition of the child as an individual justice-user and as a right-holder is still not entirely achieved. For instance, his or her meaningful participation as a standard practice and a fundamental right should be ensured in the 'modern regulated' restorative justice proceedings.

In the MENA region, particularly in Egypt, Palestine, Tunisia, Morocco, Turkey, Jordan and Lebanon, restorative justice is progressively being used as an alternative to retributive justice approaches for children in conflict and in contact with the law. Restorative justice appears as an approach and as an intervention toward the achievement of reintegration of children, pursuing the assumption of responsibility by the child offender through the understanding of the harm caused to the victim and to the community, and agreeing on a healing solution at both individual and collective levels. As such, it somehow reflects and captures the essence of customary justice mechanisms, and indeed there is a solid coexistence of formal and customary justice systems and jurisdictions, both secular and religious. Importantly, these emerging restorative justice practices under the official sphere of justice are also rapidly evolving and positively challenging non-gender-responsive patterns, where the notion of gender justice is surfacing through the Women, Peace and Security agenda[13] and survivor-centered approaches (e.g. in gender-based violence offenses) are being incorporated, mainly by female justice actors, both at formal and customary levels (Pely, 2011).

Most countries in the region have legally embraced the concept of restorative justice into their formal systems, but more as a conceptual approach, rather than through the regulation of concrete restorative justice processes as such, although they are also turning up. Indeed, the laws and regulatory instruments, such as the Circular No. 7/2018 of the Egyptian Attorney General on Restorative Justice, the Palestinian Law 4/2016 on Youth Protection, the Jordan's Youth Law 32/2014, the Lebanese Law 422/2002 on the Protection of Children in Conflict with the Law or at Risk and the Turkish Youth Protection Law 5393/2005, include principles of restorative justice in legal provisions, stressing particularly diversion, alternatives to detention, victim-offender mediation procedures, family group conferences and peace circles. While diversion and

13 The Security Council adopted a landmark resolution (S/RES/1325) on Women, Peace and Security on October 31, 2000. MENA countries have approved national action plans toward its implementation, strongly framing restorative justice mechanism for conflict resolution.

alternatives to detention are essential in building up a child-friendly justice system and can be compatible with a restorative justice approach, they do not always or necessarily involve the victim and the offender in the resolution of matters arising from the crime and, thus, in the healing process that it entails. However, it is worth noting that the region has taken a huge step forward, in the alignment and incorporation of Articles 37 and 40 of the Convention of the Rights of the Child and related recommendations of the CRC Committee into their national legal instruments. The pathway taken for this contemporary restorative justice grounded in customary justice practices indeed follows the guidance stated in the General Comment CRC Committee 24/2019 (p. 102-104) which highlights that 'such systems can serve as an alternative to official proceedings against children, and are likely to contribute favorably to the change of cultural attitudes concerning children and justice' and that 'restorative justice responses are often achievable through customary … justice systems, and may provide opportunities for learning for the formal child justice system'. Despite the efforts at the level of regulatory development, implementation remains a challenge, where victim/survivor-centered approaches, real participation of children and change of perception of child offenders are key priorities to be yet addressed.

Nevertheless, the MENA region presents a very unique scenario for the flourishing of concrete restorative justice practices, grounded in the synergies of community-based and formal justice systems. In particular, conciliation (where the facilitator of the process proposes a solution to the parties affected by the conflict) has been largely practiced at the community level, led by influential people, mostly male figures, and named differently depending on the country/community (e.g. Islah, Mukhtars, Elders, Sheiks, Imams). It is common that these actors, particularly when linked with faith-based communities, are also the official religious judicial figures applying personal status laws in the official justice system (e.g. Sharia Institution and others). This 'double-hat' position of facilitators reflects the confluence of the justice systems mentioned above.

The use of victim-offender mediation (where an impartial mediator accompanies the parties to find their solution to the conflict) and family group conferencing is also advancing in the MENA region. While some laws explicitly include mediation (called juvenile mediation in these laws), bylaws supporting the process, the governing rules, the principles of participation of the parties, the role of the mediator and the accountability mechanisms are yet to be instated. For instance, following Article 23 of its Juvenile Law 4/2016, Palestine is currently in the process of developing its child mediation process, with regard to the figure of 'social mediators' proceeding from outside the formal justice system (for instance customary justice actors), monitored by the Public Prosecutorial Offices and the Ministry of Social Development. Jordan is studying the possibility of learning from the practical experience of family mediation processes, organized within the Sharia Judicial Institution, to transfer elements of this practice into the formal child mediation process in the secular sphere (i.e. within the criminal justice system). Turkey has already enacted victim-offender mediation processes during criminal prosecutions, which have been advised by several regional and international restorative justice experts (Geske, 2012). In 2018, Lebanon approved the Judicial Mediation Law and, while it does not precisely contemplate youth mediation, it opens the door for a specific development of mediation within the child justice system. Since 2014, Tunisia also is practicing victim-offender mediation within its transitional justice process, which includes judicial and non-judicial mechanisms (UNODC, 2020).

Family group conferencing is solidly coming forth as part of diversionary measures and alternatives to detention processes. It aims to involve the offender, victim and their families into drawing individual reintegration plans that are based on children's rights (for the child offender and the victim) and rely on support from people in the close circle of the children, including professionals (e.g. social workers, psychologists, school counselors) directly linked with the child welfare and child justice systems. Egypt and Tunisia are good examples of the development of this concrete restorative justice practice, with context-based differences.

Finally, Lebanon is piloting youth restorative peace circles as a way to resolve community disputes involving children from different communities and religious identities. By using non-formal education settings rather than justice-related spaces, the narratives of collaborative problem solving, reconciliation and healing are fostered among peers.[14]

The above-mentioned practices are relatively new restorative justice practices in the MENA region that are embraced by the formal justice systems. They use different processes but are all truly promising. They require further legal development, piloting and harmonization in order to advance toward a much more comprehensive child justice system that responds to crime, respects the dignity and equality of each person, avoids stigmatization, builds understanding and promotes social harmony through the healing of victims, offenders and communities alike.

3.2 Emergence of restorative justice in Southeast Asia

Restorative justice in Southeast Asia is found mainly in the area of child justice. This is partly in response to the CRC. Other factors are at play as well, such as a need for the modernization of the criminal justice systems, emphasis on the outcomes of punishment, as well as the issue of overcrowding in prisons, all of which led to the greater use of alternative forms of conflict resolution. The development of restorative justice can also be attributed to the promotion of the concept by occidental and western-directed non-governmental agencies. Support from ruling parties, governmental bodies and heads of

14 Youth Development Program, Lebanese Conflict Resolution Network (LCRN).

state has further enthused relevant agencies to consider, develop and implement restorative justice practices (UNODC, 2015).

The example of Thailand clearly illustrates this. The Department of Juvenile Observation and Protection (DJOP), Ministry of Justice (MOJ), strongly believes in the use of restorative justice in the management of children and young people in conflict with the law. The first national seminar on restorative justice was organized in 2002 and was attended by Princess Bajrakitiyabha. The Princess's involvement in the criminal justice system reform led to several significant changes, including the Bangkok Rules.[15] In 2003, a family group conferencing initiative was set up by the Department of Juvenile Observation and Protection in Thailand. The following year, the Department of Probation implemented victim-offender mediation for adult offenders. Such efforts highlight the Thai Ministry of Justice's mandate to use restorative justice alongside the conventional criminal justice system (see O'Brien & Foussard, 2020). Between 2005 and 2007, Thailand has hosted several regional conferences and training sessions through the Asia Pacific Council for Juvenile Justice (APCJJ), with the intention to raise public awareness concerning restorative justice approaches at the national and regional level. Thailand has also been focusing on training its judiciary. In 2017, the International Commission of Jurists organized a training program specifically targeting judges and involving foreign delegates. In 2020, the Second Edition of the Handbook on Restorative Justice was co-published by the United Nations Office on Drugs and Crime and the Thailand Institute of Justice (TIJ). This handbook aims to disseminate knowledge on restorative justice practices and its implementation worldwide.

The principles of restorative justice are, indeed, not new to the Thai people. Prior to the transformation of the legal system, the Thai people lived in communities and engaged in community justice to resolve conflict. The essence of restorative justice is community involvement and this is aligned with Buddhism, the main religion in Thailand.

The Philippines is another country that implements restorative justice as part of its legal framework. The Republic Act 9344 highlights the principles of restorative justice, to be applied in all laws, policies and programs applicable to children in conflict with the law. According to this law, the application of restorative justice is done in the context of resolving conflicts, and done with the maximum involvement of the victim, the offender and the community. The outcomes are based on the reconciliation of the young person with the victim and the community. The reassurance that the young person can be integrated into society helps to secure the future of the young person, reducing the likelihood of further conflict with the law.

Indonesia has also made changes to its law, firstly to address the soaring number of young offenders in prison and to ease the overcrowded facilities, and secondly, to align

15 The Bangkok Rules were endorsed at the 65th session of the United Nations General Assembly on 21 December 2010, to serve as guidelines on the treatment of female inmates for prisons across nations, in consideration of gender differences and the specific needs of women.

with international guidelines. Law Number 11 of 2012 of the Juvenile Criminal Justice System requires children in conflict with the law to be treated separately from adult offenders. The shift away from retributive justice to the application of restorative justice is noted mainly in the area of diversion. As in the case of Thailand, restorative justice is not a new concept here. It is embedded in the customary law of Indonesia, and people are generally supportive of the implementation of restorative justice (Zulfa, 2011). Apart from being diversionary, Indonesia has also been trying to use restorative justice in the rehabilitation process of young people, mainly in the context of social reintegrative programs that are organized and supervised by probation officers.

Statutory requirements create important impetus for the development of restorative justice in some countries, but a large part of the development is also based on the guiding principles of the CRC. This can be seen particularly in two other Islamic countries in Southeast Asia, namely Brunei Darussalam and Malaysia. Both countries apply Shariah Law with variance, and adopted the CRC with reservations (Muller, 2016). In this context, sentencing is considered with regard to the beliefs and principles of Islam. However, both countries have reformed child justice legislation in order to comply with international standards. For children in conflict with the law, there are community-based rehabilitation measures, such as diversion and probation. The Youth Development Centre is one example of providing support and education for those children in conflict with the law. In Malaysia, the Child Act calls for the establishment of the Court for Children, with the inclusion of lay persons as court advisors, including a requirement for one of them to be a woman. Apart from probationary measures, there is also the option of diverting children who commit minor crimes away from the criminal justice system.

Similarly, Singapore has adopted a diversionary system for children and young offenders in conflict with the law (Chan, 2013). Legislation pertaining to the treatment of children requires those in conflict with the law to be diverted away from the broader criminal justice system. The Children and Young Persons Act and Probation Offenders Act stipulates both the requirements for institutionalization and the need for diversion and community-based rehabilitation, such as probation, to be available options. The Probation and Community Rehabilitative Service oversees the diversion and probation programs. The Probation Service works closely with the youth court in the rehabilitation process of the children and young offenders. One unique feature of the Youth Justice System in Singapore is the involvement of victims and families in the context of Project Heal. It is a type of alternative of family group conferencing and it provides an offender an opportunity to listen to the impact of his or her crime on the victims, including the families and the larger community.

In 1990, Vietnam became the first country in Asia, and the second in the world, to ratify the CRC. Although there is no clear statutory requirement in Vietnamese law for restorative justice or its related principles, the country has been developing specialized services for at-risk youth and young people in conflict with the law using the principles of restorative justice. Non-governmental bodies such as Save the Children and the Blue Dragon Children's Foundation promote differentiated treatment of children and young people in conflict with the law.

Myanmar became a signatory to the CRC in 1991, and then in 1993 the national Child Law was enacted. This is the main instrument that focuses on child justice, and it incorporates the international guiding principles. In Myanmar, restorative justice is used as a diversionary measure. Diversion was also already being used based on the culture and tradition of the country. However, despite these efforts, children in Myanmar lack access to justice and this makes it harder to apply restorative justice widely (UNICEF, 2011).

Cambodia and Laos face similar issues when it comes to access to justice for children and young people in conflict with the law. According to Cambodian law, there is provision to refer children to institutions other than prisons (Vijghen, 2013). There is also the traditional form of conflict resolution rooted in religion. For instance, Cambodian Buddhism influences a large part of the social roles within its society. While the country's justice framework was deeply affected by the immense social and economic trauma incurred during the Vietnam War and Khmer Rouge period, the Cambodian culture and religion are supportive of the principles of restorative justice, as noted in the use of community justice. Similarly, in Laos, despite the lack of expertise and access to resources, there is a movement to bring justice to children in rural places. The use of mediation is an example of the application of restorative justice. The Village Child Mediation Units (UNICEF, 2019) are a fundamental mediation unit at the village level. These units formally operate under the auspices of the Ministry of Justice and with involvement from the community.

Finally, in Timor-Leste, community or informal justice is a prominent feature. In particular, the Timor-Leste Truth and Reconciliation Commission (CAVR) aligns with restorative justice principles (Androff, 2012). The reconciliation and recovery from the harm caused are often negotiated by the local tribunal and relevant parties. Mediation procedures allow the parties involved to agree upon compensation and work toward ending the conflict by promoting peaceful relations in the future (Burgess, 2006).

4 The way forward

Restorative justice is a real paradigm shift in the way justice for children and young people is perceived in most of the world's societies. As demonstrated above, there is a willingness to make this shift from a retributive to a restorative model of justice a reality. Restorative justice will make it possible to safeguard and strengthen children's rights, whether they are directly linked to the judicial system or more broadly, such as the right to education, rights relating to health, protection against violence, etc. There are also broader benefits to the model, including the potential for restorative justice practices to reduce recidivism and pressure on prisons. This is especially relevant in the context of the COVID-19 pandemic and the need for greater social distancing, a period of time when diversionary measures and alternatives to detention should be promoted to reduce the prison general population. For instance, currently, new practices are being developed around the globe to maintain restorative justice approaches and measures through communication technology during the pandemic, which do not require face-to-face meetings. This experience could strengthen and increase the use of restorative justice even in a non-presential context, which could accelerate justice length and decision-making.[16]

However, restorative justice will not always be a silver bullet. There is much work to be done. Firstly, all states should undertake an assessment of their current restorative justice approaches and practices (at the legislative and the law enforcement levels, but also the incorporation of restorative justice elements coming from customary roots, whether secular or faith-based) in order to ensure compatibility with international standards. In some cases, the best interests of the child are still very inadequately protected. There may be legislative barriers in some national contexts to removing children from the criminal justice system in order to enable the effective implementation of restorative justice. The actors concerned (police, prosecutors, lawyers, mediators, etc.) may not have access to advanced and continued training. It is necessary that they acquire skills to promote dialogue and resolve conflicts while ensuring the safety and meaningful participation of children. Training focusing on children's rights through the lens of diversionary and non-custodial measures is essential. The lack of coordination between the different actors in the justice services may hinder the full effectiveness of restorative justice. Collaboration must be established at the national, regional and local levels between all actors, whether public or private, even those involved in customary justice systems, secular or faith-based.

Secondly, further work is also needed on data collection, research and the development of child justice programs, in order to monitor the progressive impacts of restorative justice process on the child/youth and come up with proven recidivism prevention interventions. Evidence collection and behavioral analysis will help to strengthen policies to be more child-friendly, but will also help to dispel societal misconceptions about the involvement of children in crime.

Finally, awareness-raising campaigns should be undertaken at different levels (national, regional and local) with all parties concerned, including religious and community leaders, the media and the academia. The aim is to improve the understanding of restorative justice and to promote the most appropriate practices.

16 For more information at www.euforumrj.org/sites/default/files/2020-07/Vol_21_2_17_July_2020.pdf.

Cross-regional learning, exchange of information on good practices and dissemination of experiences with good restorative justice initiatives can be a very appealing and strategic way to broaden the scope of restorative justice for children. Support to civil society organizations toward specialization and institutionalization of restorative justice processes vis-à-vis judicial authorities are also necessary for the effective implementation and sustainability of these programs.

REFERENCES

American Bar Association Resolution 107B 2019 (US). *Declaración de Costa Rica sobre la Justicia Restaurativa en América Latina* 2005 (COS).

Amour, M. (2012). Restorative justice: some facts and history. *Tikkun*, 27(1), 25-65. doi: 10.1215/08879982-2012-1012.

Androff, D. (2012). Reconciliation in a community-based restorative justice intervention. *Journal of Sociology and Social Welfare*, 39(4), 73-96.

Beale, S. (2003). Still tough on crime? Prospects for restorative justice in the United States. *Utah Law Review*, 1, 413-417. doi: 10.2139/ssrn.358440.

Burgess, P. (2006). A new approach to restorative justice – east Timor's community reconciliation processes. In N. Roht-Arriaza & J. Mariezcurrena (eds.), *Transitional justice in the twenty-first century: beyond truth versus justice* (pp. 176-205). Cambridge: Cambridge University Press.

Burgos Mata, A. (2018). Una mirada a las actuales manifestaciones alternativas del Derecho Penal Juvenil en Costa Rica. In C. Tiffer Sotomayor (ed.), *Derecho Penal Juvenil: experiencias y buenas prácticas* (pp. 261). San Jose: Editorial Jurídica Continental.

Caldwell, B. (2011). Punishment v. restoration: comparative analysis of juvenile delinquency law in the United States and Mexico. *Cardozo Journal of International and Comparative Law*, 20(1), 105-142.

Canadian Resource Centre for Victims of Crime. (2011). *Restorative justice in Canada: what victims should know*. Retrieved from https://crcvc.ca/docs/restjust.pdf (last accessed 25 October 2020).

Carranza, E. (2017). El delito violento en la población menor de edad y joven en América Latina y el Caribe. *Revista de derecho Penal y Criminología*, 5, 236-248.

Chan, W. (2013). Family conferencing for juvenile offenders: a Singaporean case study in restorative justice. *Asian Journal of Criminology*, 8, 1-23. doi: 10.1007/s11417-011-9122-y.

Council of Europe. (2011). *Guidelines of the Committee of Ministers of the Council of Europe on child-friendly justice*. Strasbourg: Council of Europe Publishing.

CRC Committee. (2005). *Concluding observations: Belize* (CRC/C/15/Add.252).

CRC Committee. (2010). *Concluding observations: Nicaragua* (CRC/C/NIC/CO/4).

CRC Committee. (2011). *Concluding observations: Costa Rica* (CRC/C/CRI/CO/4).

CRC Committee. (2015). *Concluding observations on the combined fourth and fifth periodic reports of Honduras* (CRC/C/HND/CO/4-5).

CRC Committee. (2018a). *Concluding observations on the combined fifth and sixth periodic reports of El Salvador* (CRC/C/SLV/CO/5-6).

CRC Committee. (2018b). *Concluding observations on the combined fifth and sixth periodic reports of Guatemala* (CRC/C/GTM/CO/5-6).

CRC Committee. (2018c). *Concluding observations on the combined fifth and sixth periodic reports of Panama* (CRC/C/PAN/CO/5-6).

CRC Committee. (2019). *General comment no. 24 on children's rights in the child justice system* (CRC/C/GC/24).

Department of Justice Canada. (2013). *The youth criminal justice act: summary and background.* Ottawa: Department of Justice Canada.

ECOSOC. (2002). *Basic principles on the use of restorative justice programmes in criminal matters* (E/RES/2002/12).

Ellis, J. (2009). First nations justice initiatives in Canada. *Totem: The University of Western Ontario Journal of Anthropology*, 17(1), 37-42.

Espinach Rueda, L. (2018). La justiciar restaurativa en el proceso penal juvenil. In C. Tiffer Sotomayor (ed.), *Derecho Penal Juvenil: experiencias y buenas prácticas* (pp. 247). San Jose: Editorial Jurídica Continental.

Federal-Provincial-Territorial Working Group on Restorative Justice. (2016). *Restorative justice in the Canadian criminal justice sector.* Retrieved from www.csc-scc.gc.ca/restorative-justice/092/003005-4012-en.pdf (last accessed 25 October 2020).

Feld, B.C. (2018). Punishing kids in juvenile and criminal courts. *Crime and Justice*, 47, 417-474. doi: 10.1086/695399.

Frías Armenta, M. & Gómez Martínez, L. (2014). Juvenile justice in Mexico. *Laws*, 3(3), 580-597. doi: 10.3390/laws3030580.

Geske, J. (2012). *Victim/offender mediation in Turkey.* Retrieved from https://law.marquette.edu/facultyblog/2012/04/victimoffender-mediation-in-turkey (last accessed 21 October 2020).

Jimenez Bolaños, J. (2015). Breve análisis de la justicia restaurativa. *Revista de Ciencias Jurídicas*, 136, 161-174.

Leung, M. (1999). *The origins of restorative justice.* Retrieved from www.cfcj-fcjc.org/sites/default/files/docs/hosted/17445-restorative_justice.pdf (last accessed 25 October 2020).

Ley Nacional del Sistema Integral de Justicia Penal Para Adolescentes 2016 (MEX).

Ley Nº 7576, Ley de Justicia Penal Juvenil (COS).

Ley Nº 7727, Ley de Resolución Alterna de Conflictos y Promoción de la Paz Social (COS).

Ley Nº 9582, Ley de Justicia Restaurativa (COS).

McAra, L. & McVie, S. (2010). Youth crime and justice: key messages from the Edinburgh study of youth transitions and crime. *Criminology & Criminal Justice*, 10(2), 179-209. doi: 10.1177/1748895809360971.

Mena Pacheco, O.M. (2008). Justicia restaurativa y sistema de sanciones alternativas en el Derecho Penal Juvenil. *Revista de Ciencias Jurídicas*, 116, 13-56.

Models for Change. (n.d.). *Models for change: systems reform in juvenile justice*. Retrieved from www.modelsforchange.net/index.html (last accessed 25 October 2020).

Muller, D. (2016). Paradoxical normativities in Brunei Darussalam and Malaysia: Islamic law and the ASEAN human rights declaration. *Asian Survey*, 56(3), 415-441. doi: 10.1525/as.2016.56.3.415.

Nowak, M. (2019). *United Nations global study on children deprived of liberty*. New York: United Nations.

O'Brien, W. & Foussard, C. (2020). *Violence against children in the criminal justice system: global perspectives on prevention*. London: Routledge.

OJJDP. (n.d.). *About the balanced and restorative justice*. Retrieved from https://ojjdp.ojp.gov/sites/g/files/xyckuh176/files/pubs/implementing/about.html (last accessed 25 October 2020).

Parker, L. (2002). *The use of restorative practices in Latin America*. Retrieved from http://restorativejustice.org/10fulltext/parker-lynette.-the-use-of-restorative-practices-in-latin-america.pdf (last accessed 25 October 2020).

Pavelka, S. (2016). Restorative justice in the states, an analysis of statutory legislation and policy. *Justice Policy Journal*, 2(13), 1-23.

Pely, D. (2011). Women in Sulha – excluded yet influential: examining women's formal and informal role in traditional dispute resolution, within the patriarchal culture of Northern Israel's Arab community. *International Journal of Conflict Management*, 22(1), 89-104. doi: 10.1108/10444061111103643.

Terre des hommes. (2014). *Justicia Juvenil Restaurativa*. Retrieved from www.tdh.ch/sites/default/files/f8154866-2c88-4019-8f41-07861493226b_tdh_pol-thema2014_jj_es_light_original.pdf (last accessed 7 January 2020).

Terre des hommes. (n.d.). *Restorative juvenile justice*. Retrieved from www.terredeshommes.org/causes/restorative-juvenile-justice (last accessed 7 January 2020).

Tiffer Sotomayor, C. (2012). La desjudicialización penal juvenil como un camino hacia la justicia restaurativa. In C. Tiffer Sotomayor (ed.), *Justicia penal juvenil: entre la justicia retributiva y la justicia restaurativa* (pp. 21-94). San Jose: ILANUD.

UNGA. (1985). *United Nations Standard Minimum Rules for the Administration of Juvenile Justice ("The Beijing Rules")*.

UNICEF. (2011). *Report of the first consultative workshop on the Review of the Child Law, Sedona Hotel Yangon, 8-9 December 2011* (internal document).

UNICEF. (2019). *Child rights are human rights – how a small village is protecting children.* Retrieved from www.unicef.org/laos/stories/child-rights-are-human-rights (last accessed 21 October 2020).

UNODC. (2015). *Introducing the United Nations model strategies and practical measures on the elimination of violence against children in the field of crime prevention and criminal justice: a new tool for policymakers, criminal justice officials and practitioners.* Vienna: United Nations.

UNODC. (2020). *Handbook on restorative justice programmes: second edition.* Vienna: United Nations.

UN CCPCJ. (2017). *A summary of comments received on the use and application of the basic principles on the use of restorative justice programmes in criminal matters* (E/CN.15/2017/CRP.1).

Vijghen, J. (2013). *Assessment of juvenile justice practices in Cambodia: comprehensive reference guide on child rights in the justice system.* Retrieved from www.academia.edu/2771317/Assessment_of_Juvenile_Justice_Practices_in_Cambodia (last accessed 21 October 2020).

Wong, N. (2020). *'Path forward together': province, community works for restorative justice in Northern Manitoba.* Retrieved from https://winnipegsun.com/news/provincial/path-forward-together-province-community-works-for-restorative-justice-in-northern-manitoba (last accessed 25 October 2020).

World Bank. (2011). *Crime and violence in Central America: a development challenge - main report.* Retrieved from https://openknowledge.worldbank.org/handle/10986/2744 (last accessed 7 January 2020).

Wright, W.A. & Montoya Gonzales, R. (2016). Restorative justice takes hold in Mexico's criminal justice system. *Alternative Resolutions*, 25(4), 31-39.

Youth Criminal Justice Act (S.C. 2002, c.1) 2002 (CAN).

Zulfa, E. (2011). Restorative justice in Indonesia: traditional value. *Indonesia Law Review*, 1(2), 33-43. doi: 10.15742/ilrev.v1n2.81.

Zumbado, O. & Herrero, V. (2010). *Central America: restorative juvenile justice and a region's important choices.* Retrieved from www.creativeassociatesinternational.com/stories/central-america-restorative-juvenile-justice-and-a-regions-important-choices/ (last accessed 2 January 2020).

Chapter 7
Restorative justice in European youth justice systems

Contextual, legal, practice-related and analytical aspects

Frieder Dünkel and Andrea Păroşanu

1 Introduction

Over the past few decades, numerous countries across Europe have introduced restorative justice into their criminal justice systems, often in the context of youth justice. Various international and regional standards have increasingly highlighted and supported the application of restorative justice, including with young people in conflict with the law. Restorative justice attributes greater consideration to the needs of those involved in an offense – victim and offender – as well as the community. There is a growing body of research that has repeatedly highlighted the benefits and reintegrative potential for both victims and offenders, and the promising effects restorative justice can have on recidivism.

The European restorative landscape is a heterogeneous one – while some countries have succeeded in situating restorative justice in a more prominent position in the criminal justice context, others have struggled to move it beyond the margins of the criminal justice system.

The present chapter aims at providing a comparative overview of restorative justice in European youth justice systems with a focus on contextual and legal aspects as well as practice implementation and findings from research. Consideration is given to standards relating to restorative justice, such as relevant Council of Europe recommendations. The chapter draws on the findings of two European research projects coordinated by Greifswald University: 1) a comparative study on restorative justice in 36 European countries and jurisdictions,[1] and 2) comparative research on restorative approaches in

1 See Dünkel, Grzywa-Holten & Horsfield, (2015). Participating countries/jurisdictions were: Austria, Belgium, Bosnia-Hercegovina, Bulgaria, Croatia, Czech Republic, Denmark, England/Wales, Estonia, Finland, France, Germany, Greece, Hungary, Ireland, Italy, Latvia, Lithuania, Macedonia, Montenegro, The Netherlands, Northern Ireland, Norway, Poland, Portugal, Romania, Russia, Scotland, Serbia, Slovakia, Slovenia, Spain, Sweden, Switzerland, Turkey, Ukraine. The project was funded by the EU Criminal Justice Programme (JUST/2010/JPEN/AG/1525) and the University of Greifswald.

28 EU-Members states' youth justice systems.[2] These projects sought to identify inter alia key factors contributing to the successful application of restorative justice as well as the main barriers in implementing it throughout Europe. The chapter will highlight good and promising practice models regarding youth justice. First, contextual aspects relating to European standards and their relevance for young people in conflict with the law will be highlighted.

2 Contextual background – European standards on restorative justice

Besides international standards such as the UN Basic Principles on restorative justice (2002), regional standards have increasingly attached importance to restorative approaches in the context of criminal justice. Of particular significance are recommendations from the Council of Europe, as well as further European Union instruments, which have contributed to the development of restorative justice in numerous countries across Europe.

In 1999 the Council of Europe, for the first time, addressed the issue of restorative justice in its Recommendation No. R (99)19 on mediation in penal matters. The recommendation emphasized that mediation should be a generally available service (Rule 3) and applicable at all stages of the criminal justice process (Rule 4). The impartiality and training of mediators, and the voluntariness of participating parties as well as some general principles for handling of individual cases were enshrined in the recommendation. However, in the early 2000s it became clear that the recommendation needed an update in order to further develop a nationwide practice of the extant, rather reluctant and selective practice in most countries. At the end of 2007, the European Commission for the Efficiency of Justice (CEPEJ) presented guidelines for a better implementation of the existing recommendation concerning mediation in penal matters (see CEPEJ (2007)13) as a result of the working group of the CEPEJ set up in 2005. The guidelines emphasized the strengthening of principles of mediation and other restorative justice approaches in the member states and suggested that further work should be undertaken on updating the recommendation. The report referred to large variations in the member states and a reluctant implementation of restorative justice practices in most countries. It identified

- a lack of awareness of restorative justice including victim-offender mediation,
- a lack of availability of victim-offender mediation before and after conviction,

2 See Dünkel, Horsfield & Păroşanu, (2015). Participating countries were all EU-member states, respectively 30 jurisdictions (the UK representing three jurisdictions, England/Wales, Northern Ireland and Scotland), i.e. in addition to the EU-member states covered already in the first study (see fn. 1) which were Cyprus, Luxembourg and Malta.

- the power to refer parties to mediation limited only to a single criminal justice institution,
- relatively high costs of mediation and
- a lack of specialized training and disparities in qualifications of mediators.

It took another ten years to draft and pass the new Rec. (2018)8 on Restorative Justice in Criminal Matters. The drafting was based on a comment to R (99)19 by Ian Marder in 2017 (see Penological Council under PC-CP (2017) 6), which emphasized that the scope of a new recommendation should be widened from victim-offender mediation to restorative justice approaches in general, by keeping the general outline of the 1999 recommendation, but adding specific rules on restorative justice in prisons and probation services (PC-CP (2017) 6, 2). The new recommendation has embraced this wider scope. The language of the Rec. (2018)8 is more modern, using, for example, desistance instead of rehabilitation as the aim of restorative justice approaches (see Preamble, Clause 8).[3]

The Rec. (2018)8 now contains 67 much more detailed rules, which emphasize a wider implementation of restorative justice approaches (Council of Europe, 2018).

> Restorative justice may be used at any stage of the criminal justice process including both adults and children. For example, it may be associated with diversion from arrest, charge or prosecution, used in conjunction with a police or judicial disposal, occur before or parallel to prosecution, take place in between conviction and sentencing, constitute part of a sentence, or happen after a sentence has been passed or completed. (Rule 6)

Basic principles such as

> voluntariness; deliberative, respectful dialogue; equal concern for the needs and interests of those involved; procedural fairness; collective, consensus-based agreement; a focus on reparation, reintegration and achieving mutual understanding; and avoiding domination (Rule 14)

are more clearly specified throughout the recommendation.

The scope is extended beyond the criminal procedure by proposing the use of restorative justice principles within the criminal and youth justice system after trial such as during the execution of non-custodial and custodial sanctions (within prisons

3 The text specifies: 'Considering the importance of encouraging the offenders' sense of responsibility and offering them opportunities to make amends, which may further their reintegration, enable redress and mutual understanding, and encourage desistance from crime' (Preamble, Clause 8).

and probation services, see Rules 60, 61). Much emphasis is given to clarify the relation and cooperation between criminal and youth justice and restorative justice agencies (see part III. and IV. of the Rec.) and to the training and supervision of mediators and facilitators of restorative justice approaches (see part V. of the Rec.). In terms of young people involved in restorative justice processes, the recommendation underlines that the same legal safeguards as in youth justice proceedings should be applied to them and their legal representatives (Rule 24).

Overall, the new Rec. (2018)8 is a further step to enhance the implementation of restorative justice in the Council of Europe member states. That such an effort is highly important was demonstrated by the empirical data the research of the Department of Criminology at Greifswald revealed in 2015 (see below).

Besides the latest Council of Europe recommendation, several earlier documents highlight the use of restorative justice. The EU victim's rights directive (2012) recognizes the benefits of participating in restorative justice and highlights the need for safeguards to ensure that 'victims who choose to participate in restorative justice processes, have access to safe and competent restorative justice services' (Art. 12).

In the context of youth justice, earlier Council of Europe documents, such as Recommendation No. R. (2003)20 concerning new ways of dealing with juvenile offenders and the role of juvenile justice, refer to restoration and reparation. The standards emphasize the need for more innovative and effective responses when dealing with more serious and violent offenses, and encourage the use of mediation as well as reparation to the victim in appropriate cases (Council of Europe, 2003, Rule 8).

The 'European Rules for Juvenile Offenders Subject to Sanctions or Measures' of 2008 (Council of Europe, 2009) encourage the use of mediation and other restorative interventions at all stages of criminal procedure (Basic Principle 12), and highlight the preference of mediation and restorative measures when resolving conflicts with and among incarcerated juveniles and young adults (Rule 122.2).

Furthermore, the Council of Europe (2010) Guidelines on Child Friendly Justice aim to promote the principles of the best interest of the child and encourage the use of alternatives to judicial proceedings including mediation, diversion and alternative dispute resolution (No. 24) (see also previous chapters in this book).

3 Key factors for introducing restorative justice in European youth justice systems[4]

3.1 *Reforming criminal justice systems (for adults) and juvenile justice systems (for youth)*

The modern development of restorative justice in Europe was particularly influenced by abolitionist thinking of scholars, such as Nils Christie in Norway. His notion of 're-appropriation of conflicts' demands that criminal justice professionals give the conflicts back to those directly involved in a harmful incident, to better address their needs and restore their rights (Christie, 1977). Early bottom-up movements in Austria, Norway and Finland in the 1980s were inspired by such abolitionist reasoning, and it has subsequently played an important role in other countries.

The ideas of restoration and reparation increasingly gained importance since the 1970s and were part of efforts to reform the criminal justice system. Overall, developments in numerous countries sought to bring about an overall shift in criminal thinking, away from purely retributive toward more rehabilitative and reintegrative approaches. Of significance in this context was the aim of reducing the rates of imprisonment and providing community-based alternatives to prison, focusing on offender rehabilitation and reintegration.

Criminal justice reforms, including youth justice reforms, were also reflected in the expanding use of diversion and discretionary decision-making among key gatekeepers such as prosecutors or police. Restorative elements and interventions were introduced in numerous youth justice systems to either dismiss the charge and keep young people out of the court, or to mitigate their sentences. In responding to youth offending, justice systems have increasingly sought to employ approaches based on 'education' rather than punishment, focused on providing alternative processes and measures to seek to positively influence the young person with the aim of reintegration and avoid stigmatization. Such reform developments toward diversion and decarceration were key contextual factors in introducing restorative justice in many European youth justice systems.

3.2 *Victims' rights movements*

Further roots of restorative justice developments can be found in the victims' rights movement starting in the 1970s. Strengthening the position of the victim in criminal

4 This subsection is based on information drawn from the 36 national reports from the Greifswald project, as the EU-member states project did not focus on this matter.

justice proceedings and providing enhanced responses to meet the manifold needs of victims were some of the driving factors that contributed to the emergence of restorative approaches.[5] Legal reforms increasingly included opportunities for victims to be involved in restorative processes or introduced provisions that sought to facilitate the making of reparation and the alleviation of caused harm by adult and young offenders, which the restorative ideal could cater to very well (Hartmann, 2019).

3.3 *The influence of international and regional standards*

More recently, compliance with international and regional standards as outlined above (Section 2) were further factors that motivated the implementation of restorative approaches in the justice sphere. Particularly in the context of Eastern European countries' EU accession, harmonization with EU standards and legislation was of relevance for introducing restorative processes or elements into national legal frameworks. Such instruments have provided guidance on how to implement restorative strategies at legal and policy level, drawing on 'best practices' identified in the field. The EU victim's directive, for example, positively affected the practice of restorative justice in several countries. In Finland, for instance, it provided clearer guidance for a tested nationwide system of victim-offender mediation that has been in place for a few decades for both adult and young offenders.

Table 7.1 highlights the key driving forces leading to the introduction of restorative justice into the context of responding to criminal and youth offending. In many countries, the emergence of restorative justice was influenced by more than one factor, as they are partly interrelated.[6]

Table 7.1 Factors influencing the introduction and implementation of restorative justice in criminal matters in Member States of the Council of Europe

Abolitionist thinking; traditional criminal justice system deemed inappropriate forum for resolving conflicts	*Austria; Belgium; Croatia; Finland; Latvia; the Netherlands; Spain*
Strengthening victims' rights; victim movements	*Croatia; Denmark; England and Wales; France; Germany; Greece; the Netherlands; Poland; Scotland; Slovakia; Spain; Sweden*
Inefficient/overburdened criminal justice system	*Bulgaria; Croatia; Greece; Hungary; Ireland; Latvia; Portugal; Romania; Slovakia; Slovenia*

5 See in summary also the detailed analysis in Kilchling (2019).

6 Please note that these factors are not exhaustive, as the introduction of restorative justice has to be considered within country-specific political, social, economic and cultural contexts as well.

Rehabilitation and reintegration over retribution and punishment; diversion	*Austria; Belgium; Croatia; France; Germany; Hungary; Ireland; Italy; the Netherlands; Northern Ireland; Portugal; Romania; Scotland; Slovenia; Spain*
Reforms in particular in the field of juvenile justice or youth assistance and welfare	*Austria; Belgium; England and Wales; Estonia; Germany; Ireland; Italy; Northern Ireland; Portugal; Romania; Spain*
Curbing custody rates	*Estonia; Hungary; Ireland; Northern Ireland; Poland; Romania; Scotland; Slovakia; Slovenia*
Compliance with international standards, EU harmonization	*Bulgaria; Croatia; Czech Republic; Estonia; Hungary;* the *Netherlands; Poland; Portugal; Romania; Slovenia*
Lack of trust in the judiciary following period of transition	*Bulgaria; Czech Republic; Northern Ireland*

Source: Dünkel, Grzywa-Holten & Horsfield (2015: 1032).

4 Restorative approaches and their implementation

4.1 *Restorative justice models*

Across Europe, the predominant form of restorative justice in the area of youth justice is victim-offender mediation. During the 1980s, victim-offender mediation pilots targeting young people who offend were the first ones trialed in several countries (i.e. Austria, Belgium, Finland, Germany). As both research projects mentioned above have shown, nearly all countries and jurisdictions covered by the research have since introduced victim-offender mediation schemes, albeit with variations regarding legal and practical implementation.

Conferencing and circle processes involving a wider range of participants are by far less widespread. Restorative conferencing, inspired by the New Zealand model of family group conferencing, has been introduced to a wider extent, for example, in Belgium, Northern Ireland and Ireland, and is sought to be used in cases of more serious offending. Especially in Northern Ireland, they are considered to be a core response to youth crime, and have been mainstreamed in the youth justice system. Furthermore, the use of conferencing as well as circle practices, in the sphere of youth justice, has been trialed in some other countries.

4.2 *Use of restorative processes within the youth justice systems*

Youth justice reforms have, over time, led to extending diversionary approaches in a number of countries. In suitable cases, key youth justice decision-makers will advise whether diversion from prosecution or sentencing into alternative including restorative processes should be considered. Particularly at prosecution level, charges can be withdrawn if certain conditions have been met, such as 'reconciliation'[7] between the victim and the offender or the making of reparation. Such legislative provisions are in place in almost all of the countries covered by the present research projects, but usually limited to certain offenses, i.e. those that carry a lower penalty. Less widespread than prosecutorial diversion is diversion at court level. Courts can use their discretionary powers and refrain from convicting or sentencing a young offender, or they can mitigate the sentence on similar grounds. Legal provisions relating to prosecutorial or court diversion as well as sentence mitigation serve as the most central 'access points' through which restorative processes can enter into the youth justice procedure.[8]

Further, restorative processes can be initiated at the post-sentencing stage, during the serving of a sentence of imprisonment or detention, upon release or as conditions for early release. Restorative approaches can also be applied as a means of resolving conflicts within prisons and detention centers. About half of the countries covered in the studies referred to the use of restorative justice in prison settings, with only very few (i.e. Belgium, Germany, Portugal) making legal provision in youth and adult prison legislation that seeks to incorporate reparation and a focus on victims' needs into correctional programming. In Belgium, prison legislation provides for restorative justice measures since 2005. In 2008, a nationwide implementation was established. Since 2007, the prison law reforms for young offenders as well as for adults in Germany provide that offenders should participate in restorative justice programs and measures (aimed at efforts to restore damages, victims' awareness, victims' empathy-programs etc.; see Hartmann, Haas & Steengrafe, 2013: 41 ff., 44 ff.). However, the implementation of such programs is far behind the legislative aim of providing them nationwide. Nevertheless, victim-oriented prison regimes are more at the center of prison policy in Germany than before (see e.g. § 7 Prison Act of North-Rhine Westphalia, see in general Höffler, Jesse & Bliesener, 2019).

Overall, only a few countries provide access to restorative processes regardless of the stage of criminal proceedings and regardless of offense and offender characteristics (i.e. Belgium, Denmark, Finland, Germany, the Netherlands, Norway and Sweden). However, in practice, certain offense and offender characteristics play a major role as preconditions: the (individual) victim and offender must agree, and very serious interpersonal violence (e.g. sexual offenses) are selected for consideration only exceptionally (see for a widening of the application the Recommendations under 6. below). Meanwhile, restorative justice approaches in prison settings focus just on these more serious crimes.

---

7 The term 'reconciliation' does not always mean a restorative encounter, as in numerous – particularly Eastern European – countries. A 'reconciliation' process can also take place without an impartial facilitator before a judge or prosecutor who seeks to help the parties reach an informal solution to the offense.

8 However, it is worth noting that reparation and reconciliation can also be achieved without there necessarily having been a restorative process involved.

The degree of actual service coverage varies substantially throughout Europe, with nationwide coverage of service provision in place in Austria, Belgium, the Czech Republic, Denmark, Finland, Germany, Hungary, the Netherlands, Latvia and Norway. In all other countries, VOM services (not legislation) are limited to certain geographical areas where local partnerships and initiatives have been established. By contrast, conferencing is far less common in Europe, being available on a nationwide scale in only five jurisdictions (Belgium, England and Wales (with major reservations), Ireland, the Netherlands and Northern Ireland).

Looking at the role restorative justice plays in practice, it has to be noted that measuring the use of restorative interventions is not an easy task. Specific data on young people are not always available, as is the case with general data as well. Official statistical data on the use of restorative justice are sometimes entirely lacking or are fragmented in a number of countries. Also, statistical data are rarely refined to take into account the total population of the country, or the total number of young offenders brought to justice.

Having these methodological and statistical problems in mind, overall it can be said that, both for adults and for young people, restorative justice plays a major role in the criminal and youth justice practice in only a small handful of countries. The clear leaders in youth justice practice are Finland, Northern Ireland, France, Belgium, Austria and, with some limitation due to the lack of nationwide statistics, Germany. Although in Eastern European countries, major efforts can be seen to implement restorative justice practices, in particular in youth justice, the numbers still remain relatively low, as in many of the Western European countries. (Dünkel, 2019: 111 ff; Dünkel, Grzywa-Holten & Horsfield, 2015: 1059 ff; Dünkel, Horsfield & Păroşanu, 2015: 210 ff).

5 Findings from research and evaluation

There has been a growing body of research-evidence over the last decades that indicate beneficial outcomes for all stakeholders in an offense. However, one has to admit that most of the research covers the Anglo-Saxon world and (continental) European research is less extensive.

Research has, for instance, measured high rates of satisfaction among victims and adult and young offenders who have participated in restorative processes (i.e. Latimer, Dowden & Muise, 2001; McCold & Wachtel, 2002; Umbreit, Coates & Vos, 2008; Braithwaite, 2002). These experiences imply that victim-offender mediation and conferencing can be implemented in a fashion that meets the needs and interests of both victims and offenders very well.

What also emerges from the research literature is that restorative practices are often associated with promising effects on recidivism,[9] as evidenced by a growing pool of research results (i.e. Bonta, Jesseman, Rugge & Cornier, 2008; Braithwaite, 1999; Hayes, 2007; Shapland et al., 2008; Sherman et al., 2015a, 2015b; Sherman & Strang, 2007; Umbreit et al., 2008). Despite certain methodological shortcomings,[10] the overall impression stemming from the studies is that restorative justice does not have a negative impact on re-offending (Aertsen, Mackay, Pelikan, Willemsens & Wright, 2004).[11] In a comprehensive meta-analysis, Sherman and Strang concluded that in two projects in the United Kingdom a 25 percent reduction in recidivism could be observed among violent (adult and young) offenders after participation in restorative justice processes.[12] Bonta et al. (2008: 117), who also conducted a meta-analysis of restorative programs, state that

> restorative justice interventions, on average, are associated with reductions in recidivism. The effects are small but they are significant. It is also clear that the more recent studies are producing larger effects.[13]

Sherman and Strang (2007) point out that restorative justice also has the potential to reduce the costs of criminal and youth justice. On the one hand, restorative practices in the context of diversion can reduce court caseloads and thus the expense involved in bringing offenses to justice. Furthermore, reducing the number of offenders coming before the courts can have down-tariffing effects on overall sentencing practices, as has recently been experienced in England and Wales with the Youth Restorative Disposal and

9 It has to be highlighted that reducing recidivism is not the primary aim of restorative justice-processes (see Hayes, 2007: 440), but instead to trying to reach an agreement, accountability and the fulfilment of the agreement by the offender and the satisfaction of the victim. In this regard, there is a broad consensus that for the participants of restorative interventions the results in the large majority of evaluation are very positive, see e.g. Braithwaite (2002); Hartmann (2019: 132 ff).

10 In this regard, see Bonta et al. (2008).

11 Piggott and Wood summarize the research on this aspect by stating that the large majority of the evaluation studies come to positive findings and only a few to negative effects, these mixed results being 'attributed to substantial differences between restorative justice programs in policy and practice (Piggott & Wood, 2019: 359)'.

12 Sherman and Strang (2007: 69); Sherman et al. (2015a: 12 f). (comparing effect sizes for young people versus adults a slightly stronger effect size was to be seen for adults, see p. 13).

13 Small, but significant effects on reducing recidivism were also reported by Bergseth & Bouffard, 2007; for more recent studies see Sherman et al. 2015a and 2015b; Wilson, Olaghere and Kimbrell, 2017; see also Lyness & Tate, 2011, for positive outcomes of youth conferences in Northern Ireland; see also Hayes & Daly, 2003).

Triage Programmes.[14] These deflationary effects can spread across the entire sentencing spectrum and thus reduce the use of costly custodial sentences.[15]

Recently also, the perspective of desistance research has been addressed by describing the potentiality of restorative processes as means of cognitive decision-making for 'making good' and repairing the negative consequences of the crime and thus even resulting in turning points that ease the way to a law-abiding lifestyle (Claes & Shapland, 2016; Lauwaert & Aertsen, 2016; Maruna, 2016). Theories of and research on desistance show that the development of a crime-free lifestyle is the result of structural conditions and factors (finding employment, stabilizing personal relationships, good marriage, etc.) and cognitive changes (the decision for leaving the criminal lifestyle; change of attitudes; developing empathy to (possible) victims). Victim-offender encounters can help develop or reinforce these desistance processes and further social integration (ibid.). Although most of desistance research is focused on adults, it is of major importance for young persons (children and young adults) in the transitional stage from childhood to adulthood and, in addition, may be seen in the context of neuroscientific evidence of brain maturation. Internal self-control mechanisms and structural as well as cognitive skills develop dramatically in the transitional stage up to the age of 25.[16]

Little research has been conducted on restorative justice approaches in youth detention and prison settings. In Germany, several federal prison laws provide for victim-oriented reintegration programs including sentence planning which demands the efforts of the offender to make reparation or even to undergo mediation by contacting the victim (see e.g. Baden-Württemberg, North-Rhine-Westphalia). In the federal state of Baden-Württemberg, a pilot project of victim-offender mediation with prisoners in four prisons started in 2013. The evaluation of Kilchling (2017) in a prison setting for adults after one year revealed that only a small group of offenders could be motivated to get into contact with the victim and that the interactions were seen as positive by both sides.[17] Another study revealed that prison officers in Germany are highly accepting of restorative justice measures, but that the structural problems in implementing them are considerable (see Hartmann et al., 2013). Comparable evaluation in the Thames Valley pilot project in London and of the nationwide implementation of restorative approaches in prisons in Belgium since 2008 revealed

14 See the report on *England and Wales* by Doak in Dünkel, Grzywa-Holten et al. (2015). See also Horsfield (2015: 197 f).

15 See Horsfield (2015: 364 ff.), who emphasizes the role of political pressure to expand such alternative sanctions due to the economic limits of the criminal justice system and budgetary restraints.

16 Neuroscientific evidence has been the major argument for raising the upper age of applying youth justice sanctions or measures to the age of 23 in the Netherlands by a reform law in 2014; it should be considered for the further reform development toward a young (adult) offender perspective in youth justice in other countries as well (see Dünkel, 2016; Dünkel, Geng & Passow, 2017 for further references).

17 The main problem was to get into contact with the victims, whose residence was often unknown (40 out of 91 cases). Only 11 percent of the victims explicitly refused to participate (see Kilchling, 2017: 49).

great potential for mediation and other (more indirect) restorative measures, but also approved the only moderate participation rates due to various difficulties independent from restorative efforts being organized as an offender treatment or a victims'-oriented measure (see Aertsen, 2012; Emerson & Hallam, 2015; Hartmann et al., 2013).

Not much evaluation has been carried out about the other dimension of restorative justice in prison settings, such as resolving conflicts between prisoners and prisoner-staff relations. An exception is a small research effort in a Dutch youth correctional center in 2010, where so-called 'internal mediations' were initiated when the youth had conflicts in the institution among themselves or with staff. This format worked well but was not imbedded structurally (Wolthuis & Vandenbroucke, 2010).

6 Summary and recommendations

Overall, it can be said that all countries covered, both in the study of Dünkel, Horsfield & Păroşanu (2015) and of Dünkel, Grzywa-Holten & Horsfield (2015), provide, in legislation or practice, forms of restorative justice in the context of resolving criminal conflicts. The landscape is dominated by victim-offender mediation; however, the degree of service availability varies considerably throughout Europe.

There are a number of predominant and interconnected themes when looking at the key driving factors for restorative justice to be implemented. The first relates to the traditional abolitionist thinking, which deems that the criminal and youth justice system is an inappropriate forum for resolving conflicts between offenders and victims. Accordingly, in some countries (particularly those in which the first experiences with restorative justice have been made in Europe, like Austria and Finland) the focus was on providing an informal forum that better meets the needs of those affected by the crime. This ties in to a second impetus - that restorative justice is regarded as a means for improving the standing of victims in criminal cases in the context of strong victim movements in some countries. In other jurisdictions, restorative justice came to be regarded as a promising element in a general shift in criminal and youth justice thinking, away from retribution and punishment toward rehabilitation and reintegration, objectives to which the restorative ideal can cater very well if implemented correctly due to its focus on positive reintegration. Such developments were particularly prominent in the field of youth justice, together with the broader development of children's rights (CRC 1989 etc., see below). Likewise, youth justice reform in Europe has served to provide gateways into the youth justice procedure, as the focus has increasingly been on diversion away from formal into informal processes and the use of rehabilitative and educational measures. The influence of international instruments, also relating to the promotion of children's rights, such as the Convention on the Rights of the Child and the drive for EU membership, are further prominent factors that cannot be ignored. International standards are regarded as depicting 'best practice' and thus provide the template for a criminal and youth justice system that is 'up to the standards' of Western society. Numerous countries, particularly in Eastern Europe (e.g. Bosnia and Herzegovina, Bulgaria, Croatia, the Czech Republic, Estonia, Hungary, North-Macedonia, Poland, Romania, Slovenia, Serbia, Ukraine), indicated that such instruments provided vital guidance to harmonizing their systems to Western standards, and this also covered standards relating to restorative justice. Countries like Albania and Georgia have more recently developed legislative frameworks that aim to promote restorative approaches. Hopefully the new Council of Europe recommendation Rec. (2018)8 will constitute an incentive for a wider use of restorative practices at all stages of criminal procedures and in the execution of sentences, in particular in prison settings.

The driving forces for reform such as abolitionist thinking, the emphasis on victims' rights, the shift toward more rehabilitative ('educational') youth justice measures, or just the pragmatic orientation to international human rights standards in the process of integrating into the EU have shaped the need for youth justice reforms. Youth justice reform has seen expansions in the powers of decision-makers throughout the justice system to divert cases from prosecution, conviction and/or sentencing into alternative procedures and measures that bear superior reintegrative and rehabilitative potential rather than purely retributive intervention. Overall, the big picture that remains is that the availability of restorative justice decreases the deeper one delves into the youth justice procedure. There are only a few exceptions to this rule that provide access to victim-offender mediation or conferencing regardless of the stage of criminal proceedings and regardless of offense and offender characteristics (see above under 4.2).

Regarding the use in practice, it is obvious that – except for some countries like Belgium, Northern Ireland, Austria and Finland – restorative justice unfortunately plays only a marginal role in most of Europe (see Dünkel, Grzywa-Holten et al., 2015: 1059-1062), albeit with a slightly upward trend if one takes the 'dark figure' of restorative action into account.

There is a vast pool of research on the benefits and potentials of restorative justice – therefore, the potential that restorative justice brings to the table is well-known. The role that restorative justice plays in the practice of the criminal and youth justice system, by contrast, does little to underline this view. What has indeed also become clear is that there is great potential for restorative justice to gain a more prominent role in the criminal and youth justice systems in Europe than is the case today in most countries. Restorative justice is a promising and desirable strategy that achieves the best outcomes when restorative processes are involved.

In light of the positive experiences with restorative practices, the question arises as to why they play such a peripheral role in the criminal and youth justice systems of most countries in Europe.

The reasons for an often reluctant and restricted use of restorative justice are manifold. In some countries, implementation is difficult as judges and prosecutors are reluctant to use new alternatives which lack the traditional elements of punishment. The lack of will among judicial gatekeepers to use restorative justice can be based, for example, on the distrust in the legitimacy of mediators and facilitators as deliverers of justice. In some countries, a lack of, or inappropriate, unclear legislative basis reduces the faith in restorative justice. Finally, the availability of other diversionary options that are more in line with traditional understanding of appropriate intervention may play a role.[18]

Another reason for the underuse of restorative justice in practice is the lack of information and awareness of its benefits among legislators, politicians, judicial gatekeepers and the general public. In addition, in some jurisdictions, a lack of will among legislators and politicians can be seen (in turn connected to issues of poor/lack of statutory basis, funding, lack of information/awareness and a punitive climate). As the good practices in Belgium,[19] Finland or Northern Ireland demonstrate, these obstacles may be overcome if the political climate is favorable for restorative ideas and values (in Northern Ireland, for instance, after a long period of civil war, restorative justice was in line with the general peace-making approach in politics). The EU-directive 2012-29 seems to have had some impact in furthering the idea of restorative measures being applied more often than before (see, for example, the Netherlands).

One particular challenge remains. Implementing restorative justice elements into the criminal and youth justice system may also bear the risk of 'institutionalization' that legislation brings with it, in that the values underpinning restorative justice could come to be 'watered down' so as to be accommodated within the existing criminal and youth justice system (see Aertsen, Daems & Robert, 2006 for further references). In practice, this implies that certain key ideals and values that support restorative justice are sacrificed for the benefit of achieving outcomes that are geared more toward the aims of criminal and youth justice rather than restorative justice (Vanfraechem & Aertsen, 2010). Therefore, careful implementation strategies and professional standards need to be provided.

Based on the results of Dünkel, Horsfield and Păroşanu. (2015) and the discussions in the International Juvenile Justice Observatory (IJJO),[20] Chapman has developed a 'European Model of Restorative justice with children and young people', which provides for restorative justice on four levels:

> Level 1: Restorative parenting, family group conferences, mediation and restorative relationships in schools, restorative circles and mediation in the community
> Level 2: Mediation to divert from entry into the criminal justice system

18 See in summary Dünkel, Grzywa-Holten & Horsfield, (2015: 1064 ff).
19 It has to be noted, however, that case numbers in Belgium did not increase anymore in the last years.
20 The IJJO is an NGO and lobby organization to promote European youth justice policies and practices.

Level 3: Restorative conferences and circles of support and accountability to divert from detention
Level 4: Restorative culture and practices in detention and for reintegration (Chapman, 2017: 82 f)[21]

Finally, some recommendations may be made.[22] Restorative justice is not yet available to all offenders at all stages of the criminal and youth justice procedure in all countries, as is recommended in Basic Principle No. 6 of the CM/Rec. (2018)8. Rather, access is usually restricted along the lines of proportionality and public interest, as restorative justice enters the system via diversionary pathways in most cases, or is a matter of discretion for decision-makers in the criminal and youth justice procedure. It therefore tends to be restricted to less serious forms of offending from the outset, and whether or not it is applied lies in the hand of practitioners who are likely unaccustomed to what restorative justice entails and what benefits it can bear for victims, offenders, communities and society. Therefore, it is recommended that access to restorative justice not be restricted on grounds of offense severity.

There is a need to provide forms of restorative justice that are promising for resolving conflicts between offenders and victims in cases of greater severity, and that involve the community in a greater fashion than is the case with victim-offender mediation. In this regard, conferencing has proven to be a viable and promising tool, in particular in youth justice. Recent experiences in Europe (Northern Ireland, Ireland and Belgium) have shown that positive outcomes can be achieved through conferencing in terms of satisfaction with processes and outcomes, perceptions of fairness, and re-offending.[23] However, to date very few countries have sought to apply conferencing in Europe. The same applies to experiences with circle processes. Therefore, it is recommended that countries seek to promote initiatives to introduce restorative conferencing and circles into their youth and criminal justice systems.

An often-neglected stage of the procedure is the serving of youth detention and prison sentences. Only rarely is the situation in theory and practice simultaneously such that restorative justice can come into play in correctional settings. This is regrettable, since prisons represent a large pool of yet 'untapped conflict', and are at the same time increasingly coming to be regarded as institutions of rehabilitation in which restorative approaches could be promising elements in sentence planning and programming (see, for instance, Germany). Offenders who are in prison and youth detention facilities will usually have committed offenses that made them ineligible for diversion, and thus for

21 See also www.ejjc.org/eumodel.
22 The following recommendations have been extracted from Dünkel, Grzywa-Holten & Horsfield. (2015: 185 ff.) and Dünkel (2019: 125 ff.) and further developed for the present publication.
23 See for an evaluation of the Northern Ireland conferencing schemes i.e. Doak and O'Mahony (2019); Chapman (2017 for further references).

restorative practices, although when they do their time in prison they also have time to think and work on victim understanding and can possibly take steps toward meeting their own victim. Prison legislation should encourage the implementation of victim-oriented treatment programs (see below), but also encourage restorative efforts of the society in general ('Making good', see the idea of restorative prisons). At the same time, restorative justice can be a viable means for resolving conflicts within prisons, between either prisoners or prisoners and staff. Thus, it is recommended that legislative provision be made for the making of reparation and raising awareness of victims' needs as an element in sentence planning. Likewise, it is recommended to explore ways of reforming the penitentiary climate and culture using restorative practices. Increasing empathy of offenders toward victims (e.g. through victim awareness programs) is an appropriate rehabilitative means for preventing further victimizations after release.

A recurring problem stated in many European countries has been a lack of political will to pass legislation and/or to implement or fund restorative justice initiatives, either because there is a lack of information on behalf of politicians and legislators, or because of a predominating punitive climate in society, or both. There is, therefore, a need to generate pressure 'bottom-up' on legislators to implement the aforementioned recommendations by establishing local initiatives that involve partnerships between the justice system and NGOs, universities and research institutes. Such endeavors need to be evidence-based in their approach and subject to continuous evaluation. Likewise, they need to be linked to strategies for raising awareness of the benefits of restorative justice, for all involved, that extend from relevant criminal and youth justice practitioners to the media and to the public, to generate public demand for restorative approaches in youth and adult justice systems.

Even where there is political will to implement restorative justice on a wider scale, any legislative endeavors should be based on knowledge and experiences of 'what works'. Countries that have seen the best experiences, in terms of introducing and sustaining a network of nationwide coverage and yielding decent caseloads (for example, Germany, the Netherlands, Northern Ireland, France, Finland, Belgium and Austria), provide a strong legislative basis for restorative justice. What these countries all have in common is that their legislation is based on years of experience with systems that have gradually grown from local initiatives to nationwide practices that have been subject to evaluation and adaptation. Therefore, a sound, evidence-based legislative basis will more likely be adequate for achieving the desired outcomes in its given context, and at the same time can increase faith in decision-makers to refer to it.

Finally, one should emphasize that restorative justice values and procedures are not restricted to youth justice systems, but they are an important innovation and should be further developed in conflict regulations in general, e.g. in schools, civil and administrative law litigations and in the society in general. Restorative justice 'is not a panacea against all social evils (Walgrave, 2017: 95)',[24] neither in criminal or youth justice, nor in other areas where restorative justice is practiced, but its values may contribute to a more humane and peaceful society (Braithwaite, 2019: 2 f).

References

Aertsen, I. (2012). Belgium – restorative prisons: where are we heading? In B. Barabás, B. Fellegi & S. Windt (eds.), *Responsibility-taking, relationship-building and restoration in prisons. Mediation and restorative justice in prison settings* (pp. 262-276). Budapest: National Institute of Criminology.

Aertsen, I., Daems, T. & Robert, L. (2006). (eds.). *Institutionalizing restorative justice.* Cullompton: Willan Publishing.

Aertsen, I., Mackay, R., Pelikan, C., Willemsens, J. & Wright, M. (2004). *Rebuilding community connections – mediation and restorative justice in Europe.* Strasbourg: Council of Europe Publishing.

Bergseth, K.J. & Bouffard, J.A. (2007). The long-term impact of restorative justice programming for juvenile offenders. *Journal of Criminal Justice*, 35, 433-451. doi: 10.1016/j.jcrimjus.2007.05.006.

Bonta, J., Jesseman, R., Rugge, T. & Cornier, R. (2008). Restorative justice and recidivism: promises made, promises kept? In D. Sullivan & L. Taft (eds.), *Handbook of restorative justice* (pp. 108-120). Milton Park: Routledge.

Braithwaite, J. (1999). Restorative justice: assessing optimistic and pessimistic accounts. In M. Tonry (ed.), *Crime and justice: a review of research* (Vol. 25, pp. 1-127). Chicago: University of Chicago Press.

Braithwaite, J. (2002). *Restorative justice and responsive regulation.* Oxford: Oxford University Press.

Braithwaite, J. (2019). The future of restorative justice. In T. Gavrielides (ed.), *Routledge international handbook of restorative justice* (pp. 1-3). London, New York: Routledge.

Chapman, T. (2017). Community and restorative justice. In H. Soleto, G. Varona & I. Porres (eds.), *Justicia Restaurativa y Terapéutica. Hacia Innovadores Modelos de Justicia* (pp. 75-85). Valencia: Tirant lo Blanch.

---

24 See the headline of the chapter of Walgrave (2017: 95), who presents an excellent summary of the critical aspects of RJ. Social injustices, gendered and racial violence, social inequalities and other structural social problems, cannot be expected to disappear if RJ is further expanding, but it 'should set the conditions to begin the gradual attainment of full participation of all stakeholders in social life' (Walgrave, 2017: 108).

Christie, N. (1977). Conflicts as property. *British Journal of Criminology* 17, 1-14.

Claes, B. & Shapland, J.M. (2016). Desistance from crime and restorative justice. *Restorative Justice,* 4(3), 302-322. doi: 10.1080/20504721.2016.1245912.

Council of Europe. (ed.). (1999). *Recommendation No. R (1999) 19 of the Committee of Ministers to member states concerning concerning mediation in penal matters, 15 December 1999.* Strasbourg: Council of Europe Publishing.

Council of Europe. (ed.). (2003). *Recommendation No. R (2003) 20 of the Committee of Ministers to member states concerning new ways of dealing with juvenile delinquency and the role of juvenile justice, 24 September 2003.* Strasbourg: Council of Europe Publishing.

Council of Europe. (ed.). (2009). *The European Rules for juvenile offenders subject to sanctions or measures.* Strasbourg: Council of Europe Publishing.

Council of Europe. (2010). *Guidelines of the Committee of Ministers of the Council of Europe on child friendly justice.* Adopted by the Committee of Ministers of the Council of Europe on 17 November 2010. Strasbourg: Council of Europe Publishing.

Council of Europe. (2018). *Recommendation CM/Rec (2018)8 of the Committee of Ministers to member States concerning restorative justice in criminal matters.* Adopted by the Committee of Ministers on 3 October 2018. Strasbourg: Council of Europe Publishing.

Doak, J. & O'Mahony, D. (2019). Evaluating the success of restorative justice conferencing. A values-based approach. In T. Gavrielides (ed.), *Routledge international handbook of restorative justice* (pp. 211-223). London, New York: Routledge.

Dünkel, F. (2016). Juvenile justice and human rights: European perspectives. In H. Kury, S. Redo & E. Shea (eds.), *Women and children as victims and offenders: background, prevention, reintegration* (pp. 681-719). Zürich: Springer International Publishing Switzerland.

Dünkel, F. (2019). Restorative justice in juvenile and adult criminal law: European comparative aspects. In G. Fornasari & E. Mattevi (eds.), *Giustizia Riparativa – Responsabilità, Partecipazione, Riparazione* (pp. 49-142). Trento: Università degli Studi di Trento, Quaderni della Facoltà di Giurisprudenza, Nr. 40.

Dünkel, F., Geng, B. & Passow, D. (2017). Erkenntnisse der Neurowissenschaften zur Gehirnreifung ("brain maturation") – Argumente für ein Jungtäterstrafrecht. *Zeitschrift für Jugendkriminalrecht und Jugendhilfe,* 28, 123-129.

Dünkel, F., Grzywa-Holten, J. & Horsfield, P. (2015). (eds.), *Restorative justice and mediation in penal matters – a stocktaking of legal issues, implementation strategies and outcomes in 36 European countries.* Mönchengladbach: Forum Verlag Godesberg.

Dünkel, F., Horsfield, P. & Păroșanu, A. (2015). *European research on restorative juvenile justice. Volume 1: research and selection of the most effective juvenile restorative justice practices in Europe: Snapshots from 28 EU member states.* Brussels: International Juvenile Justice Observatory.

Emerson, G. & Hallam, M. (2015). Thames valley. In R. Lummer, O. Hagemann & S. Reis (eds.), *Restorative justice at post-sentencing level in Europe* (pp. 60-73). Kiel: Schriftenreihe Soziale Strafrechtspflege Band 3.

Hartmann, A. (2019). Victims and restorative justice. Bringing theory and evidence together. In T. Gavrielides (ed.), *Routledge international handbook of restorative justice* (pp. 127-144). London, New York: Routledge.

Hartmann, A., Haas, M. & Steengrafe, F. (2013). Täter-Opfer-Ausgleich im Strafvollzug – Ergebnisse des MEREPS-Projektes. *Bewährungshilfe*, 60, 39-55.

Hayes, H. (2007). Reoffending and restorative justice. In G. Johnstone & D. W. van Ness (eds.), *Handbook of restorative justice* (pp. 426-444). Cullompton: Willan.

Hayes, H. & Daly, K. (2003). Youth justice conferencing and reoffending. Justice Quarterly, 20(4), 725–764.

Höffler, K., Jesse, C. & Bliesener, T. (2019). (eds.). *Opferorientierung im Strafvollzug.* Göttingen: Universitätsverlag.

Horsfield, P. (2015). *Jugendkriminalpolitik in England und Wales.* Mönchengladbach: Forum Verlag Godesberg.

Kilchling, M. (2017). *Täter-Opfer-Ausgleich im Strafvollzug. Wissenschaftliche Begleitung des Modellprojekts Täter-Opfer-Ausgleich im baden-württembergischen Justizvollzug.* Berlin: Dunker & Humblot.

Kilchling, M. (2019). Restorative justice: incorporating victims' rights and needs. In G. Fornasari & E. Mattevi (eds.), *Giustizia Riparativa – Responsabilità, Partecipazione, Riparazione* (S. 3-34). Trento: Università degli Studi di Trento, Quaderni della Facoltà di Giurisprudenza, Nr. 40.

Latimer, J., Dowden, C. & Muise, D. (2001). *The effectiveness of restorative justice practices: a meta-analysis.* Ottawa: Research and Statistics Division, Department of Justice Canada.

Lauwaert, K. & Aertsen, I. (2016). With a little help from a friend: desistance through victim – offender mediation in Belgium. *Restorative Justice: an International Journal,* 4(3), 345-368. doi: 10.1080/20504721.2016.1245913.

Lyness, D. & Tate, S. (2011). *Northern Ireland youth re-offending: results from the 2008 cohort.* Belfast: NI Youth Justice Agency.

Maruna, S. (2016). Desistance and restorative justice: it's now or never. *Restorative Justice: an International Journal*, 4(3), 289-301. doi: 10.1080/20504721.2016.1243853.

McCold, P. & Wachtel, T. (2002). Restorative justice theory validation. In E. Weitekamp & H.-J. Kerner (eds.), *Restorative justice: theoretical foundations* (pp. 110-142). Cullompton: Willan Publishing.

Piggott, E. & Wood, W. (2019). Does restorative justice reduce recidivism? Assessing evidence and claims about restorative justice and reoffending. In T. Gavrielides (ed.), *Routledge international handbook of restorative justice* (pp. 359-376). London, New York: Routledge.

Shapland, J., Atkinson, A., Atkinson, H., Dignan, J., Edwards, L., Hibbert, J., Howes, M., Johnstone, J., Robinson, G. & Sorsby, A. (2008). *Does restorative justice affect reconviction? The fourth report from the evaluation of three schemes.* London: Ministry of Justice.

Sherman, L.W. & Strang, H. (2007). *Restorative justice: the evidence.* London: The Smith Institute.

Sherman, L.W., Strang, H., Barnes, G., Woods, D.J., Bennett, S., Inkpen, N., Newbury-Birch, D., Rossner, M., Angel, C., Mearns, M. & Slothower, M. (2015a). Twelve experiments in restorative justice: the Jerry Lee program of randomized trials of restorative justice conferences. *Journal of Experimental Criminology*, 11, 501-540. doi: 10.1007/s11292-015-9247-6.

Sherman, L.W., Strang, H., Mayo-Wilson, E., Woods, D.J. & Ariel, B. (2015b). Are restorative justice conferences effective in reducing repeat offending? *Journal of Quantitative Criminology*, 31, 1-24. doi: 10.1007/s10940-014-9222-9.

Umbreit, M.S., Coates, R.B. & Vos, B. (2008). Victim-offender mediation: an evolving evidence-based practice. In D. Sullivan & L. Taft (eds.), *Handbook of restorative justice* (pp. 52-62). Milton Park: Routledge.

United Nations Economic and Social Council. (2002) (ed.). *Basic principles on the use of restorative justice programmes in criminal matters.* No. 2002/12 of 24 July.

Vanfraechem, I. & Aertsen, I. (2010). Empirical research on restorative justice in Europe: perspectives. In I. Vanfraechem, I. Aertsen & J. Willemsens (eds.). *Restorative justice realities – empirical research in a European context* (pp. 267-278). The Hague: Eleven.

Walgrave, L. (2017). Restorative justice is not a panacea against all social evils. In I. Aertsen & B. Pali (eds.), *Critical restorative justice* (pp. 95-110). Oxford, Portland: Hart Publishing.

Wilson, D.B., Olaghere, A. & Kimbrell, C.S. (2017). *Effectiveness of restorative justice principles in juvenile justice: a meta-analysis.* https://doi.org/10.3886/ICPSR37000.v1.

Wolthuis, A. & Vandenbroucke, M. (2010). Schade herstellen tijdens jeugddetentie. *Proces*, nr. 3, 150-164.

Chapter 8

Restorative child justice: South Africa, Namibia and Zimbabwe

Julia Sloth-Nielsen

1 Introduction

Restorative justice as a part of the proposed youth justice (now child justice) system formally appeared in policy documents in 1994, with the publication in South Africa of a booklet titled Juvenile Justice for South Africa: Proposals for Policy and Legislative Change.[1]

The paper offered proposals for policy and legislative changes to create an effective juvenile justice system in South Africa. The proposals emphasized accountability and encouraged young people to take responsibility for their behavior, promoting restorative justice and conflict resolution, bringing young people and their families to the center of the decision-making processes, protecting the rights of young people and victims, and offering alternatives at every stage of the juvenile justice process to minimize the need for institutionalization. Ensuring cultural appropriateness was a central theme. There was some knowledge transfer to newly independent Namibia at the time, including in relation to restorative justice, which also gained, in practice, a toehold. A South African non-governmental organization undertook training of diversion officers in Zimbabwe as a prelude to the launch of the Pre-Trial Diversion Project (described later), which was thereafter built on restorative justice principles. Restorative justice in the three countries under study stems from common antecedents, arguably warranting a comparative approach. That is what this chapter seeks to undertake.

2 South Africa

Restorative justice has been around in the annals of South African child justice reform processes since the early 1990s, when, at the dawn of the new democracy, a delegation from New Zealand visited South Africa to explain the functioning of restorative justice in their (then new) legislation. Their enthusiastic approval fell on fertile ground here –

1 Skelton, Pinnock & Shapiro (1994).

South Africa was searching for innovative solutions for the post-apartheid era that was almost upon us, and healing, amends and forgiveness were the hallmark of the Truth and Reconciliation Commission that was to be established to bring to light South Africa's dark history of repression.

The period that followed saw much enthusiasm, and some practice experimentation with family group conferences in particular, based on the New Zealand model. Somewhat skeptical, I launched, in conjunction with curious criminal justice functionaries, an informal pilot study to test the waters, as it were. This scheme was designed so that the first case on the juvenile court roll every Tuesday morning[2] would be referred to a family group conference, irrespective of the charge or the circumstances of the child offender, his or her family, or that of the victim. A variety of skilled volunteers were drawn in as facilitators – a youth development professional, a mediator and a social worker. Of course, the young offender or victim could have refused to participate, although, to my recollection, none did.

Sadly, the notes on each case, and the eventual results, were never formally written up or published. Nevertheless, all stakeholders were able to agree upon a few key findings, which did shape the discourse during the law reform process that followed. First, it was clear that automatically referring cases to a family group conference was ill-conceived: for some of the 'easy' or petty cases, such an intensive process was unnecessary and consumed precious (human) resources; for others, the intervention merely exacerbated existing welfare and family problems, which should never have entered the criminal justice system in the first place; and third, managing victims (and their expectations) was almost more troublesome than engendering remorse and an apology on the part of the offender.

In addition, during the tenure of the Inter-Ministerial Committee on Young People at Risk, a cabinet committee which was set up in 1998 and 1999 to make proposals for the transformation of the entire child and youth care system (Sloth-Nielsen, 2017), a dedicated and funded restorative justice pilot project, involving family group conferencing, which ran for a year, took place under their auspices (Skelton, 2002). The project was functioning at around the time that the law reform process was unfolding. The project dealt with approximately 47 cases involving economic offenses as well as offenses against the person, such as assault and even assault with intent to do grievous bodily harm, and the results of the study were published along with an implementation manual. The main findings centered around the processes needed to set up and manage family group conferences, especially managing victim expectations of compensation and redress what they saw as the primary benefit to themselves.

Overall, formal child justice law reform spanned the period 1996 to 2008, after a project Committee of the South African Law Reform commission was appointed to

2 Mondays were regarded as being too busy, after the build-up of cases that had occurred over the weekend.

lead a consultative process to prepare a Bill for Parliamentary consideration. The Bill was initially introduced in Parliament in 2002, but after short deliberations, fell by the wayside, until it was resurrected and properly reconsidered in 2007. This culminated in the adoption of the Child Justice Act 75 of 2008. The Act came into force in 2010, and has now been implemented for a decade.

This period spanning the 1990s and the early part of the millennium saw much innovation with diversion in particular. Diversion programs commenced in 1992, spearheaded by a non-governmental organization, and to date most diversion programs are offered by non-governmental organizations, who receive a per capita subsidy from the state for the programs they present, to children in conflict with the law. Diversion now occupies a central place in the legislative scheme. Not only does an entire chapter of the Act deal with diversion, but a new pre-trial procedure, the preliminary inquiry (a roundtable case conference), was introduced to make it mandatory for diversion to be considered in all cases before the matter is set down for plea and trial.[3] The Child Justice Act established a system of national accreditation of service providers and their programs, with programs having to comply with minimum criteria (section 55) and service providers being held accountable to the Department of Social Development (which bears responsibility for diversion) (section 56). Re-accreditation is undertaken at periodic intervals (every four years). Whilst the names of the approved programs are officially gazetted, it cannot be established to what extent these programs contain a restorative justice element, although the Child Justice Act itself is clear that several legislated objectives of diversion encompass restorative justice principles (diversion must 'encourage the child to be accountable for the harm caused by him or her'; diversion must 'provide an opportunity to those affected by the harm done to express their views on its impact upon them'; diversion must 'encourage the rendering to the victim of some symbolic benefit or the delivery of some object as compensation for the harm'; diversion must 'promote reconciliation between the child and the person or community affected by the harm caused by the child' (section 51 (b);(e), (f) ;(g)). It stands to reason, therefore, that registered diversion programs must meet these restorative objectives.

The 2008 Child Justice Act further provides expressly for referral to family group conferences as a form of diversion (section 61: Sloth-Nielsen & Gallinetti, 2011). Family group conferences are described as informal procedures which bring together the child who is alleged to have committed the offense and the victim, together with the support of their families or other appropriate persons, with the aim of developing a plan on how the child will address the effects of the offense. Both the child and the victim must consent to

3 There is no limit on the age of the child or the nature of the offense for which the child has been charged. However, for certain serious offenses (listed in a schedule to the Act), the written permission of the Director of Public Prosecutions must be obtained before the matter may be diverted (section 52(3)(a)). Diversion is possible at any time, even after commencement of a trial in court.

the family group conference taking place. It is mandated that a probation officer (i.e. social worker), appointed by a magistrate, convene the family group conference (section 61(3)). This plan should contain specified objectives to be achieved by the child (and the period within which they are to be achieved), contain details of any services and assistance to be provided to the child and his or her parents, specify which person or organization will provide these services and assistance, state the responsibilities of the child and his or her parents, provide details of personal objectives for the child and for the parents, and include any other matters relating to employment or education as are relevant (section 61(4)). A written record of this must be kept.

The Child Justice Act also provides for victim-offender mediation, which differs from family group conferencing insofar as it includes only the child and the offender, without the broader participation of family and support persons being required. For this reason, it is allegedly not a favored option for non-governmental organizations and probation officers.

Restorative justice can also be used as a mode of imposition of sentence. Section 73 of the Child Justice Act, titled 'Restorative Justice Sentences', provides for referral to a family group conference, to victim-offender mediation or to 'any other restorative justice process which is in accordance with the definition of restorative justice'.[4] In this case, the plan developed at the family group conference must be approved by the sentencing officer (section 73(2)), and if the court does not approve, it may impose another sentence but must enter the reasons for substituting the plan with its own sentence (section 73(3)). The Annual Report of the Department of Justice 2017-2018 shows that only a few such sentences are imposed nationally every year (one in 2015-2016, three in 2016-2017 and four in 2017-2018). The 2015-2016 Annual Report on the implementation of the Child Justice Act provides a historical account of figures for restorative justice sentences since 2011; they have shrunk from a high of 508 such sentences in 2012/2013, to 402 in 2013/2014 to the one recorded for 2015-2016.[5] The Annual Report of 2017-2018 (the most recent available) of the Department of Social Development gives overall diversion figures, but does not break these down into the various programs to which children in conflict with the law were referred. It is therefore impossible to detect whether restorative justice processes are being utilized as diversionary options. What has become clear is that, since the implementation of the Act commenced in 2010, the numbers of children in

4 The definition of restorative justice is that found in section 1 of the Act, namely 'an approach to justice that aims to involve the child offender, the victims, the families concerned and community members to collectively identify and address harms, needs and obligations through accepting responsibility, making restitution, taking measures to prevent a recurrence of the incident and promoting reconciliation'.

5 It is possible that this very low figure is a result of incorrect data capturing. The 2015/2016 report is the last combined interdepartmental report that was tabled in Parliament. Thereafter, the Child Justice Act was amended to enable departments to report individually. This was because numerous challenges arose in collating the data from the respective departments, which delayed the submission of the report to Parliament. This report is required by section 96(3)(b) of the Child Justice Act.

conflict with the law entering the system have dropped sharply, by around 40 percent. The reasons for this are not yet in the public domain, as research commissioned by the Department of Justice in 2018 to explore this has not been released. It is speculated that the more onerous procedures imposed on the police (they have to write a report and submit this to court if they do not release children charged with less serious offenses from police custody, for instance) have led to a drop in arrests of children. Nevertheless, the impact of the lower rate of entry into the system has impacted all further processes mandated by the Child Justice Act, including a sharp decrease in children placed on diversion programs as well as those ultimately convicted and sentenced. It will also inevitably have impacted referrals to restorative justice, if indeed this is occurring at all at present.

But numbers aside, it can be concluded that the enthusiasm for restorative justice endeavors that led to the restorative provisions of the Act being developed seems to have waned significantly as time has passed since the heady early post-apartheid days. Although speculative, some reasons can be put forward for this decline.

First, preparing participants, setting up and convening a family group conference is a time-consuming endeavor. Probation officers and social workers are notoriously overworked. It is likely, therefore, that they favor less intensive diversion options such as supervision and guidance orders (contemplated in section 53(f)) of the Child Justice Act). Indeed, the Department of Social Development reports a significant number of home-based supervision visits (more than 3,000), which tends to support this theory. Second, the involvement of non-governmental organizations in the delivery of restorative justice programs more generally (e.g. in cases involving adult defendants) remains obscure; the only national organization with dedicated expertise in this area closed its doors due to lack of funding a couple of years ago, after 20 years of existence. This organization was also able to provide mentoring and training, which is no longer possible. For accredited diversion services providers, it is likely that the presentation of programs to groups of children will be more cost- and time-efficient than running dedicated one-on-one conferences for individual child offenders, and their victims and their respective families. Third, with the passage of time since both the Truth and Reconciliation Commission and the heady days of the initial pilot projects, many skills have been lost to the sector as formerly enthusiastic and trained people have moved on in what is a notoriously mobile sector (social service delivery).

A recent judgment from the Constitutional Court of South Africa affirmed that at least there is support for restorative justice at that level. In *Centre for Child Law v. Media 24 and others* (CCT 216/18), the issues at stake were twofold: one, that the provision in the Criminal Procedure Act 51 of 1977 which protected the identity of children until they reached 18 years applied only to children accused of offending, and to child witnesses, leaving out child victims who had not yet testified, or who were not called to testify.[6] The Court agreed that this was unconstitutional, and contrary to the best interests of the child. The second issue was whether the prohibition on revealing the identity of an accused child or child witness should persist upon the child reaching the age of 18 years. Since the statutory protection extended only until the age of 18, the media were free to publish identificatory details once this age threshold had been reached (and often did so).[7] The Court ruled that despite the importance of the principle of open justice in a democracy, which serves the public interest (paras. 91-95), other competing principles (such as the child's right to dignity, privacy and her best interests) outweighed the need for the public to be fully informed of all details of matters, including the identification of a child accused, victim or witness.

When it comes to child accused, accountability and shame should be reintegrative rather than stigmatizing. Once the child offender turns 18 and is identified, this could be considered a form of stigmatization known as 'disintegrative shaming', which fails to reconcile the relationship between the accused and the community, and labels them a potential repeat offender. This is in contrast to 'reintegrative shaming' which aims to strengthen the relationship and ties between the accused and the community. In the context of a child accused, 'reintegrative shaming' is more appropriate and consistent with a restorative justice approach. Since restorative justice is a long-term process, it requires ongoing protection (para. 81).[8]

Restorative justice is understood to be both 'backward-looking' as it deals with the 'aftermath of the offense', and 'forward-looking', since it takes into account the implications for the future. Restorative justice encourages rehabilitation and reintegration. These worthy objectives may assist in holding child accused responsible but restoring them to 'the status of a moral being who can make and act on choices'; it is necessary for us to understand that 'a restorative justice approach can be a catalyst to create possibilities for a crime-free life for the offender, and by doing that create a safer environment for all' (para. 77).

6 As was the case in the matter which first gave rise to the court action: it concerned a child who had been kidnapped when only 2 days old, whose true identity was coincidently discovered by her biological parents when she was 17 years of age. The woman who had abducted and raised her was prosecuted and convicted. The victim did not testify against the woman who had brought her up.

7 The girl at the center of the issue in this case had a *curator ad litem* appointed to look after her interests, and an application was successfully made to court to suppress details of her identity begin leaked after she turned 18, during the course of ongoing proceedings. A few years later, she herself applied for the order to be lifted, as she was ready to share her story and had written a book about it. This too was granted. The agency of a protected person to reveal their story (and identity) if they wanted to was affirmed in the Constitutional Court judgment.

8 This probably refers to the fact that ongoing protection of the accused's identity after 18 years is more in keeping with a restorative justice approach.

Hence, an important strand of the Court's reasoning was based on the key justification for ongoing protection being that it would give effect to restorative justice. Apart from serving as a jurisprudential concept though, it seems that a dedicated effort will have to be made for the day-to-day functioning of the restorative justice provisions of the Child Justice Act to be brought to life again in South Africa. Ann Skelton (Skelton & Batley, 2019), well-known advocate for restorative justice and children's rights expert, expresses her disappointment thus:

After being in development since 2009, the Restorative Justice National Policy Framework appears to have been completely sidelined. There is no implementation plan and no attention to resourcing issues. There are significant gaps in data from government agencies, and data from CSOs suggest lower levels of implementation than a decade ago. The information provided by practitioners from the CSO sector indicates some worrying trends regarding cases being resolved through restorative justice processes and outcomes. Many have shifted their attention away from child offenders toward young adults. While that group also deserves attention, the implication is that the state is presumably providing restorative justice services to children, but there is limited transparency in the content and quality of such programs, and a dearth of independent evaluations. The fact that some NICRO offices and the RJC have closed doors is a very worrying sign, and points to a deep problem in the partnership between government and civil society. The reduction in the number of cases coming into the child justice system (and a concomitant reduction in the number of cases being referred for a diversion – at least in numbers, if not as a percentage) gives the impression that diversion practice is dwindling rather than burgeoning as had been expected. The increased use of referral to 'ADRM' by the prosecuting authority may be seen as a positive factor, but the extent to which the process and outcomes are restorative is questionable. Mediation projects run by CSOs have mostly been terminated due to a lack of funding. Restorative justice work with sentenced offenders continues, but it is patchy and characterized by precarious relationships with Correctional Services authorities. In the criminal justice sphere, therefore, we observe a dwindling of restorative justice work, compared with a decade ago, when the Child Justice Act was poised for implementation and expectations for restorative justice expansion were high.

3 Namibia

Namibia is a very sparsely populated country of 2.5 million inhabitants, in a country of 825,615 square kilometers. Namibia's child justice law reform process has been underway for a very long time. In 1994, a first draft Child Justice Bill was prepared, and a further unfinished version is dated 2012 and the process is still not complete. In its response to the country report submitted to the UN Committee on the Rights of the Child in 2012, the Committee voiced concerns about the 'exceptional delay' in finalizing the Child Justice Bill, also noting that the minimum age of criminal responsibility, which is 7 years of age in the State party, is unacceptably low. It also highlighted the children's courts not being operational in all regions, the absence of information in the State party report and in the public domain on the situation of children in conflict with the law, and the lack of special detention facilities for children, both boys and girls – children were being incarcerated with adults, experiencing poor conditions of detention, including in prisons. However, one reason for the long process of reform in the sphere of child justice, was the parallel process of developing the country's child protection legislation. This consultative process took some years (more than nine years) and was concluded only when the omnibus Bill was passed in Parliament in 2015. However, it could not be promulgated until February 2019, due the fact that the regulations (subsidiary legislation) required to underpin implementation had not been finalized until then.

I acted as a consultant to the Ministry of Justice in 2018 to prepare an updated version of a Child Justice Bill, which was due to be tabled in Parliament in 2019; however, this did not happen, possibly because of the arrest of the Minister of Justice toward the end of the year on corruption charges. A new minister has only recently (March 2020) been appointed.

All previous versions of the Child Justice Bill, and the current one, contain elaborate restorative justice provisions. The enthusiasm for restorative justice was predicated upon the sharing of lessons learned between South Africa and Namibia in the 1990s, and a receptive population to restorative justice principles and objectives on account of the fact that they harmonize with customary justice tenets.

The Bill in its current version elaborates particularly the benefits to all concerned – child, victim and community – of restorative justice (Sloth-Nielsen, 2018). Part 2 of Chapter 7 is devoted entirely to the process of entrenching restorative justice as a diversion option and permits a referral to be effected by a probation officer, a prosecutor or a court. The process for referring and convening a family group conference is detailed in the Bill, and its intended result, namely the formulation of a written plan with resolution(s) appropriate to the child (including possible referral to a diversion program), his or her family and to local circumstances which are consistent with the principles contained in the Act is outlined. The plan must state the responsibilities of the child, the child's parent or an appropriate adult in lieu of a parent or guardian; state the personal objectives for the child, the child's parent or an appropriate adult; and include such other matters relating to the education, employment, recreation and welfare of the child as are relevant. Provisions for monitoring its implementation and the fulfilment of its conditions are spelt out.

Amongst both practitioners and policy makers in Namibia, there appeared to be significant support for these extensive restorative justice provisions at the time that the

Bill was being consulted upon during 2018 and 2019. However, what is equally true is that the measure of success of restorative justice efforts lies in the (uncertain) future.

At the moment, pending the adoption of the Child Justice Bill, the Criminal Procedure Act No. 51 of 1977 (as amended in 2003) continues to apply. The minimum age of criminal responsibility remains at 7 years, echoing that of South Africa from the time that Namibia was a colony of South Africa. The new legislation would seek to change that. Since 1994, diversion has been possible; currently the two diversion options used are pre-trial community service and referral to a life skills program. The social workers at the Gender Based Violence Police Units are responsible for the assessment of children at the courts, and for providing supervision for pre-trial community service. Other stakeholders involved are officers from the Ministry of Youth responsible for presenting the life skills program. In Namibia, detention of a child refers to either detention at a police station awaiting trial or detention in a prison due to a court order carrying a custodial sentence.

Namibia has made some reasonable progress in the area of juvenile justice despite insufficient resources, poor levels of decentralized services (detention facilities and police cells) and legislative shortcomings.

4 Zimbabwe

Pre-trial diversion was launched in Zimbabwe in 2009 and is currently being implemented in 16 districts. Again, there was capacity-building from neighboring South Africa during the period prior to implementation of diversion, which meant that restorative justice was a stated objective of diversion (National Pre-trial Diversion Committee: Guidelines on Pre-Trial Diversion, undated). A National Pre-trial Diversion Steering Committee was established under the auspices of a high court judge. Initially donor-funded, diversion officers[9] were appointed in the initial five districts selected for the pilot, but the program was taken over by the government in June 2016. Amongst the objectives of the pilot program were: where appropriate, to encourage restoration, restitution or compensation to the victim, thereby bringing closure to both the victim and the offender; to ensure that the child understands the impact of his/her crime on others including the victim, the respective families and the community; and to promote forgiveness of the child for the crimes committed, reconcile the child with the victim and the community, and promote and support rehabilitation and reintegration of the child offender back into the community (National Pre-trial Diversion Committee: Revised Guidelines on Pre-Trial Diversion, 2017: 8).

9 The Diversion Officer is a social worker specifically appointed and trained to manage the various activities of the diversion program.

During the pilot phase, there were a range of diversion options that were available for the diversion committee to recommend: a formal caution; reparation; community service; counselling and/or education; constructive use of leisure time; victim-offender mediation and family group conferencing. However, an evaluation found that the most commonly used forms of diversion are cautions (formal and informal), reparation, counseling and victim-offender mediation (Penal Reform International, 2016). Family group conferences were used in six percent of the diverted cases in the study. Victim-Offender Mediation was described as a key diversion option, to promote restorative justice.

In 2017, revised guidelines for the implementation of pre-trial diversion were agreed upon and adopted. These state that, in practice, the protection of the best interests of the child (the best interests of the child principle is constitutionalized in the 2013 Constitution of the Republic of Zimbabwe in sections 19 and 81) means that the traditional objectives of criminal justice, such as repression/retribution, must give way to rehabilitation and restorative justice objectives in dealing with young people. The Guidelines detail (apart from other diversion measures such as a caution or referral to community services) victim-offender mediation and family group conferencing as possible restorative justice avenues.

> Victim-offender Mediation also called Victim-offender Dialogue is a process that provides interested victims an opportunity to meet their offender, in a safe and structured setting, and engage in a mediated discussion of the crime ... With the assistance of a trained mediator, the victim is able to tell the offender about the crime's physical, emotional and financial impact; to receive answers to lingering questions about the crime and the offender; and to be directly involved in developing a restitution plan for the offender to pay back. During the mediation, the facts of the case, the feelings of the victim and the question of compensation and/or apology are discussed. The objective is to work out, with the assistance of a mediator, an agreement which could consist of an apology, monetary compensation and/or indirect compensation for losses suffered by the victim... The main purpose of the family group conference is to bring together all persons with an interest in the case such as local leaders, church leaders and others who have a stake in the matter. This option may be particularly beneficial in victimless crimes or where the victim is corporate e.g. graffiti, vandalism of public property etc. ... The following should be observed when conducting Family Group Conferencing: ... All interested stakeholders should be present; the Diversion Officer moderates the conference .... (National Pre-trial Diversion Committee: Revised Guidelines on Pre-Trial Diversion, 2017: 33-36)

As a consultant engaging with stakeholders in the lead-up to the adoption of a new Child Justice Act during 2019, however, I observed that many diversion cases were not finalized because of the inability on the part of the child or his or her family to pay compensation to the victim. In my view, restorative justice is not solely about compensation to the victim, and in a resource-poor country such as Zimbabwe, it should not be a bar to completing cases as other forms of restoration could be implemented – such as a formal apology or symbolic restoration. Nevertheless, this understanding was evidently not shared by program implementers, who viewed financial reparation as integral to the restorative justice outcome.

The proposed Child Justice Bill of Zimbabwe is at an advanced stage of preparation prior to it being tabled in Parliament – likely during 2020 (references included here are to a version of the Bill that was debated at a writing retreat attended by stakeholders in December 2019). Restorative justice is allotted several pages in a briefing memorandum developed and endorsed by cabinet in the lead-up to the law-making process (Briefing paper on the development of a Child Justice Act, 2019). One objective of the Bill is to promote rehabilitation and restorative justice principles, and clauses 56-66, which fall in a dedicated part of the chapter on diversion, spell out how family group conferences are supposed to unfold and be conducted. A referral to a family group conference can be effected by a prosecutor, a diversion committee, or a court, having regard to the nature of the offense, the harm suffered by anyone in the community because of the offense, whether the interests of the community and the child would be served by having the offense considered or dealt with in an informal and participative way, and whether a family group conference is particularly beneficial because of the fact that there is no identifiable victim of the offense. With strong local support amongst stakeholders for restorative justice as a key objective of child justice, it is highly likely that these provisions will feature in the final legislation, once adopted. Until then, the minimum age of criminal capacity remains at 7 years, and the general provisions of the Criminal Procedure and Evidence Act (Chapter 9:07) form the basis for arrest, detention, trials and sentencing, subject to the 2017 National Pre-trial Diversion Committee's Revised Guidelines on Pre-Trial Diversion.

Zimbabwe introduced a progressive Constitution in 2013, with a wide array of children's rights, including a provision that detention shall be used only as a last resort and for the shortest appropriate period of time. However, data on the numbers of children deprived of their liberty is not readily available. Incompatibility with the constitutional prohibition on torture and on inhuman and degrading treatment or punishment has led to a Constitutional Court ruling in 2019 that the sentence of juvenile whipping be declared unconstitutional (*S v. Chokuramba* (Justice For Children's Trust Intervening As Amicus Curiae; Zimbabwe Lawyers For Human Rights Intervening As Amicus Curiae) case CCZ 10/19 of 3 April 2019). Finding the judicial sanction of corporal punishment to be in conflict with the constitutional prohibition on inhuman and degrading punishment, the Court said that

> the deliberate and systemic assault with a cane on the buttocks of an individual, inflicted by strangers as a form of punishment authorized by a judicial tribunal, is inherently a demeaning invasion on the inherent dignity of the person punished. It must in the circumstances be degrading and inhuman. It does not become less so because a juvenile might conceivably recover from such assault on his inherent dignity sooner than an adult might in similar circumstances.

Hereby, the Court has removed this as a punishment option which was frequently used in the juvenile justice system. Undoubtedly, this will also foster and support the goal of extending the reach of diversion and alternative community-based sentences.

5 Conclusions

Restorative justice has gained a toehold in the southern African sub-region in child justice legislation and, to an extent, in practice. However, sustaining promising initiatives seems to present challenges, as the South African experience, in particular, shows. Support in practice has wavered, as illustrated by the diminishing use of restorative justice practices, even though they appear in, and are adequately regulated by, legislation. In contrast, commitment to restorative justice in neighboring Namibia and Zimbabwe continues unabated, as evidenced in recently drafted child justice law proposals which continue to be received positively by stakeholders from all quarters at workshops (non-governmental organizations, police authorities, prosecutors and so forth). The reasons for this must necessarily be speculative, but it could be that the ties that restorative justice has to indigenous values is still felt more strongly in these countries, in comparison to South Africa (which is much more populous, too). It could simply be that South African functionaries prefer the 'easier' diversion options which the Child Justice Act provides,[10] as they are less time-consuming and labor intensive.

In this regard, it would be naïve not to reflect on current developments and their impacts on restorative justice. The global pandemic COVID-19 has hit Africa in 2020 as elsewhere, although for reasons that yet have to be fully researched, it may be that its effects might have been experienced differently in comparison to the global north.[11] At

10 The Act provides for a series of orders, such as a 'good behavior order', a 'positive peer association order', and a supervision order (to name three) that can be imposed simply by filling out the prescribed form and adding any conditions. See section 53(1)(a)-(f).

11 Speculatively, this could be because of lower life expectancy rates anyway, since it appears to target the elderly disproportionately.

the time of writing, isolation, confinement and social distancing have become the hallmark of responses to curb the spread of the virus, although this will be, to some extent, progressively eased in order to allow economic activity to resume. Initial indications are that limitations on gatherings will be imposed as part of the efforts to contain the spread of the virus. Of all the countries discussed here, South Africa has experienced the highest infection rate, and the most intensive lockdown provisions.

Restorative justice processes are crucially dependent on encounters; the reintegrative shaming dimension cannot occur in the absence of face-to-face dialogue between offender, victim and families. Skelton (2010) notes that Judge Albie Sachs, formerly of the Constitutional Court, has explained the principles of restorative justice as encompassing the following:

> In the *Dikoko* judgment Sachs J described the following elements of restorative justice: encounter; reparation; reintegration; and participation. [Justice Sachs explained that encounter – which he also refers to as dialogue – enables the victims and offenders to talk about the hurt caused and how the parties are to get on in future].

This is of course impossible under current lockdown regimes, but may prove equally undesirable even after they are relaxed. Given the digital deficit in Africa, replacement of 'in-person' mediated meetings with online versions is simply not a prospect in the foreseeable future. This then poses considerable challenges for 'in-person' meetings, at least in the short to medium term.

There is another caveat: the COVID pandemic has exposed huge flaws and gaps in child protection systems across the continent, rendering children far more vulnerable to violations of their physical and psychological integrity as they remain concealed at home, out of school and as frontline responders are unable to detect or get access to children in need (Williams, 2020). Scaling up the social workforce has become a priority in order to respond to the emerging child protection crisis. For instance, on 11 May 2020, the South African Minister of Social Development announced that 2,800 additional social workers would be appointed with immediate effect to respond to the social dimensions of COVID-19, including reintegrating children in alternative care into families, deinstitutionalization of persons with disabilities, assisting with foster care placements and so forth (Legalbrief, 2020). Predictions abound that the public health crisis is going to become a children's rights crisis (Williams, 2020). The post-COVID period is likely going to see social services geared to addressing the economic devastation and upsurge in child protection requirements that the emergency has caused. This may leave less room for social services aimed at responding to crime.

A third hurdle is the need for reparations to victims as an outcome of conferencing. It has already been noted that in the Zimbabwean context, cases remain open for years due to children being unable to fulfil agreements concerning reparations (albeit that this 'requirement' is not necessarily a cornerstone of restorative justice). With the economic devastation that COVID is wreaking, fulfilment of financial reparations or restitution may be even more arduous than was previously the case.

Nevertheless, the above should not be seen as a call for a return to retributive justice or to repressive punishments, such as corporal punishment or deprivation of liberty. Rather, it should spur the ongoing development of diversion options which are feasible and pragmatic in the changing social environment in which we now live. Cognizant of the need to avoid incarceration at all costs to limit the spread of COVID-19 in institutions, these should be community-based, and draw on indigenous practice and skills.

References

Briefing paper on the development of a Child Justice Act. (2019). (Copy on file with the author).

Centre for Child Law v. Media 24 and others (CCT 216/18) (RSA).

Child Justice Act 75 of 2008 (RSA.).

Criminal Procedure Act 51 of 1977 (as amended in 2003) (RSA.).

Government of the Republic of South Africa. *Annual report on the implementation of the Child Justice Act 2015/2016*. Retrieved from https://www.justice.gov.za/vg/cj/cja-anr-2015-2016.pdf (last accessed 12 August 2021).

Legalbrief. (12 May 2020, Copy on file with author).

National Pre-trial Diversion Committee: Revised Guidelines on Pre-Trial Diversion. (2017). (Copy on file with author).

Penal Reform International. (2016). *Pre-trial Diversion Programme in Zimbabwe end of pilot programme evaluation* (copy on file with the author).

S v. Chokuramba (Justice For Children's Trust Intervening As Amicus Curiae; Zimbabwe Lawyers For Human Rights Intervening As Amicus Curiae) CCZ 10/19 (3 April 2019) (Zim.).

Skelton, A. (2002). Restorative justice as a framework for juvenile justice reform. *British Journal of Criminology*, 42(3), 496-513. doi: 10.1093/bjc/42.3.496.

Skelton, A. (2010). Face to face: the restorative justice jurisprudence of Justice Albie Sachs. *Publiekreg/SA Public Law*, 25(1), 94-107.

Skelton, A. & Batley, M. (2019). *W(h)ither restorative justice in South Africa – an updated status review.* Retrieved from www.rjc.co.za/images/pdf/RestorativeJustice-Monograph2019.pdf (last accessed 9 September 2021).

Skelton, A., Pinnock, D. & Shapiro, R. (1994). *Juvenile justice for South Africa: proposals for policy and legislative change.* Cape Town: University of Cape Town Institute of Criminology

Sloth-Nielsen, J. (2017). Child justice. In T. Boezaart (ed.), *Child law in South Africa* (pp. 677-725). Cape Town: Juta.
Sloth-Nielsen, J. (2018). Towards a new juvenile justice system in Namibia. In M. Brinig (ed.), *International survey of family law* (pp. 205-218). Cambridge: Intersentia.
Sloth-Nielsen, J. & Gallinetti, J. (2011). "Just Say Sorry?" Ubuntu, Africanisation and the Child Justice Act 75 of 2008. *Potchefstroom Electronic Law Review*, 14(4), 63-90. doi: 10.4314/pelj.v14i4.3.
Williams, C. (2020). Deputy Director Child Protection, UNICEF, New York, in an online lecture to LLM students in Leiden, 11 May 2020.

Part III

Local practices and challenges for restorative justice approaches with children

Chapter 9
Introducing restorative practices in the child justice system of Georgia

Maia Chochua

1 Background

Georgia is a country of 3.16, 9 million people that declared its independence from the Soviet Union in 1991 (National Statistics Office of Georgia, 2020). It has a parliamentary form of government with the President serving as head of state. The Ministry of Justice is part of the executive branch of government with the Minister appointed by the Prime Minister with the approval of Parliament.

In more than three decades since Georgia gained its independence from the Soviet Union, efforts to establish a nation built on the rule of law have been made jointly by the state institutions and civil society. The legacy of the Soviet system left the Prosecutor's Office with excessive power over the entire justice system and allowed that office to exert control over nearly every criminal case. The role of a defense attorney in that 'justice' system was limited to that of a negotiator in backroom deals. Under this system, if a deal was struck between a judge, prosecutor and defense attorney, it was delivered in the form of a verdict (Judicial Reform Index Report, 2007). During the early independence years, a new Constitution and new Civil, Criminal and Administrative Codes were adopted and the entire corps of judges was replaced. Sadly, these changes were unable to alter a system that protected the financial interests of the various law-enforcement bodies, and in which neither the rights of the victim nor those of the defendant were fully respected. Corruption was commonplace within the criminal justice system, as well as in all aspects of Georgian life (Taylor & Francis Online, 2009).

Ultimately, the Georgian government initiated a number of democratic reforms to eliminate its communist traditions. Specifically, it took action to combat widespread corruption and organized crime, which received high marks from the World Bank due to its outcome (Eriksson, Interview with Dr. Tamara Kovziridze, 2017). Implementation of a policy of 'zero tolerance' resulted in decreased crime and also virtually eradicated institutionalized corruption (World Bank Report, 2012).

These radical reforms had a downside; however, they gave rise to harsh criminal justice policies that affected the entire population. These policies resulted in prison overcrowding, and human rights abuses in Georgian prisons (OSGF Report Crime and

Excessive Punishment, 2014). Punishment was the only response to young offenders. The initial decision to lower the age of criminal responsibility from 14 to 12 was one of various policies that was highly criticized by civil society and was ultimately rescinded (Human Rights Watch, 2007).

In the last 10 years, Georgia's primary focus has shifted to a liberalization of criminal justice policies. This shift represents a significant change from the approach seen before not only in Georgia but throughout the entire former Soviet Union countries. This is a change that has lead from a repressive approach toward a restorative justice approach.

2 Early efforts toward change

In 2010, a coalition of representatives of the Georgian civil society and the international community, that supported restorative justice approaches, successfully led the Georgian government to boldly move to introduce restorative justice mechanisms for children in conflict with the law. These approaches originally were applied at the pre-court stage only and were accompanied with rehabilitation and resocialization programs at the post-sentencing stage.

The original approaches were introduced through amendments to the Criminal Procedure Code of Georgia and included diversionary and mediation programs for first-time offenders aged 14 to 18 and for a range of serious and less serious offenses. It should be noted that initially, mediation was always a diversionary program.[1] In the initial 3-year period, these approaches were piloted in several cities, for minor offenses at the discretion of public prosecutors. These early years saw tentative steps toward reform, with law-enforcement agencies exercising extreme caution in using these new options. Ultimately, criminal justice system agencies gained confidence in their case selection and implementation of restorative justice solutions. The process was complex and included multiple trainings, motivation of staff and internal monitoring and multidisciplinary cooperation between agencies. The commitment and hard work of the professionals, their belief to change the system, was instrumental in this process.

The goal of these programs was to offer first-time child offenders an opportunity to be diverted from the child justice system and have the opportunity to be released from criminal liability, take responsibility for his/her actions and be offered the chance to participate in the restorative process through victim-offender mediation. As a precondition to participation in the program, the first-time offender needed to be prepared to apologize and reimburse the victim. The program was piloted and

1 Diversion and victim-offender mediation was introduced as one single program, with the possibility of applying diversion without victim-offender mediation, but no possibility of applying mediation without it being diversionary. Only after a few years, restorative justice measures could be applied independently. Currently, victim offender mediation can be applied at various stages of juvenile justice proceedings.

gradually expanded until it became an integral part of the justice system in August 2013. The outcomes of the pilot program allowed decision-makers to improve the program (Annual Report of the Ministry of Justice on Diversion and Mediation, 2014).

Along with the wider implementation of the program came modifications, including the elimination of the requirement for a young offender to apologize as a necessary precondition to participate in the program, the expansion of diversionary and mediation programs to serious offenses and an increased role for the mediator. Instead of a prosecutor, it is the mediator who contacts the victim, offers participation in victim-offender mediation and invites him/her to participate. Since the introduction of these changes, the number of victims consenting to participate in the mediation process has significantly increased (Crime Prevention Centre, 2019).

Five years of experimentation, development of specific regulations and standards, introduction of reform initiatives, accumulation of knowledge through multiple trainings and exchanges and, most importantly, changed attitudes and a willingness among justice professionals and policy-makers resulted in the development and adoption of the Juvenile Justice Code (2015). As a party to the United Nations Convention on the Rights of the Child, which requires State Parties to develop and implement a comprehensive child justice policy in the 'best interests of the child', Georgia was committed to reform its child justice system. Thus, the Minister of Justice, supported by EU4Justice Judiciary Support Technical Assistance Project[2] and UNICEF, moved to draft a new Code (Georgian Media Coverage, 2015). As a result of intensive work – research, drafting, consultations between state institutions and civil society – the Code was adopted in 2015 as a product of consensus between various stakeholders (OSGF, 2018).

Today, these bold steps led to almost 4,500 juveniles and young adults having participated in diversion-mediation programs, resulting in a recidivism rate that has never been over 16 percent, and approximately 60 percent of victims receiving financial restitution following their participation in restorative justice processes (Prosecutor's Office Analytical Report on Diversion and Mediation, 2019). From the individual young person's perspective, it has meant a chance to rethink, take responsibility, apologize and reconcile with the victim, find peace and continue on with their lives (EU Delegation to Georgia Press Release, 2018).

Unfortunately, restorative justice programs are only available in Georgia in case if the offender is a child (14-18) or a young adult (18-21). Neither legislation nor practice offers access to restorative justice programs to child victims in cases with an adult offender. Currently, professionals in Georgia are developing new initiatives, piloting several projects, for the legislation as well as practice, to fill this gap.

2 EU Criminal Justice Reform support information, retrieved from https://ec.europa.eu/budget/euprojects/support-criminal-justice-sector-georgia_en (last accessed 10 May 2020).

In 2020, the Minister of Justice reflected on these reforms at the International Conference on Child-Friendly Justice in Europe and said the following:

> Adoption of a separate Juvenile Justice Code in June 2015 served both for changing institutions and changing the institutional culture – the Code introduced an entirely new philosophy of Juvenile Justice where application of the non-custodial measures to children in conflict with law was made a default and criminal sanction an exceptional rule. In 2019, only 10 accused juveniles were placed in the penitentiary system of Georgia (while in 2010 and 2011 their number was 31 and 46 respectively). The tangible results are visible in case of convicted juveniles as well – here the number in 2019 was 37 (compared to 2010 and 2011 – 160 and 146 respectively). – Minister of Justice of Georgia, Thea Tsulukiani. (Statement Minister of Justice, 2020)

In promoting restorative justice in Georgia, we have seen how transformation works, how individuals can be reintegrated back into the society and how victims of crimes can have their voices heard and become the best supporters of young offenders. The restorative justice process has given a measure of peace and replaced isolation with rehabilitation. Considerable number of criminal justice professionals are now convinced that this is the only way forward if our society is to be safe. Watching these programs work is both encouraging and inspiring and serves as a driving force to continue these reforms, even under difficult circumstances. Violations are still occurring at the investigation phase, there is a lack of infrastructure and human resources as well as lack of awareness and public support in favor of restorative justice. Changes are significant and child justice practitioners seem to be convinced that they are doing the right thing, and there is no alternative to carrying on with the reforms.

3 The Georgian Juvenile Justice Code and its implementation

Since January 2016, the Juvenile Justice Code of Georgia has been supplemented by additional decrees and orders by the Minister of Justice. These actions have defined the rules of diversion-mediation program, established standards for quality and procedures for mediators involved in victim-offender mediation and regulated the operation of restorative justice systems. There are several pieces of secondary legislation that define the scope and actions of various agencies in cases when coordination and cooperation is required. These operations include victim-offender mediation. The Georgian model of victim-offender mediation includes a conference at the end of the process. Diversionary measures are always accompanied by rehabilitation and reintegration programs for young people. Key principles of the diversion-mediation program defined in the secondary regulations issued by the Minister of Justice are voluntariness, proportionality, confidentiality, prohibition of stigmatization and prioritization of the best interest of a child.

The Juvenile Justice Code of Georgia is based on the idea that restorative justice uses a multidisciplinary approach that includes professionals involved in the system united around the best interest of a child. The Code requires specialization of professionals, the use of detention as a last resort, and introduced alternative measures and alternative sentencing mechanisms, individual approaches to children in conflict with the law, provisions for child victims, witnesses of crime and children participating in administrative proceedings. The Code is in line with the UNCRC and ensures that the best interests of the child are a priority in the justice system, which means that traditional objectives of criminal justice, such as punishment and retribution, are replaced by rehabilitation and restorative justice when dealing with child offenders. It also means that the best interest of an individual child will always prevail against any other purpose of criminal justice, including public safety or general prevention.

Some of the safeguards enshrined in the Juvenile Justice Code are the prohibition of all forms of discrimination, the right to harmonious development, proportionality of the sanctions imposed, primacy of the most lenient means and alternative measures, imprisonment as a measure of last resort, prohibition of delay in child justice procedures, revocation of previous conviction immediately after serving a sentence and strict privacy rules. Some of the procedural rights include access to free legal aid for all defendants, incarcerated individuals and victims as well as insolvent witnesses. Other provisions are ensured as well, such as access to all information or correspondence related to the offender's development, an interpreter, a legal or procedural representative at every stage, consular assistance as well as the involvement of psychologists and social workers when necessary at every stage of the proceedings. Additionally, the Code provides for pre-sentence reports, individual sentence reports and biographic and psychological social assessment reports for diversion and assessments for early release consideration made by multidisciplinary groups.

The Juvenile Justice Code prohibits interrogations at night and restricts the use of force, special means and firearms. Fines are limited to amounts within the personal income of a juvenile. Jury trials are restricted since it is impossible to ensure specialization of jury members and privacy safeguards. The Code requires full separation of juveniles from the adult inmates in detention facilities and provides for access to medical services, education and rehabilitation services, contact with family and the functioning of an early conditional release system, including preparation for release and after care, for young people in prison. A significant expansion that was realized since the adoption of the Code is the application of diversion-mediation as well as other procedural rights to young offenders aged 18 to 21.

According to the Georgian legislation, victim-offender mediation can be applied before trial, by the prosecutor, in combination with diversion, at the judicial review stage when the judge can return a case to the prosecutor and refer it for diversion-mediation program, and at the sentencing stage as an additional measure. Since 2019, the Ministry of Justice has piloted a program offering victim-offender mediation to convicted persons, both in prison and under probation, as well as to former convicts as part of rehabilitation and resocialization service – the latter is available both for juveniles and adults and has no restriction on the category of crime involved. The initiation of this program is essential for the further development of restorative justice in Georgia with victim-offender mediation as a stand-alone program.

Even though the use of diversion and mediation programs was already widespread by 2015, the new Juvenile Justice Code provided more safeguards for their effective implementation. Before the adoption of the Code, prosecutors were obliged to submit a reason for application of diversion. Under the new Code, the prosecutor has to consider application of diversion-mediation as the default choice for eligible cases, with any denial requiring justification. The decision to deny access to diversion-mediation can be appealed, first before a superior prosecutor and later before a court. The court, either based on the appeal on its own initiative or on a motion of a party, can return a case to the prosecutor with the instruction to apply for diversion-mediation. This change strengthened the role of a judge and placed effective safeguards against prosecutorial abuse of discretion. It has resulted in a higher number of diversions (mostly through mediation). This served as one of the reasons for the higher percentage of diversions-mediation processes compared with commenced criminal prosecutions that ended with sentences (Crime Prevention Centre, 2019).

Diversion-mediation program is implemented through the following procedures:[3] once a prosecutor receives a file and makes a preliminary decision to apply for diversion; the prosecutor meets with the young offender and their legal representative and presents the concept of diversion, conditions and procedures. If there is consent to diversion, the prosecutor then meets with the victim and provides general information regarding diversion-mediation program. The prosecutor informs the victim that a mediator will get in contact and will provide further details about the program. Subsequently, the prosecutor officially initiates the diversion procedure and refers the case to the Crime Prevention Centre, Enforcement of Non-Custodial Sentences and Probation Agency, of the Ministry of Justice to assign a mediator and social worker. The social worker has ten working days to prepare a comprehensive assessment on

3 Legal Framework regulating Diversion and Mediation Program; Juvenile Justice Code, General Conditions and rules of diversion and mediation program; Methodology for the preparation of the individual assessment report and its standards; Mediation rules and supporting documents; Standards of psycho – social rehabilitation service providers working with juveniles in conflict with the law (available in Georgian). Retrieved from http://diversion.ge/?action=page&p_id=803&lang=geo (last accessed 10 May 2020). English translation available upon request.

biographic, psychological and social factors and to draft an individual assessment report. Along with other circumstances, the social worker has to analyze risk factors of possible recidivism. Meanwhile, the assigned mediator works with the victim to well inform him/her on the concept and benefits of participation in the mediation process. The mediator may also recommend against further participation in a mediation based on unique factors in the case. In case mediator believes that the process might be counterproductive for either party, he /she will have to provide reasoning on this. Diversion procedures may proceed even without mediation.

After receiving the individual assessment report from the social worker, the mediator then has ten working days to meet with the parties and prepare them for the mediation conference. This preparation stage also includes a preliminary agreement on the conditions and possible obligations that the young offender has to undertake as part of the diversion agreement. Finally, the mediation conference takes place at a neutral location – The Mediation House. Participants in the mediation conference include the young person and their legal representative – meaning a family member, a social worker, or their lawyer (if there is one) – and the victim. The prosecutor and the social worker may also attend the mediation conference, but their attendance is not common.

The mediation conference is led by the mediator who establishes seating arrangements, the speaking order and timing as well as ensures that all participants have the opportunity to speak openly and sincerely. The mediator has the responsibility of maintaining the good order of the conference and enabling all participants to speak freely. Should there be any difficulties, the mediator can call for a break and meet with participants individually before reconvening the session. The mediation concludes with a signed agreement outlining the obligations of the parties that may last for one to twelve months. The social worker is responsible for ensuring that the young person meets the obligations under the agreement. Along with obligations, the offender is also offered the opportunity to participate in educational or vocational activities based on their individual needs. In the case of a serious breach of the agreement, the prosecutor is entitled to suspend the diversion-mediation agreement and to refer a case to regular court proceedings.

At the court stage, mediation can be requested either by the victim or the offender, or the case can be referred to the Crime Prevention Centre, Enforcement of Non-Custodial Sentences and Probation Agency by the court or another involved institution such as the prosecutor's office or the penitentiary department. Mediation procedures and standards for mediators are similar to those applied at the pretrial stage for diversionary purposes.

The results of the new law and regulations are clear – in 2011 there were 80 diversionary orders with 28 successful mediation conferences (concluded by an agreement), while in 2019 there were 437 child diversionary orders and 360 young adult diversionary orders with 408 victim-offender mediations and 328 completed agreements (Analytical Report of the Prosecutor's Office, 2019).

The total number of diversionary measures (juveniles and young adults) since 2010 is 4,430. Sixty percent of these cases were resolved through victim-offender mediation. For the total number of diverted cases, the re-offense rate varies between 9 to 16 percent (UNICEF Press Release, 2017).

4 Structural resources

Mediators in Georgia are affiliated with the Agency for Crime Prevention, Probation and Enforcement of Non-Custodial Sentences under the Ministry of Justice. This Agency was created through the merger in 2019 of the Crime Prevention Centre (established in 2010) and the Probation Agency. However, the Mediation Department functions as a separate unit, with seventeen full-time positions. Mediators are required to complete special induction training courses at the Ministry of Justice Training Centre. Course subjects in this training include adult and child criminal justice (theory and practice), restorative justice, victim-offender mediation and the psychology of victims and offenders. Practical training on conflict resolution and facilitation of communication are also included in these courses. Upon completion of training, examinations are administered and successful candidates are required to participate in an internship with an experienced mediator, who also serves as a mentor. The mentor must submit a positive evaluation of the new candidate before final approval is given to become a member of the Mediation Department.

5 Monitoring, evaluation and challenges

Continued training is also provided to a wide range of practitioners in the criminal justice system, in individual and multidisciplinary formats. In addition, judges, prosecutors, police officers, investigators, social workers, defense lawyers, probation and penitentiary officers and mediators have various platforms for cooperation and coordination at both the national and local levels. These exchanges allow practitioners to build networks for team work, as well as to harmonize practices and discuss challenges to ensure that the system operates in the best interests of children. An Action Plan, coordinated and monitored by the Criminal Justice System Reform Inter-Agency Coordination Council, affiliated with the Ministry of Justice and its working group on child justice, guides this work (Ministry of Justice, 2009). It ensures that reforms are planned and carried out in a coordinated manner between the state institutions and in cooperation with civil society.

There are internal monitoring mechanisms developed by the criminal justice agencies that supervise the work of professionals and ensure standards are maintained. Annual statistics and program reports are prepared by the Prosecutor's Office (Annual Report and Statistics of the Prosecutor' Office, 2020). The Crime Prevention Centre,

Enforcement of Non-Custodial Sentences and Probation Agency of the Ministry of Justice publishes annual reports that include both narrative and statistical information on diversion-mediation programs (Annual Reports on Diversion and Mediation Program, 2017-2020). Mediators have biannual evaluations and regularly attend supervision workshops, to discuss practice, open issues and complex cases, led by the national and European experts.

While the Ministry of Justice and the Crime Prevention Centre, Enforcement of Non-Custodial Sentences and Probation Agency have developed internal monitoring mechanisms, there is still a need to develop external monitoring mechanisms and conduct in-depth evaluative studies in order to make evidence-based decisions drawn on thorough analyses. The European Union support mechanisms provide funding opportunities to nongovernmental organizations to monitor developments in this area. However, it is important that the State has its own resources to fund external monitoring schemes. The most recent report had been prepared by a coalition of nongovernmental organizations funded by the European Union Delegation to Georgia (Civil Society Organizations' Study on Juvenile Diversion and Diversion and Mediation Program in Georgia, 2018). The report offers a comparison of domestic legislation regulating the diversion-mediation process with international standards and practices, description of types of diversionary programs, overview of diversion-mediation practice, data on first contact of a minor with the justice system, overview of services offered, analysis of diversion-mediation agreements and quality of individual assessment reports, and description of quality assurance system, study findings and recommendations.

One of the important aspects of the diversion-mediation process is offering rehabilitation and resocialization services to child offenders according to their needs. Currently such services are available, but the majority of them are funded by international partners, and in other cases, social workers need to search and find one among various service provider organizations to find such services. It is important that the State provides funding and ensures access to such services, trainings and treatments that young offender and victims might need.

Even though Georgia has made significant advances, challenges remain. The Juvenile Justice Code requires mandatory specialization for practitioners in child justice proceedings and hundreds of trainings have been organized. However, this is a long-term process and there is still much to be done to fully sensitize all criminal justice agency representatives to child-friendly justice (Civil Society Organizations' Report on Juvenile Specialization, 2018). The civil society organizations report that most of the breaches of the procedural rights of young people take place at the stage of investigation, whereas it is of utmost importance that first contact with children is handled in a proper manner and according to the standards set out in the Code. There seems to be a consensus between the state and nonstate actors that there is insufficient vocational and educational programs for children in conflict with the law making it difficult for the involved specialists and requires a lot of creativity to find appropriate services or programs to offer.

Also, looking at the effectiveness of the diversion-mediation program, it is clear that its scope of application could still be widened, which could be achieved, for instance, by not limiting its application to first-time offenders.

6 European Union and Georgia

Child justice reform efforts in Georgia have been supported and recognized by the European Union Delegation as one of the most successful examples of systemic cooperation.

> The European Union has been a staunch supporter for justice reforms in Georgia for the last two decades, including the introduction of a Restorative Justice Mechanism. The protection of children's rights is a core element of EU-Georgia cooperation in the justice sector. The adoption of the Juvenile Justice Code in 2015 that complies with all major international standards was a huge step forward and reiterated the obligation of the State to provide care and protection of children from violence and stigma. It provided a solid ground for increased application of restorative justice practices for children in conflict with the law and young offenders. Today we are happy to observe that since 2010 over 4,000 children and young offenders have been diverted and most of them participated in the restorative justice processes of victim-offender mediation. Restorative processes provide a response to the needs of victims and studies confirm that restorative justice also helps victims repair their harm. A decreased re-offence rate in Georgia is evidence of the fact that restorative justice strengthens individuals and helps them choose not to engage further in criminal activities. – Carl Hartzell, European Union Ambassador to Georgia (Handbook on University and Professional Teaching of Restorative Justice, 2019).

The child justice system in 2020 is drastically different from that in 2010. There are several key factors that led to this progress. The Ministry of Justice, through significant assistance from international partner organizations and cooperation with the civil society, started to implement a Juvenile Justice Reform Strategy, with an associated action plan. As often occurs, these changes were spearheaded by inspired, motivated and hardworking practitioners whose efforts were strongly supported by international partners, including the European Union and UNICEF. Early experiments with diversion-mediation programs were often met with astonishment among criminal justice practitioners who had never conceived of practices other than punishment and isolation as a solution to child offending. It took a combination of training sessions on child justice law, international standards and the psychological aspects of child development to convince the skeptics. "I wish more diversions are carried out through victim-offender mediation. Children radically change during the victim-offender mediation conference. Sometimes, their apology is much more powerful than anything else." – Prosecutor from Akhaltsikhe, Georgia spoke to a journalist for the publication prepared by the EU-Funded Project.

Equally effective was educating practitioners on European and international developments in the field through conferences in Georgia with recognized experts coupled with study visits to European justice systems. These visits exposed Georgian practitioners to real-life examples of how restorative justice works. As a result, Georgians became members of the European Forum for Restorative Justice and the European Restorative Justice Policy Network, benefiting from the valuable intellectual resources of the Network and its experts.

Two experts, Justice Renate Winter and Professor Ivo Aertsen, should be individually recognized for their long-term commitment and motivation in assisting Georgia to reach this point in its child justice reform effort. They were a source of inspiration and role models for this work in Georgia (Video interview with Professor Ivo Aertsen). This progress could not have been made and the challenges could not be met without them. While they have led the work, countless others – Georgians and international supporters – have helped change lives and make a true difference in Georgian society.

Georgia's success in implementing child justice reforms has raised interest not only in the Caucasus region but also beyond and has brought practitioners to Georgia to see these reforms for themselves. In 2019, Georgia, with the support of the European Union and in cooperation with the European Forum for Restorative Justice, organized the 'International Conference on Restorative Justice towards a Safe Society'. Delegations from nine countries met with international experts and heard speakers from eight countries, generating significant interest among conference participants (Video on International Conference on Restorative Justice, 2019).[4] These types of international conferences, which expose participants to the latest international developments in the field of restorative justice, create significant opportunities to expand the reach of new ideas and practices to different countries and to Georgia (Materials of the International Conference on Restorative Justice, 2019).

The European Union supported the Ministry of Justice in its effort to develop a special certified course for mediators, including the newly completed *Handbook on teaching*

4 International Conference on Restorative Justice 'Towards Safe Society' organized by EU4Justice Judiciary Support Project in cooperation with the European Forum for Restorative Justice. Video available at: https://drive.google.com/drive/folders/1Rc4lv-OwktDABgPUy5X6fle4FqITaIfd?fbclid=IwAR0qgUnyIxnE-FJEQFJmLFJ2_9OB2VAwUOQbH6yLjoPJornaspfCZ-kL7wU (last accessed 10 May 2021).

restorative justice at the universities and professional training institutions. Training of trainers was delivered for university professors involved and practitioner trainers.

EU Ambassador, Carl Hartzell says in his foreword to the *Handbook on university and professional teaching of restorative justice*:

> The application of Restorative Justice is rapidly growing throughout Europe. We acknowledge Georgia's increased approximation to European standards and the willingness of state institutions to further develop restorative justice in Georgia. Today, restorative justice practices are being successfully piloted for adults and EU supports the Ministry of Justice with the development of further legislation.
>
> It requires a societal transformation to replace a conventional punitive approach with restorative, rehabilitative measures, including among professionals and the general public. I am therefore pleased to present the Handbook for Teaching Restorative Justice to key faculties in universities – including law, social work, psychology, and journalism – as well as to judges, prosecutors, social workers, mediators, police, penitentiary and probation officers. This Handbook seeks to assist professors and trainers to acquire good knowledge of the history of restorative justice, its international regulations and development – including the development that has taken place in Georgia – the understanding of victims, offenders, psycho-social factors, and models of restorative justice, its interaction with society at large, media and community involvement. I hope that it will make an important contribution to the further integration of restorative and rehabilitative measures into the justice system for the benefit of a safe society.

7 Current planning

The Georgia Ministry of Justice is currently working in close collaboration with the European Union Judiciary Support Project to draft a chapter on restorative justice to be included in the Criminal Procedure Code as well as making amendments to the Juvenile Justice Code. The aim of these pieces of legislation would be to encourage mediation for a young victim, adult offenders as well as child offenders in a more direct way (apart from as a diversion-mediation program) and in different crime categories. The chapter on restorative justice would also include the overall restorative justice principles.

Meanwhile, the Ministry of Justice plans to continue piloting the victim-offender mediation program for young and adult convicted persons. The Ministry of Justice, with EU support, organized and plans to organize more workshops and trainings on restorative justice in general as well as referral skills for the respective professionals to encourage more referrals. Georgia will continue to celebrate the international week of restorative justice in November that coincides with the introduction of the diversion-mediation program in Georgia, which has already become a good tradition and platform for gathering professionals, decision-makers and civil society organizations to analyze past year challenges and achievements and present and discuss innovations. This occasion has also become an effective motivator to encourage practitioners to continue to refer cases by awarding them for their distinguished role in implementing the diversion-mediation program (Annual Conference 'Tbilisi Mediation Days', 2018).

Not surprisingly, child-friendly justice became a major focus of the Georgian Presidency of the Council of Europe in 2020. Georgia presently chairs the Committee of Ministers of the Council of Europe and, in this framework, the Council of Europe and the Georgian Presidency of the Committee of Ministers jointly organized an online event 'Child-Friendly Justice in Europe – Participation and Restorative Justice' on Tuesday, 12 May 2020.[5]

The Minister of Justice of Georgia, Thea Tsulukiani said:

> The Ministry of Justice is currently setting up new Child Referral Mechanism and Referral Centre. Creation and starting of the operation of a Child Referral Mechanism and Referral Centre in January 2020 was an important step forward in realizing the philosophy of child-friendly justice – the mechanism provides non-criminal responses to offenders under 14 whereas it plays a role of first and second degree crime prevention for those above this age. Major competences of the Child Referral Centre are:
> - Coordination of the identification process of children with difficult/antisocial behavior by different agencies and relevant procedures;
> - Assessment of child conditions and individual needs;
> - Creation of family-type school;
> - Inclusion of the child in the relevant programs/services;
> - Monitoring and supervision of participation of a child in the appropriate services/programs. (COE International Conference 'Child-Friendly Justice in Europe –Minister of Justice of Georgia')

Moreover, the Ministry of Education, through EU support, is developing a school mediation program, under the guidance from the Chair of the European Forum for Restorative Justice, Mr. Tim Chapman. The EU is working closely with leading Universities in Georgia to assist in designing courses on restorative justice. A special training course on restorative justice is being developed for judges and prosecutors.

5 'Child-Friendly Justice in Europe – Participation and Restorative Justice' Conference concept note and programme. Retrieved from https://rm.coe.int/concept-note-and-programme-en/16809e5053 (last accessed 12 May 2020).

These efforts by the government are supplemented by programs that raise awareness on restorative justice among professional groups, universities and the general public. Practitioners continue to share experiences and best practices on a regular basis throughout the country. Civic education and increased public awareness of the benefits of restorative justice are also key parts of current planning efforts. These include publishing stories, producing videos and delivering public lectures (International Conference on Restorative Justice 'Towards Safe Society', 2019). According to practicing mediators, the biggest challenge for them is convincing victims to participate in the victim-offender mediation process. According to the latest figures (as of 2019), mediation was conducted in 55 percent of eligible cases, in which there was an identifiable victim (Annual Report on Diversion and Mediation, 2019). Mediators, bearing in mind key principle of voluntary participation, use a mix of creativity and hard work to motivate victims to participate in these programs and help 'spread the word' about the benefits of these mediations. The challenges and needs often seem endless – more services, more trainings, more offenders and victims involved in the process. But there is now also a more certain stream of individuals ready and willing to make restorative justice work in Georgia. This path leads only forward to a better life for young and old alike.

References

'Child-Friendly Justice in Europe – Participation and Restorative Justice' Conference concept note and programme. Retrieved from https://rm.coe.int/concept-note-and-programme-en/16809e5053 (last accessed 12 May 2020).

Analyzes of the Diversion and Mediation Program as of 2019 prepared by the Prosecutor's Office (available in Georgian). Retrieved from http://pog.gov.ge/uploads/429f65a7-ganrideba-2019-weli-converted.pdf (last accessed 10 May 2021).

Prosecutor's Office Analytical Report on Diversion and Mediation, 2019. Retrieved from https://pog.gov.ge/uploads/429f65a7-ganrideba-2019-weli-converted.pdf (last accessed 5 August 2021).

Annual Conference 'Tbilisi Mediation Days'. (2018). Conference materials and Programme. Retrieved from https://tbilisimediationdays2018.sched.com/event/IwF3/restorative-justice (last accessed 12 May 2020).

Annual Report and Statistics Prepared by the Prosecutor's Office of Georgia. (2020). *Report of the prosecutor general.* Retrieved from https://pog.gov.ge/uploads/746d8d16-Annual-Report-of-the-General-Prosecutor-compressed-1.pdf (last accessed 10 May 2021).

Annual Report of the Ministry of Justice on Diversion and Mediation. (2014). *Annual report of the crime prevention, enforcement of non-custodial sentences and probation agency of the ministry of justice* (available in Georgia). Retrieved from http://diversion.ge/res/files/52/Diversion%20Report%202014.pdf (last accessed 10 May 2021).

Annual Report on Diversion – Mediation (2019). *Prepared by the Crime Prevention Centre of the Ministry of Justice of Georgia* (available in English language). Retrieved from https://drive.google.com/file/d/1sh6IEUWzYqCH2Xx-QjJhcNQFiSPGw7Ka/view (last accessed 10 May 2021).

Annual Reports on Diversion and Mediation Program. (2017-2020). *Annual reports on the implementation of diversion and mediation program prepared by the crime prevention centre, probation and enforcement of non-custodial sentences* (available in English). Retrieved from http://diversion.ge/?action=page&pid=51&lang=eng&fbclid=IwAR20kTRAYh5e-u58ZKar4gprwDCj2lfW8WxlmwjxiFcAKZFayJ6v40lLTkc (last accessed 10 May 2021).

Eriksson, F. (2017). *The rapid economic liberalization and ruthless fight against corruption in Georgia – Interview with Dr. Tamara Kovziridze.* Retrieved from www.cmi.no/publications/6145-the-rapid-economic-liberalisation-and-fight (last accessed 10 May 2021).

EU Ambassador to Georgia, Carl Hartzell's foreword to the Handbook on University and Professional Teaching of Restorative Justice prepared by the EU4Justice Judiciary Support Project. (2020) Georgian version available at: https://drive.google.com/file/d/1PXglX0SIe1Uzxg21YvqPCrG_gaBem06f/view?fbclid=IwAR3bh9F71uNYQZF1lLGXjTXOy9D7c8dXYhuwbe8aV7noDfuEluYbCzsFjEY (last accessed 10 May 2021).

EU Criminal Justice Reform Support Information. Retrieved from https://ec.europa.eu/budget/euprojects/support-criminal-justice-sector-georgia_en (last accessed 10 May 2021).

EU Delegation to Georgia Press Release. (2018). Press release on the occasion of Minister of Justice, EU and UNICEF celebrating 3,000 youth who benefitted from revised Juvenile Justice Code in Georgia. Retrieved from https://eeas.europa.eu/delegations/georgia/53087/node/53087_pl (last accessed 10 May 2021).

Georgian Media Coverage. (2015). Foreign experts say Georgia's Juvenile Justice Code is 'innovative'. Retrieved from https://agenda.ge/en/news/2015/2548 (last accessed 10 May 2021).

Human Rights Watch. (2007). Report on Georgia: lowering the age of criminal responsibility flouts international standards. Retrieved from www.hrw.org/news/2007/06/10/georgia-lowering-age-criminal-responsibility-flouts-international-standards (last accessed 10 May 2021).

International Conference on Restorative Justice "Towards Safe Society". (2019). International Conference on Restorative Justice "Towards Safe Society" organized by EU4Justice Judiciary Support Project in cooperation with the European Forum for Restorative Justice. Interviews with key note speakers available at: www.facebook.com/EU4JusticeJudiciary/videos/645269859271684/?__tn__=%2Cd%2CP-

R&eid=ARCzq8A8kgZWO3jhEbM7lOeRIilx_idsr5yguQ9LS-PZY7rHeJQ4APzIHuE D93TQ3T9VKwh3Pu7a6o8r (last accessed 12 May 2020).

Introduction of the diversion and victim-offender mediation as one program, with the possibility of applying diversion without victim-offender mediation, though no possibility of applying mediation independently, was always source of confusion and misunderstanding among practitioners. Only after years, restorative justice measures could be applied independently. Maia Chochua 2021.

Judicial Reform Index Report Prepared by ABA ROL. (2007). Retrieved from www.americanbar.org/content/dam/aba/directories/roli/georgia/georgia_lpri_volume_ii_11_2007.pdf?fbclid=IwAR2AES8XfPlGrKme9ftw5bpaDwYTEdYaIYzOPjTSPue4hdvsRXAlEIGYSVE (last accessed 10 May 2021).

Juvenile Justice Code of Georgia (available in English). Retrieved from https://matsne.gov.ge/en/document/download/2877281/0/en/pdf (last accessed 10 May 2021).

Kukhianidze, A. (2009). *Corruption and organized crime in Georgia before and after the 'Rose Revolution'*. Retrieved from www.tandfonline.com/doi/abs/10.1080/02634930903043709?journalCode=ccas20& (last accessed 10 May 2021).

Legal Framework regulating Diversion and Mediation Program; Juvenile Justice Code, General Conditions and rules of diversion and mediation program; Methodology for the preparation of the individual assessment report and its standards; Mediation rules and supporting documents; Standards of psycho-social rehabilitation service providers working with juveniles in conflict with the law (available in Georgian). Retrieved from http://diversion.ge/?action=page&p_id=803&lang=geo (last accessed 10 May 2021). English translation available upon request.

Materials of the International Conference on Restorative Justice. (2019). International Conference on Restorative Justice "Towards Safe Society" organized by EU4Justice Judiciary Support Project in cooperation with the European Forum for Restorative Justice. Presentations and other materials available at: https://drive.google.com/drive/folders/19dwF_PB1GcqlfunHIyYdNxUzu0D3dtvU?fbclid=IwAR0qgUnyIxnE-FJEQFJmLFJ2_9OB2VAwUOQbH6yLjoPJornaspfCZ-kL7wU (last accessed 10 May 2021).

Ministry of Justice. (2009). Ministry of Justice information regarding Criminal Justice Reform Strategy and Action Plan. Retrieved from www.justice.gov.ge/Ministry/Index/237 (last accessed 10 May 2021).

National Statistics Office of Georgia. (2020). Retrieved from www.geostat.ge/en/modules/categories/316/population-and-demography (last accessed 10 May 2021).

Open Society Georgian Foundation. (2018). *The need for improving child access to justice in Georgia*. Retrieved from http://osgf.ge/wp-content/uploads/2018/09/Angarishi-A4_-Child_ENG.pdf (pg.2 Juvenile justice reform as a progressive part of child access to justice) (last accessed 10 May 2021).

Report Crime and Excessive Punishment. (2014). *The prevalence and causes of human rights abuse in Georgia's prisons*. Retrieved from www.osgf.ge/files/2015/Publication/Final_Report_ENG.pdf (last accessed 10 May 2020; 10 May 2021).

Research on the Specialization of Professionals in Juvenile Justice System prepared by the 'Georgian Centre of Psychosocial and Medical Rehabilitation of Torture Victims' (GCRT) with the partner organization 'Rehabilitation Initiative for Vulnerable Groups' (RIVG) through EU funding. The research is focused on one of the priority directions of criminal justice reform strategy, such as establishment of selection criteria for professionals involved in juvenile justice system, their specialization and continuous training. (2018) Retrieved from http://gcrt.ge/uploads/publications_doc/114_1.pdf (last accessed 10 May 2021).

Statement Minister of Justice. (2020). International Conference 'Child-Friendly Justice in Europe – Participation and Restorative Justice' Minister of Justice of Georgia statement. Retrieved from https://rm.coe.int/statement-minister-of-justice-georgia/16809e4f67 (last accessed 12 and 13 May 2020).

Statistics on Diversion and Mediation Program. (2019). Prepared by the Crime Prevention Centre of the Ministry of Justice (available in English). Retrieved from https://drive.google.com/file/d/1sh6IEUWzYqCH2Xx-QjJhcNQFiSPGw7Ka/view (last accessed 31 August 2020).

Study on Juvenile Diversion and Diversion-Mediation Programme in Georgia prepared in the framework of the project 'Improving Secondary Crime Prevention Process for Juveniles and Children in Conflict with the Law in Georgia', funded by the European Union and implanted by the 'Georgian Centre of Psychosocial and Medical Rehabilitation of Torture Victims' (GCRT) in cooperation with the partner organizations 'Rehabilitation Initiative for Vulnerable Groups' (RIVG) and 'Civil Development Agency' (CIDA). (2018) Retrieved from www.rivg.ge/media/1001537/2018/03/29/232152dd2374aea097770853801dba69.pdf (last accessed 10 May 2021).

UNICEF Press Release. (2017). *The rate of committing a crime by juveniles has considerably dropped as a result of restorative justice and diversion*. Retrieved from www.unicef.org/georgia/press-releases/rate-committing-crime-juveniles-has-considerably-dropped-result-restorative-justice (last accessed 10 May 2021).

Video interview, on restorative justice reform initiatives undertaken by Georgia, with Ivo Aertsen, Professor Emeritus of the Leuven University, Expert of the EU4Justice Judiciary Support Project. Retrieved from www.youtube.com/watch?v=TDIw2eFhw2Y (last accessed 10 May 2021).

Video on International Conference on Restorative Justice. (2019). International Conference on Restorative Justice "Towards Safe Society" organized by EU4Justice Judiciary Support Project in cooperation with the European Forum for Restorative Justice. Video available at: https://drive.google.com/drive/folders/1Rc4lv-OwktDABg

PUy5X6fle4FqITaIfd?fbclid=IwAR0qgUnyIxnE-FJEQFJmLFJ2_9OB2VAwUOQbH6yLjoPJornaspfCZ-kL7wU (last accessed 10 May 2021).

World Bank Report. (2012). Fighting corruption in public services chronicling Georgia's reforms. Retrieved from http://documents.worldbank.org/curated/en/518301468256183463/pdf/664490PUB0EPI0065774B09780821394755.pdf (last accessed 10 May 2020).

Also consulted

Chapman, T. & Törzs, E. (eds.). (2018). *Connecting people to restore just relations. Practice guide on values and standards for restorative justice practices*. Leuven: European Forum for Restorative Justice.

Christie, N. (1977). Conflicts as property. *British Journal of Criminology*, 17, 1-15. doi: 10.1093/oxfordjournals.bjc.a046783.

Miers, D. & Aertsen, I. (eds.). (2012). *Studies in criminology and forensic sciences regulating restorative justice a comparative study of legislative provision in European countries*. Frankfurt am Main: Verlag für Polizeiwissenschaft.

Miers, D. & Willemsens, J. (2004). *Mapping restorative justice – developments in 25 European countries*. Leuven: European Forum for Victim-Offender Mediation and Restorative Justice.

Zehr, H. (1990). *Changing lenses: a new focus for crime and justice*. Scottdale: Herald Press.

Zehr, H. (2002). *The little book of restorative justice*. Intercourse: Good Books.

International and European instruments

Council Europe – European Commission for the Efficiency of Justice (CEPEJ). (2007). Guidelines for a better implementation of the existing recommendation concerning mediation in penal matters.

Council of Europe Recommendation CM/Rec(2018)8 of the Committee of Ministers to member States concerning restorative justice in criminal matters.

European Union Directive 2012/29/EU of the European Parliament and of the Council of 25 October 2012 establishing minimum standards on the rights, support and protection of victims of crime, and replacing Council Framework Decision 2001/220/JHA.

UN ECOSOC Resolution 2002/12 on Basic principles on the use of restorative justice programmes in criminal matters.

National laws and regulations

Decree on Mediation for Adult Convicts.

Decree on the Operation of the Diversion-Mediation Programme for Juveniles.

Juvenile Justice Code 2015.
National Regulation of Mediation.
Rules of Procedure and Working Documents for Mediators Involved in Mediation and Diversion Programme for Juveniles.

Chapter 10

Restorative justice and children's rights in Aotearoa New Zealand

Convergence and divergence

Andrea Părosanu and Nessa Lynch

1 Introduction

This chapter considers how two conceptual frameworks or ways of thinking (restorative justice and children's rights) converge and diverge in their application to children in conflict with the law. Our enquiry is sparked by the general assumption that both frameworks are in alignment (see e.g. the recent General Comment from the Committee on the Rights of the Child (2019)). We refer to 'restorative justice' in this chapter as an alternative way of responding to offending behavior or conflict that focuses on repairing harm. Restorative justice aims to give people who are harmed an opportunity to actively participate in the process and have their views and needs considered. People who have harmed have the chance to reflect upon the impact of their behavior and how to contribute to promote repair. We use the term 'children's rights' here to describe the human rights framework as it applies to children, including the general human rights conventions (children are humans after all) and the specific principles and protections set out in the United Nations Convention on the Rights of the Child (CRC) and its associated international and regional standards.

In this chapter, we use the youth justice system[1] in Aotearoa New Zealand[2] to illustrate some case studies of potential tensions in how the frameworks operate in practice. First, we give an overview of the youth justice system and the children in it, and discuss how restorative justice is used in the youth justice system. Second, we discuss the principles of a children's rights approach to youth justice, and how the principles and practice of restorative justice may converge and diverge with a children's rights approach. Third, we focus on two particular issues – the capacity of children to

1 We acknowledge the – interchangeably used – term 'child justice system' as being referred to by the UN Committee on the Rights of the Child in their recent General Comment 24. As in Aotearoa New Zealand, the term 'youth justice system' is commonly being applied, we refer to this notion throughout the chapter.
2 Aotearoa is the Māori word for New Zealand.

participate in restorative justice processes and the rights and interests of child victims, to illustrate these points of convergence and divergence.

A note on terminology – this chapter uses the term child in its CRC (Art. 2) sense to refer to all those aged less than 18. The youth justice system in Aotearoa New Zealand does differentiate in liability, jurisdiction and procedure between children (those aged less than 14) and young persons (those aged 14 to 18).

2 The youth justice system in Aotearoa New Zealand

The youth justice system in Aotearoa New Zealand both mirrors comparable jurisdictions and has particular challenges (Lynch, 2019; Lynch & Liefaard, 2020).

2.1 Trends in reported crime

Over the last two decades, reported offending by children has been decreasing in Aotearoa New Zealand, indicated by lower rates of apprehensions, prosecutions and convictions. This youth crime drop may also be observed globally (McAra & McVie, 2018). Between 2010 and 2018, the overall offending rate for children aged 10 to 13 declined by 55 percent, and the rate for those aged 14 to 16 fell 58 percent (Ministry of Justice, 2019). The rate of Youth Court appearances for 14- to 16-year olds has halved since 2010 (Ministry of Justice, 2019), and the number of persons under the age of 20 serving prison and community-based sentences has also fallen (Department of Corrections, 2015).

2.2 Characteristics of children who offend

Like in comparative jurisdictions, children in conflict with the law have multiple vulnerabilities (Lynch & Liefaard, 2020). Māori (the indigenous people of Aotearoa New Zealand) children are overrepresented at different stages of the criminal justice system, both as victims and offenders (Ināia Tonu Nei, 2019). A snapshot of 2018 statistics (Ministry of Justice, 2018c) reports that the majority (78 percent) of children in the youth justice system are male. Most children (40 percent) charged in court are 16 years old, 33 percent are 15 years of age, 23 percent 14 years old and a small share (2 percent) are aged 10 to 13 (Ministry of Justice, 2018c). Worldwide, it is estimated that about 50 to 75 percent of children who offend have been diagnosed with at least one mental health disorder, compared to 13 percent of the general population (summarized in Lambie, 2018; see also Young, Greer & Church, 2017). A recent study investigating risk factors for 184 youth female offenders in Aotearoa New Zealand found that about three-quarters had a mental health diagnosis (Lim, Lambie & van Toledo, 2019). A further aspect of concern is the increased vulnerability of children and adults who offend and who have had traumatic brain injury. People involved in the justice system have higher rates of traumatic brain injury than their non-offending counterparts. More than one-third experienced multiple injuries, many before age 15 (Lambie, 2020). Māori children in conflict with the law experienced higher rates of mental health problems than non-Māori (see Lambie (2018) for further references).

Most children who offend have experienced high rates of abuse and neglect. 97 percent of children aged 10 to 13 and 89 percent of children who offend aged 14 to 17 who were referred to a youth justice family group conference (FGC) came to the attention of Oranga Tamariki[3] in 2018 for care and protection concerns (Ministry of Justice, 2019). The above cited study by Lim et al. (2019) on youth female offenders found that 90 percent had experienced at least one form of maltreatment, and 50 percent were victims of sexual abuse. Eighty percent of child and youth offenders had been exposed to family violence. Children who have experienced recurrent or more than one form of maltreatment are at higher risk of engaging in offending behavior (see Lambie (2018) for further references). Further risk factors are related to substance-abuse disorders – the majority (79 percent) of children who offend in Aotearoa New Zealand were found to have used alcohol and two-thirds (66 percent) of offenders between 17 and 24 had used methamphetamine in 2017 (see Lambie (2018) for further references). Moreover, many children in the youth justice system are vulnerable due to other forms of neurodevelopmental disorders, including communication disorders (Lambie, 2020), which will be discussed more in detail later in this chapter.

2.3 Principles underpinning youth justice

Aotearoa New Zealand's youth justice legislation has long been a model for jurisdictions worldwide (Morris & Maxwell, 1993). This is due to its (then) innovative focus on diversion, delegation of power to families and communities, and the inclusion of consideration of the interests of victims of crime. Recent changes to the legislation have shifted the conceptual base somewhat (Lynch, 2019). The legislation now centers on the concept of 'well-being', requiring a more holistic analysis of the child and their circumstances. The purpose of the youth justice system explicitly recognizes the rights and interests of victims and the aim of preventing and reducing offending, indicating a more 'crime control' focused approach. But, consideration of best interests and protection of rights are required, indicating a child-centered lens. The recently introduced legislative term 'mana tamaiti' means that decision-makers must recognize

3 Oranga Tamariki – Ministry for Children is the state care agency and was established in 2017. 'Oranga' is the Māori word for well-being, and 'tamariki' means children.

the 'intrinsic value and inherent dignity', which is derived from a child's whakapapa [genealogy] and their belonging to whānau, hapū, iwi or a family group, in accordance with tikanga Māori [custom] or its equivalent in the child's culture (Cleland, 2019).

2.4 *Use of restorative justice processes in the youth justice system*

Aotearoa New Zealand's youth justice system places a strong emphasis on alternative resolution. The majority of child apprehensions are diverted from prosecution, mainly through the police youth diversion scheme. Only about 20 to 30 percent of children face prosecution (District Court of New Zealand, 2019). Although there are numerous forms of diversion, it is the FGC which has most been associated with restorative justice. The FGC plays a central role as a decision-making process in youth justice both in diversion and when a case is prosecuted. It is a process that involves the child and their (extended) family, the victim, support people and professionals such as police officers and social workers in decisions to respond to wrongdoing and repair harm. In 2017/2018, approximately 4,600 youth justice FGCs were held, involving 2,250 individual children (Oranga Tamariki, 2018). FGCs are used for more serious or persistent offending where other diversionary measures are not sufficient.

When the FGC was created in 1989, the term restorative justice was not used in the legislation as the concept of restorative justice was not widely recognized. It was only later that FGCs were recognized as being a restorative justice process (Morris & Maxwell, 1993), though it is probably more accurate to describe the FGC as a process with the potential for restorative justice to occur (Lynch, 2010). It is important to note that the FGC is essentially mandatory in nature, in contrast to adult restorative justice conferences, which are entirely voluntary (see Lynch, 2019). Low victim participation may also reduce the potential for restorative practice. In 2018, only 18 percent of victims attended FGCs in person, and 33 percent made written submissions.[4] The reasons for low participation rates are manifold. Maxwell, Kingi, Robertson, Morris, and Cunningham (2004) found that while the main reason for victims' nonparticipation was a reluctance to meet the child or their family, organizational or logistical aspects, such as venue and timing, may also play a role.

Under legislative amendments that took force in July 2019, the FGC is now required to consider what restorative justice actions could be undertaken. This can include apologizing to the victim, paying compensation or providing a service to the victim, making a gift or other amends, providing victims the chance to explain how the offence has impacted him or her and have a say about how to repair the harm.[5]

---

4 Oranga Tamariki, personal communication (25 October 2019).

5 Section 258 (2) Oranga Tamariki Act. The act does not further define the term 'restorative justice action.' Examples for restorative justice actions are listed on Oranga Tamariki's Practice Centre website.

3 The children's rights framework

3.1 *A principled approach to children in conflict with the law*

The primary international standard for children's rights is the United Nations CRC. The CRC stands out from other human rights standards as having reached 'virtual universality' (Rios-Kohn, 1998: 140). As well as general principles, such as the primacy of the best interest of the child, it provides for specific rights for children in conflict with the law. These principles are developed in the recently revised General Comment 24 on the rights of the child in the child justice system (Committee on the Rights of the Child, 2019). Processes and outcomes must promote the child's sense of dignity and worth and emphasize respect for human rights, and reintegration (Art. 40.1 CRC). Alternatives to formal criminal proceedings are encouraged (Art. 40(3)(b) Convention; Committee on the Rights of the Child, 2019). The child's privacy must be respected at all stages of proceedings (Art. 40(2)(vii) and Art. 16 CRC). Custody is to be a last resort (Art. 40.1 CRC). Effective and meaningful participation is a key plank of a children's rights compliant system (Art. 12 CRC).

In regional standards, the Council of Europe has established guidelines for 'child-friendly justice', taking a broad and holistic approach to proceedings and processes involving children:

> justice that is accessible, age appropriate, speedy, diligent, adapted to and focused on the needs and rights of the child, respecting the rights of the child including the rights to due process, to participate in and to understand the proceedings, to respect for private and family life and to integrity and dignity. (Council of Europe, 2010, II.A.c.)

3.2 *Restorative justice and the children's rights framework*

As mentioned in other chapters in this book, the CRC does not specifically mention restorative justice, but the Committee on the Rights of the Child in its recent commentary 24 recommends restorative justice be employed in a number of contexts: diversion (2019, para. 17) and as a noncustodial disposition (2019, para. 74). Restorative justice is also linked to the need to empower indigenous peoples in the resolution of offending by their children (2019, para. 104):

> Restorative justice responses are often achievable through customary, indigenous or other non-State justice systems, and may provide opportunities for learning for the formal child justice system. Furthermore, recognition of

such justice systems can contribute to increased respect for the traditions of indigenous societies, which could have benefits for indigenous children.

European regional standards also encourage the use of restorative justice in the context of criminal justice and provide basic principles for restorative justice (Council of Europe, 2018). The principles provide *inter alia* that restorative justice should be a generally available service (Rule 18) and should be available at all stages of the criminal justice process (Rule 19). The recommendation underlines that the same special regulations and legal safeguards relating to participation of children to be applied in restorative justice measures (Rule 24). Further, the European Rules for Juvenile Offenders Subject to Sanctions or Measures (Council of Europe, 2008) highlight once again that restorative measures should be used at all stages of dealing with children including at the stage of serving a sentence (Basic Principle 12); and that restorative approaches should be preferably used when applying community sanctions and measures (Rule 23.2) as well as when resolving conflicts with and among prisoners (Rule 122.2).

Having outlined the principles underpinning both frameworks, and having set the context of the Aotearoa New Zealand youth justice system, what follows are two in depth examples considering how children's rights may be safeguarded within the principles of restorative justice.

4 Implementing the child's right to participate

Involvement in criminal justice proceedings is challenging for *all* children due to the complexity of the legal system. It presents an even greater barrier for those children who experience particular difficulties with communication and comprehension. Such aspects might be of particular concern in restorative processes, which rely on oral communication and where the views of the child are central in decision-making. Family group conferencing is strongly based on verbal interaction. Children, families, victims and professionals come together in a conversation about the impact of the wrongful incident on the victim, the repair of harm and the addressing of the needs of the child. The process relies on participants to communicate and to understand the narratives and emotional aspects. Children need the capacity to understand the questions posed by professionals, comprehend the sometimes-complex narratives, articulate their views and explain what happened and have the appropriate nonverbal behavior skills (Snow & Sanger, 2011). The question arises as to what extent children have such a capacity to understand the process and its outcomes, and hence exercise their right to participate.

There is a growing body of research highlighting the impact of language impairment on children's engagement in the youth justice system, including in restorative processes.

Oral language competence refers to a range of everyday verbal skills including in both the receptive and expressive areas, and it is the means by which people form and maintain relationships (Snow & Sanger, 2011). The research indicates that children who offend are more likely to have learning disabilities and language difficulties compared with non-offending youth (see Snow & Powell (2012) or Lount, Purdy & Hand (2017) for further references). In Aotearoa New Zealand, a very high prevalence of learning disabilities was identified among young people in youth justice residences. 92 percent of youth from two youth prisons were found to have at least one learning disability in the areas of reading, mathematics or oral language. Particularly reading comprehension was found to be very low. In contrast, youth in communities were found to have much lower rates of learning disabilities (Rucklidge, McLean & Bateup, 2013). Another Aotearoa New Zealand-based study revealed that 64 percent of male sentenced and remanded in youth justice residences had language impairments, compared with 10 percent of the control group. One of the findings relates to hearing – youth justice residents were more than seven times more likely than controls to have some form of hearing loss in one or both ears (Lount et al., 2017). Further qualitative research into oral language and youth justice processes found that a small sample of young people from a youth justice residence experienced difficulties in understanding the court process and, in turn, felt that they had no 'voice' and control (Lount, Hand, Purdy & France, 2018). Evidence from Australia shows that over 50 percent of a community sample of young male offenders had significant oral language disorders, relating to figurative/abstract language, sentence repetition and narrative language skills (Snow & Powell, 2008). A recent, small-scale qualitative study focused on young people's experiences with the youth justice system, including FGCs (Metzger, Savaii, McKee & Kedge, 2018). The research found that young people perceived communication in general often led to negative consequences for them. Many of the thirteen interviewed male young people (aged 12 to 21 years) reported having difficulties in understanding institutional language. Often, they used strategies to hide their communication difficulties. These findings are supported by anecdotal evidence from practitioners in the youth justice system.

How can these difficulties impact participation in restorative justice processes? Often, children's language deficits are undetected, and they may be labeled as lazy, rude, uncooperative or unmotivated in restorative processes. Deficiencies in verbal competences and nonverbal behavior may lead to the impression of low empathy and shallowness (Snow & Powell, 2008; Snow & Sanger, 2011). It is also estimated that a considerable part of children who offend experience language deficits due to the difficulty or even inability in expressing emotions (Hayes & Snow, 2013). Limited communication skills have implications for children's participation in family group conferencing, which focus on an exchange of experiences and feelings. Children may not be able to clearly express their views and acknowledge their wrongdoing in a meaningful way and thus not fully engage in the process. Language impairments and comprehension difficulties may also affect the capacity of children to fully understand the legal consequences of family group conferencing and thus may affect their right to meaningful participation in the process.

How can a child's right to participation be implemented in the FGC? Early identification of language impairments is of importance in ensuring that children can access appropriate professional assistance. In Aotearoa New Zealand, specialized communication assistance has been made available to support children who struggle with language. The model has been inspired by the role of the intermediary in England/Wales and applied in Aotearoa New Zealand since 2012 (Howard, McCann & Dudley, 2020). Since then, communication assistance has been increasingly used in youth justice proceedings, including FGCs (see Lynch, 2018a).[6] Speech-language therapists, appointed by the Court, assess children's language and communication skills and assist them to engage more effectively (Kedge, 2018a, 2018b). They ensure children are able to understand what others are saying and support them in communicating and expressing their perspectives and needs. The involvement of specialist support also provides the opportunity to develop more creative and culturally appropriate FGC plans and increase engagement of children in the process and its aftermath. Local projects based on collaboration between speech-language therapists from the organization Talking Trouble and Oranga Tamariki youth justice teams have been carried out to develop strategies and resources for working with children and their families (Kedge, 2018a, 2018b). This interdisciplinary collaborative approach is intended to be rolled out more widely to cover a number of youth justice sites around the country.

Recent research (Howard et al., 2020) relating to professionals' perspectives on communication assistance in the Aotearoa New Zealand youth justice system identified overwhelmingly supportive views. Respondents valued the model for enhancing understanding and participation of children by tailoring processes to their needs and resulting in better outcomes, including therapeutic approaches and more workable FGC plans. A further benefit referred to was greater awareness of children's communication difficulties and reflection on the way of interacting with children, leading even to individual practice changes. Key challenges professionals reported related to communication assistance being a new profession with a developing identity, deciding about who needs help and when, the lack of standard practices and the need for wider recognition within the youth justice sector (Howard, McCann & Dudley, 2019).

From a children's point of view, research by Metzger et al. (2018) identified factors that children found essential to support a better communication. These included the importance of building trust and rapport between adults and children, being spoken to respectfully and listened to actively and with empathy and creating an environment where children feel emotionally and physically safe in. Good relationships between staff

6 Communication assistants can be appointed for witnesses and defendants of all ages and all types of crime, see Howard et al. (2020).

and children have consistently found to be one of the factors leading to better outcomes for children who offend.

5 Child victims – role and participation

Over the last few decades, the role of the victim in the criminal process has received more attention, and reforms have contributed to strengthening victims' rights. Besides protective rights and rights to compensation, reforms also focused on enhancing victims' right to participation in the criminal justice process (which, however, remains partial). Reforms have been less extensive in regard to child victims, and rather focused on child defendants and child witnesses (see Lynch, 2018b).

The exact extent of how many youth justice cases would involve victimization of another child is difficult to depict. Limited data are available as child victimization studies are rare in most countries (see Lynch (2018b) for further references). Reported data on the extent of child victimization in Aotearoa New Zealand are provided by the New Zealand Crime and Safety Survey. However, it has to be noted that this survey does not cover offences against children up to the age of 14. According to this survey (Ministry of Justice, 2018a), 30 percent of 15- to 19-year olds reported being victimized once or more. 20- to 29-year olds experienced the highest risk of victimization (40 percent). In terms of personal offences, the New Zealand survey reveals that the abovementioned age groups experienced higher levels of victimization compared with other age groups. Twenty percent of 15- to 19-year olds and 21 percent of 20- to 29-year olds reported being victims of personal offences. The findings showing that children have an increased risk of being victimized are consistent with international research (i.e., Finkelhor, 2008; Finkelhor, Turner, Shattuck, Hamby & Kracke, 2015). It is also acknowledged that children who had been victimized have an increased risk of experiencing future victimization (Finkelhor et al., 2015).

The right to participation is one of the essential rights anchored in the CRC (Art. 12), emphasizing the opportunity for the child to express his or her own views in matters affecting the child and to be heard. Victims' involvement and participation is one of the central characteristics of restorative justice processes. International standards encourage the use of restorative justice as discussed above, such as the Committee on the Rights of the Child (2019) and the United Nations Office on Drugs and Crime's Model Law (2013). Restorative justice is an approach to crime that invites victims to actively engage with the offender in a respectful dialogue, placing the victims' interests and needs arising from the harmful incident at its core. The needs of victims including child victims of crime are manifold and complex. Common themes are a need for procedural justice, more precisely to be treated fairly, to be able to express their views and to be listened to. Further common themes are a need for empowerment and control, a safe encounter with the offender, social acknowledgment and reparation (i.e., Gal (2011) for further references). Furthermore, child victims are often found to have a need for support from within and outside the family (Gal, 2011), such as the involvement of parents (particularly for younger children) and peer support networks.

In terms of victims' experiences with restorative justice processes, research shows overall encouraging results. A wide range of international studies have shown that victims experienced high levels of satisfaction with the restorative process and outcomes (Bolívar, Aertsen & Vanfraechem, 2015; Doak & O'Mahony, 2006; Shapland et al., 2007; Sherman & Strang, 2007; Strang, Sherman, Mayo-Wilson, Woods & Ariel, 2013). Victims appreciated being treated fairly (i.e., Latimer, Dowden & Muise, 2005; Van Camp, 2014), and experiencing lower levels of fear and post-traumatic stress symptoms as well as a lower desire for revenge (Sherman et al., 2015).

According to the New Zealand Restorative Justice Survey (Ministry of Justice, 2018b), most victims (75 percent) aged 19 or younger reported to be satisfied with their restorative justice conference involving adult offenders. The survey further revealed that the vast majority of victims aged 19 or under were likely to recommend the restorative justice process to others (92 percent), similar to those aged 20 to 29 years (90 percent). Interestingly, the age group of 19 or under (83 percent) was most likely to state that they felt a lot better or slightly better after the restorative conference. However, a study conducted by Gal and Moyal (2011) on Australian conferences found that young victims were a little less satisfied with restorative conferences than with the court process, compared with adult victims. The authors also observed that child victims experienced a sense of lacking control due to aspects such as power imbalances between participants and inexperience in speaking up in the conversation.

Consideration needs be given to restorative dialogues ensuring that child victims have their equal voice in the process and feel treated with respect. Facilitators need to be sensitive and aware of any power imbalances and address these to provide for a fair process for children who have been harmed. Further attention must be paid to child victims having less capacity to engage in the restorative process due to language impairments and other special needs. As with children who offend, specialist assistance to support these children to participate effectively in restorative processes is essential, and it further ensures that children's rights are respected.

6 Concluding remarks

Aotearoa New Zealand's youth justice system is regarded as progressive and tolerant, with its focus on diversion and participatory decision-making processes embodied in the FGC. It seems that some efforts are underway to strengthen the restorative nature and quality of youth justice FGCs and increase victim involvement in these approaches.

For children who offend, child-friendly justice in practice depends on their meaningful participation through communication and understanding of these processes. As has been shown, many of these children have communication difficulties, and adequate approaches are required to respond adequately to their needs. Communication assistance has become an increasing topic of interest among youth justice professionals in Aotearoa New Zealand in recent years and has led to greater awareness of children's speech-language needs. Further training for justice practitioners would be of use to better recognize communication difficulties and address children's needs. The involvement of specialist assistance provides an opportunity to increase children's voices in the decision-making process including the FGC, and support them in better understanding the proceedings. There seems to be particular potential for communication assistance in the FGC, being a flexible approach, which can be tailored to the needs of the child and that can include a culturally appropriate lens. An increased use of speech-language specialists is one primary factor to enhance children's participation in the youth justice system including the FGC and enhance its restorative potential. Such involvement would also be of benefit for child victims with communication needs in supporting them having their say in the process and engaging in a meaningful conversation with the offender. More research needs to be done to further explore the communication and participation needs of child victims.

References

Bolívar, D., Aertsen, I. & Vanfraechem, I. (eds.). (2015). *Victims and restorative justice: an empirical study of needs, experience and position of the victim within restorative justice practices. Country reports*. Leuven: European Forum for Restorative Justice.

Cleland, A. (2019). Oranga Tamariki reforms: can law be implemented where understanding is lacking? In N. Lynch (ed.), *Children's rights in Aotearoa New Zealand – reflections on the 30th anniversary of the Convention on the Rights of the Child* (pp. 55-56). Wellington: Law Foundation/Michael & Suzanne Borrin Foundation.

Council of Europe. (2008). Recommendation No. R (2008) 11 of the Committee of Ministers to member states on the European Rules for juvenile offenders subject to sanctions or measures, 5 November 2008. Strasbourg.

Council of Europe. (2010). Guidelines of the Committee of Ministers of the Council of Europe on child friendly justice. Adopted by the Committee of Ministers of the Council of Europe on 17 November 2010 and explanatory memorandum. Strasbourg.

Council of Europe. (2018). Recommendation CM/Rec (2018) 8 of the Committee of Ministers to member States concerning restorative justice in criminal matters.

Adopted by the Committee of Ministers on 3 October 2018 at the 1326th meeting of the Ministers' Deputies. Strasbourg.

Department of Corrections. (2015). *Top series: young offenders.* Wellington: Department of Corrections.

District Court New Zealand. (2019). *Reports, Publications & Statistics.* Retrieved from www.districtcourts.govt.nz/reports-publications-and-statistics/annual-reports/page-2342/youth-court/ (last accessed 7 February 2020).

Doak, J. & O'Mahony, D. (2006). The vengeful victim? Assessing the attitudes of victims participating in restorative youth conferencing. *International Review of Victimology,* 13(2), 157-177. doi: 10.1177/026975800601300202.

Finkelhor, D. (2008). *Childhood victimization: violence, crime and abuse in the lives of young people.* New York, Oxford: Oxford University Press.

Finkelhor, D., Turner, H., Shattuck, A., Hamby, S. & Kracke, K. (2015). Children's exposure to violence, crime, and abuse: an update. *Juvenile Justice Bulletin.* U.S. Department of Justice.

Gal, T. (2011). *Child victims and restorative justice: a needs-rights model.* New York: Oxford University Press.

Gal, T. & Moyal, S. (2011). Juvenile victims in restorative justice. findings from the reintegrative shaming experiments. *British Journal of Criminology,* 51(6), 1014-1034. doi: 10.1093/bjc/azr052.

Hayes, H. & Snow, P. (2013). *Oral language competence and restorative justice processes: refining preparation and measurement of conference outcomes.* Canberra: Australian Institute of Criminology.

Howard, K., McCann, C. & Dudley, M. (2019). 'It's really good, much needed, why hasn't it happened earlier?' Professionals' perspectives on the benefits of communication assistance in the New Zealand youth justice system. *Australian and New Zealand Journal of Criminology,* 53(2), 265-284. doi: 10.1177/0004865819890377.

Howard, K., McCann, C. & Dudley, M. (2020). 'I was flying blind a wee bit': professionals' perspectives on challenges facing communication assistance in the New Zealand youth justice system. *The International Journal of Evidence & Proof,* 24(2), 104-120. doi: 10.1177/1365712719877893.

Ināia Tonu Nei. (2019). *The time is now: we lead, you follow.* Wellington: Ministry of Justice.

Kedge, S. (2018a). *Presentation to South Pacific Council Youth Children's Courts on 17 October 2018.* Wellington. Retrieved from https://safeandeffectivejustice.govt.nz/about-this-work/hui-maori/ (last accessed 17 August 2020).

Kedge, S. (2018b). *Transforming the communication involved in justice processes in New Zealand.* Paper presented at the 31st Annual Conference of the Australian and New Zealand Society of Criminology, 5 December 2018, Melbourne.

Lambie, I. (2018). *It's never too early, never too late: a discussion paper on preventing youth offending in New Zealand.* Auckland: Office of the Prime Minister's Chief Science Advisor.

Lambie, I. (2020). *What were they thinking? A discussion paper on brain and behaviour in relation to the justice system in New Zealand.* Auckland: Office of the Prime Minister's Chief Science Advisor.

Latimer, J., Dowden, G. & Muise, D. (2005). The effectiveness of restorative justice practices: a meta-analysis. *The Prison Journal*, 85(2), 127-144. doi: 10.1177/0032885505276969.

Lim, S., Lambie, I. & van Toledo, A. (2019). Characteristics of female youth offenders in New Zealand. *International Journal of Offender Therapy and Comparative Criminology*, 63(2), 198-217. doi: 10.1177/0306624X18799002.

Lount, S.A., Hand, L., Purdy, S. & France, A. (2018). Tough talk: youth offenders' perceptions of communicating in the youth justice system in New Zealand. *Australian and New Zealand Journal of Criminology*, 51(4), 593-618. doi: 10.1177/0004865817740404.

Lount, S.A., Purdy, S.C. & Hand, L. (2017). Hearing, auditory processing, and language skills of male youth offenders and remandees in youth justice residences in New Zealand. *Journal of Speech, Language and Hearing Research*, 60(1), 121-135. doi: 10.1044/2016_JSLHR-L-15-0131.

Lynch, N. (2010). Restorative justice through a children's rights lens. *The International Journal of Children's Rights*, 18(2), 161-183. doi: 10.1163/157181810X12592206285646.

Lynch, N. (2018a). *Neurodisability in the Youth Justice System in New Zealand: How Vulnerability Intersects with Justice* (May 30, 2016). Dyslexia Foundation of New Zealand. Summarising the Contributions of Participants at the 2016 Neurodisabilities Forum, Hosted by DFNZ in Wellington, 12 May 2016, Victoria University of Wellington Legal Research Paper No. 16/2018, Available at SSRN: https://ssrn.com/abstract=2869502.

Lynch, N. (2018b). 'The other child' – the rights of the child victim in the youth justice system. *International Journal of Children's Rights*, 26(2), 228-250. doi: 10.1163/15718182-02602002.

Lynch, N. (2019). *Youth justice in New Zealand* (3rd ed.). Wellington: Thomson Reuters.

Lynch, N. & Liefaard, T. (2020). What is left in the 'too hard basket'? Developments and challenges for the rights of children in conflict with the law. *The International Journal of Children's Rights*, 28(1), 89-110. doi: 10.1163/15718182-02801007.

Maxwell, G., Kingi, V., Robertson, J., Morris, A. & Cunningham, C. (2004). *Achieving effective outcomes: youth justice in New Zealand.* Wellington: Ministry of Justice.

McAra, L. & McVie, S. (2018). Transformations in youth crime and justice across Europe: evidencing the case for diversion. In B. Goldson (ed.), *Juvenile justice in Europe* (pp. 73-103). London: Routledge.

Metzger, N., Savaii, K., McKee, A. & Kedge, S. (2018). *Youth voices about youth justice. Listening to young people's experiences of communication within the youth justice sector in New Zealand.* Auckland: Talking Trouble Aotearoa New Zealand.

Ministry of Justice. (2018a). *New Zealand crime and victims survey. Key findings.* Cycle 1 (March-September 2018). Descriptive statistics. Wellington: Ministry of Justice.

Ministry of Justice. (2018b). *Restorative justice survey. Victim satisfaction survey 2018.* Report Prepared by Gravitas Research and Strategy Ltd. Wellington: Ministry of Justice.

Ministry of Justice. (2018c). *Trends in children and young people in court.* Wellington: Ministry of Justice.

Ministry of Justice. (2019). *Youth justice indicators summary report.* August 2019. Wellington: Ministry of Justice.

Morris, A. & Maxwell, G.M. (1993). Juvenile justice in New Zealand: a new paradigm. *Australian & New Zealand Journal of Criminology*, 26(1), 72-90. doi: 10.1177/000486589302600108.

Oranga Tamariki. (2018). *Annual Report 2017/2018.* Wellington.

Rios-Kohn, R. (1998). The convention on the rights of the child: progress and challenges. *Georgetown Journal on Fighting Poverty*, 5, 139-160.

Rucklidge, J.J., McLean, A.P. & Bateup, P. (2013). Criminal offending and learning disabilities in New Zealand youth: does reading comprehension predict recidivism? *Crime and Delinquency*, 59(8), 1263-1286. doi: 10.1177/0011128709336945.

Shapland, J., Atkinson, A., Atkinson, H., Chapman, B., Dignan, J., Howes, M., Johnstone, J., Robinson, G. & Sorsby, A. (2007). *Restorative justice: the views of victims and offenders. The third report from the evaluation of three schemes.* London: Ministry of Justice.

Sherman, L.W. & Strang, H. (2007). *Restorative justice: the evidence.* London: The Smith Institute.

Sherman, L.W., Strang, H., Barnes, G., Woods, D.J., Bennett, S., Inkpen, N., Newbury-Birch, D., Rossner, M., Angel, C., Mearns, M. & Slothower, M. (2015). Twelve experiments in restorative justice: the Jerry Lee Program of randomized trials of restorative justice conferences. *Journal of Experimental Criminology*, 11(4), 501-540. doi: 10.1007/s11292-015-9247-6.

Snow, P.C. & Powell, M.B. (2008). Oral language competence, social skills and high-risk boys: what are juvenile offenders trying to tell us? *Children & Society*, 22(1), 16-28. doi: 10.1111/j.1099-0860.2006.00076.x.

Snow, P.C. & Powell, M.B. (2012). Youth (in)justice: oral language competence in early life and risk for engagement in antisocial behaviour in adolescence. *Trends and Issues in Crime and Criminal Justice*, 435, 1-6.

Snow, P.C. & Sanger, D.D. (2011). Restorative justice conferencing and the youth offender: exploring the role of oral language competence. *International Journal of Language and Communication Disorders*, 46(3), 324-333.

Strang, H., Sherman, L., Mayo-Wilson, E., Woods, D. & Ariel, B. (2013). *Restorative justice conferencing (RJC) using face-to-face meetings of offenders and victims: effects on offender recidivism and victim satisfaction. A systematic review* (p. 12). Oslo: Campbell Systematic Reviews.

UN Committee on the Rights of the Child. (2019). General comment No. 24 (2019) on children's rights in the child justice system. CRC/C/GC/24, 18 September 2019.

United Nations Office on Drugs and Crime (2013). Justice in matters involving children in conflict with the law. Model law on juvenile justice and related commentary. Vienna.

Van Camp, T. (2014). *Victims of violence and restorative practices: finding a voice.* London, New York: Routledge.

Young, S., Greer, B. & Church, R. (2017). Juvenile delinquency, welfare, justice and therapeutic interventions: a global perspective. *BJPsych Bulletin*, 41(1), 21-29. doi: 10.1192/pb.bp.115.052274.

Chapter 11

The potential of restorative justice to fulfill the children's right to be heard

The experience in Chile

Daniela Bolívar, Alejandra Mera and Iván Navarro

1 Child justice system and the right of the child to be heard

As child justice procedures are distressing and unknown situations, children might feel uncomfortable and unnerved by the experience (Etcheberry & Fuentes, 2017: 115). Likewise, Bernuz (2015: 78) argues that often the mere provision of information about their rights does not imply that children understand their meaning or that they can freely exercise them, because in general, justice procedures do not allow the spontaneous expression of views by the involved parties. The former, in addition to the stress produced by the experience and the complexity of legal language, can cause the child not to understand the charges against her or him, nor the characteristics or the consequences of the procedure (Bernuz, 2015: 85), impairing her or his right to a defense (Couso & Duce, 2013: 75).

We must also remember that, historically, children have been a part of the 'silenced social collectives', either because they have been thought not to be mature or capable enough to participate in decisions that affect them, or because their views are not given weight against the opinions of adults and/or experts (Bernuz, 2015: 68). The UN Convention on the Rights of the Child (CRC), however, particularly in Art. 12, contradicts such conception of the child as incompetent, not responsible or incomplete (Krappmann, 2010: 502), and conceives her or him as a subject of rights, who is able to significantly participate in the matters that affect their lives. In this sense, Morrow (1999: 149) states that the CRC 'represents a potentially dramatic shift in approaches to children's rights.'

As a corollary of these facts, one might wonder how can young people's experience with child justice procedures be improved and to what end. A pivotal issue here is the recognition of children's rights by the UN CRC (UN, 1989). Within this, the principle of the specialization of the justice proceedings for children and adolescents (UN, 1985; UN, 1989) has been widely recognized (Duce, 2009; Hernández, 2007). This principle demands that States should have regulations on criminal proceedings for children and adolescents, separate from the ones on general procedures for adults. Besides, it requires that administrators of justice have specialized training. This separation of legal processes is based on the specific characteristics of children and young persons, which give rise to the need for differentiated treatment, and it is expressed through the provision of specific guarantees and rights, which are additional to the ones established for the general population.

General Comment N°12 (2009) of the Committee on the Rights of the Child, in the second paragraph,[1] states that the CRC is based on four fundamental principles: the right to nondiscrimination, the right to life and development, the right to be heard and the primary consideration of the child's best interests. According to the same paragraph, these rights do not only constitute rights in themselves, as they should also be considered in the interpretation and implementation of the other rights of the CRC.

The right to be heard is the focus of this chapter. Article 12 of the CRC states that the child, who is capable of forming his or her own views, has the right to express those views freely during the different stages of the procedure and to be duly informed about the characteristics and consequences of the criminal procedure. All of this serves the purpose that children are able to make their choices freely and voluntarily, with the best possibilities of effective participation. In order to achieve that, the CRC and the GC N° 12 (paras. 42, 34, 60, 61) give a relevant role to the quality of the dialogue between the child and the authorities involved in the case.

Regarding child offenders, in general terms, the rights to be heard and to actively participate in the procedures have been connected more directly to the right to a fair trial and other procedural guarantees, like the right to a defense. Nevertheless, one could argue that the right to be heard could be considered from a wider perspective of analysis. It provides both the potential of expanding and enriching the content of the right to a fair process and the possibility to address the child offender's needs and interests in order to promote better conditions for effective participation in the child justice system.

In this chapter we explore, based on a pilot restorative justice experience in our home country, what 'being heard' might mean, and the extent to which a restorative approach could contribute to fulfilling such a right. In order to do that, we first describe the Chilean experience and share our observations of the practice, after which broader reflections on the topic are presented.

1.1 Chilean child justice system

The Chilean child justice system is regulated by Law N° 20.084 (2007) and is applicable to offences committed by 14- to 17-year-old youngsters. This law was created within the

1 CRC/C/GC/12 20 July 2009.

framework of several reforms aimed at modernizing the Chilean justice system that started in the 1990s, after Chile's return to democracy.[2]

Law N° 20.084 eliminated the old tutelary system that had been the dominant child justice model in Chile during most part of the 20th century. The law aimed at establishing a system based on the particular responsibility[3] of adolescents who committed a criminal offence. This was reflected in Law N° 20.084 by means of Article N° 20, which states that measures and penalties were established with the objective of 'making effective the adolescent's responsibility for criminal offences in a way that the penalty is part of a broader socio-educational intervention oriented towards a complete social integration.' Consequently, the reform allowed the country to move to a new system that offered young offenders some guarantees and rights that protected them, as a way to establish a response to young offenders more consistent with the CRC (ratified by Chile in 1990).

During the years, that Law N° 20.084 has been in place, different evaluations have been completed and, in general, they concluded that the child justice system encounters multiple challenges that made a review very necessary. Particularly, evaluations showed that institutions that take part in the operation of the child justice system should have a deeper organic and functional specialization. Currently, though, there are no specialized courts, and there is a scarcity of public prosecutors and judges who specialize in cases involving young offenders (Espejo, 2014). Moreover, the trial and judgment process is currently very similar to that for adult offenders. Only some differences are relevant and they are related to the repertoire of legal actions and penalties (Mera, 2018: 35-36).

At the time of writing this paper, a reform of the Chilean child justice system is being developed,[4] oriented to take care of observed deficiencies and to promote better conditions for fulfilling guarantees and rights that are established in international instruments that are binding for Chile.

This reform has both an institutional and a legal component. The institutional component involves the creation of a National Juvenile Social Reintegration Service. The reform not only recognizes restorative justice as one of the paradigms that orients its policies and interventions, but it also establishes a national mediation service. Even though such service has been designed mainly as a diversionary strategy, the new law leaves the door open for its use in a broader repertoire of offences, even in the stage of execution of the sentence.

In order to implement this reform, the Ministry of Justice and Human Rights (from now on Ministry of Justice) has developed a series of actions intended to reinforce the

---

2 As part of that context, it is worth mentioning the reform of the Chilean Criminal Justice System that took place in 2000. Such reform replaced a system created in the early 20th century and introduced an accusatorial oral system, as well as new institutions, such as the Public Prosecutor's Office (Fiscalía), the Public Defence Attorney's Office (Defensoría) and the Guarantee Courts (Juzgados de Garantía). More can be seen in Criminal Procedural Code (2000), Law 19.696, available at: www.leychile.cl.

3 History of the Law 20.084, p. 11, available at: www.leychile.cl.

4 Chilean Senate, Law Project Number 11174-07.

process of designing public policies and for the permanent inclusion of mediation in the child justice system. One of them consists of a Pilot Victim-Offender Mediation Programme being developed since 2017.

The pilot program was designed and implemented in different steps. A working model of a mediation program was established by the team of the Ministry of Justice in consultancy with the European Forum for Restorative Justice, the external supervision and evaluation of an expert team of the Universidad de Chile (Bolívar et al., 2017). Subsequently, a second supervision contributed to establish quality indicators and a supervision system for mediators (Miranda et al., 2018). The new program also received the recognition and support of EUROsociAL+ to strengthen its implementation (2018-2019). Currently, the program operates in six cities (Santiago, Valparaíso, Viña del Mar, La Serena, Coquimbo and Copiapó).

During the first year of implementation (2017), the Santiago pilot program was evaluated. The findings from this evaluation inform the observations presented in this chapter, in light of exploring the possibilities offered by restorative justice in order to promote effective fulfillment of procedural guarantees, particularly the right to be heard that offenders have in child justice procedures.

1.2 The Chilean Pilot Victim-Offender Mediation Programme

In 2017, the first Pilot Victim-Offender Mediation Programme for young offenders was implemented in the northern area of Santiago de Chile and led by the Ministry of Justice. Mediation between the victim and the offender would allow diverting the case from the child justice system. At the time, the mediator[5] was concentrated in a particular zone in Santiago de Chile, in order to produce a manageable number of cases.

In order to promote this initiative, the Ministry of Justice and Human Rights established a collaborative panel at a national level with the Public Ministry and the Public Defence Attorney's Office. In December 2016 a Protocol for case referral was signed by the national authorities of those institutions and the Minister of Justice and Human Rights. The content of this protocol established referral criteria, confidentiality commitments, legal implications of mediation, and indications for local implementation and coordination. As Chile has no specific law on mediation, this agreement offered formal and institutional legitimacy to carry out mediations in penal matters. The legal framework used was the alternatives measures already established in our law. This became very important, as it allowed the referral of cases that, without the existence of mediation, would have actually been prosecuted and punished. The protocol did not establish a priori what kind of agreements would be acceptable as an outcome of

5 One single mediator was part of the pilot during the first year. Others were involved later.

mediation, so it was up to the parties to define its content, to be later confirmed by judicial authorities.

At that time, the pilot project fulfilled the following criteria: a) it was considered an autonomous intervention outside of the criminal justice system and subject to the supervision of the Ministry of Justice; b) it was oriented toward the first stages of the criminal investigation process; c) the cases were referred mainly by prosecutors and defense attorneys; and d) it adopted a territorial approach, which involved focusing on specific jurisdictions, enabling coordination with local organizations and on-site interviews.

During the evaluation period, the Public Prosecutor's Office and the Public Defence Attorney's Office diverted 27 cases to mediation. Some referrals took place after the case was sent to Court and others were selected during the investigation process.

2 Case study

The process evaluation that was carried out during the first year of the pilot program involved a case study in which six cases were followed up. Information about these cases was collected through: a) pre- and post-interviews with participants (victims and young offenders); b) observations of pre-mediation and mediation sessions; c) interviews with the mediator; and d) analysis of relevant documentation (such as police report). This data collection allowed producing a detailed record on how each case evolved, what participants experienced and what contextual elements were relevant throughout the process.

In the cases included, the ages of offenders ranged from 15 to 17 years. In five cases the victim was adult (older than 18 years old) and in one case the victim was a 16-year-old-boy. Three cases involved more than one offender. Three cases ended with a final agreement (two through direct mediation and one through indirect mediation), and three cases were closed with no agreement. In all the cases, the young offenders were accompanied by a responsible adult (i.e., parents, grandmother).

In general, information collected from these cases gave us a good idea of what 'being heard' could mean when dealing with young people and how this could be encouraged by professionals. In what follows, we first enlist the different ways children either could express themselves or be taken into account during the mediation process. Thereafter, we indicate the conditions that facilitate these ways of 'hearing' children.

2.1 *Some ways young people were 'heard' during the mediation process*

Our records included different types of narratives young offenders shared with the mediator. These narratives could be expressed in different moments of the mediation process, i.e., during the first informative session, preparatory meetings or during the direct encounters with the victim.

We could see that young offenders were able to:

- Tell or explain their motives and the personal, familiar or social context related to the offence, the judicial procedure or the mediation process;
- Express concerns and ask questions related to the consequences of the offence and penalties as well as questions about the victim and a potential encounter;
- Express negative emotions (fear, anger) connected to the offence, the judicial procedure or the mediation process;
- State their own worldview about their acts and those of others, including the victim;
- Express positive emotions, such as thankfulness, empathy and satisfaction related to the process and the involved parties;
- Show self-motivation, of any nature, with no fear of being judged. These motivations could be material or utilitarian (e.g., participating in the program in order to avoid sanctions or penalties) or symbolic (e.g., having the opportunity to tell others that she or he is not a criminal);
- Especially when trying to reach agreements and defining action plans, to state what they were (or were not) willing to do.

These expressions of 'being heard' include two elements we consider relevant to point out. First, such narratives can be shared even in cases that do not include face-to-face mediation. In other words, young offenders could express themselves and tell their own stories during the very first encounters with the mediator, which means that the right to be heard is protected (and must be protected) already at the beginning of the intervention. Second, given the nature of mediation, which involves other people, child offenders had the opportunity to share their narratives not only with the mediator, but also with others (e.g., parents, victims). This means that the young person could be heard not only by the mediator but also by actors that are highly important for them and for their social reintegration process.

We could also see that the mediation process facilitated 'emotional development', especially for those young people who were able to finish the mediation process with an agreement. There were opportunities of emotional growth and opportunities to address issues that were relevant in order to solve the conflict that affected the young person. Consider the following situations:

- In two cases, the mediation process allowed young offenders to solve conflicts that needed to be covered before the resolution of the case with the victim, giving rise to an active process of communication and dialogue, of hearing and being heard. For example, in one of these two cases, in which three offenders were involved, the conflict among the offenders and their families was addressed. In the other case, the child offender was able to solve a problem that he had with his parents.

- It was observed in two cases that were solved by direct mediation, that the process gave the young offender the possibility of changing his position during the sessions: Child offenders were given the right to change their views about the other party (the victim) and about her or himself in relation to the offence and its consequences.
- During the process, young offenders were able to know and to contrast their views with those of the other people involved (including the information about the victim shared by the mediator during the preparation phase), and also to consult and share opinions with relevant judicial actors, such as public prosecutors, and other professionals.
- As the process was more informal and friendly, resistance associated with the judicial system was reduced, making child offenders more receptive to the information that they received, promoting the construction of new meanings and fostering participation. The relationship established with the mediator and the fact that meetings were usually held in the mediation center (instead of in court) or at the offender's home helped to reduce resistance.
- The program also allowed young offenders to take on different degrees of engagement, motivations of different types and different degrees of responsibility. The mediator was also willing to listen to offenders' narratives and allow them to adjust them during the intervention.
- In both cases that were ended by direct mediation, the young offenders (and their victims) felt that justice had been served in their case; not only because 'both parties have been heard' (direct quotation from an offender) but also because the agreement reached was heard (ratified) by the judicial authority.
- The process gave offenders the opportunity to show themselves to the victims and to the judicial system as a *person*, without being classified into only one category ('delinquent').

Finally, the cases that resulted in an agreement (in these cases: the returning of the robbed item, monetary compensation or an apology) were ratified by means of legal remedies. That means that the process allowed young offenders being attentively heard by the judge, who took the agreement into account in their final resolution. 'Being attentively heard by the judge' was symbolic, as the judge officially accepted the agreement between the parties and made it valid in legal terms. But 'being heard' was also a concrete moment, as demonstrated in two of the three cases we analyzed: the young persons involved had the opportunity to express in the hearing itself, that is, in front of the judge and together with the victim, how the mediation process went. One of these judges was interviewed afterward and commented on how she had experienced a different hearing than those she was used to: 'I did not see a delinquent in front of me but a young person very proud of what he had achieved' (Bolívar et al., 2017).

In conclusion, in a restorative justice experience, the child could be heard not only in relation to the concrete contents and emotions that he could share with the mediator or with significant others (including the victim) throughout its process. The young person can also 'be heard' when the process takes into account his developmental stage, because as the process is flexible and inclusive, it allows him to evolve his narratives and explanations, opening opportunities for development and learning.

2.2 *Conditions that facilitate the right to be heard in a mediation process*

Adequate conditions to be heard must exist. We have learnt from the Chilean experience that the most important factor for the young person was that she or he felt that they were in a space in which they were safe and free of criticism. We believe this is a response to the nature of the relationship with the mediator. Young people discovered that the mediator differed from other legal professionals: the mediator was close to the child offender but she or he was not an ally; the mediator accepted the offender without judgment, was active but did not exert control, and was proactive but did not impose her ideas.

Aside from this general framework, we learnt that there are some elements that can further facilitate (or hinder) 'being heard':

- Setting. The meeting room at the mediation center was a facilitating condition when it provided a more informal atmosphere than that of settings where legal procedures are traditionally carried out. Besides, the preparatory meetings were carried out at the child offender's house or at a care center located in her or his neighborhood. Choosing these settings proved that the mediator was interested in the offender and able to know the context and take it into consideration.
- Parents' role. Parents may play different roles that facilitate or not that the child offender 'is heard'. In one case, the father adopted a leading role at the meeting and prevented the young offender from expressing her or himself and giving account of her or his needs. In another case, the father was able to communicate his feelings while allowing the offender to be free to express her or his emotions and concerns as well.
- Strategies used by the mediator. The mediator uses specific strategies that allow the child offender to be heard by her or himself as well as by the adults that surround the young person (besides the victim). The mediator may decide who should attend a meeting and be flexible enough to refocus or change the dynamics of the meeting, depending on the needs of the young offender and the victim. For example, the mediator can decide whether it is or is not advisable for parents to attend a meeting, and how to support a young offender in their decision which adult (or adults) will accompany her or him during mediation if there is more than one

responsible adult. Another strategy is for the mediator to understand underlying meanings in a young person's narrative and to delve into the child offender's motivations and expectations, beyond what she or he has been able to express.

- Confidentiality. It is important to remember that the space given to the young person to express her or himself in an open and honest way will be influenced by the confidential and private nature of the meetings with him. This confidentiality context is relevant even when the young person meets the mediator accompanied by a friend. In one case, for example, the mediator met simultaneously with two youngsters involved in the same offence. Maybe due to peer influence, this joint meeting seemed to prevent them from expressing personal emotions and both tried to maintain a certain role at the meeting ('being cool').

3 The right to be heard and restorative justice: some additional reflections

We have already mentioned that the CRC gives a relevant role to the quality of the dialogue between the child and the authorities involved in the case in order to exercise their rights. In a restorative process, the nature of the relationship with the mediator, which starts with the young person's free consent to participate, allows a friendly context, which would encourage a child's understanding of both the process dynamics and consequences. Moreover, a necessary condition to safeguard voluntary participation in the process is precisely to inform the child in advance and in a clear manner about all the aspects involved; for instance, who the parties are, what will be discussed, when and to whom she or he is expected to give her or his opinion, or how her or his opinion will be taken into account in the final decision. This context allows, as seen in the section above, the young person to express all kinds of narratives, and for these narratives to evolve throughout the intervention.

Hearing children in an appropriate way is a complex task that involves recognizing different aspects regarding their development and to be able to understand and interpret them in a proper manner to address their needs and interests. Based on the observations made in the Chilean pilot program, we can argue that a restorative procedure enables compliance with these requirements, given the special features of the process and because people who conduct these processes (facilitators or mediators) are required to be properly trained.

Additionally, the relevance given to the views of the child during the procedure presents interesting challenges. The CRC states that the child should not only be heard, but that her or his opinions should be given due weight. This requires that the child be duly explained what decisions are being made in the procedure and how her or his views have been considered in those decisions (Bernuz, 2015: 82; Krappmann, 2010: 507). The former does not mean that children have the final word in the matters in which they take part, but that they do play a significant role in the process. As Morrow states (1999: 155), children 'want to have a say' but not necessarily decide: the demand is for inclusion, not for total decision-making autonomy.

Restorative processes are characterized by significantly including the views of the child. The child is expected to take responsibility for the consequences of the offence in front of the victim and to play a leading role when agreeing to the type of reparation to be implemented (Chapman, Gellin, Aertsen & Anderson, 2015). For this reason, it is essential for the child to perceive that her or his opinion is taken into account throughout the process and to see the extent to which it is incorporated in the mediation agreement. This aspect is closely associated with the concept of procedural justice, since it requires the views of children to be seriously weighed and considered during the procedure, a principle that has often proven to be more important for children than the outcome in the final decision (Gal, 2011: 46). As mentioned before in this chapter, one young offender who participated in mediation considered that the procedure he went through was 'fair' because he and the other party (the victim) had been heard.

In conclusion, a restorative justice process that allows a young person to be heard is a determining factor for children to perceive a sense of justice, since it is precisely defined as a justice of participation and dialogue, in opposition to an imposed justice (Bernuz, 2014: 13). If we add to this that offenders are more likely to respond in a positive manner before criminal justice when they perceive the procedures as fair (Braithwaite, 2003), we could expect more involvement and better results than in traditional procedures.

4 Conclusions and final reflections

The States adhering to the CRC have the obligation to provide complete protection to children under the law, and criminal child justice procedures must safeguard all children's rights enshrined in the Convention. In that sense, an essential component in the due process is the right of the child to be heard. Restorative justice provides a better scenario to protect this right, as the process is generally conducted in a friendly and confidential way, with less formality, and usually in a context that is neutral or independent from the formal justice system. Also, youngsters' willingness and involvement in the process guarantee that she or he 'has a say' about how the case is 'dealt with', making sure that the child offender has all the information that she or he needs in order to make relevant decisions. This involvement and participation may take the form of an agreement that is adapted to her or his expectations and possibilities as well as those of the victim. This agreement is also shared with judicial authorities. In other words, children are attentively heard in order to provide a 'fair' restorative justice process.

In addition to these procedural factors, it is essential to delve into the meaning of the right to be heard. Based on the observations of the Chilean experience, we identified three core aspects: (i) the child's life story, narratives, emotions, questions and fears could be attentively heard; (ii) the restorative process is be able to address the child's present needs and the ones that have arisen as a consequence of the offence and/or the judicial procedure; and (iii) the restorative process can take into account the developmental stage of the child, giving her or him opportunities for development and growth, that is to say, to evolve her or his meanings and narratives. Restorative justice procedures have the potential for 'hearing' the child in these three dimensions. It is interesting to mention that the process does not only allow the child's voice to be heard by the mediator or the judicial authority, but also by their family, the victim or other meaningful people, having a magnifying effect and allowing the child to develop her or his social capital.

The change introduced by the CRC regarding the conception of the child does not guarantee the change of mentality and practices required from the administrators of justice to make it effective. In the General Comment N°24 (2019), para. 4, the Committee on the Rights of the Child establishes that state parties require significant investment to achieve full compliance with the Convention. In this regard, we also learned that having a skillful mediator is not enough. In our experience (Bolívar et al., 2017), the right to be heard can only be upheld when there exists a judicial system that incorporates restorative justice as a valid approach, and when judicial authorities and professionals are highly trained and have become fully aware of restorative justice implications. The former will enable an opportune diversion – and consequently, the access of children to restorative justice programs in different stages of a criminal process –, and the validation of its results, making this 'act of hearing' real, concrete and significant. Training, sensitization and involvement of prosecutors and defense attorneys in the process of implementing the Chilean pilot program not only allowed valuing the program and its results, but also an increase of referrals and more flexible selection criteria (Bolívar et al., 2017). The principle of accessibility to the mediation service is a structural condition for youngsters to be effectively heard and for the system not to give priority to some cases or profiles over others.

Finally, the right to be heard is not only a matter of individual young people, but an issue that concerns us all, as a society. Gal (2011: 44) argues that the participation of children in the decision-making processes would be highly educative and would be a contribution to democratic societies, as it would train children to be tolerant and respectful of the views of others. Bosisio (2012: 145) adds that the children's right to participation 'would help them understand the meaning and working of democracy.'

References

Bernuz, B. (2014). La legitimidad de la justicia de menores: entre justicia procedimental y justicia social. *InDret, 1*, Barcelona.

Bernuz, B.M.J. (2015). El derecho a ser escuchado: El caso de la infancia en conflicto con la norma. *Derechos y Libertades*, N° 33, Época II, 67-98.

Bolívar, D., Ramírez, A., Baracho, B., de Haan, M., Castillo, F., Fernández, M. & Aertsen, I. (2017). *Estudio Proyecto Capacitación, Asesoría y Estudio Práctico Mediación Penal Juvenil. Informe Final.* Santiago: Facultad de Ciencias Sociales, Universidad de Chile.

Bosisio, R. (2012). Children's right to be heard: what children think. *International Journal of Children's Rights*, 20, 141-154.

Braithwaite, J. (2003). Does restorative justice work? In J. Johnstone (ed.), *A restorative justice reader: texts, sources, context*, 320-352. Cullompton: Willan Publishing.

Cámara de Diputados de la República de Chile. (2015). Informe Ejecutivo de la Evaluación de la Ley 20.084. Comité de Evaluación de la Ley.

Chapman, T., Gellin, M., Aertsen, I. & Anderson, M. (2015). *European research on restorative juvenile justice (vol. 2): protecting rights, restoring respect and strengthening relationships: a European model for restorative justice with children and young people.* Brussels: International Juvenile Justice Observatory; European Council for Juvenile Justice.

Código Procesal Penal de Chile aprobado mediante la Ley 19.696. (2000). Retrieved from www.leychile.cl (last accessed 10 February 2020).

Couso, J. & Duce, M. (2013) *Juzgamiento penal de adolescents.* Santiago: LOM.

Duce, M. (2009). El Derecho a un Juzgamiento Especializado de los Jóvenes Infractores en el Derecho Internacional de los Derechos Humanos y su Impacto en el Diseño del Proceso Penal Juvenil. *Ius et Praxis*, 15(1), 73-120.

Espejo, N. (2014). *Hacia una reforma integral del sistema del sistema penal de adolescentes en Chile: el desafío de la especialización. Serie de Reflexiones: infancia y adolescencia N° 18.* Chile: UNICEF.

Etcheberry, L. & Fuentes, C. (2017). El derecho de los niños a ser oídos. In A. Quesille (ed.), *Constitución Política e Infancia* (pp. 111-147). Chile: UNICEF.

Gal, T. (2011). *Child victims and restorative justice: a needs-rights model.* New York: Oxford University Press.

Hernández Basualto, H. (2007). El Nuevo Derecho Penal de Adolescentes y la Necesaria Revisión de su "Teoría Del Delito". *Revista de derecho (Valdivia)*, 20(2), 195-217.

Krappmann, L. (2010). The weight of the child's view (Article 12 of the Convention on the Rights of the Child). *International Journal of Children's Rights*, 18, 501-513.

Mera, A. (2018). *Los derechos de los niños, una orientación y un límite. Reforma a la justicia penal adolescente. ¿Por qué no dar un giro hacia la Justicia Restaurativa?* Chile: UNICEF.

Miranda, P., Bolívar, D., Farah, J., Fernández, M. & Baracho, B. (2018). Elaboración de un Sistema de Supervisión para la Mediación Penal en el Marco del Nuevo Servicio de Reinserción Social Juvenil. Informe final. Escuela de Trabajo Social, Pontificia Universidad Católica de Chile.
Morrow, V. (1999). 'We are people too': children's and young people's perspectives on children's rights and decision-making in England. *The International Journal of Children's Rights*, 7, 149-170.
Senado de la República de Chile. (2017). Proyecto de Ley que Crea el Servicio Nacional de Reinserción Social Juvenil e introduce modificaciones a las Ley 20.084 y a otras normas que indica. Boletín 11174-07. Retrieved from www.senado.cl/appsenado/templates/tramitacion/index.php?boletin_ini=11174-07 (last accessed 18 January 2020).
United Nations (1985) United Nations Standard Minimum Rules for the Administration of Juvenile ("The Beijing Rules"). Retrieved from https://www.ohchr.org/documents/professionalinterest/beijingrules.pdf.
United Nations (1989) Convention on the Rights of the Child. Office of the High Commissioner for Human Rights. Retrieved from https://www.ohchr.org/en/professionalinterest/pages/crc.aspx.

Chapter 12

When child-friendly justice meets restorative justice in a welfare model

The case of France

Jessica Filippi

If childhood is the sleep of reason ... I am, however, very far from thinking that children have no reason to think. On the contrary, I see that they reason well in everything they know about their present and sensible interest. (Rousseau, 1792[2009]: 132)

1 Introduction

In France, a general legal framework introduced by the law of 15 August 2014 relating to the individualization of penalties and the reinforcement of the effectiveness of penal sanctions put in place measures of restorative justice in the Code of Criminal Procedure (Law, 2014). Article 10-1 provides a broad implementation for restorative justice measures, more particularly 'in all criminal proceedings and at all stages of the proceedings, including the execution of the sentence'. A restorative justice measure can be 'proposed' during all the stages of a criminal procedure, from the moment a crime is reported to the execution of sentences, or even beyond (Law, 2014).[1] Three years later, a Circular presented how practically restorative justice measures can take place in judicial proceedings (Circular, 2017).[2] Three legal conditions permit to propose measures of restorative justice to offenders and victims. The first one is a minimal recognition of the fact by the offender, the second condition is that all participants have a complete informations about what restorative justice is and to finish and the third condition is

1 Art. 707-IV-2 du code de procédure pénale de la loi du 15 aout 2014 relative à l'individualisation des peines et renforçant l'effectivité des sanctions pénales, "D'obtenir la réparation de son préjudice, par l'indemnisation de celui-ci ou par tout autre moyen adapté, y compris, s'il y a lieu, en se voyant proposer une mesure de justice restaurative"; Art. 707-IV-2 of the Criminal procedure code of the law of the 15 August 2014 on the individualization of sentences and strengthening the efficiency of criminal sanctions 'To obtain compensation for his/her loss, compensation for it or any other appropriate means, including, where appropriate, being proposed a restorative justice measure'.

2 A circular is a document with instructions on the substance of the law or the procedure. It is an infra-regulatory text and is only here to comment on existing law, adapt its concrete application to local circumstances. This circular is written by several ministers (interministerial circular) for the attention of the decentralized services which will have to apply it.

that participants consent expressly to participate in such a process. The legal authority has to control the implementation of these three conditions to permit to the process of restorative justice to pursue. However, the 'welfare model',[3] adopted in France with youth justice system, limits the capacity of the interested parties to be involved in such a process, especially for juveniles (child victim or offender).

Even if restorative justice for juveniles is legislated, its practices are very limited. Since 2019 and until 2021, restorative justice experimentations are taking place in the criminal justice system, involving professionals from public and private services of the ministry of justice, on ten sites (regions of Thionville, Nevers, Toulouse, Marseille, Gironde, Saint Nazaire, Porcheville, Juvisy-Sur-Orge, Amiens and Valence). The establishment of partnership agreements with the various professionals of the juvenile justice system has made it possible to define the roles and places of each professional in the information, orientation and implementation of restorative justice (RJ). While some regions have agreements with different partners (public service, national education, police and victim association) in place, others are not yet finalized (three out of ten sites). The lack of agreement and the lack of training are obstacles to these experimentations. Professionals in these sites are not familiar with the participatory and empowerment process of restorative justice (Filippi, 2021a).

Furthermore, the way restorative justice is presented in the French Circular and its place in the criminal justice system are also barriers for implementation. There are tensions and contradictions between the welfare model and the concept of child-friendly justice, which includes principles and processes of restorative justice. This may be one of the reasons why restorative justice has been difficult to implement in the welfare system in France. It seems that a power relation is established 'against' restorative justice by the welfare model. If the ideology of the welfare model limits the implementation of restorative justice, amendments and recommendations are necessary to permit a real and broad implementation and appropriation of restorative justice by children.

2 Participation in justice: from 'child-friendly justice' to restorative justice

Child-friendly justice, as a concept, is also an approach in line with the philosophy and the process of restorative justice. The European (Children's Directive, EU2016/800; Council of Europe, 2010) and international rules (Committee of the Rights of Children, CRC) contribute to a framework of 'child-friendly' justice. This concept is applied to all

3 The welfare model is a protectionist logic and an approach based on the assumption that juvenile wrongdoing is the product of social or environmental factors for which the young person cannot be held individually responsible. The primary goal is to provide appropriate intervention and educational measure than punishment.

children in conflict with the law (Children's Directive, EU2016/800). 'Child-friendly justice' could be an encounter between the basic principles of children's rights and juvenile justice with all the processes that permit a child to participate actively in judicial proceedings that interest him/her.

A child who is capable of forming his/her views can express them freely. Those views should be given due weight in accordance with his/her age and maturity (Art. 12.1 CRC) in any judicial and administrative proceedings affecting the child, either directly, or through a representative in a manner consistent with the procedural rules of national law (Art. 12.2 CRC). Children have the right to express themselves, speak their mind and give their views in all decisions that affect them (Art. 40.1 CRC, Art. 40(3)(b) CRC, Art. 40(2)(vii) CRC). The child should be given the opportunity to express his/her views concerning the (alternative) measures that may be imposed (Art. 39 CRC; Art. 40.1 CRC, Art. 40(3)(b) CRC) and the specific wishes or preferences he/she may have in this regard should be given due weight.

Restorative justice is a process that permits children to implement those rights and approaches. In the scientific literature, some definitions place the emphasis on the participatory aspect of the process and on encounters and active participation through dialogue. Others stress restorative outcomes such as 'reparation, victim recovery and offender reintegration' (United Nations, 2020: 4). In restorative justice, the participatory dimension is also present; it could be assimilated as the process of empowerment, which is a fundamental value of restorative justice. It can be defined in practice by two concepts: 'agency' and 'A child must be given the opportunity to express his/her views freely, and those views should be given due weight in accordance with his/her age and maturity (Art. 12, CRC), and this throughout the juvenile justice process accountability' (O'Mahony & Doak, 2017). The implementation processes of restorative justice present convincing positive results for all the people involved throughout the criminal justice system. With respect to its participants, restorative justice is a more meaningful experience of justice (Aertsen & Peters, 1998, 2003; Lilles, 2001; Morris & Maxwell, 2002; Umbreit et al., 2001). Their participation is free and voluntary. They can withdraw from the process at any time. Restorative justice gives participants the opportunity to take an active role in the regulation of conflict. The victims are valued by the process, they can have the information they need ('when', 'why', 'how') and share their concerns, their feelings and their emotions. By involving the offenders and inviting them to listen to the victims, answer questions and feel empathy, they develop understanding of the harmful act. From this position, the offender is better able to propose solutions and feels more invested in the modalities of their implementation. The association of the community in the process of restorative justice can offer support to the offender and victim and the resources needed to achieve their goals. The process of accountability is not only dedicated to the offender, but to all those who 'feel concerned' about the offense. Participants then can take responsibility for addressing the impact and consequences of the offense on themselves and others (Bolitho, 2015; Bolivar, 2019; Hallam, 2014).

Very young children or children without full capacity to pursue their rights are bearers of rights. For these children, alternative systems of representation need to develop in order to avoid discrimination. Every juvenile justice intervention should aim to reintegrate the child into society and allow him/her to play a constructive role. Child inclusive practices give children and young people the opportunity to have a conversation (verbal, written, through play and storytelling) with professionals who are assisting their parents to make arrangements for the children's future. It enables consenting children and young people to share their experiences and express their concerns and views and for these to be sensitively considered with their parent's concerns and views so that their developmental needs and concerns can be better understood and taken into account within the dispute resolution process.

More precisely, restorative justice is a process based on active and voluntary participation, listening, free exchanges, respect and empowerment of each participant in the process. It is important to include all those who have an interest in finding a way out of the conflict crystallized by the offense. Both are processes with child inclusive practice, and both empower children and young people to participate in justice. Restorative justice allows them the choice to have a conversation about conflict or offenses and to express their opinions and views in a process that is complementary to judicial proceedings. Also, 'child-friendly justice' is based on the right to self-expression and/or legal representation, the right to be heard and the right to take part in a decision. Restorative justice is a communicative process. Children (offender and/or victim) are heard and are free to participate. In addition, it is a dynamic process, which requires the participation of all parties. By encouraging the participation and understanding of the people in the process, restorative justice allows for offenders, victims and the community to have a role and a place in juvenile justice and to increase their belief in the justice institution. Child-friendly justice also permits an atmosphere of understanding and allows juveniles to participate in this sphere and to express their needs. Both, based on children's rights, 'child-friendly justice' and 'restorative justice', are appropriate processes to implement those rights in the best interest of the child. To implement those rights in good order and in an effective way, professionals should provide this information to the participants (Council of Europe, 2010).

In a restorative justice process, in order to repair and redress the harm done to the victim, the community and the offender, all parties should be actively involved in the process. In this sense, the promotion of the responsibility and accountability of the participants are highlighted. (Filippi, 2018a, 2018b) (Table 12.1).

Table 12.1 Common points between child-friendly justice and restorative justice

Children's rights	Child-friendly justice	Restorative justice
The right to be heard (Art. 12 CRC, to express their view, to be informed, to participate in justice (Art. 40.1, CRC; Art. 40 (3)(b), Art. 40(2)(vii) and Art. 16).	Child-friendly justice is an approach which implement international (Committee of the Rights of Children, CRC) and European rules (Children's Directive, EU2016/800; Council of Europe, 2010). Child-friendly justice is a way to create an environment and to adapt justice for children in order to help them to participate actively and to take part in it. Child-friendly justice includes the rights to due process, to participate in and to understand the proceedings, to respect for private and family life, and to integrity and dignity.	Restorative justice is a way for the implementation of these rights in a voluntary and secure place. Restorative justice is a way to balance the expectations and needs of its participants after a conflict to find the best solutions to resolve the conflict. Opinions, views and feelings are considered, solutions proposed are related to the discernment at level of maturity of the child.
The best interest of the child (BIC) (Art. 2 CRC, Art. 3 CRC, Art. 6 CRC, Art. 40.1 CRC).	Child-friendly justice is accessible, age-appropriate, diligent, adapted to and focused on the needs and rights of the child. Opinions, views and feelings are considered, intervention are related to the best interest of the child.	The process of restorative justice belongs to the participants and involves them in expressing their own interests, expectations and needs. The framework of implementation of measures of restorative justice and the role of the (impartial) facilitator permit each participant to find their place in the process in a just, fair, secure and confidential atmosphere.

Meanwhile, there is a real discrepancy within the 'welfare model' between the judicial procedure and legal and professional culture, on the one hand, and the emancipatory dimension and the processes of empowerment (agency and accountability) (O'Mahony & Doak, 2017), which characterize restorative justice, on the other hand, which will be explored in the next section. In some countries a 'welfare' model prevails, which focuses on the needs of the child, diagnosis, treatment and informal procedures, whereas other countries favor a 'justice' model, which emphasizes accountability, punishment and procedural formality. In other countries, such as Belgium and France, there is a subtle mix of these two models, creating a particular context in which restorative justice is being implemented (Filippi, 2021b).

3 Restorative justice in France narrowed by the 'welfare' model

3.1 The role of adults and legal representatives in restorative measures

While restorative justice is supposed to belong to all those who feel concerned in the conflict, the full participation of children who are suspects or accused of a crime in restorative justice measures can be threatened by the control that may be exercised by the parents of the child (both offender and victim) and the judicial authority. Even if children are interested in taking part, the current process of restorative justice in France may no longer belong to them.

We see that the 'welfare model' with its protectionist logic leaves little room for an emancipatory ideology, which could lead to a process such as restorative justice for juveniles. Restorative justice should be an intervention not to punish or to re-educate, but to set the conditions for the restoration of the participants in this process caused by the offense.

The Circular about the implementation of the measures of restorative justice mentions that:

> The implementation of restorative justice measures should be adapted to the status as child offenders or victims and to involve parents in the process … Furthermore, for child victims, special attention must be paid to the implications and impact of such a measure, including legal representatives. (Circular, 2017: 4)

While legal representatives are referred to, it seems that a mention of how they should be concretely involved is missing. Instead of just mentioning 'parents' in the text, reference should have been made to 'legal guardians of parental authority', which refers more generally to persons with a set of rights and duties whose ultimate purpose is the interest of the child. Parental authority is defined by its purpose: it ensures the protection of the child in her/his safety, health and morals, in order to ensure his/her education and enable her/his development with respect for her/his person (French civil code Art. 371-1).

In the event that one of the two legal representatives agrees on the involvement of a child in a restorative justice measure and the child also finds an 'interest' in participating in it, such a measure will continue. In the event that legal representatives do not wish the child to participate, but she/he wishes to, the decision initially envisaged can be reviewed by the same legal representatives, thus allowing the child's involvement in the restorative justice process. From a practical point of view, in measures affecting juvenile offenders and either juvenile or adult victims, it is rare for those having parental authority to refuse the participation of their child in a restorative justice measure. In the light of these elements and in the context of the Circular, preference should be given to using the notion of 'parental authority', in which case the decision to participate or not in a restorative justice measure rests with the legal representatives but would be animated primarily by the interest of the child. By clarifying the term used and its precise legal meaning, it could be ensured to some extent that the expectations and needs of the primary stakeholders in the restorative justice process are taken into account.

Moreover, the implementation of restorative justice measures in France must be adapted to the offenders' and victims' status as children. The Circular states:

> It is therefore essential to assess the adolescent's ability to measure the effects of her/his act on the victim and his willingness to engage in a restorative justice process. (Circular, 2017: 4)

Within the framework of restorative justice, a minimal recognition of the facts may be sufficient to initiate the process. The feelings and the perceptions of the child concerning actually performing an act may depend on the past and circumstantial events that she/he experienced. Although a juvenile may initially fail to 'evaluate the extent of the effects of her/his act' (Circular, 2017: 4), it is by the gradual returns and comments of the members of the community (including their parents) and/or the victim(s) that the measurement of these effects occur and she/he may take responsibility for the consequences.

In criminal proceedings for child offenders or victims, the lack of capacity or maturity is used by the legal authority as an obstacle for his/her effective participation in decision-making processes in justice. We can speculate that this consideration could be an obstacle for the implementation of restorative justice, which offers the possibility to the interested parties to express their views and their feelings. Restorative justice processes permit their participants to take an active role (accountability and empowerment) to propose and develop the best solutions to move beyond the conflict.

Restorative justice is primarily a voluntary process. Children can be encouraged but not forced to participate. Their participation in this process depend on what they want (expectations and needs) and on their capacities (their interests and their commitment in the resolution of the conflict). The Circular regarding implementation of restorative justice mentions that it is necessary to assess the willingness of the participants to engage in a restorative justice process. Once again, the intervention of an adult to evaluate this desire interferes with the needs and the interests of the child in deciding to participate in the process. The assessment of the suitability of a measure of restorative justice can only be done by a professional who is trained in restorative justice, for instance a mediator who intervenes in parallel to the judicial process. In the context of restorative justice, the sense of responsibility should not be understood as a situation where the offender is obliged to assume the consequences imposed by the system, but rather a responsibility in which the offender actively assumes the relationship between himself and the act. She/he becomes aware of being accountable for the offense in this latter, less legalistic sense and will actively participate in the social reaction to her/his act (obligations).

Through the Circular, the required involvement of an adult limits the child's participation. The involvement of an adult, following the logic of protection in the 'welfare' model, controls and decides in 'the interest of the child'. This presence undoubtedly serves a protective end, but at the same time limits the implementation of a process of empowerment of the young person(s) involved.

3.2 *A protective logic at every stage of the process*

Even if the interest of the child and her/his needs are addressed when they participate in a restorative justice measure, the degree of influence is again reduced by the central role played by the judicial authorities. The Circular envisages different ways of control and 'dispossession' of the restorative measures for the young participants. The judicial authorities play a major role in the orientation and in the qualitative evaluation of the measures of restorative justice at all the stages of the judicial procedure.

For instance, at the level of the public prosecutor's office:

> The restorative justice measure is proposed to the parties by the judicial authorities … the magistrate determines the moment when this measure can begin … the files for which this measure shall be the subject of careful selection by the public prosecutor…. When it receives a request for the implementation of a measure originating from an association, it shall exercise an appropriateness review and give its prior consent. (Circular, 2017: 8)

At the investigative stage, the magistrate must be informed by the service that is in charge of the delivery of restorative justice, about the implementation of the measure. It may obtain 'her/his prior agreement, with regard to issues of the proceedings' (Circular, 2017: 8), in front of an examining magistrate.

It is also worth mentioning that both for children and adults, the restorative justice measure:

> may be inadequate because of the risk of interaction between the parties … it is important at this stage as at the initial examination stage to preserve the word

> of the victim and not to compromise the conduct of the judicial investigation. (Circular, 2017: 9)

The precautions presented through the Circular are essentially based on two aspects. The first aspect relates to a concern for protection for the participants and more particularly for children when the facts have occurred in the family sphere. With the Circular, the intention of the ministry of justice is well on track with regard to transposing the European Directive 2012/29/EU of the European parliament and of the Council of 25 October 2012 establishing minimum standards on the rights, support and protection of victims of crime.[4] Although the transposition of this directive into the framework of the Circular on the development of restorative justice is laudable, the compatibility between this directive and the restorative justice process is questionable. Restorative justice processes can be implemented for all kind of offenses and can facilitate exchanges or encounters between offenders and victims even if they belong to the same family. According to the European Directive, contact with offenders and victims from a same family should be avoided: Member States shall :

> establish the necessary conditions to enable avoidance of contact between victims and their family members, where necessary, and the offender within premises where criminal proceedings are conducted, unless the criminal proceedings require such contact.

The second aspect refers to compliance with procedural rules (presumption of innocence, evidential rules for proof of culpability). The legal culture, which is inscribed in the Circular, seems to assimilate restorative justice process as a place where justice will be done. Restorative justice may be inadequate because it could '... compromise the conduct of the judicial investigation' (Circular, 2017: 4). In the Circular, restorative justice is associated as a process where the judicial truth can be determined. The welfare model restricts this process of justice.

These two elements, presented separately, nevertheless remain intrinsically linked through the judicial process.

4 In the European Directive 2012/29/EU of the European Parliament and of the Council of 25 October 2012, establishing minimum standards on the rights, support and protection of victims of crime, the Art. 19 provides that 'Member States shall establish the necessary conditions to enable avoidance of contact between victims and their family members, where necessary, and the offender within premises where criminal proceedings are conducted, unless the criminal proceedings require such contact'. Also, the Art. 23-3-a provides 'the following measures shall be available for victims with specific protection needs identified in accordance with Art. 22(1) during court proceedings: (a) measures to avoid visual contact between victims and offenders including during the giving of evidence, by appropriate means including the use of communication technology'.

In light of what has been stated above in relation to the impetus given by the judicial authority, there is a risk of conflict between the legal protection culture of the judicial authority in specific situations (like family cases) and the restorative justice processes. Theoretically, however, restorative justice measures can happen in all kinds of cases.

Although the right to participate permits a child to be involved in such a process, the legal authority can stop the process of restorative justice '... to preserve the word of the victim and not to jeopardize the proper conduct of the judicial investigation' (Circular, 2017: 9). This formulation relates to the victim's protection as a possible witness. The Circular, except for the three legal conditions (mentioned above), does not detail the role of initiation and control by the magistrate. Because, it is not detailed, this formulation seems to leave enough room for those interested in the process to participate in. But, to give restorative justice its full and effective place, it is essential that legal professionals have complete information on the practices and processes of restorative justice (through training). The legal authorities have reservations about restorative justice. For them only the juvenile justice system guarantees the rights of children. Because restorative justice is a confidential process, the authorities will have no means of knowing or of controlling what happens.

By ensuring confidentiality, restorative justice can neither be a means of investigation that seeks to determine the guilt of the suspect nor a process that interferes with the search for the truth. Restorative justice and its processes aim to guarantee respect and safety and protection of the participants (offenders, victims and community) through the presence and integrity of the mediator. Assessment and preparation are crucial to refine exchanges that take place between the participants as well as the modalities when implementing the process.

While the Circular should allow for a 'wide ownership' of the process by the participants, it nevertheless remains in the most serious circumstances under the authority of the magistrate (offense in family sphere, sexual assault, etc). It is undeniable that the Circular will, by some lack of precision, allow a wide potential implementation of the process by the judicial authorities, the professionals and/or the participants of the restorative justice process. However, this lack of precision could lead to the opposite effect in view of the many reservations and issues of concern listed and expressed above, also bearing in mind the principles of the French judicial procedure and the protection of the participants in the process. Without definition or precision, the magistrate could control all of the propositions of restorative justice measures for juveniles when she/he considers that the offense is too serious. By his/her control and assessment of opportunity for restorative justice, this situation could lead to a marginalized implementation of such a process and a voluntary process that can be taken out of the control of the participants. Unfortunately, in this situation, some restorative justice measures could be limited to less severe cases and may be proposed in criminal offenses that did not take place in the family setting, and mostly taking place in the post-sentencing phase. Restorative justice could offer benefits for participants beyond this if the process is proposed at all stages of procedure and for all types of offenses. From the moment the participants wish to enter a voluntary process, they can leave at any time without any consequences for the outcome of the legal proceedings. Considering that such a process is supervised and evaluated by a mediator who is trained in restorative justice, the assessment of a magistrate is not necessary.

Paradoxes arise in the interweaving of restorative justice measures and judicial proceedings for juveniles. While, on the one hand, there remains a desire to allow magistrates to control the restorative process (especially in specific field like interfamilial offenses), and, on the other hand, there are rules of confidentiality and disconnection between restorative justice and judicial proceedings, the balance remains fragile. The Circular presents restorative justice as a way of reparation and resolution of conflict. It also highlights a minimalist approach by focusing on processes of restorative justice and disconnection with the judicial procedure (Filippi, 2021: 56). In this sense, restorative justice cannot 'color' the juvenile justice system. The French approach toward restorative justice seems to 'preserve' the principles of judicial proceedings and limit the practical implementation of the principles of restorative justice to a certain extent (Zehr, 2002: 37, 2012: 98). While the legal framework of restorative justice in France permits a broad implementation at every stages of proceedings, because of the disconnect between restorative justice and judicial proceedings, it seems that practice of restorative justice for juveniles is reserved, for now, for children who are subjected to educative measures. The limitations of this way of implementing restorative justice with juveniles can be explained by the need of control by the legal authority.

4 Conclusion and recommendations

The way of thinking about restorative justice by lawmakers and professionals in judicial proceedings is currently limiting its development in France. The concepts of confidentiality and minimal recognition of facts, which are inherent to the process of restorative justice and distinguishes it from judicial procedures, seem to be problematic for legal and child protection professionals. Because of these considerations, the implementation of restorative justice is envisaged in parallel with a penal measure. It seems that professionals need to supervise and control the process (Filippi, 2021: 54).

The legalization on restorative justice measures for youth could be a departure point for France to permit young people to gain access to the right to participate actively in judicial proceedings. In the Juvenile Criminal Justice Code (JCJC, 2019, 2021), two articles address access to restorative justice for children. The first one is located at the beginning of the new code in Article L. 13-4 (JCJC, 2019). The second inscribes mediation as an alternative measure (JCJC, 2021, Article D. 422-4) and in a provisional judicial educational measure (PJEM) or an educational measure justice (EMJ) (JCJC, 2019) through the 'reparation' module (JCJC, 2019, Art. L. 112-8 and L.112-10). In Article L. 13-4 the proposal for restorative justice is located in the common provisions, thus demonstrating the importance accorded to this philosophy in the welfare model. Restorative justice practice will follow the instructions of the Circular (Circular, 2017). Unlike the Article L.13-4, the second approach of 'restorative justice' presents an integrated mediation in the criminal system. As an alternative or in an educational framework (PJEM or EMJ), these legal frameworks present mediation as an 'ordered' measure (JCJC, 2019) which have consequences on judicial procedure. The service in charge of mediation informs the judge of the difficulties observed and can request the modification of the module or its deletion (Art. D112-30, JCJC, 2021). Restorative justice is envisaged as a single measure, as a diversion measure at the beginning of the procedure and as complementary process in the context of PJEM or EMJ. Mediation here, is absorbed by the juvenile justice system and lost restorative justice values. Unfortunately, the way of implementation restorative justice and mediation doesn't answer to the welfare model's philosophy and child-friendly approach.

Restorative justice should be integrated in the youth justice system, reconciling the dimension of education and the child-friendly justice approach. For now, if restorative justice is proposed only in the case of a previous educative measure, because of the need for supervision by adults, it remains limited in its scope (Filippi, 2021, 54-55). Its implementation within the child justice system must be done in a maximalist approach and should be proposed and not ordered: the effects of restorative justice should be complementary to the criminal justice system at the heart of the socio-judicial answer and will influence the criminal justice system (Walgrave, 1993, 1999) in favor of juveniles. The adoption of such an approach would eventually lead to the adoption of a democratic welfare model for juveniles. It would not simply be a child justice system promoting restoration, but it would be about doing justice through restoration (Walgrave, 2008). It will be a way to implement restorative justice by seeing what the participants were able to decide, accept or exchange during the process. Finally, it will be a way for children to be recognized as human beings who can decide and propose things with their own life experience and with their own legal capacity. Children may, then, expect a system in which they participate actively or which enables them to participate in society, in institutions, in justice, in the name of their fundamental rights. This would be beneficial both for children and their communities. This requires that they can exercise their rights as autonomously as possible because 'they reason well in everything they know about their present and sensible interest' (Rousseau, 1792[2009]: 132).

References

Aertsen, I. & Peters, T. (1998). Mediation for reparation: the victim's perspective. In E. Fattah & T. Peters (eds.), *Support for crime victim in a comparative perspective, a collection of essays dedicates to the memory of Prof. Frederic McClintock* (pp. 229-251). Leuven: University Press.

Aertsen, I. & Peters, T. (2003). Des politiques européennes en matière de justice restauratrice. *Le Journal International De Victimologie*, 2(1), 1-13.

Bolitho, J. (2015). Putting justice needs first: a case study of best practice in restorative justice. *Restorative Justice: An International Journal*, 3(2), 256-281.

Bolivar, D. (2019). *Restoring harm: a psychosocial approach to victims and restorative justice*. London: Routledge.

Children's Directive. (2016). Directive (EU) 2016/800 of the European Parliament and of the Council of 11 May 2016 on procedural safeguards for children who are suspects or accused persons in criminal proceedings.

Circular. (2017). Circular of the 15 March relative à la Mise en œuvre de la justice restaurative applicable immédiatement suite aux article 10-1, 10-2 et 707 du code de procédure pénale. Retrieved from https://www.legifrance.gouv.fr/download/pdf/circ?id=42000 (last accessed 3 August 2021).

Council of Europe. (2010). *Guidelines of the Committee of Ministers of the Council of Europe on child-friendly justice*. The Council of Europe programme "Building a Europe for and with children". Retrieved from https://rm.coe.int/16804b2cf3 (last accessed 2 August 2021).

Filippi, J. (2018a). Restorative justice for young offenders: an analysis of the French circular confronting at European and national legal perspective. *UCL Journal of Law and Jurisprudence*, 7(1), 142-162.

Filippi, J. (2018b). La justice restaurative des mineurs en France, une approche dans une perspective juridique et scientifique. *Journal du droit des jeunes*, 375, 18-29.

Filippi, J. (2021). *Droit pénal des mineurs et justice restaurative, Approche comparée France/Fédération Wallonie-Bruxelles*, Presses Universitaires du Septentrion.

Filippi, J. (2021). Restorative justice for juveniles in France: maximalist and minimalist tendencies, *Les cahiers de la sécurité et de la justice*, Hors-série, 48-59. Retrieved from https://www.vie-publique.fr/sites/default/files/collection_number/portrait/photo/9782111574786.pdf (last accessed 2 August 2021).

JCJC. (2019). Juvenile Criminal Justice Code of the 11 september, *Ordonnance n° 2019-950 du 11 septembre 2019 portant partie législative du code de la justice pénale des mineurs*, JORF n°0213 du 13 septembre 2019. Retrieved from www.legifrance.gouv.fr/affichTexte.do?cidTexte=JORFTEXT000039085102&categorieLien=id (last accessed 2 August 2021).

JCJC. (2021). Decree of the Juvenile Criminal Justice Code of the 30 may, Décret n° 2021-683 du 27 mai 2021 portant partie réglementaire du code de la justice pénale des mineurs (articles en D), JORF n°0124 du 30 mai 2021. Retrieved from https://www.legifrance.gouv.fr/jorf/id/JORFTEXT000043555232 (last accessed 2 August 2021).

Hallam, M. (2014). *Restoring the balance: an evaluation of the project conducted through interviews with victims, offenders and those making referrals to the service.* London: Victim Support (Thames Valley Area).

Law. (2014). Law n° 2014-896 of the 15 august relative à l'individualisation des peines et renforçant l'efficacité des sanctions pénales, JORF n°0189 du 17 août 2014 Retrieved from www.legifrance.gouv.fr/affichTexte.do?cidTexte=JORFTEXT000029362502&categorieLien=id.

Lilles, H. (2001). Circle sentencing: Part of the restorative justice continuum. In A. Morris & G. Maxwell (eds.), *Restorative justice for juveniles: conferencing, mediation and circles* (pp. 161-179). Oxford: Hart Publishing.

Morris, A. & Maxwell, G. (eds.). (2002). *Restorative justice for juveniles.* Oxford: Hart Publishing.

O'Mahony, D. & Doak, J. (2017). *Reimagining restorative justice: agency and accountability in the criminal process.* Oxford: Hart Publishing.

Rousseau, J-J. (1792[2009]). *L'Emile.* Paris: Flammarion.

Umbreit, M., Coates, R. & Vos, B. (2001). Victim impact on meeting with young offender: two decades of victims-offender mediation practice and research. In A. Morris & G. Maxwell (eds.), *Restorative justice for juveniles: conferencing, mediation and circles.* (pp. 133-137). Oxford: Hart Publishing.

United Nations. (2020). Office on Drugs and Crime. *Handbook on restorative justice programmes.* Criminal Justice Handbook Series (2nd ed.). Retrieved from www.unodc.org/documents/justice-and-prison-reform/20-01146_Handbook_on_Restorative_Justice_Programmes.pdf (last accessed 2 August 2021).

Walgrave, L. (1993). Beyond rehabilitation: in search of a constructive alternative in the judicial response to juvenile crime. *European Journal on Criminal Policy and Research,* 2(2), 57-75.

Walgrave, L. (1999). La justice restaurative: à la recherche d'une théorie et d'un programme. *Criminologie,* 32(1), 7-29.

Walgrave, L. (2008). *Restorative justice, self-interest and responsible citizenship.* Cullompton: Willan Publishing.

Zehr, H. (2002). *The little book of restorative justice.* Intercourse, PA: Good Books.

Zehr, H. (2012). *La justice restaurative. Pour sortir des impasses de la logique punitive,* Paris: Labord et fides, le champ éthique.

Chapter 13
Restorative justice for young people in Poland

The law, current practices and prospects for improvement

Beata Czarnecka-Dzialuk

1 The roots of restorative justice interventions

Searching for appropriate responses to youth offending has turned attention toward the potential of the philosophy and practices of restorative justice philosophy and practices in many countries, including Poland. Reports and articles presenting mediation programs in other countries have been published in Polish since the mid-80s and provided an inspiration for searching for such alternatives to traditional proceedings. A decade earlier, the interest in the rights of the child had been raised – in Poland and abroad. The fact that the first draft of the UN Convention on the Rights of the Child (CRC) was 'made in Poland' is not surprising for those dealing with the history of pedagogical ideas in my country.

In particular, certain solutions resembling those proposed by restorative justice had already been developed in the 1920s. Widely known for accompanying children from his orphanage on their way to a Nazi concentration camp in Treblinka and sharing their fate to the very end in the gas chamber, Janusz Korczak (1921) had initiated a child-friendly court in his orphanage run by the children themselves in order to solve misconduct cases or peer conflicts among them. His initiative to involve children in making decisions for themselves has been recently described as 'an active form of solving relational problems among pupils' (Pyżalski, 2018: 40). Worth remembering also is that the idea to create UNICEF came from the Pole Dr. Ludwik Rajchman, bacteriologist and social activist (Krawczak-Chmielecka, 2017). In the 1970s, Kamiński, an eminent pedagogue, proposed methods of working with cub scouts resembling certain restorative programs. One of the methods was youth therapeutic groups: young people were first brought together to critically reflect on their behavior, to make decisions to improve it and to prepare a corrective action plan. Another one, used with the youngest cub scouts, was the 'circle of counsel' – a meeting of a whole group of cub scouts collectively searching for the solutions to problems and conflicts between its members. In these circles, even when there were strong negative opinions on certain behaviors, the reaction of the group was always restorative and far from punitive (Czarnecka-Dzialuk & Stryjek, 2019; Kamiński, 1974, 1998).

The concept of children's rights has been one of the most important justifications for restorative justice programs for youth in Poland. Let us mention again that it was Poland that proposed the children's rights conference in 1978. The first draft was produced in the Institute of Law Studies of the Polish Academy of Sciences by the team led by Professor Tadeusz Smyczyński. The working group created by the United Nations Human Rights Committee to lead the work on the Convention was chaired by Adam Łopatka,[1] a professor in the same institute (Krawczak-Chmielecka, 2017).

Analyzing the rights of the child has turned attention to certain important questions that might be the basis for implementing restorative justice. The first is the subjectivity of children, enshrined in Article 12.1 of the Convention. It points out that State Parties shall assure that the child, who is capable of forming his or her own views, has the right to express them freely in all matters affecting the child, the views of the child being given due weight in accordance with the age and maturity of the child (para. 1). For this purpose, the child shall in particular be provided the opportunity to be heard in any judicial and administrative proceedings affecting the child, either directly, or through a representative or an appropriate body, in a manner consistent with the procedural rules of national law (Art. 12.2). Other relevant matters are contained in Article 40.3 of the Convention, namely in relation to the laws and procedures concerning juveniles, stressing measures without resorting to judicial proceedings, ensuring that human rights and legal safeguards are fully respected. Also, the procedural rights of children who are in conflict with the law, enshrined in the Convention, should be mentioned in the context of restorative justice. According to Article 40, they should be treated in a manner consistent with the promotion of the child's sense of dignity and worth, which reinforces the child's respect for the human rights and fundamental freedoms of others. Obviously, restorative justice should be compatible with this principle. Active participation strengthens the children's sense of agency, as they learn about the consequences of their acts for the victim and sometimes for the community or family members. This sense of agency might also be strengthened by the fact that the juvenile's decision to take part in a restorative program is needed to make it happen. As such, a sense of responsibility is being developed by creating conditions for the juvenile to learn

1 I met him when I started my doctoral studies; he greeted everybody with the unofficial 'cześć', similar to 'hi', leaving students a bit confused on how to reply to the eminent professor!

the relationship between cause and effect and to become aware of the consequences of one's behavior. Moreover, the probability of changing the juvenile's behavior increases, as restorative practices create the circumstances to develop an empathic attitude. Such expectations might be based upon emerging evidence from neuroscience, showing the capacity of restorative dialogue to promote emotional regulation and moral development[2] This is important not only when we think about minor offenders, but also about their victims – quite often they are young people too.

2 Promising beginnings of restorative programs for youth

Most of the above-mentioned developments have contributed to the implementation of an experimental program of victim-offender mediation in young offenders' cases. Below the age of criminal responsibility, which in Poland is in principle 17, responsibility for punishable action and educational or correctional measures are being applied as a rule.[3] Educative, non-punitive responses to young offenders have a long history in Poland. Consequently, the idea of an experimental program of victim-offender mediation with its possible educative effects has been accepted, even welcomed. The program and its evaluation had been reviewed in a number of publications in English (Czarnecka-Dzialuk, 2010a, 2010b, 2015, 2018; Czarnecka-Dzialuk & Wójcik, 2000, 2005; Nowak, 2009; Staniaszek 2018; Zalewski & Păroşanu, 2015). In this chapter, only the main observations will be presented. The experimental program was initiated by a team of volunteers from different professions – academics, researchers, probation officers, family judges, NGO volunteers (in the beginning there were about ten people only). The first step undertaken by this team was to examine whether the idea of victim-offender mediation was consistent with the existing legal regulations for dealing with juveniles in Poland. As the leading principles of the law on the treatment of minors of 26 October 1982 (*Journal of Laws* No. 35 item 228) are the well-being of the child, individualization and purposefulness, it was concluded that referring a case of a young person to mediation would not be against the law. Another step was to achieve buy-in by pointing out that certain historic examples of regulations or practices concerning

2 Nowadays we know that such an expectation might be based upon emerging evidence from neuroscience, showing the capacity of restorative dialogue to promote emotional regulation and moral development. Neuroscientists have demonstrated a biological impact of facing and communicating with others, i.e. the creation of mirroring neurons, and, for that reason, some of them, for example Dan Reisel, promote restorative justice (Reisel, 2013). Also Affect Script Psychology (ASP) explains clearly how we are biologically wired to have good relationships with others and why restorative approaches to problem-solving are biologically sound (Kelly & Thorsborne, 2014; Wallis & Tudor, 2008).

3 Penalty may be applied only in exceptional circumstances provided in the law. In particular, according to Art. 10 para. 2 of the criminal code, a 15-year-old who committed one of the most serious crimes according to law might be punished as an adult when the circumstances of the case and personal characteristics of the juvenile, especially inefficiency of previously applied court measures, justify this.

children consistent with the restorative justice idea have roots in the Polish law tradition. The experimental program of mediation in youth cases was then designed in 1995, after consultation with colleagues from abroad, and was accepted by the Ministry of Justice in 1996. Thanks to the financial support of the Heinrich Böll Foundation in Germany and the engagement of councils in a few Polish towns, the program could be implemented in eight selected locations (among them big cities and small towns). The action-oriented evaluation research was possible thanks to a grant from the National Research Committee.

Worth emphasizing is that two mediation trainings lasting five days each were delivered, not only to the future facilitators (most of them were probation officers dealing with family and juvenile cases), but to everybody involved in the program implementation – family judges, researchers and representatives of local authorities. Cases for mediation (there were no formal excluding criteria) were selected by the family judges, sometimes with the help of trained facilitators (mostly probation officers). Mediation was then offered to the injured party and to the young suspect. After being given the basic information on mediation, they were asked whether they agreed to participate. If yes, and if the young suspect confirmed the basic facts of the case, there were individual preparatory meetings, followed by a face-to-face meeting (although, in some cases, mediation was limited to the shuttle mediation). The basic rules, including confidentiality, neutrality and impartiality of mediation, were respected. When a case was sent back to the family court after mediation (mostly with a mediation agreement), the family judge took the final decision about the case – mostly they discontinued judicial proceedings.

During the two years of the experimental mediation program, mediation was conducted in cases involving 174 juveniles. There were cases of different offenses, most of which were not serious acts; some could be classified as 'very petty'. However, there were also felonies, very serious in terms of degree of harm and the influence of alcohol or violence. Some cases resulted from casual conflicts. For instance, a quarrel during a football match – whether a free kick should have been allowed – resulted in a physical fight, a broken nose and other face injuries. For the victimized boy it was important to learn during mediation that this act resulted not from hostility and was an accident. After the mediation meeting the young offender said that he understood that he had harmed a boy who did not deserve this. This mediation resulted in an apology, and in the family court, a reprimand. There were also more serious cases, such as rape or robbery, some premeditated and some while the offender was intoxicated.

The comprehensive evaluation of the program, including analysis of court files and detailed reports of mediators, interviews with mediation participants and checking of criminal records, has reported exceptionally good results in various areas. There were high numbers of accepted mediation proposals (around 74 percent), high numbers of agreements reached (92.5 percent), as well as a high number of agreements fulfilled (95 percent of the agreements reached) and high satisfaction of the parties involved (90 percent). The reconviction rate was very low – 14.6 percent after 1.5-2.5 years (Czarnecka-Dzialuk, 2015). These first promising results of the experimental program of victim-offender mediation in juveniles cases influenced the Polish parliament's decision to introduce regulations allowing for mediation in adult offender cases in the criminal code in the autumn of 1997 (Czarnecka-Dzialuk, 2015).

3 Legal regulations concerning victim-offender mediation in youth cases – at present and drafted for the future?

Even though in the law on the treatment of minors of 1982 there were some possibilities to justify referring cases to mediation, it seemed obvious that a clear legal basis allowing to do so would help with implementing and promoting mediation. As the work on wider amendments to the law on youth justice was just being completed in 1999, only extremely basic legal prescriptions on mediation had been proposed, while delegating detailed solutions to secondary legislation that could be adopted few months later. Therefore, it was possible to discuss legal regulations on mediation without great pressure of time. Mediation was accepted as an alternative measure, which – according to the explanatory memorandum to the governmental bill of 28 June 1999 – 'would fulfill the requirement concluded in the section 11 of the Minimal Rules (*Beijing Rules – BCD*) and in the Article 40.3 of the Convention on the Rights of the Child' (Korcyl-Wolska, 2001: 414). Note that this is another indication of how important the rights of the child have been for justifying restorative justice interventions in Poland. Regulation on mediation appeared in the Law thanks to the amendment of 15 September 2000 (*Journal of Laws* No. 91, item 1010), and the Regulation of the Minister of Justice on mediation proceedings in youth cases of 18 May 2001 (*Journal of Laws* No. 56, item 591), entered into force at the end of June 2001. Earlier, in 1997, on the basis of the promising results of the experimental program described above, mediation was introduced to the criminal codes, allowing for mediation in adult offender cases. The law on the treatment of minors, after the amendment of 2000, allows family judges to refer cases to mediation at every stage of the judicial proceedings, upon the request of the young suspect or the victim, or on his or her own initiative when all parties of the mediation proceedings agree (Art. 3a §1). Its result is to be taken into consideration when deciding about the case. Mediation is conducted outside of court, by a trained mediator supervised by an accredited organization (it may be a specialist mediation organization or another agency that also performs such tasks in addition to rehabilitation, psychological diagnosis, protecting human rights and freedoms) or by an trained individual working privately (called in the law a 'trustworthy person') (Art. 3a §2) Article 3 §3 of the law enumerates questions for secondary legislation and indicates ground rules for mediation to be taken into account. These include the educative role of mediation proceedings, the interests of the victim, voluntary participation, confidentiality, professionalism and impartiality of mediators. A further Regulation of 2001 issued by the Minister of Justice deals with the detailed rules and procedures of handling mediation, the requirements to be met by organizations and individual mediators, standards of training, the registration of mediators, access to the court and the form and scope of the report on mediation progress and result. In short, all mediators – individual persons or representatives of justified institutions – are to be registered by the president of a district court if they meet the requirements listed in the Regulation – i.e. being older than 26 years of age, having certain personal skills and knowledge and having completed a required training that meets the standards that are included in the Regulation (indicating concrete subjects, theoretical and practical). Certain groups of people cannot be mediators, such as professionally active judges, public prosecutors, policemen and 'all people employed in the justice system' – that also means probation officers, which is unfortunate, as in the experimental program a group of them had already completed mediation trainings. The Regulation provides for the principle of impartiality (§6.3), voluntary participation (§11) and confidentiality (§12). It further provides for neutral venues for the mediation and guidance about the manner in which it should be conducted (separate meetings with both sides and, if they agree to proceed further, a face-to-face meeting as a rule; shuttle mediation is allowed when direct mediation is impossible). The child's parents or other legal representatives participate in mediation proceedings (as well as parents of the minor victim). The court indicates the time for carrying out mediation – up to 6 weeks, which can be exceptionally extended for 14 days. After this time, the court should obtain a report on the results of the mediation (and the agreement, if one is reached).

In the literature, certain questions of mediation in youth cases had been raised. First of all, its educative character has been underlined (Cwalina, 2012; Konarska-Wrzosek, 2000). It has been argued that mediation should not be seen as fully diversionary, as it does not lead to referring the case to a non-judicial body. After the mediation, the case goes back to the family court, which makes the final decision (Górecki & Stachowiak, 2007; Kotowska, 2010).

The regulation in the law on the treatment of minors concerning mediation has been found unclear and too general (Czarnecka-Dzialuk, 2013). The most important rules are to be found not in the law, but in the secondary regulation only. This has resulted in a proposal by subsequent teams of experts appointed by the Minister of Justice in 2009 and 2011 to develop new rules to deal with young offenders. They highlighted that legal regulations concerning victim-offender mediation in adult cases have been amended in 2013 in such a way that the most important rules have been transferred from the secondary legislation to the code of criminal proceedings. Despite this fact, the proposed regulations have not been included in the subsequent amendments of the law, not even when, during the parliamentary debates, it was declared that amending legal regulations concerning mediation were planned to be considered 'soon'. However, it took several years to present the new draft proposal – in a governmental draft of the new law on minors of March 2019. It has finally proposed changes in the regulations concerning mediation. This Regulation however has disappeared from the chapter of general rules and is to be found only in Article 58. It states that the family court may, on the initiative of or with the consent of the injured party and the young offender, refer the case to mediation (Art. 58.1), that their participation is voluntary and needs their consent, that this consent is to be received by the family court or by the mediator after the idea and rules of mediation proceedings have been explained and that parties may withdraw consent at any time (Art. 58.2). According to Article 58.3, mediation should aim to raise in the child a sense of responsibility for the effects of his or her punishable act and to conclude with an agreement to repair the damage or redress the harm. Article 58.4 indicates that parents or tutors participate in the mediation proceedings. The mediation process must be completed within 6 weeks (Art. 58.5). Article 58.6 regulates access (limited) of the mediator to the court files. The agreement on the child's commitment to repair the damage or to compensate the harm must be accepted by his statutory representative (Art. 58.7); parents may also conclude an agreement with the injured party (Art. 58.8). The family court considers the mediation result and the agreement while deciding about the case (Art. 58.9). To other matters not regulated by the drafted law on youth, the provisions of the code of civil proceedings on mediation (Art. 183'1-183'15) are to be applied accordingly.

Those drafted changes are, in my opinion, not favorable. They do not conform to the legal regulations concerning mediation in penal cases, amended in 2013 and in 2015. I have expressed my reservations during the public consultation. Even if those draft regulations included certain elements elaborated above (namely, adding a more concrete explanation of voluntariness and requirements concerning informed concern), it seems it would be a step backward. In the governmental draft it is declared that 'the value of mediation is not to be overestimated' and that 'the legal regulations encourage the solution of disputes between the injured party and the young suspect'. The latter statement is not realized in the proposed legal solutions. First of all, as it has been mentioned, regulations concerning mediation are moved from the general part to the fourth chapter dealing with proceedings in the first instance, so they are far less visible. Currently they are at the very beginning of the law in Article 3a. Thus, the recommendation to treat restorative justice programs as the preferred method of addressing harm caused by children and young people, contained in the European Model for Restorative Justice with Children and Young People (Chapman, Gellin, Aertsen & Anderson, 2015) is not envisaged in the proposal.

The lack of clarity regarding referring cases to mediation have not been corrected. The scope of people enabled to submit a motion to the court to refer a case to mediation has not been extended (as it was suggested earlier to include probation officers or educators from institutions in which young offenders might be placed). The proposed regulations are still very brief, concluding with a reference to those already contained in the code of civil procedure. This certainly does not make understanding the regulations 'user-friendly'. For example, the statement that mediation is possible at every stage of the proceedings, is not included in the law on juveniles and can be found only in the code of civil proceedings. The principle that mediators should be specially trained disappears completely, as the regulations in the code of civil proceedings mention only one condition to be a mediator, having the capability and full citizens' rights. This would be against Article 12.I of the Directive 2012/29/UE of the European Parliament and of the Council establishing minimum standards on the rights, support and protection of victims of crime of 25 October 2012. The draft does not contain any delegated legislation, so certain matters would not be regulated. Regrettably, the new draft of the law "on supporting and rehabilitation of minors" of 20 July 2021, prepared by the Ministry of Justice, repeats the criticized regulations concerning mediation – and placing them not in the general rules (as it is in the law currently in force), but only in Article 58 of the drafted law. During public consultations similar remarks were tabled again; the Ministry of Justice has not taken them into account in the new draft.

4 Prospects and barriers of developing restorative programs for youth in Poland

Insufficient or imperfect legal regulations may be just one of the obstacles to developing mediation in children's cases and may not be the most critical one.

A survey in 2010 found that only 5.2 percent of family judges surveyed indicated that improving legal regulations would increase their use of mediation. Most (over 60 percent) referred to other factors, such as the police informing parties about the possibility of mediation, increasing awareness in the society and its availability (Czarnecka-Dzialuk & Wójcik, 2012).

Mediation in juveniles' cases is being used far too rarely. There were only 364 cases in 2018, despite exceptionally good results in terms of the numbers of agreements that have been reached (around 70 percent[4]).

Barriers to implementing victim-offender mediation in juvenile cases include a lack of proper knowledge on restorative justice principles in society and among the judiciary, a lack of mediators in some areas and a reluctance among the judiciary to implement new ways of dealing with juveniles. Even if family judges declare their acceptance of mediation, it is not reflected in practice (Czarnecka-Dzialuk, 2016). It seems that there

4 The number of cases referred to mediation in adult offender cases by the court in 2018 was around 3,900 and by the public prosecutor, around 700; this is less than in previous years – a decrease since 2012 – respectively around 6,000 and 1,200 cases.

is a certain mental resistance, distrust and unwillingness to depart from the routine (Czarnecka-Dzialuk & Wójcik, 2005).

Other measures with a restorative character, as provided in the Act on the Treatment of Minors of 1982, such as the obligation to repair the damage or to perform certain forms of community work, are also being used very seldom. The National Commissioner of Children's Rights pointed this out in his addresses to the Minister of Justice in 2017 and 2018. However, there are examples of good practice in certain family courts. There was an experimental program of conferences, delivered by the Polish Centre of Mediation in three correctional institutions for juveniles who were about to leave the institution. Several programs based on the values of restorative justice have been carried out (as preventive-educational programs in schools, concluding with a competition to assess the knowledge gained about restorative justice, by expressing this idea in visual arts and literature). There are several schools using circles to deal with conflicts. Peer mediation and school mediation has developed more effective restorative justice for juveniles (Czarnecka-Dzialuk & Stryjek, 2019). Mediation techniques in order to prevent aggression, violence and social maladjustment have been officially accepted as important and efficient tools of psycho-pedagogical help in schools. Provisions concerning school mediation have appeared in the Regulations by the Minister of Education on the rules of delivering and organizing psychological and pedagogical help in public preschools, schools and institutions of 30 April 2013 and of 9 August 2017 (*Journal of Laws* of 2017, item 1591). According to the §24 item 6, one of the tasks of pedagogues and psychologists in preschools, schools and educational institutions is initiating and carrying out mediation in critical situations (Czarnecka-Dzialuk and Stryjek). Mediation is also one of the elements of legal education in schools.. A pilot program of school- and peer mediation was carried out by the Polish Centre of Mediation in twelve gymnasiums in 2001 and in twenty-six gymnasiums in 2002. Subsequently, there were projects carried out by NGOs such as the Society of Legal Intervention, local mediation centers in dozens of locations, local authorities and governmental educational departments, by the president of the district court in Lublin and by schools taking part in certain European programs. There is now a significant amount of experience, materials and manuals, including short films and videos. It is also worth mentioning that the program developed in the Gdańsk Centre of School and Peer Mediation is available to all public educational institutions in the whole municipality, at all levels (starting from preschools). It distinguishes itself from previous programs in Poland that were usually carried out in certain schools only.

Another positive feature is the cooperation between the municipality, courts, mediation organizations and academics. Family judges have expressed appreciation to the Centre as mediations provide the opportunity to avoid many debates in the family court, since the problem may already have been solved at school. According to the Article 32 j. §1 of the Act on the Treatment of Minors, when the family court considers the educational measures of the school to be sufficient, the legal authority may refer the juvenile's case to school (or to the NGO caring for the child); it may happen upon child consent (Czarnecka-Dzialuk & Stryjek, 2019). The court statistics referring to the whole country show, however, that this possibility is rarely used.

The idea of introducing good quality restorative justice programs for young people has been strongly supported by the respective Commissioners for Children's Rights, especially by Marek Michalak, who held this post between 2008 and 2018. He appointed a group of experts, who elaborated Standards of School and Peer Mediation. Recently the governmental Centre for Education Development (Ośrodek Rozwoju Edukacji or ORE) has created another team of experts – with mediators, judges and Ministry of Justice and Ministry of Education representatives to work on standards on the basis of those elaborated by the Commissioner for Children's Rights team.

5 Conclusion

From a legal point of view, there is a clear basis for developing restorative justice programs for young offenders in Poland. The various laws presented in this chapter should be considered as an important achievement, even if their enactment has not resulted in a frequent use of mediation yet. While these regulations should be improved, the main thing that needs to happen is the implementation of existing standards. It seems possible that mediation can be used more often. There is also a need to establish various types of restorative justice programs (Klaus, 2005).

What Zalewski and Păroşanu wrote a few years ago is still relevant today:

> Recommendations for the further promotion of restorative justice in Poland in the future will need to focus on raising awareness in society as well as among legal professionals, so as to properly inform these stakeholders of the significance of victim-offender mediation as well as of its availability per se. The potential for juveniles could be used to a far greater extent, as case numbers are significantly lower for young offenders than for their adult counterparts. After all, the experiences made with the experimental programme on victim-offender mediation for juveniles were incredibly positive. Furthermore, the scope of restorative justice could be widened further through legal amendments that allow restorative conferences to take place and that promote a wider use of victim-offender mediation. (Zalewski & Păroşanu, 2015)

For this purpose, it is important to refer to core values and the interests of society, to build the culture of dialogue, improve social skills and work on civic education, counteract hate speech, handle conflicts and prevent aggression, violence or social maladjustment.

While the great potential of the 'bottom-up' local initiatives and programs should be noted, at a certain point it is good to develop common rules and standards and to promote them on a national level. Thus, a systemic approach is needed. The support of governmental institutes or ministries and other experts or bodies – like the Commissioners for Human/Children Rights, is of great value. Do the policy-makers fully understand the value of restorative responses? Can we count on this, keeping in mind the drafted regulations concerning mediation? What should happen in Poland? We need to put laws into action, support local bottom-up initiatives, raise awareness, provide training, strengthen collaboration in the field of mediation with family courts and probation officers, teach alternative ways of solving conflicts in schools and develop peer- and school mediation programs. Other ways of reacting in a restorative way toward young people who make mistakes and offend are to be developed, bearing in mind the impact on their rights and on the rights of the victims involved. There are promising NGO initiatives, at the local level and above. The question is to what extend these developments would be accepted and supported by the current policy-makers.

References

Chapman, T., Gellin, M., Aertsen, I. & Anderson, M. (2015). *European research on restorative juvenile justice Volume II – Protecting rights, restoring respect and strengthening relationships: a European model for restorative justice with children and young people*. Brussels: IJJO.

Cwalina, M. (2012). Mediation involving a juvenile perpetrators of criminal acts. *Polish Journal of Social Rehabilitation*, 3, 253-262 2081-3767 (PRINT) / 2392-2656 (ONLINE)

Czarnecka-Dzialuk, B. (2010a). Perspektywy i ograniczenia mediacji z nieletnimi. In *Mediacja w praktyce wymiaru sprawiedliwości*. Sąd Okręgowy w Słupsku, Ustka, 4-5 października 2010, materiały konferencji, 116-127. Retrieved from http://slupsk.so.gov.pl/download/wystapienia-prelegentow-ustka-konferencja–pazdziernik-2010-www.pdf (last accessed 4 September 2021).

Czarnecka-Dzialuk, B. (2010b). The quest for sustaining research. Empirical research on restorative justice in Poland. In I. Vanfraechem, I. Aertsen & J. Willemsens (eds.), *Restorative justice realities. Empirical research in a European Context* (pp. 219-234). The Hague: Eleven International Publishing.

Czarnecka-Dzialuk, B. & Wójcik, D. (2000). Victim-offender mediation in Poland. In The European Forum for Victim-Offender Mediation and Restorative Justice (red.),

Victim – Offender Mediation in Europe. Making restorative justice work (pp. 309-336). Leuven.

Czarnecka-Dzialuk, B. (2013). O doskonaleniu przepisów dotyczących mediacji w sprawach karnych oraz nieletnich. In J. Utrat- Milecki (eds.), *Reformy prawa karnego. W stronę spójności i skuteczności* (pp. 233-247). Warszawa, Oficyna Naukowa.

Czarnecka-Dzialuk, B. (2015). Poland: twenty years of restorative justice implementation. *Restorative Justice. An International Journal*, 3(3), 396-404.

Czarnecka-Dzialuk, B. (2016). European model for restorative justice with children and young people. Conclusions for Poland, *Polish Journal of Criminology*, 2(1), 163-177. doi: 10.5604/01.3001.0010.7474.

Czarnecka-Dzialuk, B. (2018). Remarks on the Subjectivity of Juveniles. In P. Kozłowski, A. Rękas & M. Gorzko (red), *Podmiotowość dziecka w wybranych obszarach rzeczywistości społeczno-prawnej. Social Studies: Theory and Practice*, 5(2), ISSN 2544-0071 63-74.

Czarnecka-Dzialuk B. & Wójcik, D. (2005). Victim-offender mediation with juveniles in Poland. In A. Mestitz & S. Ghetti (eds.), *Victim-offender mediation with youth offenders in Europe. An overview and comparison of 15 countries* (pp. 137-156). The Hague: Springer.

Czarnecka-Dzialuk, B. & Wójcik, D. (2012). *Stosowanie sądowych środków oddziaływania wobec nieletnich w świetle koncepcji teoretycznych, statystyk oraz opinii sędziów i kuratorów rodzinnych* (p. 70). Instytut Wymiaru Sprawiedliwości, Report No. 204, Warszawa. Retrieved from https://iws.gov.pl/wp-content/uploads/2018/08/AR_W%C3%B3jcik.-Czarnecka-DzialukStos.s%C3%84%E2%80%A6dowych-%C3%85%E2%80%BAr.-oddz.-wobec-niel.pdf (last accessed 22 August 2020).

Czarnecka-Dzialuk, B. & Stryjek, K. (2019). Restorative justice in schools – lessons learned from Poland – the example of Gdańsk Centre for school and peer mediation. In D.S.W. Wong & T. Gavrielides (eds.), *Restorative justice in educational settings and policies: bridging the east and west* (pp. 53-63). London: RJAll. ISBN: 978-1-911634-07-2.

Górecki, P. & Stachowiak, S. (2007). *Ustawa o postępowaniu w sprawach nieletnich. Komentarz* (p. 36). Oficyna a Wolters Kluwer business.

Klaus, W. (2005). Sprawiedliwość naprawcza dla nieletnich w Polsce. In M. Płatek & M. Fajst (eds.), *Sprawiedliwość naprawcza: idea, teoria i praktyka*. (pp. 196-198). Liber: Warsaw.

Kelly, V.C. & Thorsborne, M. (eds.). (2014). *The psychology of emotion in restorative practice: how affect script psychology explains how and why restorative practice works*. London, Philadelphia Jessica Kingsley Publishers, 272 pages.

Konarska-Wrzosek, V. (2000). Postępowanie mediacyjne w sprawach nieletnich. *Przegląd Sądowy*, 4, 62-69.

Korcyl-Wolska, M. (2001). *Postępowanie w sprawach nieletnich w Polsce*. Zakamycze, p. 414.

Korczak, J. (1921). Jak kochać dziecko (How to love a child). Part 2 – Orphanage; first published in 1921, then all 3 parts in 1929; available at https://polona.pl/item/jak-kochac-dziecko-internat-kolonje-letnie-dom-sierot,MzM4Mzc1OA/137/#info:metadata pp.200-261 (last accessed 2 September 2021).

Krawczak-Chmielecka, A. (2017). O rozwoju praw dziecka w Polsce i na świecie. *Dziecko Krzywdzone. Teoria, Badania, Praktyka,* 11-23, (ISSN: 1644-6526, eISSN: 2545-3475) 16(2).Retrieved from https://dzieckokrzywdzone.fdds.pl/index.php/DK/article/view/629/488 (last accessed 2 September 2021).

Nowak, A. (2009). Mediation as an alternative form of the juridical proceeding toward juvenile delinquents. *The New Educational Review,* 19, 3-4, 209-218.

Pyżalski, J. (2018). Przeciwdziałanie przemocy rówieśniczej w szkole – krytyczny przegląd stosowanych rozwiązań. *Dziecko Krzywdzone. Teoria, badania, praktyka* Vol. 17 Nr 1 (2018) 31 p. 40.

Reisel, D. (2013). The neuroscience of restorative justice. Retrieved from www.ted.com/talks/dan_reisel_the_neuroscience_of_restorative_justice (last accessed 26 May 2020).

Staniaszek, M. (2018). (Not)applying mediation in juvenile cases. *Polish Journal of Social Rehabilitation,* 5, 143-154. Retrieved from http://resocjalizacjapolska.pl/index.php/rp/article/view/97/167 (last accessed 16 August 2020).

Wallis, P. & Tudor, B. (2008). *The pocket guide of restorative justice*. London, Philadelphia.

Zalewski, W. & Păroşanu, A. (2015). Poland. In F. Dünkel, P. Horsfield & A. Păroşanu (eds.), *Research and selection of the most effective juvenile restorative justice practices in Europe: snapshots from 28 EU member states, european research on restorative juvenile justice* (Vol. I); pp. 131-135). Brussels: IJJO.

Chapter 14
Child justice in the Netherlands

A boost for restorative and child-friendly interventions?

Maartje Berger and Annemieke Wolthuis

1 Introduction

For decades, restorative approaches were not integrated within the criminal procedure and were used mainly as out-of-court settlements or diversionary measures in the Netherlands. This has changed. Restorative justice is slowly finding its place in the child justice system. Since the seventies there has been an increased awareness that a criminal justice system based on punishment has a counterproductive effect on the lives and future of children in conflict with the law. Alternatives, including mediation and conferencing, found their way into the child justice system. A unique example is Halt, a diversionary measure that was introduced as many as 40 years ago, providing an alternative for young offenders and recently also including a restorative approach. Every year between 13.000 and 16.000 minors work several hours, doing learning tasks and making apologies as part of the Halt measure. During the last decade also, victim-offender mediation and mediation in criminal cases have increased as well as developments in schools and in civil society.

Since 2011, the Office of the Public Prosecutor and the police have been under a legal obligation, owing to the introduction of an article in the Code of Criminal Procedure (Art. 51h), to inform victims and suspects about the possibility of participating in mediation and, if the victim agrees, to support the parties in this process. Restorative justice has also been given more attention in upcoming government plans. The minister for legal protection (a special assignment in addition to the minister of justice and security, including procedural safeguards and responsibility for the implementation of legislation concerning restorative justice), stated in an official letter in 2018, followed by official policy rules for restorative justice provisions in January 2020, that all youth justice cases must be assessed for their eligibility for a restorative justice intervention. Additional funding was allocated to restorative services to strengthen the position of restorative justice in youth justice.

A positive development in the Dutch child justice system is the increase in awareness among policymakers and professionals to adopt and follow international standards for children's rights, including the Guidelines of the Committee of Ministers of the Council of Europe on child-friendly justice and binding EU directives, such as the Children's Directive EU 2016/800, the Victims' Directive EU2012/29 and the principles of the UN Convention on the Rights of the Child. These standards uphold a comprehensive framework and a guide for the implementation of child-friendly justice in national laws and practice. In this view, a restorative approach and meaningful participation are prerequisites for working towards a more child-friendly approach.

However, there are challenges. Young offenders are not well informed about their rights and are treated similarly to adults after being arrested by the police and charged by prosecutors.[1] Child suspects are allowed to speak in court, but prefer to remain silent for fear of incriminating themselves. Many young victims and offenders are unaware of what their right *to be heard* means and how it can be related to restorative justice interventions or mediation. The range and variety of restorative interventions that young people can be referred to are limited and not very different than those for adults.

This chapter presents an overview of the Dutch child justice landscape, including figures. This is followed by a description and short analysis of the principles of child-friendly, participative and restorative justice that need to be considered. Furthermore, restorative and child-friendly justice in practices in the Netherlands are addressed, both civil society interventions and criminal justice-related interventions, including a case example. In addition, an overview of policy developments and specific challenges is provided. The chapter concludes with innovative ideas for a more restorative, participative and child-friendly justice system.[2]

2 Child justice in the Netherlands

In recent decades, a variety of care-focused, participative, restorative and judicial interventions and measures for child victims as well as children alleged to have, accused of or recognized as having infringed the criminal law have been introduced. The impact of these measures is promising in that the numbers on youth crime and deprivation of liberty have been decreasing by nearly 50 percent since 2012. In 2020, 12.8 of 1,000 children aged 12 to 18 were registered as crime suspects.[3] However, the number of children in police custody and closed child justice centers still remains high. The following table provides an overview of children in the justice system. The country has 17 million inhabitants. On 1 January 2020, the Netherlands had 4,869,842 inhabitants under the age of 25, or 28 percent of the population.[4]

---

1 www.defenceforchildren.nl/media/2653/20171001_dc_folder-aanhouding-jonge-verdachten_a5-web.pdf.

2 The authors would like to thank Gert Jan Slump and Bas van Stokkom for some useful comments on an earlier draft.

3 Centraal Bureau voor de Statistiek (2021), see www.nji.nl/nl/Databank/Cijfers-over-Jeugd-en-Opvoeding/Cijfers-per-onderwerp/Cijfers-per-onderwerp-Delinquentie.

4 Centraal Bureau voor de Statistiek (2021) Bevolkingscijfers jongeren.

Table 14.1 Indicators of the child justice system in the Netherlands

Indicators	2016	2017	2018	2019	2020
Total number of police hearings with child suspects (unique)[a]	33.043	28.486	24.394	25.714	-
Total number of children in police custody (unique)[a]	7.101	5.244	4.605	5.129	-
Halt measure (diversion measure including a restorative approach)[b]	17.030	16.995	14.419	16.088[5]	13.421
Victim-offender (Perspectief Herstelbemiddeling) mediation in cases of minors	-	-	417	374	416
Mediation in penal cases: Referrals of youth cases to mediation	-	-	-	213	227 (1 December 2019-1 November 2020)
Number of youth justice cases in court: Verdict guilty[c]	-	-	4.135	4.220	-
Total number of children in secure child justice centers[d]	1.054	1.005	1.112	1.321	-
Total number of children aged 12 and 13 in secure child justice centers	14	13	15	26	-
Percent of minors in pretrial detention in secure child justice centers at reference date[e]	76%	80%	82%	72%	
Average number of days in pretrial detention in secure child justice centers	36	38	33	36	
Total number of children with a PIJ measure (treatment) in a secure child justice center at reference date[e]	22	8	20	25	

Source: Ministry of Justice and Safety, Dienst Justitiële Inrichtingen (DJI), unless mentioned otherwise.
[a] BVI = police database. Unique: Every action is counted as one. When a minor is interrogated twice, it is counted twice.
[b] Highlights van Halt p. 3 (2019).
[c] Criminaliteit en rechtshandhaving, WODC 2020 (C&R2019-tabellen-h03_tcm28-466), Tabel 14 door de rechter in eerste aanleg afgedane misdrijfzaken met minderjarige verdachten: schuldigverklaringen naar delictgroep.
[d] Number of minors in a closed youth justice institution on 1 January plus the number of minors placed in the institution during the year.
[e] 1 January of the following year. For example, the number over 2017 is set on 1 January 2018.

5 In 2020 the number of Halt interventions dropped to 13.421 as children spent more time at home during the lockdown.

Even though the rates of youth offending have decreased over the last several years and alternatives such as diversionary measures and community sanctions are often used, Defence for Children, Restorative Justice Nederland and other nongovernmental organizations (NGOs) have concerns about child justice in the Netherlands. While there is a broad awareness and effort to implement a child-friendly justice approach at the governmental level, in practice the criminal procedure is still focused on the prosecution of child offenders and procedural (due process) aspects.

Also, the minimum age of criminal responsibility (MACR) is still set at twelve years, which is low compared with other European countries. The Committee on the Rights of the Child (hereafter referred to as 'the Committee') mentions in *General Comment 24* (issued in 2020, rule 21 and 22) that age fourteen is the most common MACR internationally and recommends a higher age. Furthermore, children's rights are being denied when young suspects are being questioned or interrogated by the police and during police custody. At this stage of the criminal procedure, their treatment mirrors that of adult suspects, and basic rights such as deprivation of liberty as a measure of last resort and for the shortest appropriate period are not well implemented. The Dutch Council for the Administration of Criminal Justice and Protection of Youth (RSJ) has asked the government to comply with international standards advising children to be held for a maximum of 24 hours in police custody (RSJ, 2019) and to raise the age of criminal responsibility to fourteen or sixteen (RSJ, 2017). Even though some improvements have been made, such as more child-friendly ways of working by the police force, both aspects have not changed much since then, and the minister wants the age of criminal responsibility to remain at twelve owing to some severe criminal cases by youngsters aged twelve and thirteen and the need to be able to combine criminal and care aspects (Letter Minister of Legal Protection, 20 December 2017).

3 Child-friendly, participative and restorative principles to consider

As already stated in several of the previous contributions to this book, the Committee and the General Comments of the Committee describe the need for meaningful participation as part of a comprehensive child-friendly child justice system. The Netherlands has already been using participation as a basic model for its social welfare system. In the last decade, the promotion and use of child participation has also become more important (RAND Europe & Eurochild, 2021; van der Gaag, Gilsing & Mak, 2013). Children are already part of advisory, participatory and decision-making processes, taking part in youth boards or serving as counsellors in schools or youth care, for example, in their role as experienced experts informing and advising policymakers or management in institutions. Furthermore, civil court judges seem to integrate into their decisions the opinion of children over the age of twelve more often, for example in family matters (Bruning, Smeets, Bolscher, Peper & De Boer, 2020). However, in child justice, participation is less visible and not clearly embedded in law, policy and practice yet. Besides, a significant number of children in prison have intellectual disabilities and need specific attention and guidance (Kaal & de Jong, 2018).[6]

As child-friendly restorative approaches are good participatory practices for young victims, suspects and offenders, further implementation of their key principles is an urgent need. The Committee has already challenged the Dutch and many other justice systems, promoting diversion (General Comment 24, par 17) by emphasizing that the law should contain a wide variety of noncustodial measures, including restorative justice (par 73 and 74). Based on the country report of the Netherlands in 2015, the Committee said in its conclusions (rule 59c) that the member state must 'promote alternative measures to detention, such as diversion, probation, mediation, counselling, or community service, wherever possible'. This development requires systemic change, since it was noted that restorative practices were used mainly outside of the youth justice system. The Netherlands will report to the Committee again in 2021.[7] In light of the above, the Dutch NGO Collective[8] published its alternative report at the end of April 2021 in which it continued to advocate for an expanded use of restorative interventions.

In addition to the CRC, growing awareness in Europe has led to several EU directives emphasizing the importance of a child-friendly and restorative approach that includes procedural safeguards. The right to an individual assessment is thereby important, inasmuch as it aims to take into account the specific needs of children concerning protection, education, training and social integration. It has to be carried out at the earliest appropriate stage of the proceedings, considering a child's personality and maturity; economic, social and family background; and any specific vulnerabilities he or she may have (Art. 22 sub 4 EU Victims' Directive, EU2012/29 and Art. 7 Children's Directive, EU2016/800). The EU also calls on states to encourage initiatives that provide children with support, taking their needs into account and giving access to restorative justice services. The right to an individual assessment, which is part of the EU directives, can serve as a practical starting point for participation, informing children about and involving them in restorative justice at an earlier stage. It can also lead to a restorative approach at a later stage of the judicial procedure, as part of either

6 See, www.nrc.nl/nieuws/2019/01/02/jongere-met-lichte-beperking-belandt-vaker-in-gevangenis-a3127737 (last accessed 29 July 2021).

7 Report of the Kingdom of the Netherlands under Article 44 of the Convention on the Rights of the Child www.rijksoverheid.nl/documenten/rapporten/2020/11/05/report-of-the-kingdom-of-the-netherlands-answers-to-questions-1-33.

8 The Dutch NGO collective consists of six NGOs dealing with children's rights issues in the country: Defence for Children, de Nationale Jeugdraad, Kinderpostzegels, UNICEF Nederland, Save the Children and Terre des Hommes. They have a long history of cooperation and also make use of experts and cooperate with other organizations in the field.

special conditions for suspension, community service or behavioral interventions (Wolthuis & Randazzo, 2021).

3.1 *Restorative justice and participation*

Restorative justice has great potential for effectively implementing the right to meaningful participation in the Dutch child justice system. It is a response to crime in which young people fully participate, learn how to communicate about what happened, learn about the impact on the victim and other people, and take responsibility for youth offending or criminal behavior.

The close relationship with participation is addressed by the Committee, defining restorative justice as:

> any process in which the victim, the offender and/or any other individual or community member affected by a crime actively *participates* together in the resolution of matters arising from the crime, often with the help of a fair and impartial third party.

Examples of restorative processes include mediation, conferencing, conciliation and sentencing circles (GC 24, par 8).

According to Article 12 of the CRC, children have the right to be heard. The Committee emphasizes, in General Comment 12, that this right applies to all relevant judicial proceedings affecting the child, including children in conflict with the law, child victims of physical or psychological violence, sexual abuse or other crimes. Both kinds of proceedings may involve alternative dispute mechanisms such as mediation and arbitration (par 32).

The right to be heard has to be fully observed at all stages of the judicial process, from the pretrial stage to the right to be heard by the police, the prosecutor and the investigating judge. When diversion is applied, including mediation, free and voluntary consent is needed, as is the opportunity to obtain legal and other advice and assistance in determining the appropriateness and desirability of the diversion proposed (par 34).

The Committee asks member states to be aware of the potential negative consequences of an inconsiderate practice of participation and the right to be heard, requiring extra qualitative standards. Especially in cases where a child has been a victim of a criminal offense, sexual abuse, violence or other forms of mistreatment, state parties must undertake all necessary measures to ensure that the right to be heard is exercised such that full protection of the child is ensured (par 21).

3.2 *'Meaningful participation'*

Children and young adults have a right to participate in criminal cases. When young suspects or victims are not informed about the procedure and cannot communicate about what happened to them, they may miss out on opportunities that can substantially enhance their well-being. When they are taken seriously and feel listened to, they are better connected to society, making it more likely that they will understand, trust, cooperate and communicate better with authorities such as the police, youth care and social workers (McGarrell, Olivares, Crawford & Kroovand, 2000).

The Lundy model of participation is intended to focus decision makers on the distinct and interrelated elements of the provision. To implement meaningful participation, its four elements should be taken seriously: 1. Space: children must be given safe inclusive opportunities to form and express their views; 2. Voice: they must be facilitated to express their views; 3. Audience: the view must be listened to; and 4. Influence: the view must be acted upon, as appropriate (Lundy, 2007). The model was prominently endorsed by the Irish Department of Children and Youth Affairs in their National Strategy on Children and Young People's Participation in Decision-Making (2015-2020).

The Committee states that child participation is a tool to stimulate the full development of the personality and the evolving capacities of the child. The concept emphasizes that including children should not only be a momentary act, but the starting point for an intense exchange between children and adults. According to General Comment 12 participation can be made 'meaningful' through the following five steps:

1. Information: Children need to know about their right to express their opinion and about the impact that their views will have on the outcome, such as the possible decisions and their consequences;
2. Listening: Children need to be sure that the adult who is responsible for the hearing is willing to listen and will seriously consider what the child has decided to communicate. Important to note here is that child participation is voluntary and should be carried out in a safe environment where children feel free to share their views;
3. Assessment of the capacity of the child: If children are capable of forming their own views, these are weighed as a significant factor in the settlement of the issue. Good practices for assessing the capacity of the child have to be developed;
4. Feedback: Children's views are given due weight. This means that they need to be informed of the outcome of the process explaining how their views were considered;
5. Complaints, remedies and redress: When the rights of children are disregarded or violated, it needs to be clear whether mediation or a complaint mechanism can be addressed.

When we link these steps to restorative justice, we see that meaningful participation includes rights that are part of restorative approaches, such as the right to be informed and the right to be listened to. The beauty of restorative justice is that the opportunity for children to voice their opinion is embedded within a reciprocal process of information exchange, aiming to repair damage that has been done. When performed well, all five steps to 'meaningful participation' are integrated in every step of the decision-making process, ensuring that a child knows how his or her views are considered and why decisions are made. All this fits into a more humane way of dealing with harm created by criminal behavior (Chapman et al., 2019).

Recently, on 24 March 2021, the European Children's Rights Strategy was adopted by the European Commission.[9] Child-friendly justice and meaningful youth participation play a major role in this. Child-friendly justice is a broad concept, yet encompasses the effective participation of children in legal proceedings as an important element of a fair trial. Meaningful participation, according to the Strategy, means that children receive age-oriented information, can express their opinion, have the right to be heard, should be taken seriously, receive feedback and can legitimately oppose a decision. Autonomy and participation belong together, and this is confirmed in the rules of thumb on youth participation, drawn up by the Dutch Alexander Foundation. Rule 16, which deals with the attitude of professionals, says: 'Emphasize the autonomy of young people' in the sense of approaching young people more and more as independent, autonomous decision makers.

For young people on their way to adulthood, autonomy in the sense of the need for connection and competence are becoming more important as laid down in the 'self-determination' theory by Ryan and Deci. They demonstrate that supporting people's basic needs for competence, relatedness and autonomy is critically important for virtually all aspects of individual and societal functioning. It contributes to motivation, development and wellness (Ryan & Deci, 2017). Without investing in connection, behavioral interventions will lead to control of power and less autonomy.

4 Restorative and child-friendly justice in practice in the Netherlands

Restorative justice in criminal cases is used in the Netherlands through three different approaches. Practices may take place within or outside of the criminal procedure, as an addition to or as part of the procedure (Dierx & van Hoek, 2012).

In youth cases, the police, the child protection board and/or public prosecutor have to inform young suspects about potential restorative interventions. This takes place when a child suspect is subjected to risk assessment using a tool called the National Instrument

9 EU strategy on the rights of the child, p. 15. See also: https://ec.europa.eu/info/sites/info/files/1_en_act_part1_v7_0.pdf.

for Youth Criminal Justice (LIJ). In cases involving child victims, Victim Support informs them and their parents about restorative justice.

Different restorative interventions were developed independently within the Dutch civil and child justice system. The increasing emphasis on participation and child-friendly justice is leading to a more structural role for restorative justice. Depending on the case, a child can be referred to out-of-court interventions or, when prosecution starts, to the mediation desk of the local court (all courts have an office working specifically on mediation in criminal cases).

The national police and prosecution officers are working on guidelines for the use of restorative justice – the police intend to present a restorative policy plan in 2021.[10] Interventions that will be highlighted in the following paragraphs are 'peaceful' schools, youth courts, family group plans, victim-offender conversations, Halt and mediation in criminal cases.

4.1 Civil society interventions

4.1.1 'Peaceful' schools and youth courts

In the past decade, mediation outside the criminal procedure has been taking form in schools, for example where new methods such as 'peaceful schools' and 'youth courts' have emerged.

More than a thousand primary schools are registered as peaceful schools, and this number is growing. 'Peaceful schools' involve the use of peer mediation, which was inspired by successful initiatives originating from the United States (Magazine RJN, 2018). These methods integrate a restorative approach in school programs, teaching children and young adults to solve their conflicts by becoming or using a (peer) mediator. Furthermore, participation is stimulated through 'youth courts'. These are established in many schools to train young judges to make decisions in cases of conflict among their peers at school and where children get to participate in a restorative way. Since they are partly criminal offenses they work closely with the local police, and recently also with Halt, and can be described as a restorative justice-based tripartite court model (Mijnarends, Brink van den & Verkroost, 2018; Wolthuis, Claessen, Slump & Van Hoek, 2019).

4.1.2 Family group plans and conferencing

In youth care, family group plans are a common feature, and family conferencing has developed into a structural possibility embedded in law (van Pagée, van Lieshout & Wolthuis, 2012). In 2015, the new (civil) Youth Law granted citizens the right to make

10 At the beginning of 2020 a national coordinator was appointed with the task of creating this policy. She liaises with many parties in the field, including Restorative Justice Nederland.

their own care proposal: the family group plan. Such an outcome is a strategy developed by parents, but also friends, family, neighbors and sometimes professionals that belong to the social environment of the child. The 'Eigen Kracht Centrale' and some other organizations provide assistance in facilitating conferences that result in making such plans. The process entails various people coming together from the social network of the young person to discuss what is needed to make the environment of the young person safe, de-escalate conflict situations and resolve problems, all guided by a trained facilitator and following a script. Such a procedure can prevent children from being placed outside their family, as other alternatives are explored. Recent research has shown that in youth cases it is necessary to involve a broader network and make use of group conferencing (Geenen, Kalter, Van Mazijk, Uitslag & Lamkaddem, 2019). More often than not, professionals prefer to take the lead themselves in organizing a conferencing session. Parents and children then have to read and sign the agreement, potentially impacting on their ownership and commitment. This calls for more research and pilots on what works in youth cases.

4.1.3 Victim-offender mediation

Victim-offender mediation takes place outside of the criminal procedure. These mediations are carried out by an organization called Perspectief Herstelbemiddeling. It has a link with Victim Support in the Netherlands, but operates independently and is funded by the ministry of justice and security. Victim-offender mediation is a form of contact that enables victims and offenders (and if useful also other people involved or hurt), by learning about the circumstances and motives as well as asking questions and getting answers about what happened, to relate differently to each other. This can help them in dealing with the consequences of the crime. Each year, 1,500 conversations are arranged, of which, in 2018, 40 percent of the offenders and 33 percent of the victims were minors (Annual Report, 2018). In 2019, the organization received 1,550 requests (Annual report, 2019). In 2020, they registered 416 cases of minors for victim-offender mediation. On the perpetrator side, it concerned 291 youth cases. On the victim side, interviews were held with 125 minors (information received from the organization).

4.2 Criminal justice-related interventions

4.2.1 Halt

Halt, also referred to as The Alternative, is a diversionary program in the youth justice system with restorative characteristics. The program, functioning at the police level, was already integrated into law and policy as early as the 1980s. Originally, children and adolescents were, often before being charged, simply offered completion of a community service at an early stage. Recently, restorative aspects were added within the program. If young people complete the Halt program successfully, they do not end up having a criminal record. In cases such as shoplifting, outcomes may include young offenders aged 12 and over apologizing or compensating for the harm committed. In cases where more parties are involved, such as group disputes or bullying, a staff member of Halt holds a face-to-face restorative conversation. During such a conversation, all parties, including the offender, the victim, family members, neighbors and a teacher, can participate. They discuss damages and consider apologies, and the young offender may participate in an educational or vocational training program (Abraham, Buysse & Nauta, 2013; Buyse, Abraham, Hofstra & Van Dijk, 2017). Halt appears to be especially effective for young people with a low risk of recidivism and few problems. The recidivism of these youngsters in Halt is lower than in the regular criminal law approach (Buyse et al., 2017).

In 2019, 16.088 minors who committed a criminal offense took part in Halt (Halt, 2019). In 2020 the number of Halt interventions dropped to 13.421 as children spent more time at home during the pandemic and the lockdown. (Halt, 2020)

4.2.2 Mediation in criminal youth cases

Mediation in criminal youth cases is part of the criminal procedure. As soon as prosecution starts, child suspects receive information about this form of victim-offender mediation. When several criteria are met and verified, a child can be referred to the mediation desk of the local court. They can be assisted by a parent or another person of trust. When an agreement between the parties is reached during mediation, it has to be taken into consideration by the prosecutor or judge when deciding on a sanction or measure.

When a case is referred to the mediation desk of the court both parties are contacted about participating in mediation. Almost one out of two cases referred to mediation via the mediation bureau of the court does not start or is not finalized. During the intake by phone by the staff of the mediation bureau will speak to both parties about the procedure, the possible impact and ask for commitment. In half of the cases, it can seem not to be the right fit for the parties involved or one of them is not interested. If both parties agree to mediation, two mediators are appointed, and a face-to-face meeting is organized (Handleiding MiS, 2017).

Table 14.2 Figures of referrals and mediations in youth cases (December 2019 – December 2020)

Referred	Finalized	Complete agreement	Agreement with financial compensation	Partial agreement	No agreement
227	100	94 cases	25 cases	0 cases	6 cases

In 2020, in 94 percent of the cases the mediation ended with a signed agreement. A mediation process takes an average of 13 days to be finalized (Council for the Judiciary, 2020).

The following case provides insight into this process and impact of the use of mediation in youth cases.

A case: Best friends fighting (a real case, slightly adapted, including the names)
Dunya and Karin were fourteen years old and were best friends and classmates. They got into a fight in high school and Karin kicked Dunya, causing bruised ribs, pain, blood and emotional damage. How did it start? Dunya and Karin talk about it during the individual intakes and during the mediation. The fuss between the friends started with being disappointed with each other. They then blocked each other on their phone. Dunya wanted to talk it out later, but could not. Groups would have stoked each other. And negative things would have been said about Dunya's family. Karin also spent a lot of time with another girlfriend. When Dunya wanted to walk up to her at her locker that day, Karin thought she was following her. All this enraged Karin so much that she gave Dunya that kick. First, she walked on. She later learned that her ex-friend was crying and flinching. Teachers joined, and Karin was suspended for a few days. The pain and the complaints that this caused Dunya impelled her, together with her mother, to report the crime to the police.
The public prosecutor in this case thought the girls could try mediation. They would bump into one other at school or in the neighborhood anyway.

Both girls brought a parent to the meeting, and Dunya also brought her grandmother, who knows both girls. During the mediation meeting, the girls and their support persons shared what they had experienced that night. They also expressed that they never intended this to happen.
These agreements were sent back to the prosecutor, who would take them into account when deciding on the case. One of the mediators in this case said:
'This incident had a big impact on everyone involved, the girls and their parents and grandmother. And for the girls, who had not realized how much impact it had for the other one. It was emotional for all. During the mediation, they listened to each other's stories and started to show understanding. It was reassuring to see how apologies were made, how the girls agreed what they would do when they would meet again and the family members showed respect for what they wanted. The best possible outcome had been reached, I thought'.

This is but one example of a variety of cases that are dealt with through mediation within the court system. The cases vary considerably in range of severity and kinds of agreements that are reached. Young people involved explain that they are happy to participate in such a procedure, citing it as an opportunity to really be taken seriously.

5 Promising governmental policy concerning youth cases and restorative justice

On 11 July 2018, the minister for legal protection, responsible for procedural safeguards and the implementation of legislation concerning restorative justice, confirmed, in an official letter, a new approach, stating that, in principle, 'in all youth justice cases it needs to be investigated if a restorative justice intervention is possible'. He added an extra budget of €300.000 per year, starting in 2019, assuring a stronger position for mediation and the restorative approach in the youth justice system. In June 2019, a new policy plan was presented to fight youth crime and improve the youth justice system. Priorities stipulated in the plan include a more personalized approach during detention and aftercare, a faster response to criminal offenses, shorter-term detention in small-scale institutions, and attention to restorative justice. Underlining the latter, the minister guarantees a structural financial budget and an investment in information tools for professionals, victims, young suspects or offenders and their parents (Minister of Legal Protection, 2019).

Another milestone is the launch of a new policy framework for restorative justice interventions on 8 January 2020, developed by the ministry of justice and security. The rules address special attention to mediation in youth cases and conferencing and include provisions on qualifications for mediators to ensure high quality services. Collectively, they acknowledge that the child justice system offers a different range of sanctions, measures, interventions and procedural rights compared to common criminal law (Minister of Legal Protection, 8 January 2020).

5.1 Experts launch a law proposal initiative

Experts in the field of criminal and restorative justice consider Article 51h, as it now stands, to be open-ended and vague, leading to either broad or narrow interpretation. A group of specialists in restorative justice approaches (Claessen et al., 2018) have been working on a new, broader proposal of law. The group of experts working on this legislative proposal argues that mediation is an important part of the criminal procedure with a wide range of possibilities. The idea behind the legislative proposal is to ensure more legal certainty and legal equality throughout the Netherlands.

The proposal consists of seven articles to be incorporated into the (new) Dutch Code of Criminal Procedure, in addition to two articles to be added to the criminal law governing adults and minors, respectively. The seven articles will jointly form a new title of the (new) Dutch Code of Criminal Procedure, called 'Restorative Justice Services' (Wolthuis et al., 2019).

The Fourth Chapter and Article VII of the proposal contain 'Special Provisions with Regard to Youth (Use of Mediation and Group Conferences)'. These recommend that where an accusation concerns an accused who had not yet reached the age of 18 at the time the criminal offense was committed (and up to 23 when adolescent criminal law is applied), the child protection board will investigate, prior to the decision by the public prosecutor's office on whether to prosecute, whether there are grounds on which to give priority to employing mediation or group conferencing. The child protection board will advise the public prosecutor's office on the use of mediation or group conferencing. In cases involving youngsters, the public prosecutor's office or the court will *ex officio* investigate the possibility of either mediation or group conferencing. The mediator assigned to the case will investigate whether mediation or a group conference is the most appropriate form of restorative justice. This will be done by checking the family situation and who was involved or hurt by the offense. In the event of a successful outcome of mediation or a successful group conference, a custodial sentence may be imposed only if the gravity of the offense, the character of the accused or the circumstances during the commission of the offense demand such an outcome. In its judgment, the court will specifically state the reasons that have led to its decision to refer or not to restorative measures and follow the agreement between parties or not (Claessen et al., 2018).

Such innovations enhance children's rights: authorities have to motivate in every case why certain measures were taken and whether restorative approaches are considered or not involving professionals knowledgeable about child rights in the process.

However, barriers still exist. Surprisingly, in youth cases, although everybody is convinced about the positive effects, a broader restorative approach is not yet visible. The budget that was allocated by the ministry, especially to mediation in youth cases in 2019, is never fully spent. The multitude of police officers, prosecutors, child protection workers and judges are not sufficiently familiar with a restorative approach. At the time of writing there was no clear policy on how victim offender and mediation in criminal cases could be used at the police level, aiming to avoid sending youth cases to prosecution. Existing practices, such as Halt, the victim-offender mediation organizations outside the courts and the mediation bureaus within the courts, operate separately from each other. It is not always clear whether the specific restorative intervention applied is in the best interest of the child.

Although policy plans stipulate that restorative justice should always be offered in youth cases, a youth-centric method, including specialized skills for professionals, still has to be established. There are a handful of mediators specialized in youth cases, but such expertise should be shared and evaluated much more.

According to EU law, the Netherlands needs to further develop and implement the existing practice of multidisciplinary and individual assessment of child victims, suspects and offenders. In order to guarantee access to fair justice, the use and implementation of restorative principles is needed. It also serves the best interests of children, recognizing their evolving capacities and empowering them to participate in justice proceedings.

Many of the prevailing restorative practices in the Netherlands do not yet comply with child-friendly restorative justice and the five steps of 'meaningful participation'. For example, many children are unaware and lack information about what restorative justice is, and professionals are not sufficiently trained to work with and listen to young victims, suspects and offenders. Significant people around the young person, with the exception of parents, are not sufficiently involved. When the right information on restorative practices is not guaranteed and if well-trained professionals are not consistently available, promising developments in laws and policies cannot be embedded in practice.

The Committee underlines the right of children to be heard during every stage of the judicial process. As the Dutch Criminal Code and policy rules for mediation are advancing, this is the perfect moment to start inviting children to share their views and take them seriously, contributing to a more restorative, participative and child-friendly justice system.

6 CHALLENGES AND RECOMMENDATIONS FOR A PARTICIPATIVE AND CHILD-FRIENDLY, RESTORATIVE YOUTH JUSTICE SYSTEM

Even though we are proud of the developments of restorative justice in the Netherlands during the last decennium, with diversionary measures, victim-offender conversations outside the criminal procedure, mediation in criminal cases, restorative justice programs in schools and in youth care, we believe that the implementation in youth cases needs extra attention. A comprehensive rights-based and rights-needs approach is needed to ensure that restorative justice is always offered as a first option. The Committee, the Council of Europe and the European Union call upon the Netherlands to implement restorative practices and child-friendly justice. This includes an additional focus on participation. In the near future, this means, in our view, that changes, investments and innovation in the Dutch youth justice system are needed, as worked out in ten concrete recommendations:

1. The scope of Article 51h has to be extended with a law on restorative provisions and policy including specific articles on young people. The law proposal that was initiated by citizens and experts, which includes special provisions on youth (Claessen et al., 2018), needs to be implemented.
2. A restorative approach, including mediation in criminal cases, should be added to the guidelines for youth criminal procedure[11] promoting that 'in all youth justice cases it is investigated whether a restorative justice intervention can be applied'. This means that a restorative approach becomes an integral part of the youth justice procedure, being offered immediately after a report by a victim is made and after the arrest of a child suspect as a diversionary measure, but also when prosecution starts or when children are held in police custody or during pretrial detention.
3. Children should be thoroughly informed about judicial and nonjudicial proceedings and the choices they have. Child-friendly materials on alternatives and restorative justice need to be made available for children and their parents, including special

11 Guidelines and framework for the criminal procedure of youth and adolescents, including Halt.

tools for groups with disabilities or psychological challenges. The information should also explain the possible consequences of each option.

4. The right to a multidisciplinary individual assessment for children involved in criminal proceedings, as implied in EU directives, needs to be further developed, emphasizing a restorative approach. This will enable stakeholders to use restorative interventions as part of special conditions for suspension, community service and behavioral measures.
5. Stakeholders, including the child protection board, the police, prosecution and lawyers, need to receive information, training and guidelines on restorative justice in order to improve referral of cases involving children to restorative interventions. They need to be aware of children's particular vulnerabilities and protect children from harm and secondary victimization.
6. Specialized working methods for restorative justice in youth criminal cases, involving a broader social network such as conferencing and circles, need to be further researched and piloted.
7. Professionalization strategies of intermediaries and mediators need to be formulated through quality requirements, training, special skills and intervision sessions taking into account age and specific children and youth needs, including setting up a pool of experienced youth mediators who can guide others.
8. For young people with intellectual disabilities, more participation tools and restorative approaches should be made available, along with methods specifically designed to take language or learning problems into account.
9. More research needs to be conducted on the experiences and evidence-based best practices with young victims, suspects and offenders in the restorative process in criminal cases.
10. Children themselves should be involved. A real and meaningful 'participation society' allows young people to contribute to the maximum extent.

References

Abraham, M., Buysse, W. & Nauta, O. (2013). *Halt vernieuwd, procesevaluatie van de vernieuwde Halt-afdoening.* Amsterdam: DSP-groep.

Bruning, M., Smeets, D., Bolscher, K., Peper, J. & De Boer, R. (2020). *Kind in proces: van communicatie naar effectieve participatie*, Meijers-reeks nr. 335. Nijmegen: Wolf Legal Publishers.

Buyse, W., Abraham, M., Hofstra, D. & Van Dijk, B. (2017). *Werkzaamheid van de Halt-afdoening.* Amsterdam: DSP-groep.

Centraal Bureau voor de Statistiek. (2021). *Cijfers jeugddelinquentie.* Retrieved from www.nji.nl/nl/Databank/Cijfers-over-Jeugd-en-Opvoeding/Cijfers-per-onderwerp/Cijfers-per-onderwerp-Delinquentie (last accessed 29 July 2021).

Centraal Bureau voor de Statistiek. (2021) *Bevolkingscijfers jongeren*, retrieved from https://www.cbs.nl/nl-nl/visualisaties/dashboard-bevolking/leeftijd/jongeren (last accessed 29 July 2021).

Chapman, T., Gellin, M., Aertsen, I. & Anderson, M. (2017a). Protecting rights, restoring respect and strengthening relationships: European model for restorative justice with children and young people. *European Council for Juvenile Justice*, Brussels: International Juvenile Justice Observatory.

Chapman, T., Gellin, M. & Anderson, M. (2017b). Toolkit for professionals: implementing a European model for restorative justice with children and young people. *European Council for Juvenile Justice*, International Juvenile Justice Observatory.

Chapman, T., Hoek, van, A. & Wolthuis, A. (2018). *More humane approaches addressing the harm of criminal behaviour.* Amsterdam: Restorative Justice Nederland.

Claessen, J., Blad, J., Slump, G. J., van Hoek, A., Wolthuis, A. & de Roos, T. (2018). *Legislative Proposal to Introduce Provisions Governing Restorative Justice Services into the Dutch Code of Criminal Procedure and Explanatory Memorandum.* Oisterwijk: Wolf Legal Publishers.

Cleven, I., Lens, K.M.E. & Pemberton, A. (2015). *De rol van herstelbemiddeling in het strafrecht. Eindrapportage Onderzoek pilots Herstelbemiddeling.* WODC. Tilburg: Intervict.

Council for the Judiciary, 2020 Retrieved from https://www.rechtspraak.nl/Organisatie-en-contact/Organisatie/Raad-voor-de-rechtspraak/Nieuws/Paginas/Mediation-zeer-succesvol-in-strafzaken-met-jongeren.aspx

Dierx, J. & Van Hoek, A. (2012). *Mediation in strafzaken. De praktische toepassing van restorative justice en herstelrecht.* Den Haag: Sdu Uitgevers.

Gaag, R. van der, Gilsing, R. & Mak, J. (2013). *Participatie in zicht Gemeenten, jeugdigen, ouders en jeugdzorgcliënten in de transitie jeugdVMSzorg.* Utrecht: Verwey-Jonker Instituut.

Geenen, M., Kalter, M., Van Mazijk, T., Uitslag, M. & Lamkaddem, M. (2019). *Mediation in strafzaken: Geborgd in kwaliteit. Een onderzoek naar kwaliteitseisen voor mediators in strafzaken.* Utrecht: Hogeschool Utrecht.

Halt. (2019). *Jaarverslag en jaarrekening 2019.* Retrieved from https://www.halt.nl/storage/uploads/3cf35057-5a6a-4076-9fbf-1ba0db438638/jaarverslag-en-jaarrekening-halt-2019.pdf (last accessed 29 July 2021)

Halt. (2020). *Jaarverslag Halt 2020.* Retrieved from https://www.halt.nl/storage/uploads/9f63a1e4-2dec-44f7-b6a9-4d71cd45e9bc/Jaarverslag-2020.pdf (last accessed 29 July 2021).

Handleiding MiS (2017), Uitermark, J.J.M., Handleiding verwijzing naar mediation in strafzaken door Openbaar Ministerie en zittende magistratuur (OM/ZM), 31 mei 2017.

Highlights van Halt (2019). Retrieved from: https://www.halt.nl/storage/uploads/70bd751f-0ec4-4f31-901b-37c87e882b7a/High-lights-2019_toegankelijk.pdf (last accessed 29 July 2021)

Kaal, H. & De Jong, J.D. (2018). *Kom me horen. 11 Levensverhalen van delinquente jongeren met een licht verstandelijke beperking.* Amsterdam: Brave New Books.

Kamerbrief aanpak Jeugdcriminaliteit. (2019) https://www.rijksoverheid.nl/documenten/kamerstukken/2019/06/28/tk-aanpak-jeugdcriminaliteit.

Liefaard, T. (2008). Deprivation of liberty of children in light of international human rights law and standards. Vrije Universiteit Amsterdam. Mortsel Belgium: Intersentia.

Lundy, L. (2007). 'Voice' is not enough: conceptualising Article 12 of the United Nations Convention on the Rights of the Child. *British Educational Research Journal (BERA)*, 33(6), 927-942.

McGarrell, E.E., Olivares, K., Crawford, K. & Kroovand, N. (2000). *Returning justice to the community: the indianapolis juvenile restorative justice experiment.* Indianapolis: Hudson Institute.

Mijnarends, I., Brink van den, Y. & Verkroost, D. (2018). *Evaluatie pilot jongerenrechtbanken – Deel 2 Uitgevoerd in opdracht van de Stichting Jongerenrechtbanken Nederland.* Leiden: Universiteit Leiden.

Minister of Legal Protection. (2017). *Jeugdcriminaliteit* (Youth crime) Letter to the House of Representatives, 20 December 2017: Tweede Kamer, vergaderjaar 2017-2018, 28 741, nr. 40.

Minister of Legal Protection. (2019). *Aanpak jeugdcriminaliteit* (Tackling youth crime), Letter to the House of Representatives, 28 June 2019: Tweede Kamer, vergaderjaar 2018-2019, 28 741, nr. 53.

Minister of Legal Protection. (2020, January 8). *Beleidskader herstelrechtvoorzieningen gedurende het strafproces* (Policy framework restorative approaches during the criminal procedure). The Hague.

Pagée, R. van, Lieshout, van J. & Wolthuis A. (2012). Most things look better when arranged in a circle. Family Group Conferencing empowers society developments in The Netherlands, In E. Zinsstag & I. Vanfraechem (eds.), *Conferencing and restorative justice, international practices and perspectives* (pp. 217-230). Oxford: Oxford University Press.

Perspectief Herstelbemiddeling. (2018). *Contact met de ander helpt.* Annual report 2018, Utrecht. Retrieved from https://www.perspectiefherstelbemiddeling.nl/sites/default/files/2020-04/Perspectiefjaarverslag2018.WEB_.pdf (last accessed 8 September 2021).

Perspectief Herstelbemiddeling. (2019). *Herstellen doe je samen.* Annual report 2019, Utrecht. Retrieved from https://www.perspectiefherstelbemiddeling.nl/sites/default/

files/2020-05/Jaarverslag%202019%20Perspectief%20Herstelbemiddeling.pdf (last accessed 8 September 2021)

Raad voor Strafrechtstoepassing en Jeugdbescherming. (2017). *Verhoging strafrechtelijke minimumleeftijd in context Advies over verhoging van de strafrechtelijke minimumleeftijd en het belang van goede jeugdhulp*. Den Haag: RSJ.

Raad voor Strafrechtstoepassing en Jeugdbescherming. (2019). *Minderjarigen in een politiecel. Een advies over duur, verblijf en alternatieve locaties*. Den Haag: RSJ.

RAND Europe & Eurochild. (2021). *Study on child participation in EU political and democratic life, directorate-general for justice and consumers unit C2 fundamental rights policy*. Luxembourg: Publications Office of the European Union.

Ryan, R.M. & Deci, E.L. (2017). *Self-determination theory: basic psychological needs in motivation, development, and wellness*. New York/London: The Guilford Press.

Stichting Alexander (2019), *Jeugdparticipatie* (p. 25). Vuistregels. Retrieved from https://st-alexander.nl/wp-content/uploads/2020/09/PDF-Vuistregels-1.pdf (last accessed 29 July 2021).

VMSZ. (2020). *Mediation in strafzaken, Berichten uit de praktijk*. Nederlandse Vereniging van Mediators in Strafzaken (VMSZ). Utrecht: Libertas Pascal.

Wolthuis, A. (2012). *Herstelrecht, een kinderrecht. Voorstellen voor een integratie van herstel in het hart van het jeugdstrafrecht* (dissertatie). Den Haag: Boom juridische uitgevers.

Wolthuis, A. (2020). Een strafrechtmediation in het licht van kinderrechten. In G. Frerks, T. Jongbloed, M. Uitslag & T. Westra (eds.). *Insiders of outsiders? De voor- en nadelen van interne en externe mediation* (pp. 93-107). Antwerpen-Apeldoorn: Maklu.

Wolthuis, A. & Berger, M. (2017, September). Jeugdherstelrecht in Nederland, waar staan we. *Tijdschrift Jeugdrecht in de Praktijk*, (3), 15-32.

Wolthuis, A., Claessen, J., Slump, G.J. & Van Hoek, A. (2019). Dutch developments: restorative justice in legislation and in practice. *The International Journal on Restorative Justice*, 2(1), 117-133. doi: 10.5553/IJRJ/258908912019002001007.

Wolthuis, A. & Randazzo, S. (2021). *European review on individual assessment for children*. FOCUS Project on My Needs. Hungary: Terre des hommes.

Chapter 15
Rights, restoration and justice for children

Shaking the Movers in Canada

*Brenda Morrison, Virginia Caputo, Angie Osachoff and Daniella Bendo**

1 Introduction: rights, restoration and justice for children in Canada

This chapter explores the connections between restorative justice, children's rights and youth engagement. The chapter begins with an account of the development of children's rights through the work of former senator and long-time children's rights advocate the Hon. Landon Pearson, who developed a rights-respecting youth engagement model called *Shaking the Movers* (STM) with colleagues in 2007. Since then, the model has been used with children and young people to engage them in exploring their civil and political rights. Over time, the model has been modified and implemented in various regions in Canada. The chapter describes one such model developed in British Columbia (BC) that exemplifies Gal's ecological model of children's rights and needs (described elsewhere in this book by Tali Gal). This STM BC model brings together partners within universities (Simon Fraser University's Centre for Restorative Justice) and nonprofits, the primary partner being Equitas, whose mission it is to advance equality, social justice and respect for human dignity through transformative human rights education programs in Canada and around the world. In this chapter, the potential for STM to be used as a community-based youth engagement and crime prevention forum is discussed as a restorative approach to justice that enables young people to build the capacity to make responsible decisions and know their rights. STM BC enables young people to participate in decisions that affect their lives as rights holders in safe, inclusive and meaningful ways that are grounded in young people's lived experiences. The participatory process recognizes and honors interconnected relations in a shared humanity, these being two of the pillars of children's rights advocate, and STM founder, the Hon. Landon Pearson's vision. As one of Canada's prominent children's rights leaders, Pearson's vision encompasses principles of restorative justice to activate youth engagement premised on respecting children as full members of society, with the right to fully participate.

* We would like to thank STM coordinator, Precious Ile, and STM participant Allegra Nesbitt-Jerman for their helpful comments on this chapter.

Pearson's vision has been closely intertwined with the history of the development of children's rights in Canada over the past 60 years. Her efforts over six decades toward setting up an architecture for realizing children's rights focus on collaboratively bringing together a suitable structure for sustained activity in the political sphere. Pearson's work toward this goal, spanning legislative, bureaucratic and applied environments, has been driven by a firm conviction in the centrality of a rights-respecting approach. Her approach, premised on the notion that children are full rights holders, is at the heart of the way Pearson champions children's rights issues at public, political, and senatorial levels.

In her role as the spouse of a diplomat beginning in the early 1950s, Pearson encountered children living in diverse political, economic and sociocultural contexts in France, Mexico, India and the former Soviet Union. These experiences augmented her understanding of the realities of children's lives, the importance of establishing a language of children's rights and the urgency of advocating for a view of children as full members of society, alongside adults; their presence as human beings is situated *relationally* alongside adults rather than on the periphery of adult society. From the 1970s to the 1990s, Pearson continued her children's rights advocacy work, taking up various roles including that of vice-chair of the Canadian Commission for the International Year of the Child (IYC), in 1979, and as a lead participant in the delegation to the 1990 World Summit for Children. Over the decades, she garnered an international reputation for her work on promoting children's rights and participation in Canada and abroad. Indeed, Pearson collaborated with others in transforming the 1959 Declaration on the Rights of the Child into an international Convention. Canada made two specific contributions: first, to include language in the Convention on the rights of Indigenous children and second, to include children's right to play. The General Assembly of the United Nations adopted the Convention unanimously on 20 November, 1989, rapidly becoming the most widely ratified human rights treaty in history. The Convention integrated civil and political rights with economic, social and cultural rights so that children's rights could be understood contextually and relationally.

As a member of the Senate of Canada from 1994 to 2005, Pearson continued her advocacy on behalf of children and young people with her strong belief in their right to participate in matters that affect their lives. She sought out and created opportunities to open up parliamentary processes to engage children and young people in decision-making processes. For instance, she ensured that young people spoke as witnesses at parliamentary committees, including those considering the Youth Criminal Justice Act. Pearson used the party caucus system as one of the mechanisms through which to advance children's rights so that she could interact directly with other politicians and with government in building support for a rights-based and inclusive approach. Importantly, Pearson took the responsibility while in the senate to sponsor every piece of legislation that directly affected children and ensured that in this process a child rights perspective was included as it passed through the Senate standing committees on which she served to become law. Her involvement led to positive changes for youth in conflict with the law, including changes in the criminal code with respect to the protection of children from sexual exploitation as well as a new rights-based perspective in the Evidence Act with respect to children as witnesses (Ruiz-Casares, 2014).

Pearson continued to advocate for children's right to participate and to be heard throughout her career in precedent setting ways. At the United Nations' Special Session on Children in 2002, as the personal representative of Prime Minister Jean Chrétien, for instance, Pearson insisted that young people be included in the delegation to the meeting. By the time of the Special Session, 132 countries followed Canada's example by including children in their delegations.[1] The report included a *Plan of Action for Canada* to prioritize children's rights and to guide child- and family-friendly policies.[2]

When she retired from the Senate in 2005, Pearson moved, along with her children's rights resource library, to join the Centre for Initiatives in Children, Youth and Community (CICYC) at Carleton University.[3] CICYC's research in policy and practice in justice, policing, health and related contexts emphasized the core principle of youth engagement. This focus blended well with Pearson's established work in children's rights advocacy and participation. The CICYC team's research included restorative justice responses for youth in conflict with the law, homelessness and street youth with attention to well-being and justice, healthy development of young people, and crime prevention through social development and sustainable communities. Youth participation was a key component of their approach, including for sustainable crime prevention.[4] This was the context through which the STM youth participation and engagement model arose.

1 Following the Session, Pearson coordinated Canada's response by producing the report in 2004 titled *A Canada Fit for Children* with the help of a youth advisory group: Canada, Government of Canada. *A Canada Fit for Children* (2004). Retrieved from http://publications.gc.ca/collections/Collection/SD13-4-2004E.pdf.

2 Pearson's final role in the Senate was as vice-chair of the Senate Standing Committee on Human Rights that called for a Federal Children's Commissioner. The Committee issued its interim report in November 2005 titled 'Who's in Charge Here: Effective implementation of Canada's international obligations with respect to the rights of children' (2005, Canada, Government of Canada). Retrieved from http://publications.gc.ca/site/eng/398014/publication.html.

3 Pearson initially joined an established center comprising a group of sociology, criminology and anthropology colleagues. The Centre for Initiatives on Children, Youth and Community had the following team members: Dr. Tullio Caputo (Sociology, Co-Director), Dr. Katharine Kelly (Sociology, Co-Director), Michel Vallée (Criminology), Wanda Jameson (External Consultant) and Dr. Virginia Caputo (Anthropology).

4 A model developed by CICYC brought together values, structures and processes (VSP) whereby sustainable communities are those that have common values, workable governance structures and inclusive and relational processes for young people. For a video presentation by Dr. Tullio Caputo on the VSP Tool, go to https://policywise.com/resource/sustainable-community-crime-prevention/.

2 Shaking the Movers

The idea that inspired the STM model emerged from lessons Pearson learned about the importance of young people's participation in decision-making processes from her long history of children's rights advocacy in Canadian and international contexts; the model was further developed in dialogue with Professor Judy Finlay at Ryerson University and CICYC colleagues. In 2007, Pearson and CICYC members organized and hosted the first STM national workshop at Carleton University. With funding support from the Public Health Agency of Canada, 40 young people and their chaperones from across Canada attended the inaugural two-day on-campus event.

The theme of the first STM in 2007 – 'speaking truth to power' – resonates strongly with restorative justice. Pearson insisted that by ensuring a safe space operating on mutual respect and trust, young people could be supported to speak from their lived experiences to meaningfully address issues of concern to them, which could, in turn, inform decision makers who act on their behalf. STM 2007 focused on Articles 12, 19, 24 and 44 of the UNCRC (Art. 12 – Right to Participation, Art. 19 – Protection from Violence and Abuse, Art. 24 – Right to Health, and Art. 44 – State Obligations to Report Back to the United Nations). Following this inaugural meeting, and with further funding support from the Laidlaw Foundation and the National Collaborating Centre for Aboriginal Health to support Indigenous youth participation, STM workshops have been held with children and young people each year since 2007. Driven by a concern to expand the 'movers' portion of the model and require decision makers to respond directly to STM participants' concerns, the Landon Pearson Centre created a network of children's rights academics to respond to young people directly and to hold decision makers accountable to them. As with restorative justice, accountability, in this case vertical accountability, is a key principle (see Roche, 2004). The Child Rights Academic Network (CRAN) began in 2008 to hold annual meetings to respond to concerns articulated by young people in concluding reports that are circulated following each STM workshop.

In BC, STM workshops emerged as a collaborative partnership between Simon Fraser University's *Centre for Restorative Justice* and the BC office of *Equitas: International Centre for Human Rights Education*. The inaugural STM BC workshop responded to the national theme of the 'Sexual Exploitation of Children'. STM BC organizers adapted the workshop model to reflect local contexts and to amplify restorative justice principles embedded in its design, including connectivity, group safety, rights-based and relational understanding, accountability, and inclusive participation. To demonstrate how Gal's rights-needs restorative justice principles are amplified in the STM model in ways that successfully engage young people, the following section offers an overview of STM's design focusing on participation and process, followed by a discussion of the ways human rights education amplifies STM's focus on a rights-respecting and inclusive approach.

2.1 *A focus on child and youth participation*

The STM model adopts a rights-based participatory approach to providing children and young people with a unique opportunity to exercise their right to engage in important civil and political processes. Framed by the United Nations Convention on the Rights of the Child (UNCRC) Guiding Principles and Provision Articles, STM's design fosters children's participation and is attentive to transferring power to children who are central to the model's design (Caputo, 2018). The model recognizes children's rights as *relational* and fosters an interactive and collaborative approach between children and adults. Adopting a rights-based and participatory approach, the model aligns with nine essential components proposed by Lansdown and O'Kane (2014) that define quality participation. They note that quality participation results from processes that are transparent and informative, relevant to children's rights, voluntary, respectful, child-friendly, inclusive, supported by trained adults, safe and sensitive to risk and accountable to children (Lansdown & O'Kane, 2014). The STM model not only aligns with these components for meaningful participation, but also respects the four key dimensions for effective consultation with young people (space, voice, audience and influence), in accordance with Article 12 of the UNCRC. For instance, the model is used in workshop settings that are designed to be informative and transparent because youth know exactly what STM can and cannot achieve and are provided with information in order to understand the purpose of the workshop and their own role in the process. The workshops are relevant because the topics discussed are always chosen by children who attend the workshops the previous year. The spaces in which the workshops take place and the various activities are thoughtfully designed by young facilitators to open up discussions in inclusive and appropriate ways; the process is supported by adults who understand how to minimize risk yet remain on the periphery of the process. The key messages from STM workshops are captured in reports authored by a young person who acts as a recorder at each of the workshops. These reports are distributed widely by the Landon Pearson Centre to child rights academics, educators, activists, advocates, policy makers, legislators and parliamentarians with the intent to 'shake the movers' (Pearson & Collins, 2011). The Child Rights Academic Network (CRAN), comprising over 65 child rights academics from across Canada and one from the UK, gathers annually at Carleton University to respond to the STM reports and young people's recommendations and insights. The CRAN meeting is livestreamed via Instagram so that young people can hear CRAN members' responses to their concerns.

The STM workshops are usually structured over one or two days of interactive encounters with children and youth up to the age of eighteen. Youth facilitators meet prior to the event either as part of a course throughout a semester or for several intensive rights-based training sessions. They design rights-based activities and discussions to be implemented at the workshop. These activities guide the workshop for up to 30 participants. On day one, youth facilitators and participants gather for relationship development: introductions, ice-breaker activities and to share a meal. The following day of the workshop is spent in discussion and activities related to the main STM theme (Pearson & Collins, 2011).[5]

3 Children's participation in the STM model

The United Nations Committee on the Rights of the Child states that

> the concept of participation emphasizes that including children should not only be a momentary act, but the starting point for an intense exchange between children and adults on the development of policies, programmes and measures in all relevant contexts of children's lives. (United Nations, 2009: 18)

Participation is at the heart of the design of STM BC that incorporate pedagogical elements that bring together human rights education with restorative justice. Human rights education, which requires both content and process (Bajaj, 2011), emphasizes shared learning between facilitators and participants in open spaces to enable honest and intense conversations leading to social change. Like restorative justice, one of the key goals of human rights education is to contribute to long-term changes in social systems through the promotion of equality, sustainable development and participation (United Nations, 2019). As a lifelong process, it builds knowledge and skills, attitudes and behavior that lead to action for social change (Cooper, Nazzari, Kon Kam Kin & Pettigrew, 2013; United Nations, 2019).

Aligned with a restorative justice model, human rights education takes a holistic approach. It seeks to equip individuals with knowledge and skills and the motivation to transform their lives and the broader community (Equitas, 2020; Tibbitts, 2008). Human rights education enables children and youth to critically analyze situations that impact their well-being and the well-being of others as well as to thoughtfully reflect on ways to take action for change (Equitas, 2020). The educational activities reflect these goals through an interactive and learner-centered pedagogy that is experiential and activity-centered, problem-posing, participative, dialectical, analytical, healing, strategic thinking-

5 To see the different ways that workshops have been designed by local site organizers, STM reports can be accessed at the following link: www.carleton.ca/landonpearsoncentre.

oriented, and goal and action-oriented (Tibbitts, 2008). Each of these elements of human rights education closely aligns with and reflects a restorative justice approach, deepening the relational ecology of democracy (Llewellyn & Morrison, 2018).

Valuing and honoring lived experiences are key components of both human rights education and restorative justice processes. For children and youth, in particular, a participatory approach to human rights education that acknowledges and values their knowledge and lived experiences reaffirms young people as change makers with the capacity to make an impact on the interconnected world around them (Cooper et al., 2013). With the STM workshops, this primarily takes the form of play-based learning that can include art, role playing and physical activity. These diverse activities and discussions support children and youth in inclusive ways to effectively participate and learn (Cooper et al., 2013).

The design of the STM workshops held in BC is exemplary in the ways it upholds restorative justice, human rights education and child rights-based principles in specific ways. These principles flow from those articulated by the UN Committee on the Rights of the Child deemed necessary to ensure that children can effectively participate and be heard in decision-making processes (United Nations, 2009). What is evident from this list is the commonality and overlap with principles that drive and sustain restorative justice processes:

1. ***Transparent and Informative***: Child and youth participants and workshop facilitators are provided with all information about the STM BC process in advance. They are also given child-friendly consent forms that allow them and their guardians to provide consent to participate and to have their participation documented. STM BC ensures that all activities are informative and support participants' understanding of the topics being discussed and learning about human rights and how their contributions will be presented to adults and 'movers' in the community.
2. ***Voluntary***: By combining human rights education approaches with restorative justice, the facilitators are able to provide a space where youth feel comfortable and respected participating. Participation and sharing of opinions are always voluntary, and participants are able to step in or out of circles as they need. For example, during one STM BC session, a young participant who faced multiple barriers to traditional forms of participation initially expressed discomfort in voicing his opinion. On the first day, he did not participate at all and observed the process from outside the circle. On the second day, he joined the activities and the circle but, turned his chair backward during the discussion to indicate that he did not want to speak. By the third day he was participating in all of the activities and discussions. By creating a safe space where he had agency to choose to participate or not, and by not forcing participation by any one individual, the facilitators gradually brought forth voluntary participation from everyone.

3. ***Respectful***: Children are at the heart of STM BC. Their knowledge and understanding of the world around them is the foundation of the program. In order to build respect between participants and facilitators, STM BC always begins with the creation of a values charter, where participants are able to share what they need to feel safe and thrive during the process. Respect is a central value of the charter, as defined by the participants. Adult allies of STM BC demonstrate respect for the participants by participating in the circles only when invited to hear what the children and youth have to say.
4. ***Relevant***: Central to STM BC is the relevance of the topics that are chosen each year by young people. Within each topic area, there is a broad variety of subtopics. The discussions, focal points and outcome are never predetermined by the adult allies supporting STM BC. Instead, they are chosen by the children and youth through their participation. The participatory human rights education activities support the children and youth to safely explore the topic and to identify whether it is relevant to them and why, how it impacts their lives and the lives of their peers, and to suggest action items. Topics have included climate change to youth on the move, having experienced being displaced from home by wild fires or being an immigrant or refugee.
5. ***Child-friendly***: Ensuring that children and youth of all ages are able to participate equally means using activities that recognize the iterative and evolving capacity of the participants, as well as their different backgrounds, identities and realities. By using a human rights education approach with participatory game-based activities from Equitas' tested resources that are designed specifically to teach children and youth about their rights, STM BC is able to provide a child-friendly space where they are able to learn about their rights, the issues impacting their lives, and how they can effect positive change in their communities.
6. ***Inclusive***: STM BC is inclusive to all children and youth, ensuring that everyone is able to participate in the activities and discussions. Because STM BC uses human rights education, the play-based activities include art, role play, music and physical activity to support children and youth to learn while honoring their unique learning styles. For example, during one session, a young transgender participant joined STM on the first day, and, because of their involvement in the development of the values charter, and the inclusive nature of the activities, they felt respected and included throughout the day. Halfway through the first day they started to contact their friends and invited them to join, stating, 'The facilitators were really listening and including everyone.' On another occasion, a young participant who was homeless was entering the university to participate in STM BC. An acquaintance stopped this individual and questioned why she was there. The participant proudly replied, 'Because today I belong here.' By fostering inclusive spaces for everyone, STM BC supports a diversity of children and youth to actively participate and be heard.

7. ***Supported by training***: The process for ensuring that participants are able to participate fully in STM BC includes intense training for university-aged youth facilitators. These facilitators initially participate in over twenty hours of training including the essentials of human rights norms and values, the participatory approaches of human rights education and how to facilitate play-based activities and restorative justice circle processes. This training instills in the young facilitators a sense of ownership of the process that they are leading; they design the workshops and format of STM BC with the support of the adult allies.
8. ***Safe and sensitive to risk***: STM BC has addressed topics that can have negative impacts on the well-being and safety of children and youth, including bullying, exploitation and access to justice. As a result, the safety of facilitators and participants is of utmost importance. All adult allies and facilitators must submit criminal records checks to ensure that they are able to work safely with children and youth. As part of the facilitator training, they receive information on how to handle disclosures and safely address complex topics. Support from adult allies, including councilors and subject matter experts, is also on-site, but located outside of the participants' room. They are available at any time to provide support.
9. ***Accountable***: Consultations with children and youth are often described as a one-sided process, as children and youth do not know what happened after their participation. STM BC believes that authentic inclusion does not end when participants leave their session and, accordingly, shares the final report that was coauthored with children and youth and creates video recordings of adult responses to the report that are shared with the youth. Through this iterative process of engagement, participants learn that their contributions are valued, responded to, and, in many cases, lead to positive, lasting change. This instill a sense of pride in the participants.

4 STM BC and children's rights: Through the lens of restorative justice

STM BC's relational lens of children's rights builds on Zehr's (1990) *Changing Lenses,* which set the stage thirty years ago for a paradigm shift toward a relationally responsive approach to crime and public safety:

> Crime is a violation of people and relationships. It creates obligations to make things right. Justice involves the victim, the offender, and the community in a search for solutions which promote repair, reconciliation, and reassurance (Zehr, 1990: 185).

In viewing restorative justice as a relational form of justice, in the context of STM BC, the work embodies a relational approach of *reassurance* for children that validates children's inherent dignity and worth (Evans & Vaandering, 2016). In this context, the practice of restorative justice in criminal justice settings can learn from the practice of restorative justice in educational (RJE) settings (Morrison, 2017). The framework developed emphasizes the importance of being proactive as well as reactive to harmful and criminal behavior and the importance of engaged community praxis in creating learning communities that foster rights and responsibilities. Proactive learning, through community development pedagogy, nurtures *reassurance* within STM BC forums. Learning circles are a concept and practice that RJE employs to nurture relational environments, in that, circles are

> a learning community that nurtures the capacity of people to engage with one another and their environment in a manner that supports and respects the inherent dignity and worth of all. (Evans & Vaandering, 2016: 8)

Community praxis is also central to the theory and practice of restorative justice, as community bridges the relationship between the individual and the state (Asadulla & Morrison, 2021; Burford, 2018; Pranis et al., 2003). Community has the capacity to connect young people with those *small places close to home* in the context of their everyday lives; as such, community is central to the upholding of rights (Morrison, 2010). State institutions provide children's services, while communities hold children's spaces (Moss & Petrie, 2002). Both must work together. These child-friendly community spaces need to be proactive, more than reactive, to crime prevention and reduction responses. Together we need to build relational trust, through rights-based community praxis, before harm happens. Trust is nurtured through healthy relationships, when young people are offered dignity and worth (Johnston, 2018).

The role and power of dignity are central to all contexts of life, including responding to harm, for 'our desire for dignity is our highest common denominator' (Hicks, 2011: 17). Hicks further argues that 'the actions and reactions of dignity need to be learned' (p. 18). RJE learning circles are the foundation of community and school-based restorative justice, as they precede the need to respond to harm. Framed as a health and well-being practice that reaffirms the relational foundation of learning and growth, STM-BC is primary prevention that supports secondary and tertiary responses. In other words, STM BC reaffirms the relational nature of child well-being, as a foundation for responding restoratively to harm and crime, wherein participants repair and rebuild relationships (Morrison, 2007). RJE learning circles have been found to be an effective response to both the desire of children to be treated with dignity and the need to open spaces to treat one another with dignity (Morrison & Reistenberg, 2019). Hicks' (2011) 'ten essential elements of dignity' are embodied in restorative justice learning circles:

acceptance of identity; inclusion; safety; acknowledgement; recognition; fairness; benefit of the doubt; understanding; independence; and accountability.

Guiding principles for the practice of restorative justice have also been built on a human rights framework by Llewellyn (2004; 2007) and recently applied to the Restorative Inquiry for the Nova Scotia Home for Coloured Children, *Journey to Light: A Different Way Forward* (Nova Scotia Government, 2019). These guiding principles are embedded in the practice of restorative justice, seeking to deepen the relational ecology of restorative justice within complex systems (see Llewellyn & Morrison, 2018):

1. ***Relationally focused***: Resisting an isolated view of individuals or issues.
2. ***Comprehensive/holistic***: Taking into account contexts, causes and circumstances, with an orientation toward understanding what happened in terms of what matters for parties.
3. ***Inclusive/participatory***: Adopting a relational view of parties as having a stake in the outcome of the situation, with acknowledgment specifically of those parties that are affected, those that are responsible, and those that can affect outcomes.
4. ***Responsive***: Treating the practice as contextual, flexible and continuously attentive to the needs of all parties.
5. ***Responsibility-oriented***: Oriented toward identifying both individual and collective obligations, rather than placing blame.
6. ***Collaborative/nonadversarial***: Focused on collaborative engagement, rather than control over process and outcomes by one or more 'authorities'.
7. ***Forward-focused***: Oriented toward education, problem-solving, prevention and proactive (rather than reactive) responses to crime.

Gal (2011) echoes the same principles specifically in the context of the needs and rights of children, particularly as victims. She outlines eight heuristics: (1) holism, (2) tailor-made process, (3) children as partners, (4) participation as a continuum, (5) liberating children's voices, (6) adults not being risk averse, (7) restorative processes as a goal and (8) empowering advocacy. Gal's needs-rights model for children is built on six human rights principles: best interests of the child, participation, nondiscrimination, development, protection and rehabilitation. In her comprehensive work, Gal substantiates these normative principles through theories and findings of psychosocial research. She presents four evaluative clusters concerning the child's well-being in criminal or restorative justice processes: (1) the best interest cluster, focusing on rehabilitation and acknowledgment of harm; (2) the control cluster, emphasizing the need to treat children as partners who are in control of the process they are involved in; (3) the procedural justice cluster, highlighting the importance of experiencing the process as fair and just; and (4) the protection cluster, stressing the impact of victimization, special needs and vulnerabilities of individual children when their victimization experience is treated.

Using these same heuristics and system framework, Gal (2017: 57) develops an ecological model of child and youth participation:

> The ecological approach to children's rights stresses that to understand the phenomenon of child participation, it is necessary to consider conditions and processes that affect children and youths, expanding the environment under consideration to include children's families, communities, the professionals working with them, policy makers, and eventually, the entire regulatory regime.

STM BC operationalizes Gal's (2017) needs-rights based model of child and youth participation, opening child-centered spaces to hear their voices and recommendations in areas that affect their lives, from climate change to child sexual exploitation.

5 STM BC and child sexual exploitation

Reid and Gilliss (2020) describe the critical challenges to hearing the voice of youth in Canada's youth justice system. Their work amplifies the work of Bessant (2005: 5) who argues that adult policy makers try to 'imagine what young people want or what they believe they ought to want or need … as a substitute for young people'. In the words of Landon Pearson, the task of adults in the STM process is to 'open the space and get out of the way' (Pearson, 2015). This is echoed by Reid and Gilliss (2020: 132), who conclude:

> In order that we might truly understand the needs of youth, youth themselves must be consulted. The UN Convention on the Rights of the Child demands this, and as a signatory to this human rights treaty, Canada must respond.

The complexity of responding relationally to meet the needs-rights of young people is well illustrated by youth involved in systems of sex work and exploitation, as Gorkoff, Miller, Shepard and Bolton (2020: 380) stress: 'Making sense of young people involved in systems of sex work is not easy, as the role of sex work in society is deeply stigmatized and precarious.' Gorkoff and colleagues (2020: 400-401) conclude:

> For our purposes, juxtaposing the [formal institutional] terminology with the lived realities of young people on the street provides us with some contradictory themes, but it also gives us the power to question official discourse and move toward policy that is reflective of the needs of young people involved in the [sexual exploitation trade] SET.

Responding to the call of young people in Canada, the STM IX focused on engaging with and hearing the voices of young people on child sexual exploitation. In BC, the youth coordinator, who also wrote the participant-centered report that amplifies their experience and recommendations, describes the relational child/youth space created:

> Like previous Shaking the Movers (STM) conferences, youths speak their minds without adults in the room, except to ensure youths' needs for safety and other essentials are met. The conference was facilitated by youth for youth. Facilitators were SFU students and youths were mostly from Surrey and Coquitlam cities though invitations were sent across the Lower Mainland of Vancouver. Facilitators received at least 30 hours of training spread over 8 days to prepare for STM. Participants were aged 13 – 22 years. The youth facilitators were close in age to the young people and as a result, we bonded closely with one another. Youths saw facilitators as equals who could relate to their daily life challenges. Our relationship which was built on trust shaped the openness of conversations throughout the conference. (Ile, Pearson, Osachoff & Morrison, 2015: 5)

Each STM BC training includes: learning circles (based on Boyes-Watson & Pranis, 2015) and Equitas (2015) training on children's rights through experiential learning. Given the specific focus of STM IX facilitators also received training from Children of the Street and partnered with the Stop Exploiting Youth (SEY) unit of Pacific Community Resources Society. The facilitators created a safe space for the participants to share their lived experience and make recommendations. Youth facilitators estimated that 80 percent of those in attendance were at risk of sexual exploitation or experienced it at one point in their lives. As one participant stated, 'Much of modern day exploitation is hidden, [we need to] bring the next generation into dialogue.' Another youth participant shared:

> Exploitation comes from a place of hurt, pain, due to unmet needs; it can be defeated by providing better access to basic human needs like love, belonging, community, identity, education, health care, nourishment, and employment.

The full STM process is outlined in the *for youth-by youth* report, which includes recommendations that are brought to the annual CRAN meeting in Ottawa. The following were the three main recommendations from the STM IX young people:

1. Community spaces like STM BC are needed where youth are heard, respected and valued.
2. Opportunities should be provided for youth to share their knowledge as they have a lot to offer because they personally know the areas where they are negatively

impacted. The stigma that youths are lazy and unwilling to contribute in meaningful ways to society should be curbed.
3. Children's rights need to be more 'visible', and made more accessible to children/ youth.

The youth coordinator summarized the STM journey with the participants in the following words:

> *In the beginning, youths were unsure of how to put their words into recommendations. The word 'recommendations' seemed scary, almost intimidating. As youths realized that recommendations meant what they wanted to see happen, their transformation was empowering. Voices soared throughout the room, echoing their rights and stepping into leadership roles to brainstorm solutions to problems identified. One youth said,* 'Didn't expect to talk so much' *and everyone laughed to acknowledge his transformation (Ile et al., 2015: 25)*

6 Bringing rights home for children

The work of STM BC highlights the intersection of crime, crime prevention, restorative justice, child and youth engagement and the rights of children. The United Nations Office on Drugs and Crime, at the conclusion of the 13th Congress on Crime Prevention and Criminal Justice, adopted the

> Doha Declaration which highlights the importance of education as a tool to preventing crime and corruption. It emphasizes that education for children and youth is fundamental in promoting a culture that supports the rule of law, crime prevention and criminal justice.

Education for Justice (E4J) is one of the four pillars of the Doha Declaration that support a global program that focuses on four interrelated components: resilient, reliable and transparent institutions; fair, humane and effective criminal justice systems; youth crime prevention; education for justice.

The ambitious aim of these initiatives is to promote a culture of lawfulness, focusing on institutional change. In the context of E4J, the initial focus will be on primary, secondary, and tertiary education. As the work of RJE over the past 20 years shows, institutional culture change does not come easy (Morrison & Reistenberg, 2019; Morrison, Blood & Thorsborne, 2005). It needs to embrace the principles of restorative justice, holistically and collaboratively (Llewellyn & Morrison, 2018). At the heart of cultural change is community-based learning. In the context of STM BC this involved creating learning communities within the institution and with community-based partners. This is the essence of STM – creating a culture of learning and belonging within community. Creating positive communities of belonging is particularly important for vulnerable and marginalized youth, who often have negative relationships with adults and institutions. One STM BC participant stated, 'The scariest thing is an older guy with a suit.' STM BC's work with sexually exploited youth would not have been possible without our community partners who work with this community of young people every day: Children of the Street and Pacific Community Resources Society.

This work leaves the regulatory institutional silos behind and addresses the complex relational needs and rights of children. Building the relational trust with vulnerable populations takes time and deep commitment to work across institutional silos. STM BC is a small initiative with significant impact, for only a few children and youth. It will be sustainable, as a holistic crime prevention model, only through broader commitment, as a holistic rights-based crime prevention model.

In the words of Eleanor Roosevelt, in 1958, on presenting *In Your Hands* to the United Nations, in response to a worldwide, year-long observance of the Tenth Anniversary of the Universal Declaration of Human Rights:

> Where, after all, do universal human rights begin? In small places, close to home – so close and so small that they cannot be seen on any map of the world. Yet they are the world of the individual person: the neighborhood he lives in; the school or college he attends; the factory, farm or office where he works. Such are the places where every man, woman, and child seeks equal justice, equal opportunity, equal dignity without discrimination. Unless these rights have meaning there, they have little meaning anywhere. Without concerted citizen action to uphold them close to home, we shall look in vain for progress in the larger world.

Significant challenges are ahead in aligning children's rights with criminal justice systems. Only with sustained citizen education and action that includes the voice of children can we sustain the cultural change we seek to build capacity in those *small places close to home* at the community level. STM BC embodies a relational approach to rights, restoration and justice that holds promise as an effective crime prevention initiative for children and their communities.

References

Asadulla, M. & Morrison, B. (2021). *Communities are not at the periphery, rather they are at the centre of Restorative Justice in BC: an inquiry into the praxis of Restorative Justice in British Columbia, Canada.* Manuscript under review.

Bajaj, M. (2011). Human rights education: ideology, location, and approaches. *Human Rights Quarterly*, 33(2), 481-508. Retrieved 15 April 2020, from www.jstor.org/stable/23016023.

Bessant, J. (2005). Principles for developing youth policy. Policy Studies, 26(1), 103-116.

Boyes-Watson, C. & Pranis, K. (2015). *Circle forward. Building a restorative school community.* St. Paul: Living Justice Press.

Burford, G. (2018). Keeping complexity alive: restorative and responsive approaches to culture change. *International Journal of Restorative Justice*, 1(3), 356-371. doi: 10.5553/IJRJ/258908912018001003002.

Caputo, V. (2018). *What makes shaking the movers unique? The Landon Pearson Centre for the study of childhood and children's rights.* Carleton University: Ottawa, ON. Retrieved from https://carleton.ca/landonpearsoncentre/wp-content/uploads/Landon-Pearson-Centre-WHAT-MAKES-SHAKING-THE-MOVERS-UNIQUE_.pdf (last accessed 4 August 4 2021).

Cooper, A., Nazzari, V., Kon Kam Kin, K. & Pettigrew, A. (2013). Speaking rights: youth empowerment through a participatory approach. *International Journal of Child, Youth and Family Studies*, 3(1), 489-501. doi: 10.18357/ijcyfs43.1201312627.

Equitas – International Centre for Human Rights Education & Office of the United Nations/High Commissioner for Human Rights. (2020). *Evaluating the impact of human rights training.* Guidance on Developing Indicators.

Evans, K.R. & Vaandering, D. (2016). *The little book of restorative justice in education.* New York: Skyhorse Publishing.

Gal, T. (2011). *Child victims and restorative justice: a needs/rights model.* New York: Oxford University Press.

Gal, T. (2017). An ecological model of child and youth participation. *Children & Youth Services Review*, 79, 57-64. doi: 10.1016/j.childyouth.2017.05.029.

Gorkoff, K., Miller, A., Sherpherd, C. & Bolton, C. (2020). Youth involvement in systems of sex work and strategies of interventions. In J. Winterdyk, K. Gorkoff, D. Antonowicz & R. Smandych (eds.), *Youth justice: a Canadian overview* (pp. 379-406). Toronto: Oxford University Press, 379-406.

Hicks, D. (2011). *Dignity: its essential role in resolving conflict.* New Haven: Yale University Press.

Ile, P., Pearson, L., Osachoff, A. & Morrison, B., (2015). *STM IX: standing out against sexual exploitation.* Retrieved from https://carleton.ca/landonpearsoncentre/shaking-the-movers/.

Johnston, D. (2018). *Trust: twenty ways to build a better country.* Toronto: Penguin Random House.

Lansdown, G. & O'Kane, C. (2014). A toolkit for monitoring and evaluating children's participation. England, Wales and Scotland: The Save the Children Fund. Retrieved from https://resourcecentre.savethechildren.net/document-collections/toolkit-monitoring-and-evaluating-childrens-participation.

Llewellyn, J. (2004). A primer on human rights law. In J. Downie, K. McEwen & W. MacInnis (eds.), *Dental law in Canada.* Markham: Butterworths.

Llewellyn, J. (2007). A healthy conception of rights?: thinking relationally about rights in a health care context. In J. Downie & E. Gibson (eds.), *Health law at the supreme court of Canada.* Toronto: Irwin Law.

Llewellyn, J. & Morrison, B.E. (2018). Deepening the relational ecology of restorative justice. *International Journal of Restorative Justice*, 1(3), 343-355. doi: 10.5553/IJRJ/258908912018001003001.

Morrison, B.E. (2007). *Restoring safe school communities: a whole school response to bullying, violence and alienation.* Sydney: Federation Press.

Morrison, B. E. (2010). From social control to social engagement: finding the time and place to talk. *Contemporary issues in criminal justice policy.* American Society of Criminology Annual Meeting.

Morrison, B.E. (2017, September 18-19). *Community praxis: lessons for restorative justice in education.* New Advances in Restorative Justice Theory and Practice. The Centre for Criminal Justice Studies International Conference. University of Leeds.

Morrison, B., Blood, P. & Thorsborne, M. (2005). Practicing restorative justice in school communities: the challenge of culture change. *Public Organization Review*, 5, 335-357.

Morrison, B.E. & Riestenberg, N. (2019). Reflections on 20 years of restorative justice in schools. In Osher et al. (eds.), *Keeping students safe and helping them thrive: a collaborative handbook for education, mental health, child welfare, safety, and justice professionals, families, and communities.* Santa Barbara: Praeger.

Moss, P. & Petrie, P. (2002). *From children's services to children's spaces: public policy, children and childhood.* London: Routledge.

Nova Scotia Government (2019). Restorative Inquiry for the Nova Scotia Home for
Coloured Children, *Journey to Light: A Different Way Forward.* Retrieved from https://restorativeinquiry.ca/ (last accessed 4 August 2021).

Pearson, L. & Collins, T. (2011). *Shaking the movers: a model for collaborative consultation with children and youth on public policy.* The Landon Pearson Centre for the Study of Childhood and Children's Rights. Carleton University: Ottawa, ON. Retrieved from https://carleton.ca/landonpearsoncentre/shaking-the-movers/ (last accessed 4 August 2021).

Pearson, L. (2015). Personal communication. Ottawa.

Pranis, K., Stuart, B. & Wedge, M. (2003). *Peacemaking Circles: From Crime to Community*. St. Paul, MN.: Living Justice Press.

Reid, S.A. & Gilliss, S. (2020). Critical challenges in hearing the voices of youth in the youth justice system. In J. Winterdyk, K. Gorkoff, D. Antonowicz & R. Smandych (eds.), *Youth justice: a Canadian overview*. Toronto: Oxford University Press.

Roche, D. (2004). *Accountability and restorative justice*. London: Oxford University Press.

Ruiz-Casares, M. (2014). Children's rights: building from a sense of fairness. An Interview with Landon Pearson. *Canadian Journal of Children's Rights*, 1(1), 6-17. Retrieved from http://journals.carleton.ca/cjcr.

Tibbitts, F. (2008). Human rights education. In M. Bajaj (ed.), *Encyclopedia of peace education*. New York: Teachers College.

UNCRC. (2009, July 1). General Comment No 12: The Right of the Child to be Heard. 51st session, UN Doc CRC/C/GC12. Retrieved from https://www2.ohchr.org/english/bodies/crc/docs/AdvanceVersions/CRC-C-GC-12.pdf (last accessed 4 August 2021).

UNOCD. (2019, November). The Doha Declaration: Promoting a Culture of Lawfulness. Retrieved from https://www.unodc.org/dohadeclaration/en/news/2019/11/30-years-on–the-convention-on-the-rights-of-the-child-remains-relevant-and-needed.html (last accessed 4 August 2021).

Zehr, H. (1990). Zehr, H. (2015). *Changing lenses: restorative justice for our times*. Harrisonburg, Virginia: Herald Press.

Chapter 16

Strengthening rights and participation of children

A Finnish perspective on a restorative approach to education

Maija Gellin

1 Introduction

In Finland, the health and social care and youth work activities are locally organized to enable easy access to care when needed. Early prevention work is highlighted to increase the safety and health of every individual, from infants to seniors. Following this alignment, the rates of juvenile delinquency showed a decreasing trend until the end of 2018 but a slight increase in the 2019 statistics. However, the number of young people in prisons is very low.[1] According to data with the Finnish Criminal Sanctions Agency, three persons aged fifteen to seventeen years were held in custody as sentenced prisoners in 2018 and none in 2019. In 2018, 39 persons aged 18 to 21 were held in custody, and in 2019 there were 40 such persons. In 2018, there were ten remand prisoners aged fifteen to seventeen, and in 2019 there were 33. In 2018, remand prisoners aged 18 to 21 numbered 154, and in 2019, 173 (Criminal Sanctions Agency, 2018: 28; 2019: 28).

The Juvenile Punishment Act entered into force in 2005. Juvenile punishment, included in the Criminal Code of Finland, is a specific sentence for offenders under the age of 18 years. A juvenile punishment can last from four to twelve months and consists of supervision appointments, guidance and support to promote coping in society and orientation to employment. Eleven new juvenile punishments entered into force in 2018, compared with seven in 2019. (Criminal Sanctions Agency, 2018: 4, 42; 2019: 42).

In 2016 the national crime prevention Program *Working Together for Safer and More Secure Communities* was prepared by the Finnish National Council for Crime Prevention in the ministry of justice. The basic aim of the program is (1) to clarify the role of crime prevention in other municipal plans; (2) to improve crime prevention cooperation and networking with public authorities, businesses, organizations and citizens; (3) to increase crime prevention expertise at the local and national levels; (4) to promote the

1 The minimum age of criminal responsibility in Finland is 15 years.

consultation of local residents and nongovernmental organizations in the planning of crime prevention measures and (5) to improve the opportunities of citizens to influence and participate in preventing crime and increase the sense of safety and security in their communities. The focus is on situational crime prevention. The advantage of situational prevention actions lies largely in the fact that the measures may provide realistic, often practical and cheap solutions. The basic experience is that criminal activity is often a complex situational event in which a young person may have behaved violently and also experienced violence at that moment or earlier.

The same individuals can be both offenders and victims, so it is important in crime prevention to examine crimes, offenders and victims of crime as a whole. Early intervention methods include services for individuals, families, schools and communities in order to minimize the effects of risk factors. For example, maternity and child health clinics use various assessment forms to identify risk factors that are hazardous to the development of children, such as parental alcohol use and relationship conflicts. As an active response to these risks, within the day care system, children may be granted a place in day care if this is considered important for their development, while guiding parents to the health or social care systems if needed. To steer young people away from criminal activities, various forms of help have been developed, such as multiprofessional preventive practices by youth work, police and social work as well as various forms of mediation in crimes and disputes (Ministry of Justice, 2016: 9-13).

2 THE FINNISH EDUCATION SYSTEM

The Finnish education system is highly valued globally, topping the rankings of the international test PISA (the Program for International Student Assessment) in the early 2000s. Many teachers from abroad try to learn from the Finnish system. The value and success of the Finnish school system is grounded in the Constitution of Finland, in which free education is addressed as a fundamental right of every citizen. This right to free and common education for every child is a significant and unique basis in Finnish society. Parents can rely on this right without worrying about the costs, equality and quality of the school system and education. In addition, Finnish teachers are highly respected professionals with an academic education that focuses on research-based studies and active practice as well as a high range of theoretical knowledge.

Some key factors can be found to explain the high standards and achievements of the Finnish school system. The Finnish education system consists of nine years of basic education (comprehensive school), which is compulsory, and upper secondary education, which is either general upper secondary education or vocational education and training. In addition, higher education is provided by universities and universities of applied sciences. The first premise is the equal education system for every child, where the same learning targets apply to every school. Instead of competition, the Finnish system relies on collaboration, trust and collegial responsibility in and between schools (Sahlberg, 2015: 19-23). The Finnish teaching profession is based on continuous professionalization of teaching and school leadership that requires advanced academic education, solid scientific and practical knowledge and continuous on-the-job training. The quality of education is not evaluated by the level of literacy and numeracy test scores alone. Instead, education is designed to emphasize whole-child development, equity of education outcomes, well-being, and arts, music, drama and physical education as important elements of the curriculum (Sahlberg, 2015: 135-182; Sahlberg & Johnson, 2019).

2.1 Strengthening of children's participation in education

Despite these high standards of education, conflicts, bullying and misbehavior are a part of daily life in Finnish schools, as they are all over the world. In Finland, the obligation to intervene in conflict and abusive behavior in schools is based on the Basic Education Act, which states that a pupil has the right to a safe study environment (Basic Education Act 1998/268, Chapter 7, 29 §). The government's proposal in its explanatory memorandum, clarifies the content of 29 §: this provision obliges the organizers of education to ensure not only that the facilities intended for teaching are safe, but also that students are not subjected to violence or other harassment at school (HE 86/1997, 64). On the other hand, the Finnish Constitution (Chapter 2, 6 §) requires children to be treated equally as individuals so that they can express their views and have influence in their own life. The Finnish Constitution thus upholds Article 12 of the UN Convention on the Rights of the Child.

In the Finnish Core Curriculum for Basic Education (Opetushallitus 2014), the objectives of broad-based competence, such as learning how to learn, communication and expression of self, are established. Respect for human rights, the ability to appreciate interaction and the expression of one's own views are the skills needed in an increasingly diverse society. According to the Core Curriculum, a school's mission is to strengthen the involvement and active citizenship of students so that they can hone their participation and communication skills while providing a safe environment for the school community. Mediation is emphasized in chapter 3.3 of the Core Curriculum, which highlights the values of participation and influencing and building a sustainable future. The chapter points out that pupils must be given the opportunities to learn to work together and to practice negotiation, mediation and conflict resolution, and critical reflection (Opetushallitus, 2014; 20-24).

In 2018, the Finnish Ministry of Education published a report that presents development proposals related to regulatory change needs, strengthening of the participatory culture and the development of multidisciplinary cooperation, including restorative practices and mediation as an important part of daily activity. Mediation efforts are aimed at both restorative conflict management and prevention of exclusion by returning the parties to their community without stigma. Mediation reinforces a respectful, tolerant and supportive atmosphere aimed at reducing the need for punishment. Mediation produces a culture of conflict management that enables children and students to participate in decision-making on issues related to their own lives and to practice mediation and conflict resolution skills. With regard to mediation, development proposal number 9c includes the need to further strengthen the culture of mediation in schools and day care (Opetus- ja kulttuuriministeriö, 2018: 24-26, 66-67).

3 A critique of punishment-based disciplinary culture and zero tolerance

In Finland, critical discussion of the effects of punitive and zero-tolerance practices has been increasing. The development of decision-making policy at the societal level has also affected school and education policy in Finland. The shift from welfare policy to risk policy has taken place since the mid-1990s, with greater demands to ensure the safety of citizens, increase criminal justice resources, empower different types of voluntary security groups and increase the severity of penalties (Harrikari, 2008: 99-134). In the field of education this development has led to the discussion of increasing sanctions and implementing zero-tolerance policies, although the international and national research results of the effectiveness of these policies have not been convincing (e.g. Welsh & Payne 2018, 215-234; Skiba et al. 2018, 235-252). For example, with regard to the effects on young people Finnish researchers have reported an increasing risk of exclusion from society, a greater likelihood of drifting into risky behavior, the development of a criminal identity, the emergence of criminal subcultures as well as the increasing experiences of inequality and injustice, all of which drive young people toward misbehavior (e.g. Ellonen, 2008: 51-97; Korander, 2014: 184-213; Vesikansa & Honkatukia, 2018: 133-138).

The Finnish Basic Education Act (37§) identifies only punitive measures as disciplinary methods for schools. A punitive approach is still common when solving conflicts, although the National Core Curriculum emphasizes pupils' participation in conflict management, mediation and problem solving. On the other hand, the premise is that the law gives a framework to the school discipline system and the curriculum provides the content, which offers the guidelines for everyday pedagogy in schools. In the last ten years many practices in positive pedagogy and social skills learning have been introduced in schools to promote inclusion, including the restorative approach and practices, all of which are aimed at decreasing the need for using sanctions and increasing pupils' participation and opportunities for decision-making. Vesikansa and Honkatukia (2018) state that conflicts are a natural part of young people's development. It follows that pedagogically sustainable solutions should be found to deal with them. The exclusion of misbehavior in the classroom may ensure others' peace of mind and learning, but there is no evidence to support the benefits of such a policy. A more humane approach is necessary, and this challenge applies to the entire culture of the educational field (Vesikansa & Honkatukia, 2018: 143).

The restorative approach differs from punishment-based disciplinary culture and zero-tolerance programs. Instead of sanctions, face-to-face meetings, ownership and an understanding of the effects of behavior, both from the individual and from the community's perspective, are emphasized. The UN report Promoting Restorative Justice for Children (2016) highlights children's rights. Restorative justice emphasizes the significance of what has happened for both human relations and for the future and seeks solutions to prevent the recurrence of the harmful event. Restorative justice procedures are appropriate for dealing with children's situations, regardless of whether the offense is minor or serious (United Nations, 2016: 1-2).

The guidelines of the Council of Europe on child-friendly justice affirms that friends treat each other well, trust each other and listen to and understand each other, so child-friendly practices should seek to implement these ideals of friendship (European Union, 2010: 7). Liefaard, Rap and Bolscher (2016) reviewed Directive EU / 2016/800, published by the Council of Europe, on procedural guarantees in criminal proceedings against children suspected of having committed a criminal offense. The Directive stresses that a child's sense of dignity must be promoted in juvenile justice proceedings and that the child's innate right to dignity must be respected (Liefaard et al., 2016: 81-83).

4 Access to mediation services in Finland

In Finland, the development of mediation services has supported the development of child-friendly justice. The best interests of the child and other rights of the child, particularly the right to influence decision-making, are emphasized. According to several Finnish researchers (e.g. Ervasti & Nylund, 2014; Gellin, 2019; Iivari, 2010; Pehrman, 2011), mediation can be defined as a voluntary and informal procedure in which a neutral and external third party helps the parties to reach a mutually satisfactory agreement. The central premise of restorative mediation is that everyone who has been affected by a crime will be offered, with the help of a mediator, an opportunity to discuss what happened, its implications and measures needed to repair the harm.

In Finland, mediation is promoted at various levels of society. The Law on Mediation in Criminal Cases and Certain Disputes (2005/1015) came into force in 2006, although the mediation services had already been available to citizens since 1984, at least in urban areas around the country. Following the introduction of the law, victim-offender mediation services are now available free of charge to all citizens throughout Finland. The service is coordinated by the National Institute for Health and Welfare (THL). The mediation offices in Finland are staffed by mediation professionals, but mediation processes are facilitated by voluntary mediators. According to THL statistics, in 2018, 15,526 cases were referred to mediation, of which 30 percent of suspects were under the age of 21 and 9 percent of the proportion of suspects were under the age of 15. The report states that, although the under-15s are not criminally responsible, they are nevertheless obliged to compensate the damage they cause. Mediation also enables the young to take moral responsibility for their actions and can thereby reduce the risk of reoffending. Almost half (49 percent) of all mediated cases were violent crimes, 33 percent of which were violent cases in close relationships. In addition, mediation was used in cases of property damage and theft (10 percent), unlawful threats (7 percent) and violations of peace of homes (4 percent). Other unspecified cases accounted for 12 percent, and disputes accounted for 5 percent of all cases (Terveyden ja hyvinvoinnin laitos, 2019).

In addition, the Law on Court Mediation (2005/663) entered into force in Finland in 2016. Court mediation can be used, for example, in inheritance disputes or in matters of compensation for damage or in custody disputes. About 2000 cases are solved in court mediation every year, and about half of the cases relate to custody of children. The family mediation program, FASPER, has modeled the mediation required by the Marriage Act (234/1929), paying special attention to the realization of the best interests of the child. In this mediation practice the parents are participants, but the position of a child and his or her needs are the focus. Meanwhile, the Centre for Neighbourhood Mediation offers a mediation service for conflicts between neighbors and families and conflicts between different population groups in residential areas, and over 300 cases are mediated annually by the staff members. To increase the availability of this service, the staff of the Centre for Neighbourhood Mediation is also training members of local housing companies and active residents to use a restorative approach. Youth workers in different organizations also produce guidance on mediation or mediation activities for conflicts that happen in the free time after school. Street mediation is used in larger shopping malls for the misbehavior of young people (for example, cases of vandalism, thefts and rule breaking or threatening or shouting at other customers). In schools and day care centers, the VERSO program has trained pupils and staff members to mediate the everyday conflicts and bullying.

Figure 16.1. Access to mediation services in Finland (Gellin, 2019: 31).

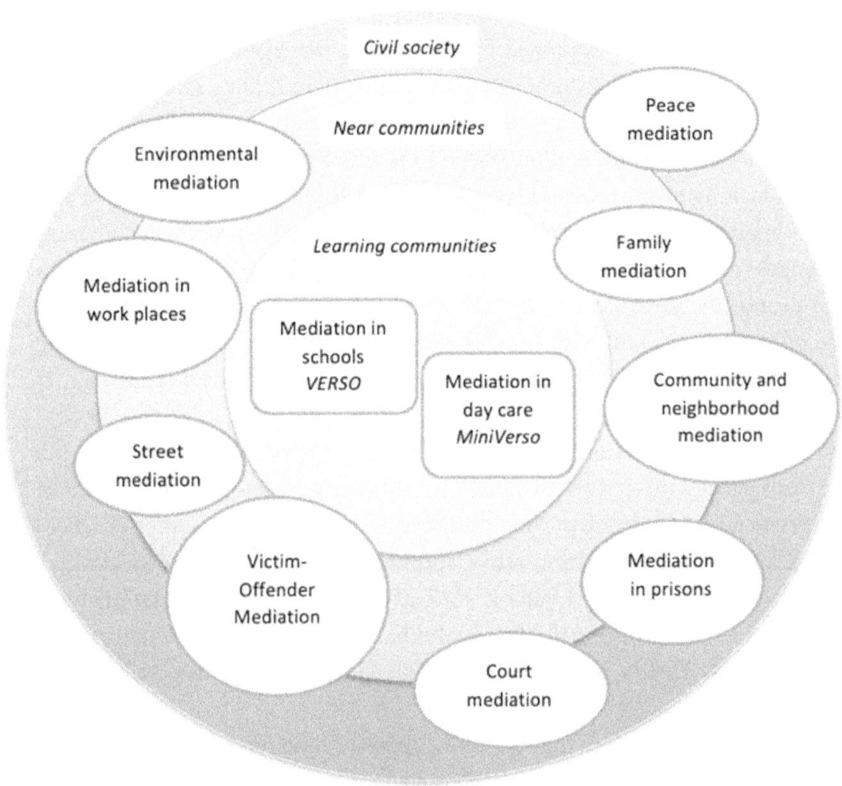

Figure 16.1 illustrates the mediation services provided by Finnish society. With regard to children's rights, the Finnish mediation services offer important avenues for juveniles to be heard and to enable their participation. In the figure, level one comprises those learning communities that are legally provided to children. For example, in a day care unit or a school that implements restorative practices, children and their parents learn the basis of mediation early on. The second level covers communities in which children live and interact outside of their learning communities as part of their families, friends or leisure activities. The third level describes the mediation services in civil society in general. However, the boundaries between the various levels and services are porous and partially overlap with different stages of life and everyday events. Strengthening the culture of mediation in Finnish society contributes to transparency and continuity in practices of conflict management, while strengthening citizens' empowerment in their local social communities and in civil society (Gellin, 2019: 30-32).

5 Restorative justice and restorative practices strengthening children's rights

Ervasti and Nylund (2014) have examined Nordic conflict management and mediation practices from the perspective of restorative justice. Rather than finding guilt, restorative mediation enables parties to discuss how the imbalance in a human relationship caused by an act can be restored. Fairness, in this sense, means rebuilding relationships, restoring the situation and looking to the future (Ervasti & Nylund 2014: 486-489). Chapman and Chapman (2016) point out that if carefully implemented, restorative process can increase a victim's willingness to overcome their anger and demands for punishment. The process itself can free people tied down by emotions, making forgiveness possible. If the victim feels that the offender is showing respect, empathy and a desire to compensate for the harm caused, forgiveness appears to be an opportunity to move forward (Chapman & Chapman, 2016: 135-152).

Restorative justice in education can be described as an approach that enables the involvement of all parties affected by a conflict or misbehavior. However, in the field of education professionals speak more of the restorative approach and restorative practices than restorative justice. The term restorative approach refers not only to restorative practices but also to philosophical values, such as fostering positive relationships, fairness, respect and taking responsibility, as the basis for restorative practices (e.g. Gellin, 2019; Hopkins & Gellin, 2016; McCluskey, 2018; Morrison & Vaandering, 2012; Woods & Stewart, 2018).

In the Finnish field of education, the restorative approach and mediation are the most used concepts professionally associated with the practices of restorative justice. In Finland, a program called VERSO has been offering training in the use of the restorative approach and mediation in schools nationwide since 2001. The restorative approach is practiced in a school context through mediation and restorative circles, as well as conference processes. In schools, mediation can be guided by students trained as peer mediators to resolve tensions between students and also by adult or conference processes under the guidance of staff members trained as mediators when conflicts between students and school staff or adults and/or school staff and parents arise (Gellin, 2019: 70-77).

Figure 16.2. Restorative practices in Finnish schools (Gellin, 2019: 72).

Figure 16.2. illustrates the restorative practices in Finnish schools that follow the VERSO program, which was developed within the framework of the Finnish Red Cross in 2000-2004. In 2005, the Finnish Forum for Mediation (NGO) received funding from the ministry of education to further develop the program. Since 2007, the program has received more permanent funding from the ministry of social affairs and health. The first level aims to have an effect on daily work in classrooms, where social relations and togetherness are strengthened by using restorative circles in teaching and cultivating the sense of community. At the second level, the conflicts are seen as possibilities to learn social skills. Through peer mediation, disputes between students are resolved as early as possible, and when needed adult-led mediation is also available. If a conflict escalates to a more serious level, conferencing or community mediation can be used to solve it. Mediation aims to both restoratively manage conflict and also prevent exclusion by returning the parties to their school communities without stigmatizing them. In the field of education, mediation strengthens a respectful environment, which aims to reduce the need for disciplinary procedures. Mediation produces a culture of conflict management that enables children to participate in a supported way in decision-making on issues related to their own lives and to practice mediation and conflict resolution. In restorative processes, children can learn to use their right to be heard, to participate, to express thoughts and emotions and to achieve solutions at the level of their age and development, thus strengthening their sense of justice and community. From this perspective, the restorative approach offers practices that are aligned with children's rights.

6 Research as an important part of the implementation of a restorative approach

Evaluation is an integral part of the VERSO program, during both the development and the implementation of the restorative practices in schools and day care. Furthermore, the ministry of social affairs and health, as a financier, requires statistics relating to program effectiveness every year. The results of the evaluation have been published in an electronic report on the website of the VERSO program since 2017. The staff of the VERSO program collect numerical data on training and participants, and evaluation data on training quality in every training session as a part of their work. However, the focus in the annual reports is on the activity in the field. Data for annual reports is collected through sampling by anonymous electronic inquiries from the schools and day care units that are applying the program. The collected data contains quantitative information about cases addressed in peer mediation, the characteristics of cases, numbers of agreements made and agreements kept. Also, numbers of peer mediators, adult advisors and mediators as well as the number of parties in mediation are recorded. In addition to quantitative data, qualitative data is collected. Information on experiences with restorative practices, use of restorative circles and mediation, success and challenges, as well as the opinions of the parties involved in mediation are collected through structured questionnaires and open questions. Staff members of the VERSO program analyze the collected data and prepare the annual reports as a part of their responsibilities.

According to the statistics, training in the use of restorative practices and mediation through the VERSO program was completed in a total of 804 basic education schools (pupils 7 to 16 years old) by the end of 2019, and of this number 67 new schools started implementing the program in 2019. About 342 different trainings (starting, maintenance and advanced trainings) were organized by the VERSO program in 2019, in which there were a total of 6,387 participants, 2,621 of whom were aged 7 to 17, and 3,766 participants were adults.

Data was collected through sampling of the parties to the mediation done in schools, with the aim of evaluating the implementation of restorative values and children's rights and the way they were experienced in mediation processes. The exceptional situation at the beginning of the year 2020 caused by the COVID-19 virus pandemic limited the amount of responding schools this year. A total of 73 students, aged 8 to 15 years, from 7 different schools managed to respond to the enquiry before the schools were closed in March in Finland. Figures 16.3 and 16.4 display some results from the 2019 statistics, and Figure 16.5 illustrates recent developments based on a comparison of some responses with the 2017-2019 surveys. The summary of the findings of the annual report 2019 is available in English on the website of the VERSO program (https://sovittelu.com/vertaissovittelu/in-english/).

Figure 16.3. Opinions of the parties participating in peer mediation 2019 (N = 73); focusing on the process.

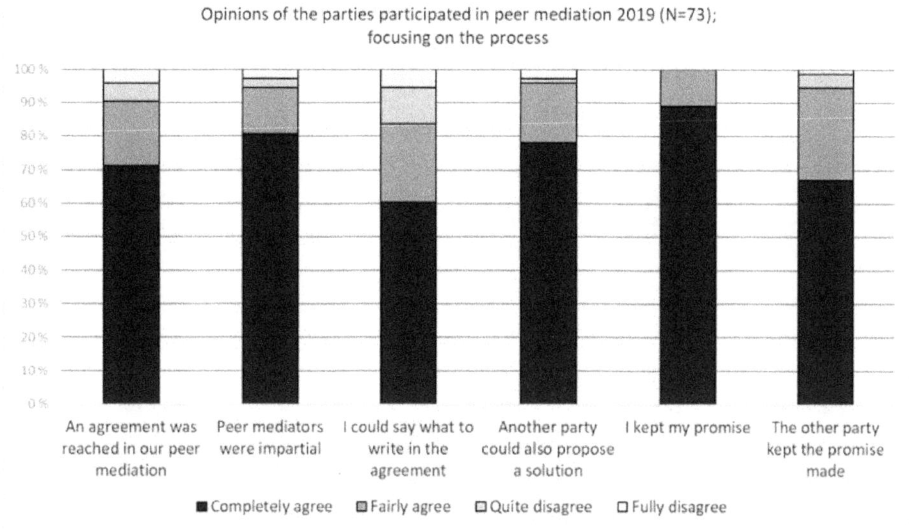

Figure 16.3 describes the responses of the parties concerning the mediation process. We had responses from 73 pupils who had participated as a party to a conflict in peer mediation. According to the results, 90 percent of the parties completely or fairly agreed with the statement *An agreement was reached in our peer mediation*. In addition, 94 percent of respondents completely (80 percent) or fairly (14 percent) agreed that *peer mediators were impartial.* The figure describes that 83 percent of respondents agreed completely (60 percent) or fairly (23 percent) with the statement *I could say what to write in the agreement*, and 11 percent and 6 percent, respectively, quite or fully disagreed with the statement. Most (95 percent) of the parties completely or fairly agreed that another party could also propose a solution. When asked about keeping promises made in peer mediation, 89 percent of respondents totally and 11 percent fairly agreed with the statement *I kept my promise.*

Figure 16.4. Opinions of the parties participating in peer mediation 2019 (N = 73); focusing on child's rights.

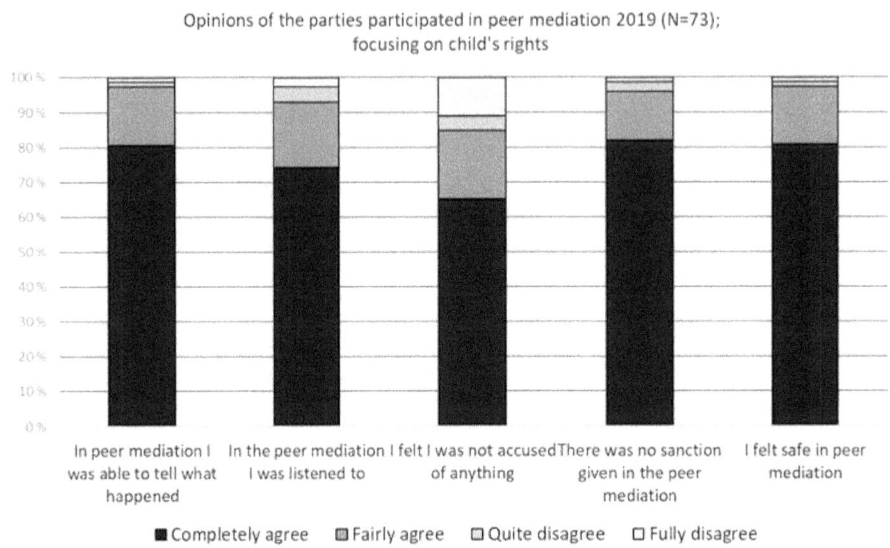

Figure 16.4 reflects the opinions of the parties involved in peer mediation from the child's rights perspective. There were also answers from 73 parties. Most (98 percent) of the respondents completely (81 percent) or fairly (17 percent) agreed with the statement *In peer mediation I was able to tell what happened.* Also, most (93 percent) of the parties completely (74 percent) or fairly (19 percent) agreed with the statement *In the peer mediation I was listened to.* In addition, 85 percent of respondents totally (65 percent) or fairly (20 percent) agreed with the statement *I was not accused of anything,* while 4 percent quite disagreed and 11 percent totally disagreed with this statement. Almost all (96 percent) the respondents either completely (82 percent) or fairly (14 percent) agreed with the statement that *there was no sanction given in the peer mediation.* In regard to the experiences of safety, 98 percent of the respondents said that they completely (81 percent) or fairly (17 percent) agreed that *they felt safe in peer mediation,* and only 2 percent disagreed with the statement. (VERSO-Programme: Annual Report, 2019: 9).

Figure 16.5. A three-year comparison of the views of the parties in the peer mediation regarding children's rights; comparing the percentages of participants' 'completely agree' responses.

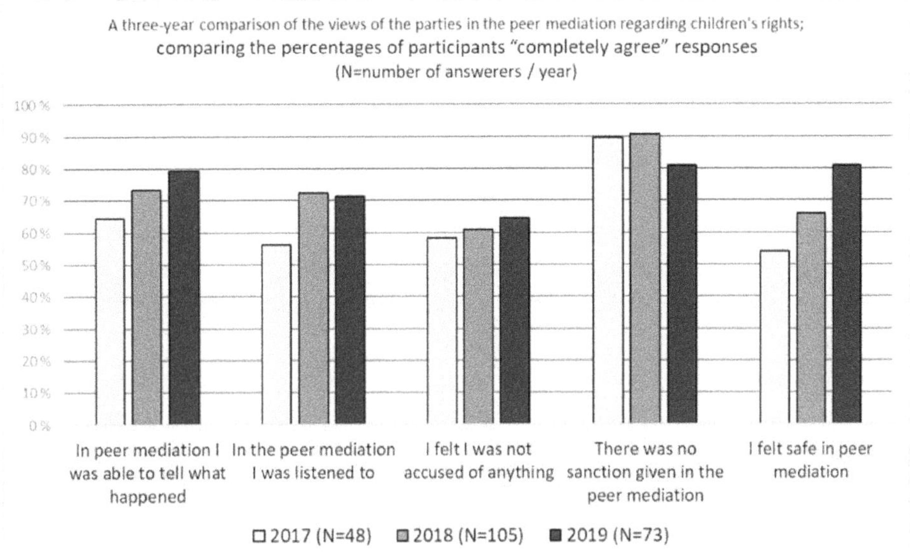

Figure 16.5 shows a three-year comparison of the answers of the parties in the peer mediation. From the children's rights perspective, parties are reporting increasing experience of being able to explain their own views. The feeling of being safe in peer mediation has also increased during the past three years. The comparison shows that there is a decrease in the view *There was no sanction given in the peer mediation*, although more and more of the parties felt that they were not accused of anything in peer mediation (VERSO-Programme: Annual Report 2019: 9).

On the basis of this data, we can conclude that there are several indications that give promising information about strengthening children's rights to be heard, to participate in decision-making and to be respected as experts of their own life at their age level in the daily practice in schools through the implementation of a restorative approach. However, more and wider data must be collected to observe and evaluate these developments.

7 The restorative school culture – realistic or utopian?

Restorative practices like circles, peer mediation and adult-led mediation in education are generating promising results. The rights of the child to be heard and to participate in a way that influences decision-making are also well respected when the restorative principles are followed in daily school practice. On the other hand, we can ask whether the results are promising because of the use of restorative methods alone or whether we need a more comprehensive restorative school approach and change of school culture to ensure that the full benefits of a restorative approach are reaped in schools. What values and principles are required in implementing a comprehensive restorative approach? These were the questions that guided my doctoral research after 15 years of experience as a restorative approach trainer in Finnish schools.

7.1 The methodology and data collection

The aim of my doctoral research was to observe how the restorative approach had been implemented in schools, what advantages such practices had brought to schools, how restorative principles were understood, and what challenges had occurred during several years of practice. The research was carried out with the Grounded Theory (GT) process. GT research approaches the phenomenon under study by creating a theory that can be assumed to work in a hypothetical context where it is used (Glaser & Strauss, 1967: 3, 249). GT research is a process that requires the simultaneous promotion of data aggregation, data coding and data analysis. The researcher is in constant interaction with their data, ensuring that a new theory is created on the basis of the data. GT, unlike other research methodologies, does not generally follow a logical order of progression, but the collection, coding and analysis of research data are in constant motion, complementing each other (Glaser & Strauss, 1967: 41-43). Although all kinds of data can be utilized in the GT process, the material collected through interviews is the most common. For this research, the data was collected from school staff members (N = 37), who had participated in advanced trainings of the VERSO program during the years 2010-2012. This includes written learning diaries collected from participants (N = 24) and interviews with an additional 13 participants. Before the start of data collection, it was ensured that all informants confirmed that they had implemented restorative practices at least one year before this research (Gellin, 2019: 85-88).

7.2 The findings

The results of the research provide a perspective on the discourse of well-being and conflict management in school communities. Both successes and challenges were reported. According to the results, the restorative approach had influenced the mindset of the teachers so that they had adopted respectful encounter, active listening, restorative circles and mediation in their daily profession and pedagogy. The data shows that the restorative approach had changed the attitudes of the teachers towards pupils in a way that children were seen as being actively involved in matters concerning their own lives. Restorative mediation was experienced as a positive and cooperative approach to conflict management. The restorative approach had changed the way the participants in a conflict were seen. Instead of seeking bullies or children who were bullied, the teacher, as a restorative facilitator, could work without labelling the parties and could support their capability to solve their conflict themselves. The teachers observed that after changing from a punitive role to a facilitative role, it was significantly easier to support the parties in their efforts to keep their promises and change their behavior. The data confirmed the necessity of proper training in order to achieve success in implementing a restorative approach. The interviewees considered the training they had received to be of very high quality (Gellin, 2019: 163-164).

The results also exposed the challenges of implementing the new restorative thinking and practices. The critical attitudes of some school staff members and parents sometimes made it difficult to use these practices. Not all adults are ready to change the sanction-based methods to restorative ones. Further, some adults could not trust the active role and expertise of pupils or participatory methods used in the restorative approach. The interviewees realized that the adoption of new practices requires planning and training but reported that there was not always time for that. The results indicate that sharing reflections and information with colleagues regularly is essential in implementing the restorative approach in daily school practices (Gellin, 2019: 162).

8 The restorative encounter is a two-way process

GT research aims to produce a theory that answers the research question, but it is important to ensure that the theory created by its methodology can also be verified and tested in contexts other than those in which it is produced. The interest in this research was to find the answer to the main question of how a restorative approach can be implemented in a community and what it produces. GT analysis revealed that *the restorative encounter* was a key concept. The restorative encounter is always a two-way process with three dimensions. It includes the adoption of restorative thinking, the understanding of restorative participation as a key factor in line with children's rights, and the use of restorative mediation as a conflict management method.

Figure 16.6. The dimensions of the restorative encounter (Gellin, 2019: 156).

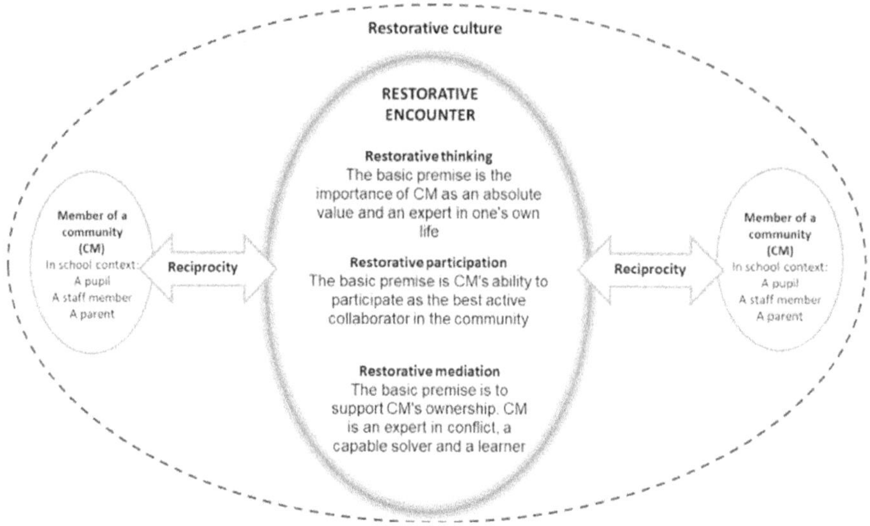

Figure 16.6 illustrates the dimensions of a restorative encounter. *Restorative thinking* emphasizes the view that the individual is valued as an expert in his or her own life without preconceived notions. This means that in encounters and interactions, community members (CM) value each other as they are, making it possible to listen to each other and understand their perspectives, even if they do not agree on everything. The experience of being valued and heard reinforces and maintains CMs' own image. In this way, restorative thinking also strengthens human relationships in encounters at different levels.

Restorative participation culminates in collaborative action in daily life in schools. Encounters and interactions take place in positions where individuals are in their community. Through restorative participation, the identities of the participators are respected as such regardless of their positions. All members of a community are seen as actors who can develop and learn through successes and failures in their cooperation with others.

The basic principle in *restorative mediation* is that conflicts are understood to be related to social relations and that they are thus accepted as part of human growth. When a conflict is experienced, the situation is understood as an opportunity for change that strengthens an individual's growth and learning. Restorative encounters do not stigmatize, but instead there is a mutual interest in increasing the understanding of CMs so that solutions support the development of CMs' self-image and capability to take responsibility for behavior and agreements. By strengthening these three dimensions when developing professional skills of school staff and social skills of children, schools can succeed in changing the school culture into an encompassing restorative school approach where children's rights are respected.

9 Conclusion

It is important to address children's rights in education. A school is a place for children to learn not only academic skills, but also social and conflict management skills for their future. Furthermore, it is where children develop their skills to act for and use their rights to be heard, to participate and to be respected as valuable individuals regardless of their age or position. The research results shared in this chapter highlight the importance of preventive and integrative action. The results show that it is possible to shift from a culture in which the focus is on sanctions to one in which a proactive and restorative attitude is cultivated. The restorative approach has contributed to the experience of dignity of an individual and the importance of a sense of community, which removes prejudice, increases understanding and responsibility, and brings respect to members of the community despite their differing views. In this respect, results inform the discussion on positive pedagogical tendencies that aim to increase positive interaction and the fulfilment of human rights among CMs.

However, the discussion on the means of achieving a restorative approach or encounter should continue along with the promotion of related research. One of the challenges that emerged from my study was the criteria for evaluation and quality of the implementation of the restorative approach in Finland's schools. The local and formal theoretical models created as part of my dissertation contribute to providing a critical platform for the realization of such a restorative approach. On the one hand, the results of this study provide some insights into what the evaluation of a restorative approach could be based on, while, on the other, the results could advance the current debate among researchers about the concern of using the concept of *restorative justice* randomly. The concern is about connecting the concept to different activities to restorative justice without critically observing and understanding the principles and background of restorative justice. This can lead to a situation where real restorative values of different practices can no longer be detected or assessed. It is necessary to examine the conditions for the implementation of a restorative approach.

Broadly, this chapter puts the relationships of children and young people and the importance of their restoration at the center of education. The school creates both visible and invisible frames, rules and norms within which it is important not only to look at how to maintain these frames but also to focus on the skills of maintaining relationships, solving conflicts and respecting human rights. Instead of a culture of accusation and sanctions, a culture of respectful and restorative encounters must be built in order to support the growth and development of children and young people, regardless of their position in a conflict or their social or economic circumstances. At the individual level, the skill of being able to participate in a restorative encounter is essential in both education and conflict management. The immediate impact of the culture of a restorative encounter has a clear link to enhanced learning and participation as well as the increasing experiences of respecting children's rights. At the community level, experiences with restorative encounters generate quality and social capital that reinforce well-being throughout the community, beginning in schools and extending to the whole society.

References

Basic Education Act 628/1998. Finlex. Retrieved from www.finlex.fi/fi/laki/kaannokset/1998/en19980628.pdf (last accessed 4 August 2021).

Chapman, T. & Chapman, A. (2016). Forgiveness in restorative justice: experienced but not heard? *Oxford Journal of Law and Religion*, *5*(1), 135-152. doi.org/10.1093/ojlr/rwv066.

Criminal Sanctions Agency. (2018). *Criminal Sanctions Agency statistical yearbook 2018.* Retrieved from www.rikosseuraamus.fi/material/attachments/rise/julkaisut-tilastollinenvuosikirja/AzNXXizez/Rikosseuraamuslaitoksen_tilastollinen_vuosikirja_2018_ENG_WWW.pdf. (last accessed 4 August 2021).

Criminal Sanctions Agency. (2019). Criminal Sanctions Agency statistical yearbook 2019.

Retrieved from www.rikosseuraamus.fi/material/attachments/rise/julkaisut-tilastollinenvuosikirja/pjeawUKaf/Statistical_Yearbook_2019_of_the_Criminal_Sanctions_Agency.pdf. (last accessed 4 August 2021).

Ellonen N. 2008. *Kasvuyhteisö nuoren turvana. Sosiaalisen pääoman yhteys nuoren masentuneisuuteen ja rikekäyttäytymiseen* (PhD dissertation). University of Tampere. Tampere: Tampere University Press.

Ervasti, K. & Nylund, A. (2014). *Konfliktinratkaisu ja sovittelu.* Helsinki: Edita.

European Union. (2010). *Guidelines of the Committee of Ministers of the Council of Europe on child-friendly justice.* Retrieved from https://rm.coe.int/16804b2cf3. (last accessed 4 August 2021)

Gellin, M. (2019). *Restoratiivinen lähestymistapa ja sovittelu peruskoulukontekstissa* (PhD dissertation). Acta Electronica Universitatis Lapponiensis 266. Rovaniemi: University of Lapland. Retrieved from https://lauda.ulapland.fi/handle/10024/63950. (last accessed 4 August 2021)

Glaser, B.G. & Strauss, A.L. (1967). *The discovery of grounded theory. Strategies for Qualitative Research.* New Brunswick: Aldine Transaction.

Harrikari, T. (2008). *Riskillä merkityt.* Nuorisotutkimusseura, julkaisuja 87. Helsinki: Nuorisotutkimusseura.

HE 86/1997. Hallituksen esitys Eduskunnalle koulutusta koskevaksi lainsäädännöksi. Retrieved from www.eduskunta.fi/FI/vaski/HallituksenEsitys/Documents/he_86+1997.pdf (last accessed 4 August 2021).

Hopkins, B. & Gellin, M. (2016). Restorative approaches in educational settings. Minori guistizia. *Rivista interdiscilinare di studi guiridici, psicologici, pedagogici e sociali sulla relazione fra minorenni e guistizia*, (1), 66-73.

Iivari, J. (2010). *Oikeutta oikeuden varjossa. Rikossovittelulain täytäntöönpanon arviointitutkimus*. Raportti 5/2010. Helsinki: Terveyden ja hyvinvoinnin laitos.

Korander, T. (2014). Rikottujen ikkunoiden nollatoleranssi. Tutkimus New Yorkin rikoksentorjunnan uuskonservatiivi-mallista Suomessa (PhD dissertation). Annales Universitatis Turkuensis C 390. Turku: University of Turku.

Liefaard, T., Rap, S. & Bolsher, A. (2016). *Can anyone hear me? Improving juvenile justice systems in Europe: A manual on how to make European juvenile justice systems child-friendly*. Retrieved from www.oijj.org/en/our-work/research/highlighted-research-projects/improvingjjs/manual (last accessed 4 August 2021).

McCluskey, G. (2018). Restorative approaches in schools: current practices, future directions. In J. Deakin, E. Taylor & A. Kupchik (eds.), *The Palgrave international handbook of school discipline, surveillance, and social control* (pp. 573-593). New York: Palgrave Macmillan.

Ministry of Justice. (2016). *Working together for safer and more secure communities*. National Crime Prevention Programme. Retrieved from https://julkaisut.valtioneuvosto.fi/handle/10024/79054 (last accessed 4 August 2021).

Morrison, B. & Vaandering, D. (2012). Restorative justice: pedagogy, praxis and discipline. *Journal of School Violence*, 11(2), 138-155. doi: 10.1080/15388220.2011.653322.

Opetus- ja kulttuuriministeriö. (2018). *Kiusaamisen ehkäisy sekä työrauhan edistäminen varhaiskasvatuksessa, esi- ja perusopetuksessa ja toisella asteella*. Loppuraportti. Opetus- ja kulttuuriministeriön julkaisuja 2018, 16. Retrieved from https://julkaisut.valtioneuvosto.fi/handle/10024/160694. (last accessed 4 August 2021).

Opetushallitus. (2014). *Perusopetuksen opetussuunnitelman perusteet 2014*. Opetushallitus, Määräykset ja ohjeet 2014, 96. Retrieved from www.oph.fi/sites/default/files/documents/perusopetuksen_opetussuunnitelman_perusteet_2014.pdf. (last accessed 4 August 2021).

Pehrman, T. (2011). *Paremmin puhumalla. Restoratiivinen sovittelu työyhteisössä* (PhD dissertation). Acta Universitatis Lapponiensis 212. Rovaniemi: Lapin yliopisto.

Sahlberg, P. (2015). *Finnish Lessons: what can the world learn from educational change in Finland*. New York: Teachers College Press.

Sahlberg, P. & Johnson, P. (2019). *What is really going on in Finland's school reform*. Retrieved from https://pasisahlberg.com/what-is-really-going-on-in-finlands-school-reform/ (last accessed 4 August 2021).

Skiba R.J. et al. (2018). Discipline Disparities: New and Emerging Research in the United States. In J. Deakin, E. Taylor & A. Kupchik (eds.), *The Palgrave international handbook of school discipline, surveillance, and social control* (pp. 235-252). New York: Palgrave Macmillan.

Terveyden ja hyvinvoinnin laitos. (2019). *Rikos- ja riita-asioiden sovittelu 2018.* Tilastoraportti 24/2019. Retrieved from www.julkari.fi/bitstream/handle/10024/138251/Tr24_19_viimeisin.pdf?sequence=6&isAllowed=y (last accessed 4 August 2021).

United Nations. (2016). *Promoting restorative justice for children.* Retrieved from. www.un-ilibrary.org/content/books/9789210582889. doi.org/10.18356/2fc79c90-en (last accessed 4 August 2021).

VERSO-Programme: Annual Report. (2019). Retrieved from https://sovittelu.com/vertaissovittelu/wp-content/uploads/2021/01/VERSO-Annual-Report.pdf (last accessed 4 August 2021).

Vesikansa, S. & Honkatukia, P. (2018). School violence as a complex social problem: trends in managing discipline in Finnish educational policy. In J. Deakin, E. Taylor & A. Kupchik (eds.), *The Palgrave international handbook of school discipline, surveillance, and social control* (pp. 129-148). New York: Palgrave Macmillan.

Welch, K. & Payne, A.A. (2018). Zero tolerance school policies. In J. Deakin, E. Taylor & A. Kupchik (eds.), *The Palgrave international handbook of school discipline, surveillance, and social control* (pp. 215-234). New York: Palgrave Macmillan.

Woods, C.A. & Stewart, M.L. (2018). Restorative justice: a framework for examining issues of discipline in schools serving diverse populations. *The International Journal of Restorative Justice*, 1(1), 81-85.

Studies in Restorative Justice (Series Editors: Estelle Zinsstag and Tinneke Van Camp)

Monographs and edited collections

Iain Brennan and Gerry Johnstone, *Building Bridges*, 2019, ISBN 978-94-6236-882-8

Annemieke Wolthuis and Tim Chapman (eds.), *Restorative justice from a children's rights perspective*, 2021, ISBN 978-94-6236-227-7

Anthologies

Lode Walgrave, *Being consequential about restorative justice*, 2021, ISBN 978-94-6236-235-2

Kathleen Daly, *Remaking justice after sexual violence*, 2021, ISBN 978-94-6236-226-0

www.ingramcontent.com/pod-product-compliance
Ingram Content Group UK Ltd.
Pitfield, Milton Keynes, MK11 3LW, UK
UKHW050954290926
15470UKWH00006B/1805

9 789462 362277